For Irwin Bardash,

A warm and generous friend of the ♡ Bach Aria Festival + Institute at Stony Brook, this book is a late offshoot of that wonderful experience.

With happy memories and best regards,

Carol K Baron

6/06

Bach's Changing World

VOICES IN THE COMMUNITY

Bach's Changing World

Voices in the Community

EDITED BY CAROL K. BARON

UNIVERSITY OF ROCHESTER PRESS

First published 2006

University of Rochester Press
668 Mt. Hope Avenue, Rochester, NY 14620, USA
www.urpress.com
and Boydell & Brewer Limited
PO Box 9, Woodbridge, Suffolk IP12 3DF, UK
www.boydellandbrewer.com

ISBN: 1–58046–190–5

Library of Congress Cataloging-in-Publication Data
Bach's changing world : voices in the community / Edited by Carol K.
Baron.
   p. cm. – (Eastman studies in music, ISSN 1071-9989 ; v. 37)
   Includes bibliographical references and index.
   ISBN 1-58046-190-5 (hardcover : alk. paper) 1. Music–Social
aspects–Germany–Leipzig–History–18th century. 2. Music–Religious
aspects–Germany–Leipzig–History–18th century. 3. Bach, Johann
Sebastian, 1685-1750. I. Baron, Carol. II. Series.
   ML3917.G3B33 2006
   780.943′212209033–dc22
                              2006002020

A catalogue record for this title is available from the British Library.

This publication is printed on acid-free paper.
Printed in the United States of America.

This book is dedicated to the memory of
Samuel Baron 1925–1997

Erklärung der Nummern.

1 Das Rath-Hauß.
2 Die Brühsche Gaße.
3 Die Peter-Straße.
4 Das Thomas Gäßgen.
5 Das Baarfüßer Gäßgen.
6 Die Heu-Straße.
7 Die Luther-Straße.
8 Das Salz-Gäßgen.
9 Die Börse.

10 Der Börsen drschlg Marckt.
11 Die Brod-Bäncke.
12 Die Fleisch-Bäncke.
13 Die Reichs-Straße.
14 Das Schuster-Gäßgen.
15 Die Niclaus-Straße.
16 Das Holdhan-Gäßgen.
17 Die Niclaus-Kirche.
18 Die Ritter-Straße.

Leipzig's marketplace and view of eastern section of the inner city. Engraving by Johann Georg Schreiber, 1712.

ßen Theil der Stadt LEIPZIG.

19 Das H: Fürsten Collegium
20 Das Rothe Collegium.
21 Das gr: Fürsten Collegium.
22 Das Grimische Thor.
23 Die Pauliner Kirche.
24 Das Pauliner Collegium.
25 Das Fürsten Hauß.
26 Der Alte Neu Marckt.
27 Raths Bibliother u: Zeug Hauß
28 Das Bernard Shauß.
29 Das Bernard Köstgen.
30 Der Neue Neu Marckt.

G. Schreiber Math: Stud: delineavit et sculpsit.

Map of Central Europe in the early eighteenth century.

Contents

Illustrations

Figures

Maps

Editor's Acknowledgments

Bach's Changing World: Voices in the Community grew out of the public humanities programs at the Bach Aria Festival and Institute. The Festival and Institute, an activity of the Bach Aria Group, was held on the campus of Stony Brook University from 1981 through 1997.

For seventeen years I enjoyed the unsurpassed privilege of hearing performances by musicians who, for intense two-week periods each year, thought of little else but Bach's music and their performances. Exchanges between colleagues could be overheard not only at rehearsals and coaching sessions but also at breakfast, lunch, and dinner, and in the "fishbowl," a large room enclosed by a glass wall that served as central office, meeting place, rest area, and snack bar. Therefore, this book owes its existence to the wonderfully gifted artist-fellows who participated in the Bach Aria Festival and Institute and to the artist-teachers of the Bach Aria Group who contributed their spirited devotion and infectious enthusiasm, and their profound identification with Bach's music.

Interaction with our informed, predominantly scholarly, general audiences inspired instituting pre-concert lectures and panel discussions, as well as open rehearsals and coaching sessions, in order to share ideas both about the process of performance and the cultural background of the music performed. These programs were very well received. My becoming acquainted with a wide range of topics in Bach musicology was a requisite for implementing these programs. As a musicologist, I found this task ever more absorbing and thought-provoking. The book itself was conceived during the implementation of the National Endowment for the Humanities' Public Humanities Programs in 1992–93 and 1993–94, which were supported with major grants. These awards facilitated invitations to scholars from other countries, in addition to those from the United States, as well as from several disciplines. The music and humanities programs strove to achieve a wide-ranging portrayal of Bach's world. Discussions with some of the scholars who gathered at the Festival resulted in the historical focus that gives this study its definition. Joining scholars from Stony Brook University, visiting scholars whose ideas greatly enhanced the Festival by their appearances and written contributions were Z. Philip Ambrose, James Anthony, Zdravko Blažeković, George Bozeman, George Buelow, Barbara Becker-Cantarino, Eugene Cox, James Day, Laurence Dreyfus, Joyce Irwin, Karl Kroeger, Herbert Kupferberg, Michael Marissen, Robert Marshall, the late John Ogasapian, Claude Palisca, Peter Reill, Charles Rosen, William Scheide, Hans-Joachim Schulze, Russell Stinson, Teri Noel Towe, Friedrich von Huene, James Winn, and Christoph Wolff. Most of the articles in this book were not presented at the Festival and Institute, but emanated from ideas sparked by discussions at the Festival. I particularly remember exchanges with feminist scholar Barbara Becker-Cantarino, who responded enthusiastically to my idea that Bach may have documented feminist issues in his music, and with Ulrich Siegele and his late wife, Leonora. These conversations encouraged me to pursue the lines of inquiry found here and find scholars whose previous work recommended them as potential contributors to the specific, overall theme of the study—a world in flux. The originality and value of their contributions speak for themselves.

Stony Brook University supported the Bach Aria Festival and Institute generously. Among the numerous people at the University who contributed to the Festival's success, I want to point to the special roles played by President Shirley Kenny and Mrs. John H. Marburger. Provost Sidney Gelber suggested that an institute devoted to Bach studies be brought to Stony Brook and was the architect behind its integration into the life of the University. The vision, encouragement, and support of James Simons, formerly Chair of the Department of Mathematics and President of Renaissance Technologies, turned a dream into reality. Faculty members of the Music, English, German, History, and Philosophy Departments at Stony Brook University made significant contributions to the humanities component of the Festival and Institute. I particularly want to acknowledge Professors David Allison, Karl Bottigheimer, Sue Bottigheimer, Robert Crease, Arthur Haas, Irwin Kra, Richard Kramer, Thomas Kranides, Victor Tejera, Ruben Weltsch, and Peter Winckler. Each year, the music library staff graciously reorganized their facility to accommodate us. Alan Inkles, Director of the Staller Center for the Arts, was a joy to work with. I am indebted to many other people on the Stony Brook campus and wish they could all be named.

Beyond the musicians and scholars who contributed directly and indirectly to this book are the many contributors who made the Bach Aria Festival and Institute possible because of their enthusiasm for Bach's music and for the musicians who made it come alive. I cannot possibly express adequately the gratitude

I feel for the members of our audiences who not only contributed financially but also hosted the musicians and performed myriad services. I have vivid memories of a community working together at many tasks. Among the many friends we had, I want to acknowledge Beverly and Harold Atkins, Irwin and Teri Bardash, Sally Faron, Paul Garfinkle, Clare Kagel, Florence Korn, Marvin Levine, Diane and Mark Orton, Marta and Tom Kastner, Mark Lederway, Eileen Rankin, James and Marilyn Simons, Laurence and Tamara Slobodkin, Mitzi Smith, and Beverly Strozier for making special things happen. I feel guilty for not being able to acknowledge all of the Festival's friends.

The unusually intelligent and committed members of the Board of Directors of the Bach Aria Group Association, including Harold Atkins, Irwin Bardash, Julia Baum, the late Adelle Blumenthal, Martin Bookspan, Betsy Noyes Britton, Andrew Feiner, Mordecai Gabriel, Paul Garfinkle, Richard Goodman, Theodore Harris, Marsha Laufer, Stanley Lampert, James Simons, Selwyn Steinberg, and Solomon Weinstock, collaborated with the University in supporting the Festival and Institute. They contributed financially and administratively and were, moreover, always interested in the programs. Marsha Laufer was especially interested in the success of this study.

Among the people who directly supported this book, I am grateful to William Scheide for his generous grant. William Scheide founded the Bach Aria Group in 1947 and directed and supported it until 1980. I invariably shared ideas with my very dear colleague in the administration of the Bach Aria Festival and Institute, Victor Ialeggio, always looking forward to his responses and suggestions. My understanding of mysticism was enhanced by Professor Shaul Magid's course in the history of Platonism and seventeenth- and eighteenth-century mysticism. He also suggested several articles and books related to my research. My studies of the Protestant reformers and mystics as well as modern Protestant theologian-scholars, which engaged me for many years, were greatly aided by conversations with Joyce Irwin, herself a theologian. Ruben Weltsch, specialist in German seventeenth-century political history, made major contributions. A remarkably knowledgeable linguist, he responded to my every call for help with a difficult German text and translated documents included in this study. Donna Sammis, head of the interlibrary loan division of the Hermann Melville Library facilitated my research at all stages. I am grateful for the generosity and kindness of librarians at the Bibliothèque Nationale, especially Mme, Elizabeth Qeuval, the Bobst Library, the New York Public Library, and the Stadtarchiv-Leipzig. Zdravko Blažeković, knowledgeable director of the Research Center for Music Iconography, made his archive available and contributed practical technical information. Christoph Wolff gave me permission to publish an abridged translation of Ulrich Siegele's article, which first appeared in *Bach-Jahrbuch*. I also want to thank several colleagues and friends, Stephen Christ, Don O. Franklin, Sarah Fuller, Neil Gillman, Julie Grim, Anita Randolfi, and Nancy Toff for their suggestions and encouragement and for reading pieces of this work.

I feel fortunate to have been able to work with the staff at the University of Rochester Press. Ralph Locke was the ideal editor, immediately grasping the significance of my objectives and then giving me the opportunity to realize them. Suzanne Guiod and her staff smoothed out stylistic inconsistencies between chapters and between German and English idioms, and took care of all the details that turn a messy manuscript into a beautiful-looking book. Production Manager Sue Smith smoothly moved the book through its many stages and was always a reassuring presence, as was Katie Hurley whose alertness made problems disappear. I also appreciate the intelligence that Mark Klemens and Timothy Madigan exercised at different stages. The Press's anonymous readers contributed valuable commentary.

Several studies, classics, inspired me to look for the unexpected in developing historical evidence. Two, which I read many years ago, made a lasting impression on me: Hugh Trevor-Roper's *Religion, the Reformation, and Social Change* and Paul Hazard's *The European Mind: The Critical Years 1680–1715,* both based on the interrelationships between society, politics, and religion. Among more recent works, Richard Popkin's *The Third Force in Seventeenth-Century Thought* had a decisive influence on this study. It pursues the complex and sometimes corrupting relationships between mysticism, theology, and religion as well as the impact of interactions between different religions in the European Judeo-Christian tradition and their respective theologies during the seventeenth century. (Ill health prevented Popkin's appearance as a lecturer at the Bach Aria Festival and Institute, but I will always treasure memories of our meeting.) A more recent book that sensitized me to new possibilities for historical scholarship was Robert Darnton's *The Great Cat Massacre and Other Episodes in French Cultural History.*

The Bach Aria Festival and Institute was the idea of my late husband Samuel Baron, the flute soloist of the Bach Aria Group from 1965 and its music director from 1980 until his death in 1997. His faith in the value of my work will always be meaningful to me. *Bach's Changing World: Voices in the Community* is dedicated to his memory.

C. B.

January 2006

Chapter One

Transitions, Transformations, Reversals

Rethinking Bach's World

Carol K. Baron

1. Introduction

Johann Sebastian Bach's life and works are neither what this book is about nor central to these chapters. They are, however, the *raison d'être* for this study that moves away from the composer and into the community in which he spent the last, longest, and most prestigious part of his professional career. The chapters highlight developments and issues that characterize Leipzig and the Saxon Electorate in an exceptional period in their history: roughly coinciding with Bach's lifetime (1685–1750), the early German Enlightenment, and the central years of the "age of absolutism," which is usually located between the end of the Thirty Years' War (1648) and the dissolution of the Holy Roman Empire (1806).

Bach moved to Leipzig when he was thirty-eight years old, an accomplished and famous organist but a less well-known, albeit mature, composer. Bach's Leipzig experiences could not, therefore, have determined his musical predilections or personal values but, rather, we can assume they contributed to his subsequent growth and to the inclinations and preferences of his later years. The portrait of Bach in Figure 1.1, one of several by a prestigious Leipzig portraitist, was painted four years before the composer died. Presumably Leipzig offered Bach a distinctive set of opportunities that were compatible with his interests and goals. Because Bach applied for this position at a stage in life when other opportunities would have been open to him—and he is known to have sought and rejected other positions—we can assume that his choice was significant and that Leipzig's reputation was a factor in his decision.

Figure 1.1. Johann Sebastian Bach, painting by Elias Gottlob Haußmann, 1748.
Courtesy of William H. Scheide, Princeton.

Leipzig was a wealthy commercial center whose favorable location at the cross-roads of important trade routes determined its success as the site of trade fairs dating back to the twelfth century. Its Saxon princes (or electors) in the capital city of Dresden, prone to a conspicuously luxuriant life-style and extravagant court displays and, furthermore, supporting an army for a series of limited but expensive and, in effect, continuous European wars, depended on the money and goods Leipzig's merchants could supply.[1] The trade fairs attracted merchants from all over Europe and Asia, and goods could be found from as far away as Russia and America. Leipzig's reputation as a commercial center is dramatically expressed in Figure 1.2. Between 1700 and 1750 Leipzig's population increased by over 50 percent to more than 30,000, and the population of Dresden, home of the Saxon court, rose from 21,000 to over 60,000—by the standards of the time, these cities were densely populated.[2] Wealthy prior to the onset of the Thirty Years' War, Leipzig reveled in an even greater acquisition of wealth during this period; its extraordinarily successful merchants commissioned mansions from leading architects that were modeled on those belonging to nobility. In addition, the merchants created public promenades and landscaped gardens and supported artists as well as musicians and composers—all with private monies (see figure 1.3). Between 1693 and 1729, Leipzig had an opera house in which fifteen performances of works using German texts were presented at each of the three trade fairs, and itinerant Italian troupes brought operas to Leipzig during the following thirty years.[3] Bach served the Leipzig community at the height of this economically burgeoning period in its history.

The city was ruled by a town council whose members were either merchants or lawyers, most often the educated sons of merchant families whose interests they represented. A patriciate consisting of Leipzig's elite, the Town Council operated with a view towards protecting and enhancing Leipzig's cosmopolitan image. Membership on the council was inherited, and members controlled the selection of new members. Outsiders could gain access for various politically feasible reasons, however, including bureaucrats representing the interests of the Saxon ruler. Chapter 5 describes the Council's functions and responsibilities.

Unlike competing German commercial centers like Frankfurt am Main and Hamburg, Leipzig was also the seat of one of Germany's leading universities. From the end of the seventeenth century, professors and other local scholars and writers published intellectually and ethically oriented periodicals that were specifically geared to Leipzig's literate population, several of which are discussed in chapters 2 and 3. Furthermore the university provided students who filled positions in local orchestras and supplied most of the actors and singers for theatrical and operatic productions.[4]

The intellectual climate in Leipzig was also influenced by the city's role as the primary center of the book trades for all of central Europe. These were run as commercial enterprises like trades in other commodities, that is, not through

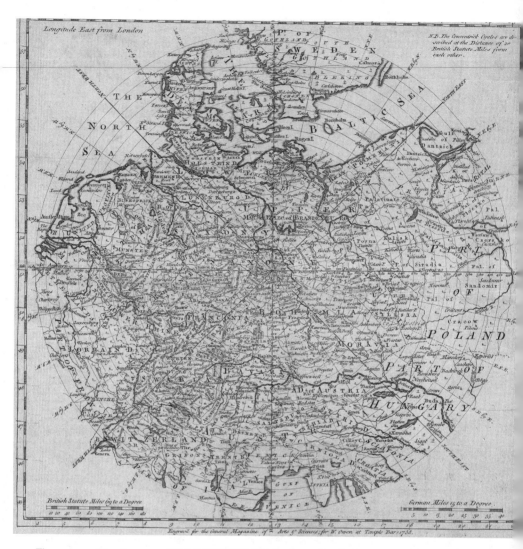

Figure 1.2. "An Accurate COMMERCIAL MAP of 440 English Statute Miles round LEIPZIG, the principal Emporium & Mart of the GERMAN EMPIRE; Shewing by Concentrick Circles the distances of all places within the compass of the present Seat of War, & also their Bearings from that City. By Eman. Bowen Geographer to His Majesty. Engraved for the General Magazine of Arts & Sciences; for W. Owen at Temple Bar, 1758." Courtesy of the Map Division, The New York Public Library, Astor, Lenox, and Tilden Foundations.

aristocratic patronage. In 1700, Leipzig, with a population of 28,000, housed eighteen publishers and booksellers, and a whole community of printers, bookbinders, and illustrators. By contrast, most central and east-central European cities, including Vienna and Prague, then had remarkably few bookshops by the standards of Amsterdam, The Hague, London, Paris, or Venice. Munich and Hanover were simply not places to buy books; Berlin reputedly had but a single bookshop and Königsberg, a university town, only three.[5] Chapter 3 discusses the shift in Leipzig publications from Latin to German and from works for scholars and theologians to devotional works and a wide variety of secular works for the public. Chapter 2 describes the freedom of the press achieved by Leipzig's commercial publishers early in the eighteenth century—with the Saxon Elector's support and a variety of ruses—who managed to avoid the censorship of fringe theologies and radical philosophical works. Leipzig's first city library opened in 1677—falling slightly behind Bremen, Lübeck, and Hamburg, commercial centers that opened libraries in 1648. The relative freedom of thought Leipzig enjoyed was noted in 1684 by a Parisian journal editor who cited Leipzig and Amsterdam for having the freest access to books from all over Europe, while French critical journals had difficulty obtaining books to review even from other Catholic countries.[6]

By contrast, in Leipzig's neighboring city Halle, which was Prussia's publishing center, publications for the public in 1717 were limited to Bibles, textbooks for the Pietist schools, collections of sermons, Biblical commentary, hymns, and autobiographical accounts of conversions and professions of faith—"overwhelmingly" dedicated to serving Prussia's "Pietist mission."[7] Halle, located only twenty miles away from Leipzig, became a Pietist center when Prussia's Elector Frederick III (r. 1688–1713; King Frederick I after 1701) founded its university in 1694. During the reign of his grandson Frederick the Great, a form of tolerance was introduced that restricted the discussion of radical and irreligious philosophies to scholars and their publication to French and Latin texts. As late as 1761, writing from Prussia's capital city Berlin, Johann Georg Sulzer could still write: "As long as books remain only in the hands of professors, students, and contributors to journals I do not think it is worth the trouble to write for the present generation."[8]

Leipzig's reputation is captured in these verses from a contemporary popular song text: "The pleasant Athens-on-the-Pleisse/ Holds glory for all/. . . . Go and note . . . / The magnificent palaces/ And what order, skill, and industry/ Can indeed conceive/. . . . Here must be an angelic life!/ Here it must be an Eden!"[9] Similar sentiments are expressed in a 1725 chamber of commerce brochure quoted in chapter 2 and in the final section of the document by Johann Kuhnau in chapter 9. This was the Leipzig to which Bach aspired. We may well ponder what gaining a position in this prestigious community, instead of at a court, for example, meant to Bach.

Figure 1.3. Leipzig: Promenade outside the Small Thomas Gate, begun
1702–1703. Engraving by J. A. Rosmaesler, 1777.

2. Incentives and Problems

Since Bach left few personal documents, the illustrious successes of modern
Bach scholarship have been accomplished despite, and possibly to compensate
for, that fact. Christoph Wolff's recent biography goes far towards alleviating
gaps in our knowledge about Bach's life.[10] Yet a recent article by George Stauffer
in the *New York Times* is entitled "Beyond Bach the Monument, Who Was Bach
the Man?" Without the biographical evidence on which scholars can usually
depend, conjecture about the composer and even some of his major works—
their meaning, purpose, and reception—has been unavoidable.[11] Robert
Marshall recently lamented that a consensus about Bach's image never developed and listed the ongoing competing images: " 'a progressive,' a radical revolutionary with a political agenda, an anti-Enlightenment social critic, a
profound—and profoundly orthodox—Lutheran theologian, and a trans- or
supra-historical unicum." Marshall also noted that these various depictions are
based "mostly on the testimony of his music" and suggested the need to expand
the evidential resources.[12] Authoritatively defended theses about Bach's religious allegiances and sensibilities and about who his friends were or weren't,
and brilliant hermeneutic analyses of his music remain challenged by equally
authoritative and contradictory theses and analyses. Focusing too closely on
Bach and his music alone may have obscured aspects of his life.

In addition to contending with the paucity of personal documents, Bach
scholars are deprived of reliable *a priori* assumptions in the religious, social, and
political spheres on which both history and biography depend: unsettled institutional structures characterize Bach's world. The Thirty Years' War ushered in
the "age of absolutism," a period when political restructuring initiated profound
changes in socio-economic institutions that dated back to the medieval social
organization of feudalism.[13] These changes affected not only Bach's life but all
of Europe. During the war, which was particularly devastating in the German
territories, the rulers of several hundred political entities had aggressively
maneuvered for land and wealth while, concurrently, Catholicism and new
Protestant systems of belief competed to establish dominance. At the end of the
war, the German-speaking territories were a conglomeration of newly formed,
larger, independent political entities—shown in Frontispiece 2.[14] By definition,
absolutism placed political power—which had previously been shared under the
feudal system with the two major Estates, the nobility and the cities, as well as
with other political bodies with less power, such as the clergy—in the person of
the ruler. In this interterritorial culture, which remained intensely competitive,
the German rulers needed increased revenues to secure their borders and establish their prestige. The paths they followed included building armies, expanding
their courts, and, notably, centralizing the administration of their governments
through a bureaucratic structure. However, the political goals and governing
styles of the individual territorial sovereigns, and the practical problems they

faced or imagined—"a matter of personalities as well as institutions"—determined their differences and the diverse paths they took.[15]

Centralization and the bureaucratization of government required a new professional class. Bureaucracies, in theory at least, would replace the nobility and cities in collecting taxes and be responsible for carrying out internal protectionist economic policies. Expert advisors could plan and recommend foreign policy decisions. By the early eighteenth century, cameralism, the new science of bureaucratic practice, was an academic subject setting new standards for statecraft. Consisting of both aristocrats and commoners, an educated class was trained or sought training to analyze every aspect of social and political life and assume responsibility for the success of the state—to be bureaucrats. Broad variations existed throughout Europe as well as within the German territories regarding, on the one hand, the replacement of aristocrats in prestigious government positions by upwardly mobile commoners who became professional administrators and, on the other hand, the ongoing traditional bonds between the aristocracy and sovereigns. Social ambiguity was inherent in this situation, where estate was identified with birth and "classification by estate emphasized rank and hierarchy in such a way as to obscure the actual lateral boundaries that set one social and political world off from another."[16] In this period, talent and industry could advance social and economic mobility and compete with the inherited privileges of the aristocracy. Newly educated commoners functioned as government consultants and bureaucrats, professors and philosophers, as well as lawyers and doctors. In commercial cities like Leipzig, opportunities for educated commoners and the independence and bargaining power of the well-established merchant society combined to formulate criteria for status by accomplishment and wealth. In the so-called "free" or imperial cities of Hamburg, Lübeck, and Bremen, these socio-political ambiguities led not only to disrespect for the nobility but even to their exclusion from city councils, an example of which the writer-publicist Johann Michael von Loën (1694–1776) targeted in 1752 in Der Adel.[17] Acquiring an aristocratic title or marrying one's daughter to a nobleman would still carry honorific value for some merchants, but feudal hierarchies were losing their significance.

Structural and attitudinal changes—profoundly affecting also the religious sensibilities discussed in chapter 2—did not await the new political constructions that would be legally enacted in the next century. Situations existed in which the conventional legal and social classifications of the estates as nobles, Bürger [that is, urban dwellers] and peasants simply didn't work "even in the political sociology of the eighteenth century," because they "left the civil service [that is, the new government bureaucrats] out of account altogether. . . . Similarly estate categories obscured the place of the German nobility, which might be either administrative or agrarian"—significant because land ownership was the traditional source of aristocratic prestige. Placing everyone "who was neither noble nor peasant in the Bürger estate" was also misleading,[18] because

> the merchant class, inasmuch as its activities freed it from "ties to the earth and to the locality," did not "realistically" belong to the Bürger estate, either socially or ethically; "by his rootless character [*unbodenständigen Art*] the merchant blends systematically into the general estate [defined early in the nineteenth century by Hegel], the estate of the officials." The world of learning was in it too, since officials "are simultaneously men of learning." The quality of personal ambition set the civil servant, merchant, and scholar off from actual Bürger.[19]

Although it is perhaps peripheral to this study, we are nevertheless going to introduce a theoretical controversy in modern scholarship that has arisen in addressing this issue of institutional ambiguity. It may be more a problem of scholarly consensus than lived eighteenth-century reality, but it does influence the ways in which the issue is being discussed and, therefore, interpretations of the socio-political sphere in Bach's time. The controversy reflects concern with appropriately representing the interconnected development of structurally functional socio-economic change—especially the movement of commoners into new roles in cities, courts, and land ownership—and the concurrent preservation, legally and in practice, of aristocratic authority and prestige. Those theories acknowledging absolutism as a transitional stage to constitutional government have been reduced to "two main variants." In brief, "one regards absolutism in political terms as the intermediary stage between the medieval and modern state," a "modernizing" factor leading to constitutional government. The other variant "sees the transition in socio-economic terms with absolutism as the intermediary between feudal and capitalist society" and is "featured prominently in Marxist interpretations of absolutism." The latter "gave rise to the designation 'late feudal epoch,' " the term used by East German historians, or "early modern period (*Die frühe Neuzeit*)," the term used in the West.[20] Self-conscious terms used to describe the new class, including "educated elite," "civil servants," or "bureaucrats," designate groups later understood unambiguously as segments of the "middle class." The religious questions arising from this ambiguity are addressed in chapter 2: for example, whether Luther's doctrine of necessary temporal hierarchies and obedience to secular authority, which was retained in the peace treaties of the Holy Roman Empire, retained its validity for the wealthy and upwardly mobile members of the Leipzig community after the Thirty Years' War, although Saxony was legally a Lutheran orthodox territory.

Further compounding difficulties for Bach scholars, modern German scholarship seems not to have studied the agents of socio-political change in the Wettin dynasty's Saxon-Thuringian territorial orbit, where Bach lived his entire life. The decidedly Prusso-centric bias in seventeenth- and eighteenth-century German studies concentrates on the decisions and actions of the highly profiled princes who ruled Brandenburg-Prussia. Although some work focuses on other large German territories, and there are numerous monographs on individual cities and regions, Saxony has, in general, been ignored. Modern monographs about Leipzig have literary or musicological orientations, and the few about Dresden are centered on court life. Modern European studies include comparisons of Brandenburg-Prussia with France and England, and some studies configure parameters for territorial comparisons that use combinations including Württemberg, Austria, and Russia, as well as other nations.[21] Only Saxony's defeat in international politics and war seems to have been addressed seriously and, even here, with less concern for consequences in Saxony than for those in Prussia.[22]

The lacunae in Saxon studies may have had their origin in the period when the archives of the German Democratic Republic were closed to scholars.[23] An interest in Germany's modern period may also be a factor. Prussia's domination of the German territories during the second half of the eighteenth century under the aggressive policies of Frederick II, "the Great" (r. 1740–86)—setting up the collision course with Austria and the circuitous path toward future unification—certainly was a factor in establishing Prussia's paradigmatic role for modern German studies. However, the influence of accessible archival materials from the central state archives of Brandenburg-Prussia, published as the *Acta Borussica* around the turn of the twentieth century, may have been even more influential. H. M. Scott suggests that its influence even led to inclusive, misleading interpretations of seventeenth- and eighteenth-century socio-political developments in other European countries by basing even them on the Prussian model.[24] Stefan Berger traces the problem back to Frederick William, the "Great Elector" (r. 1640–88), who initiated the idea of writing an "official" state history and hired court historians to do so. (The political scientist Samuel Pufendorf was hired as historian at the Brandenburg-Prussian court between 1688 and 1694.) Frederick William set a tradition followed by his successors that culminated in the *Mémoires pour servir à l'histoire de Brandenbourg* (1746) by Frederick the Great. The influence of these documents, Berger says, "has never really been overcome and remains one of the key shortcomings of today's historical writings" in "German historiography."[25]

Yet until Prussia outperformed Saxony in the middle of the eighteenth century, Saxony was one of the most prestigious Protestant electorates in the Holy Roman Empire and probably the wealthiest; in fact Leipzig continued, even after that time, to be a conspicuously successful commercial center engaged in international trade, as can be seen in figure 1.2. The point is this: studies of the German territories prior to the end of the eighteenth century cannot generalize or legitimately speak of "German" social and political history—the absolutist governments were politically and culturally too disparate. In a comprehensive German history, endemic socio-political factors and related religious beliefs can only be handled comparatively.[26]

3. Rethinking Bach's World

"Transitions"

Leipzig's unusual features and the divergence of Saxony's history from Prussia's are clarified by comparing the agents of social change in Saxony and Prussia after the Thirty Years' War. While showing some examples of shared policies, we can introduce the diverse paths that led, on the one hand, to Prussia's centralized and militarized state economy and, on the other, to the relatively freewheeling entrepreneurial economy on which Saxony depended. Furthermore, throughout this period, these territorial governments crossed paths in ways that informed their respective ambitions for land, power and prestige, and their religious—and irreligious—affinities.

The personalities of the Prussian and Saxon sovereigns and the problems and institutions characterizing these states were already articulated when they first started implementing their absolutist governments. Yet it would be incorrect to assume that these changes were initiated out of whole cloth after the Thirty Years' War, and evidence exists of dynastic "personalities" already in existence. (We note that arguments about various issues now available in Prussian historiography extend far beyond the scope of this study.) Looking both forward and backward, it seems likely that Leipzig's truly unique qualities could only have blossomed in Saxony, where a symbiosis of electoral government and city government, of electoral goals and city goals may even have been instrumental in shaping the character of Saxony's Wettin dynasty, going back to the late Middle Ages. In the end, the roles played out in the Saxon-Prussian competition—Saxony's hapless experiences on the battlefield and Prussia's primarily successful ones, their disparate levels of war preparation and strategic political planning, Saxony's luxurious court and Prussia's alternatively parsimonious or non-existent one until Frederick the Great, their reversals in fortune culminating in Saxony's thwarted political ambitions and Prussia's emergent leadership under Frederick the Great—can be ascribed to the confrontation of these dynastic cultures with a defining stage in history. Saxony's political and military passivity and expansionist vision limited to patrimony, diplomacy, and marriage contracts ran counter to Prussia's aggressive expansionist practices and to the centralizing and nationalistic direction that was, at this time, the wider European model for independent statehood:[27] The Prussian vision led to Germany's future. A comparison of how Prussia and Saxony handled the single most discussed development during the absolutist period, the expansion of central administrations through bureaucratization, highlights how these sovereigns envisioned glorifying their dynasties as well as how they defined the problems they faced.

The Prussian "Model"
After the Thirty Years' War Frederick William, the Great Elector, established the Prussian path toward state building: a "military, centralizing monarchy" that

would be followed more or less closely by his successors.[28] Prussian history of this period—and the paradigm misleadingly projected as "German"—is solidly based on the archival materials compiled and published in *Acta Borussica* and confirmed in many studies. This path, however, influenced by a history of territorial instability, mini-divisions, and the disabling divisiveness of power in the hands of the nobility, had already been anticipated and documented prior to the war in the Ordinance of 1604 during the reign of Joachim (r. 1603–8). Otto Hintze, one of the original scholars who worked on the *Acta Borussica*, finds that in this earlier document "for the first time in the history of Brandenburg, the dominating interests of modern raison d'état—the financial and the military—. . . appeared alongside . . . religious interest as the main aims of the Elector's policy." The term "economic policy" also appears in this state document for the first time.[29] Hintze associates the parallel articulation of economic, military, and religious concerns to the regime's affinity to Calvinism. Several influential noble families had already joined the Calvinist or Reform Church; the Hohenzollern dynasty's Elector John Sigismund (r. 1608–19) openly announced his conversion in 1613. Both Hintze and the modern historian Bodo Nishan emphasize the political ramifications of Brandenburg-Prussia's religious history from the early period of the Lutheran Reformation in the 1520s, when the popular conversion to Lutheranism of most nobles and their subjects took place, through the "Second Reformation" marked by the conversion of the Hohenzollern dynasty to Calvinism (known also as the Reform Church) and the "pan-Protestant awareness" in the 1630s.[30] Nishan emphasizes that the success of the earlier Lutheran Reformation in these territories contributed to the failure of the "Second Reformation," which generated interest only among the ruling elite.

Thus, at the end of the Thirty Years' War the Great Elector inherited the oppositional force of his landed Lutheran nobility along with the dangers his geographically separated and socially diverse territorial possessions presented. These were the factors that led to the nature of Prussia's absolutist reforms toward centralization and bureaucratization. To unite and protect the non-contiguous territories he gained during the Thirty Years' War, Frederick William built a centralized administration and a large, disciplined army. Since the success of his state-building goals was contingent on large revenues, he destroyed the autonomy of the noble estates and municipal governments and usurped their prior tax-collecting privileges, rendering them subservient by the 1670s to his centralized administration.[31] However he compensated the nobility by enlisting their sons as army officers and giving them major roles in administering the state's affairs.[32] Frederick William's most discussed innovation is the compromise in 1653 which, in exchange for new taxes, gave the nobility the right to hold dominant roles in the army's officer corps.[33] In addition, the legal power of the nobility as the religious protectors of their Lutheran subjects was abrogated, although this privilege had been renewed at the end of the Thirty Years'

War in the Treaty of Westphalia, specifically directed to circumstances of sovereign conversions.[34]

Thus Frederick William initiated a pattern designed to destroy the political and religious resistance of his Lutheran nobles and subjects to Hohenzollern policies. It culminated in Prussia's adoption of an authoritarian form of Pietism as its state religion. When the university at Halle was founded in 1694, it became tactically important for Prussian state-building: it was the center for educating church officials and clerics whose role was geared toward enhancing the state's political and cultural authority. It promoted an educational system throughout the Brandenburg-Prussian territories that destroyed Lutheran authority.[35] Other universities in these territories were soon answerable to the Prussian monarchs in all matters, even decisions about hiring and firing. The university in Leipzig, by contrast, although supported by the Town Council, firmly protected its autonomy, as shown in chapter 5.

In contrast to the productive steps taken by the Saxon government in the administration of its cities—Leipzig and other ones described below—Frederick William imposed excise taxes beginning in the 1660s on the goods manufactured in cities, which resulted in losses from competition with rural and noble products that were tax-exempt. Under later regimes, although cameralist theory received its fullest development at the university in Halle, where administrators and bureaucrats were trained to serve in the progressively centralized government, Prussia's economic policies continued to be unsuccessful. Karen Friedrich studied these policies and compared the successful commercial development before the war of a city like Königsberg, located in distant Polish Prussia, with the municipal economies developed under the Prussian regimes. She concluded that by comparison with Königsberg, Berlin, the Brandenburg capital, "looked like a poor country cousin."[36]

Saxon Inventiveness

In place of the acknowledged deficits in Saxon history, I am presenting the hypothesis proposed by German literary historian Hans-Gert Roloff to explain the early history of Saxon absolutism. Roloff's hypothesis is based on impressive statistics from publishing history and, I would add, the sometimes unaccountable, intangible, and serendipitous elements of the human agency. The statecraft that supported Saxon absolutism seems to have been largely fostered by commoners: Saxon bureaucracy and its underlying "theory," that is, Saxon cameralism, developed from the bottom up, so to speak. According to Roloff, Christian Weise (1642–1708), a popular writer and teacher, perceived that the Saxon Electors' absolutist style had distanced them from the administrative responsibilities of government and created a vacuum that could be filled by commoners and increasingly disenfranchised aristocrats. Weise recognized interrelationships between the needs of the Saxon government and opportunities for social change among its subjects; he alerted lawyers, trained mainly to be advocates for family businesses, to the government's needs and to opportunities for their self-advancement at court.[37]

Christian Weise was endowed with a dynamic combination of analytical gifts, rhetorical brilliance, and a bold personality. He was born in the Saxon city of Zittau and attended the university in Leipzig, where he was drawn to problems in political science. Leaving Leipzig after ten years, he held a court position as secretary to a minor Saxon nobleman, in which his duties included drafting letters and speeches for his employer, delivering speeches and producing literary materials under his own name, and analyzing the challenges of governing. This experience had a profound impact for Weise's career as a teacher at the gymnasium in Zittau, where he returned in 1678. Weise's school curriculum was both practical and creative, emphasizing problem solving and oratorical skills in German, which was slowly replacing Latin as the language of government. His goal was to create "*homo politicus*," a person trained in the political skills, wisdom, and manners needed to work at court. Weise believed that a polished rhetorical style was essential for tackling the challenges of political and social life, and he made rhetoric and logic relevant by applying them to current political topics.[38] Weise also wrote plays for student performances and scheduled frequent debates to teach self-assurance, adroitness, and speaking skills.[39] The Zittau gymnasium was renowned throughout Europe and attracted members of the lower nobility as well as commoners. Gottfried Lange, described in chapter 5, who represented the interests of August the Strong on the Leipzig Town Council and was mayor when Bach was hired as the new cantor, attended Weise's gymnasium.

Weise's fame among the reading public, however, far surpassed his fame as a teacher in Zittau. His years in politics had taught him that university graduates were not being prepared for what they would confront if they wanted to enter government service. Therefore in numerous handbooks, Weise taught rational views of statecraft, religion, and private economic interests to literate commoners. These handbooks satisfied the need for practical, vocationally oriented education, containing everything needed to prepare for the qualifying examinations that led to political jobs. For two decades, each one was reprinted in ten or twelve editions, and they were among the best-selling books in the German lands. While still working in government, Weise wrote *Klugen Hofmeister* (The Clever Court Administrator, 1676), which became the guide for an entire generation of administrators in the late seventeenth century. The following publications convey Weise's output and focus. His instruction books in rhetoric were *Der politische Redner* (*Political Speaker*, 1677); its revision in 1684, *New Erläuterten politische Redner*, and *Institutiones Oratoriae* (1687), which added systematic instruction in oratory. The titles of other handbooks were *Deutsche Staatsgeographie* (1687), *Politischen Fragen* (*Political Questions*, 1690), and *Curiöse Gedanken von deutschen Briefen* (1691), lessons in letter writing. He also wrote *Hofmeister* (*Court Administrator*, 1675) and *Politische Academicus* (1684).

Weise's poetry, novels and plays—which he started writing during his Leipzig years—also contributed to his renown. All his works had the same didactic purpose: teaching "political" behavior. His most famous novel, *Die drey ärgsten Ertznarren in der gantzen Welt* (*The Three Most Arrant Fools in the Entire World*), started in Leipzig in 1665 and published in 1672, was a humorous novel that became the model for *Der musicalische Quacksalber* (*The Musical Charlatan*) by Johann Kuhnau, Bach's predecessor at the Thomaskirche.[40] By highlighting foolish behavior, Weise used humor to instruct the reader in "correct" behavior. Weise's literary success was "much greater" in his time than that of writers like Opitz, Gryphius, Lohenstein, Hallman, and even Grimmelshausen, who are all better known today.[41] His novels were especially popular in Saxony and Thuringia in the 1670s and 1680s.[42]

Roloff's hypothesis is compatible with what we know about the character of the Wettin rulers after the Peace of Westphalia. Unlike the Hohenzollern rulers, they did not rely on religious calling, missionary enthusiasm, and territorial expansion, as such, in forming their self-image. They tended to be aloof rulers, indifferent military leaders, politically passive, and more interested in establishing their dynastic prestige through conspicuous displays and titles. The history of the Saxon electors as patrons of the arts is impressive—this was their path toward dynastic glorification. Art historians trace the origins of modern collecting in the Protestant capitals to the Saxon rulers in the sixteenth century. In a time when the arts and crafts were not differentiated, they flourished in Saxony and achieved high artistic levels. During the period of recovery after the Thirty Years' War, "religious reservations . . . disappeared, and works of art, as such [no longer restricted by Protestant iconoclasm], were bought in increasing numbers." A document from 1671 refers to an international roster of artists that mentions "paintings by Dürer, Cranach, Rubens, Lucas van Leyden, Titian, and Tintoretto."[43] Such expenditures contrast with the parsimony of Johann Georg III (r. 1680–91) in 1690, who was reluctant to spend money to support his armed forces in defense of the Empire against France. A leader on the battlefield, he was nevertheless "determined that the services of . . . [his Saxon troops] should not be at the expense of ruining Saxon finances." He insisted that they "winter close to the front . . . to spare him the cost of billeting and transport home each spring and autumn."[44] Saxon art collecting would reach its highest levels during the reign of August "the Strong" (r. 1694–1733), who ruled when Bach arrived in Leipzig.

Weise's early cameralist handbooks, judging from their multiple reprints and adoptions in juridical curricula in universities, appear to have played a major role in facilitating Saxony's state bureaucracy. Weise's work instilled aspiration for social and political advancement in the absolutist state and, Roloff concludes, drew so many readers because he convincingly presented possibilities to create new and better lives. Weise changed his readers' image of reality—hitherto based on the inflexible feudal hierarchy—and supplied practical tools to facilitate change.[45] According to Klaus Günzel, although Weise did not seek revolutionary social change, he earned his place in history, first, by having been responsible for first articulating emancipatory thoughts about the middle class and, second, by actually guiding his students into this newly forming class.[46] As the Saxon state welcomed its professional bureaucracy, another alliance with entrepreneurial commoners—in addition to that with merchants—was formed.

Political historians in the future may substantiate—or disprove—the impact of Weise's prolific and popular works on restructuring Saxony's absolutist government. The sociologist Gianfranco Poggi could very well have found for the theory's validity, having written the following:

> There was a broad tendency for the urban groups, once they had gained a legitimate position within the system of rule, to support the territorial ruler's drive to restrict the political significance of the feudal element. They did so by lending him their financial and military support and, increasingly, by manning his growing administrative apparatus. . . . In Germany, centralization was carried out at comparatively low levels by territorial rulers. . . . In most parts of Germany, the failure of high-level centralization meant that the establishment of strong political-administrative structures of rule was retarded at all levels. The main exception was Prussia.[47]

The philosopher-mathematician Gottfried Leibniz (1646–1716)—born and educated in Leipzig, a contemporary of Weise, and himself a beneficiary of court patronage—articulated these social transformations as early as 1679: "Aren't the myriad of princely courts . . . a glorious means to allow so many people to distinguish themselves who would otherwise remain lying in the dust?"[48]

"Transformations"

Comparing key developments in Saxony and Prussia highlights those features of the Saxon world, particularly in Leipzig, that have not emerged in the Prusso-German histories. Dynastic glorification in Prussia remained invested in its army, which "embodied most clearly and most palpably the new idea of state—that of the powerful, centralized, absolutist greater state. Maintenance of the army became the chief task of the state's financial administration. . . . This kind of thinking resulted in the full-blown system of commercial regulation that is associated with mercantilist economic policy. . . . The absolutist military state developed into the tutelary police state."[49] By retaining the nobility as the sole constituency of the officer corps—with few exceptions for technical expertise—the state controlled the aristocracy and was assured of its loyalty and financial subsidies. That loyalty, on which Frederick the Great would later also rely, was a significant incentive for Prussia to support the feudal Estate.

The militaristic cast of the Prussian administrative system set it apart from that of Saxony and other German states. Outside Prussia, criticism of Prussia's militaristic policies reached a broad population through the works of popular German writers. The social critic-playwright Gotthold Ephraim Lessing

(1729–81) made a Prussian tax collector-army officer, Major von Tellheim, the hero of his 1767 comedy *Minna von Barnhelm*, which he wrote for the new Hamburg National Theater. In empathy with the suffering of the defeated Saxon-Thuringian districts under his command, Tellheim is made impecunious by advancing his own money to pay the reparations he was ordered to collect. The Prussians then accuse him of having taken a bribe because he stipulated too low a rate of interest on his loan.[50]

The religious convictions that drove political and economic efforts in Prussia ran counter to the religious indifference of the Saxon dynasty. Frederick William I, Prussia's "Soldier King" (r. 1713–40), obsessively concerned with his destiny as a religious leader, controlled the administrative details of government and his army as personal religious responsibilities.[51] In his 1722 testament, he warned of the threat from the elite Lutheran nobility, as had the "Great Elector" seventy years previously. The attitudes in Prussia and Saxony toward large-scale entrepreneurs could not have diverged more. Frederick William I's mercantilist obsessions turned on irrational assumptions, despite his having cameralist theorists in the service of the state. These assumptions were based on an ideology demanding the total submission of the individual to the interests of the state.[52] If, as a consequence, Prussia's centrally controlled mercantilist policies were a failure for the general economy, they were successfully manipulated to more than adequately support the growth of the army.[53] Thus, although his father, King Frederick I, had improved Berlin's economy by encouraging craftsmen and artists when he expanded court life, the city's "economic upturn" was interrupted when Frederick William I "reject[ed] luxury production and . . . attempt[ed] to force manufacturers into producing utilitarian goods and army supplies, especially cloth for uniforms." Berlin's population was 45,000 to 50,000 in 1700; in 1730, it was 58,000 but "over 14,000 belonged to the military garrison."[54] Frederick William I's chief adviser documented the Prussian attitude during the 1720's and 30's: "Merchant-manufacturers were 'poor patriots' because they paid low wages during prosperous times, laid off workers during recessions, and then took their enhanced supply of capital out of the country without even indemnifying the state for having to take care of unemployed ex-workers reduced to beggary." Therefore, "though the state could not completely dispense with entrepreneurs, it used them only selectively and subjected them to extensive regulation."[55] The contemporary essayist-writer Johann Michael Loën responded with these thoughts about ruinous, state-mandated economic controls: "They [merchants] provide food for a country, they maintain the necessary circulation of money within it, and are the surest means for making it rich and mighty." An interfering prince, because of his own greed and the jealousy of the nobility, causes severe declines in trade and commerce; Loën concludes that "one must allow freedom for business and restrain it only by seeing to it that trust and faith, truth and justice are observed."[56] He echoed attitudes in Saxony.

The Saxon government depended primarily on funds received from the commercial success of its entrepreneurs, a pattern established in the Middle Ages. In turn, the success of its cities depended on the dynasty's trust of and support for autonomously run businesses. Saxony's economy and business enterprises flourished during the period under examination. Leipzig's accomplishments have been amply demonstrated. During the reign of August the Strong, "more manufacturing plants were established . . . than during the previous century and a half."[57] The porcelain industry, a great success story, began in 1710 in Meissen, a town outside Dresden, and held a monopoly on European porcelain production for many years. The secret to manufacturing porcelain was discovered in alchemical experiments supported by August the Strong, who was hoping to produce gold. The Saxon Electors had also subsidized the practical technological experiments of Ehrenfried Walther von Tschirnhaus (1651–1708) that culminated in his perfecting glassmaking techniques and founding the glassworks in Dresden in 1700, and then in several other towns as well. The Saxon rulers also commissioned Tschirnhaus and other scientists to look for semi-precious stones and valuable minerals.[58]

Structural changes in Saxony subjected both wealth and the ownership of land, on which aristocratic privilege was based under feudalism, to a gradual process of redistribution. Commoners who provided outstanding service to the Saxon electors as either state bureaucrats or merchants were rewarded with special privileges, sometimes even elevated to noble status. By 1720, three years before Bach arrived in Leipzig, wealthy commoners owned thirty-two of the fifty-eight estates in the countryside surrounding Leipzig.[59] Bach's *Peasant Cantata*, presented in 1742, celebrated the acquisition of the agrarian estate Klein-Zschocher—previously owned by an aristocrat—by Leipzig's superintendent of tax collection (see figure 1.4).[60] The cantata *Angenehmes Wiederau* had been composed in 1737 for a similar occasion.

Sovereign attempts to achieve unlimited power are noted much later in Saxony than in Prussia, and they never succeeded in dominating the Estates. Although chapter 5 documents the Leipzig Town Council's resistance to attempts by August the Strong to diminish its autonomy, the chapter also demonstrates Council members' pride in their participation at court. August the Strong first acted totally on his own authority when he converted to Catholicism to become the Polish king in 1697, pursuing a title for dynastic prestige. Between 1701 and 1707, he imposed taxes without the consent of the Estates and developed a Private Cabinet responsible only to him. Then in 1711, August limited the Estates' power to approve taxes. Having reorganized the Privy Council to eliminate the Estates, by 1719 August ruled independently with the aid of his minister Count Jakob Heinrich von Flemming. However, in 1727, intending to abolish the Estates' right to approve taxes, August was persuaded by Flemming not to proceed because he needed their support, particularly under the circumstances of his conversion. August periodically reassured the Estates of his support for Lutheranism as the state confession, continuing to grant the Estates, particularly

Figure 1.4. "Klein-Zschocher," a lithograph, circa 1820.

the nobility, the privileges of exercising religious authority over subjects on their lands and negotiating with the political power inherent in that authority.

The first account of August's interfering with Leipzig's local government—an infrequent occurrence—was in 1701 when he imposed a mayoral appointment. The appointee, Conrad Romanus, persuaded the Leipzig Town Council to make large amounts of money available to the King. In 1705, the Council arrested Romanus for treason: He was overheard proposing to Elector-King August "that the cities should be stripped of their autonomy and transformed into state entities." He was also accused of embezzling city funds. August did not follow Romanus's suggestion but he did intercede to save his life. Romanus was nevertheless imprisoned until he died in 1746.[61] This Romanus, incidentally, was the father of Marianne von Ziegler, Bach's sometime librettist, participant in the women's literary movement in Leipzig, hostess of the leading salon, and a leading protagonist in the culture wars discussed in chapter 7.

"Reversals"

Reversals in Saxony's fortunes during the final decade of Bach's life were politically far-reaching. Overextended by her commitment in Poland—August's acquisition so he could become a king—Saxony could not defend itself against the Prussian army. When Frederick the Great, soon after gaining the Prussian throne, used the disciplined military force he inherited to pursue ambitions for power and land, he precipitated the outbreak of a European-wide war that lasted intermittently for two decades. In October 1744, Prussian troops marched through Saxony on their way to invade Bohemia. Then, during the last month of the Second Silesian War, Prussian troops occupied Leipzig until the Treaty of Dresden was signed on Christmas Day, 1745 (see figure 1.5). Prussia officially gained the territory of Silesia, hitherto closely related culturally and economically to Saxony, and exacted reparations from Saxony. Saxony suffered a loss of prestige from which it never recovered. Peter Wilson writes that at this time "Prussia already showed signs of treating Saxony as a potential base, forcibly inducting 1,600 militiamen into its army and prefiguring more extensive exploitation during the Seven Years' War" (1756–63).[62] T. C. W. Blanning says Saxony "financed Prussia's achievement of great-power status, for their involuntary sacrifices financed fully one third of the Prussian war effort." He quotes Frederick as saying, "Saxony was like a flour-sack— no matter how hard or often one hit it, a puff of flour would always come out."[63]

Questions regarding the immediate effect of Prussia's new-found political power on Leipzig's social, religious, and political institutions during the final decade of Bach's life would justify another study. In the meanwhile, two musicologists have speculated about Bach's musical response to Frederick—the response of a Leipziger. Although their scenarios regarding Bach's relationship to Frederick are as speculative as other interpretations of Bach's inner life, they are nonetheless compelling. Bach, who composed the *Musical Offering* for Frederick, seems to have shared the reaction of most of the philosophers Frederick invited to his court: they avoided or limited their contacts with the King, preferring their freedom to the "servitude" he demanded. Their attitude, says Peter Gay, was "a commentary on their political thought, but beyond that, it was a commentary on Frederick's conduct."[64] Is it merely coincidence that, according to Forkel's history of Bach, the composer resisted Frederick's invitations for a period of seven years before agreeing to a visit in 1747?[65] Jean-Jacques Rousseau described Frederick as someone "who does not love virtue, but who considers it as a bait with which to amuse fools."[66] Similarly, musicologist Michael Marissen concludes that Frederick's enthusiastic assessment of Bach's improvising a fugue derived from nothing more than its value as "an entertaining and exciting diversion."[67] Bach knew about Frederick from his son Carl Philipp Emanuel, who entered the king's employ in 1740 as accompanist on clavier.

The work Bach composed for Frederick and flatteringly dedicated is one of the most contentious in musicology. Comprising ten canons, including several in puzzle notation, two fugues, and a four-movement trio sonata, the *Musical Offering* is an anomaly in music history. It is neither a musical genre nor a collection of sub-pieces that are noticeably connected beyond their use of Frederick's "royal theme," upon which Bach was asked to improvise during his Potsdam visit. Bach's reason for composing such a collection continues to draw interest. Scholars have also speculated about a musical and/or rhetorical logic for the order of the pieces as well as the significance of these possible orders.

Da die Sächsische Armee den gefährlichen Anschlag gefasset hatte, samt den Oesterreichern in das
sich gezwungen gesehen, Sr. Hochfürstl. Durchl. dem regierenden Fürsten zu Anhalt-Deßau, er
zerstreuen, und sich dieser Stadt bemächtigen, mögten. Dieses ist auch den 30. Nov. 1745. gli
sich in der größten Unordnung zurück gemacht, daß also der Fürst von Anhalt am besagten
ausserhalb des Thores auf das submisseste empfangen un

Figure 1.5. Leipzig's surrender to Prussian troops on November 30, 1745.
Contemporary engraving.

...deburg, wie auch in die Chur-marck einen Einfall zu thun; als haben Ihro Königl. Majst. von Preussen
...a, daß Dieselben mit ihrer Armee gerade auf Leipzig der feindlichen entgegen ziehen, dieselbe
...gefühlet worden, immaßen die feindl. Armee des Fürsten Ankunft nicht erwartet, sondern
...ne einigen Schwerdtschlag in Leipzig eingezogen ist, nachdem er von dortigem Magistrat
...olet worden.

Michael Marissen and Joel Sheveloff, the two scholars suggesting a scenario for Bach's response to Frederick, challenge the assumption that Bach intended to honor the monarch with his "musical offering." And, although their points of departure could not be more contrary, they both draw attention to Frederick's lust for power and reputation for arrogance. Also, both scholars point to Bach's using the most complex counterpoint ever composed as purposeful and fraught with meaning, because contrapuntal procedures were negated in the gallant homophony Frederick favored. To very briefly summarize their richly argued positions: Michael Marissen's reading proposes an order that has an "increasingly theological character." Its significance lies in Bach's intention to preach "'glorification through abasement,' a view tied to Luther's 'theology of the cross'" and decidedly not in keeping with Bach's "stated intention" to glorify Frederick in either the dedicatory preface or in the inscriptions the composer added to the canons.[68] Joel Sheveloff's reading proposes musical puzzles on both local and global levels of the composition, citing an overall palindromic order with symmetries at key points. According to Sheveloff, Bach was avenging himself, both personally for being treated disrespectfully during his visit to Potsdam and as a Saxon patriot. His stratagem involved presenting music to Frederick, also a composer, that was greater than any he could have imagined and too complex for him to understand.[69] In either case, Bach's response to Frederick, like the responses of the philosophers who avoided this monarch, remained concealed. Even if Frederick had been capable of understanding such messages, there is no evidence that he ever looked at the work dedicated to him.

4. Chapter Themes

The chapters in this study address issues that emerged in the course of new social and intellectual opportunities becoming available. Its authors are from different disciplines: musicology, literary criticism and history, theology and religious history, political history, feminist studies, and linguistics. The interdisciplinary perspectives brought to bear on the entire study also operate within individual chapters, because they all incorporate findings from outside the respective disciplines of their authors: combining feminist literary criticism and musicology, musicology and social and religious history, literary criticism and socio-political history, and so forth.

The period of Bach's lifetime marks an era in Saxon-Thuringian culture in which private society was able to develop an autonomous voice, distinct from that of either the Saxon state and its larger-than-life Dresden court or the religious establishment. Constituting the rise of a public sphere, these private voices emerged in Leipzig with the consent of the Saxon government.[70] Except for the limited confrontations described above, the Saxon ruler and the Leipzig merchants remained tied by mutual interests as they had been for several hundred

years. The prosperity that provided leisure time for Leipzig's citizens to patron-
ize the arts, cultivate intellectual pursuits, and envision and desire a vital, par-
ticipatory bourgeois culture was realized in an absolutist context.
Leipzig was in a uniquely favored position to develop a public sphere. Its cosmopolitan bourgeois population had the wealth to acquire what it admired in its
aristocrats, in Parisian dress codes, and in stylish architecture. Leipzig's theater,
described in chapter 3, emulated French literary values while engaging the
Leipzig audience in issues specifically relevant to them. The Saxon comedies
and moral weeklies articulated the values of the educated professionals—whose
members authored these works—and served as vehicles for their "continuing
education" and entertainment. At the same time, they tried to "modernize" the
conservative merchants, mainly for the benefit of their families. Chapter 7
describes how, for an all-too-short period, women were able to emulate their
French literary heroines and break through the male hegemony in public culture. Both chapters describe social settings where moral, religious, political, and
literary issues were the center of attention and music was performed: men at a
coffeehouse, women at a *kaffeeklatsch* or *kaffeekränzchen,* and mixed company at
salons. Leipzig's educated elite read novels and literary criticism, were introduced to the works of philosophers, and argued about religious ideas, as
described in chapter 2.

Women assumed new roles during this period. During their short-lived prominence in the literary sphere, the right to drink coffee became one of the battles
they fought; Bach's charming cantata was associated with the "gender wars."
Women were welcomed at Pietist meetings, a well-documented source of friction
between Lutheran Pietists and Orthodox, and works by female English mystics
were published and discussed, as chapter 2 demonstrates. The Leipzig comedies
discussed in chapter 3 articulate the need to educate women to be compatible
partners for their educated husbands. Gottfried Scheibel's document in chapter 9
argues for the use of female singers in church, which he acknowledges is controversial but nevertheless supported within the music profession. Bach used
nine texts written by Marianne von Ziegler for sacred cantatas.

Leipzig was exposed to different kinds of music criticism. Johann Kuhnau's
"Treatise on Liturgical Text Settings," chapter 8 in this volume, was designed to
teach his congregants discriminating listening. It was published in 1709 and
accompanied a set of cantata texts to use at services during the season from
Advent until the end of that year. The religious implications of this treatise and
Scheibel's (chapter 9) are discussed in chapter 4. Between 1737 and 1739, controversial criticism of Bach's music was disseminated in Leipzig. The protagonists were Johann Adolph Scheibe in *Der critische Musikus* (1737–40), published
in Hamburg, and Leipzig respondents Johann Abraham Birnbaum and Lorenz
Christoph.[71] At issue were questions of style. At about the same time, literary
critics from Switzerland attacked the aesthetic premises of Johann Christoph
Gottsched, whose multiple roles in Leipzig as literary reformer, mentor,

Enlightenment leader, and translator-editor of radical texts are discussed in chapters 2, 3, and 7.

Public opinion became a force to be reckoned with, and chapter 5 describes the Town Council's use of newspapers to influence it during their "infamous" negotiations to choose Kuhnau's successor as cantor for the Thomasschule. Bach, a famous organist at that time, was deemed inferior to their first-choice candidates, who were all from the world of opera, in a clear statement of the community's aesthetic taste. However, the legal status of Lutheran orthodoxy in Saxony created ambiguous situations that have resisted consensus in modern Bach scholarship. Chapter 5 demonstrates that the Leipzig clergy's "examination of faith"— a step in the hiring process that scholars cite as evidence of the strength of Lutheran orthodoxy—was a *pro forma* exercise that conformed to traditional, official expectations but no longer represented "the theological tendencies and inclinations of the examiners or the individuals who were examined." Johann August Ernesti, the Thomasschule rector and University theologian, professed faith according to Lutheran orthodoxy but incongruously also pursued Biblical criticism as human history—a branch of Rationalist scholarship. Moreover, the clause in Bach's contract requiring that he not compose "operatically"[72] is ironic since the "theatrical style" had been recognized in cantatas by Kuhnau and, particularly, those by Telemann before Bach arrived in Leipzig. Was this clause hypocritical or simply unexamined, or was it a formal concession to the clergy but unrelated to the reality of musical practice?[73] Such inconsistencies project subtler, more nuanced views onto Bach's image and work.

During this entire period, there was a lack of consensus and concern among theologians about what constituted an appropriate style for church music. The documents in chapters 8 and 9, along with other writings discussed in chapter 4, attest to the fact that distinctions between church and theatrical styles had significantly weakened; there is support in these chapters for the idea that these aesthetic changes could be justified theologically. Pointing to the similarities between liturgical music and the music heard in operas performed in Leipzig between 1693 and 1720, chapter 6 asserts that church services became an alternative musical experience after the Leipzig opera ceased its operations, particularly for visitors to the fairs. Bach's congregants had many reasons for attending church services—religious and musical sensibilities were among them.

The clerical estate under the Empire, that is, an independent political entity like the aristocracy and cities, Lutheran orthodoxy was represented on the Town Council by members of its consistory. These members were councillors who, in the Council, also represented the merchants, the Elector-King, and other constituencies. The breakdown of the clergy's privileges, although they were still legally protected, is demonstrated in the government and church archives reported in chapter 5, which show, for example, that the clergy did not participate in the negotiations to choose a cantor for the St. Thomasschule, a musician presumably hired primarily to conduct services at the two principal churches.

The clergy were not even invited to approve the decision or Bach's contract. Council business was not always conducted even-handedly, at least not according to traditional privileges.

Among the many ironies and contradictions underlying the negotiations in the Leipzig Town Council when Bach was hired as cantor are those that illustrate the tensions between the electorate's aspiring absolutism and the city's traditional autonomy. Chapter 5 argues that Bach's professional problems stemmed from competition between councillors supporting absolutism and councillors representing the city's patriciate. Using records from government and church archives, chapter 5 brings an unusual level of immediacy to these negotiations and to their implications for Bach's professional problems with the Leipzig Town Council.

The distinctively worldly character of Saxon absolutism made its mark on Leipzig's religious milieu: eschewing control, openness to diverse religious and philosophical ideas, and support of a free press. Chapter 2 illustrates ways in which the Saxon dynasty actually encouraged philosophical and religious exploration. For example, one may question whether Johann Georg III's subsidizing the publication of one of the most prestigious and successful international journals in 1682—thereby making available new intellectual norms—was contingent on a redeeming intellectual facet of the prince's dynastic image or his attempt to deflect criticism of luxurious court life and mold public opinion. One German critic at the end of the seventeenth century, Immanuel Weber (1659–1726), was cynical:

> The craze for opera, ballet, theatre, masquerades, and other such pleasure-seeking . . . instills irresistibly precisely those most addicted to foreign novelties with a yearning for philosophy with which to stifle qualms of conscience and fear of divine retribution. Hence the fad for philosophy now sweeping the German courts, far from being designed to edify and uplift . . . has an essentially irreligious and immoral purpose.[74]

In either case, the state protected the Leipzig community's freedom to explore the Enlightenment's radical challenges. In effect, the separation of church and state at the level of the central government resulted from August's conversion. The title of chapter 2 refers to the disputatiously pluralistic religious world in which Bach lived and worked. Contemporary thought was fragmented, intellectually complex, and, indeed, unable to assimilate the multiplicity of ideas, beliefs, and values that were simultaneously current.

5. Rationale and Conclusion

The chapters in *Bach's Changing World: Voices in the Community* suggest possibilities for understanding how Bach fit into his Leipzig community. These chapters look at contemporary religious and philosophical literature, various kinds of secular and devotional publications, works for theater, official records, and theological commentary. Entertainment venues and all forms of commercially available literature are used to study topical issues, which range from electoral and clerical law enforcement objectives to changes in the social and educational values that the merchant and professional classes articulated. The chapters privilege sources that were available to the literate population in Bach's day and, moreover, could be considered "popular," that is, produced commercially, widely distributed by the commercial standards of the day, and available in book shops. Works written by earlier generations are included as long as they were still selling. Individuals in the community are identified whenever feasible: from this community's now mainly anonymous members, several have gained attention because their stories amplify our knowledge of Bach.

The chapters in this study also look at how Leipzig citizens and, peripherally, neighboring German communities responded to the religious, social, and political demands that emerged during the lifetimes of the composer and the previous generation, whose experiences and memories still had resonance with their progeny. Thereby, the chapters suggest contexts for understanding Bach's life within the ambiguous and transitional structures of the early modern German world.

The rationale for our approach lies in the fact that Bach was an accepted, admired, and trusted member of the Leipzig community. Evidence of his standing is seen in the commissions he received from royalty, academics, and merchants alike, in addition to the fact that he held positions as the city's principal church, municipal, and court composer. He could only have acquired such prestige by participating in that community as a responsible citizen attuned to its values and concerns.

Unlike the slow, steady flow of events and accomplishments blending into the future, the progression that describes most historical periods, Leipzig's history during Bach's lifetime may have progressed in an exceptional way. Consider the period as a self-limiting moment in history. Since the Lutheran Reformation, religion had provided the strongest reason for societal identity and division, regionally and internationally. Now transforming circumstances, the progression of Saxony's secular absolutism and the early *Aufklärung*—two paths being defined in Leipzig by the time Bach was born—were interacting with Lutheran orthodoxy. Between the last two decades of the seventeenth century and the middle of the eighteenth, this interaction provided the catalyst for the development of a bourgeois culture in Leipzig: a culture strong enough to support its own specific concerns and objectives. A public sphere emerged in which people socialized in neutral, private settings—independent of government and ecclesiastical institutions—in theaters, beer halls and coffeehouses, libraries and bookstores, at salons and Pietist study groups.

Yet Bach's greatest music was composed for religious reasons and was heard in church, in a traditional religious setting. Coming at the end of the tradition of music composed for the Protestant liturgy, and composed in an era when the community's aspirations were no longer passively centered on the blessed afterlife of Lutheran orthodoxy, Bach's music nevertheless retains the authenticity of its idealized religious vision; its aesthetic power is still unmistakable today. Like the Leipzig community, Bach's music folded the world and the world-to-come into one experience: "Here must be an angelic life! / Here it must be an Eden!"[75] Politically ambiguous and vulnerable, religiously and philosophically pluralistic in ways that defy definition, Leipzig during this period in its history contributed to the inconsistencies that are part of the Bach legacy.

Bach's allegedly "uneventful life"—a widely accepted "fact"—may appear less so when his responsiveness is assumed to exist alongside the documented responses of colleagues and congregants. The issues discussed in this volume contributed to the anxieties of active, involved members of the Leipzig community. The stories about Bach's belligerent personality gain new dimensions when thought of as responses to shared problems. Although we may never fully determine whether or to what degree Bach maintained positions independent of his community and state and which of their values and beliefs he shared, Bach's portrait, when viewed against the background of this community, gains greater depth. Questions about Bach and his music may always be with us, but a deeper understanding of the cultural world Bach inherited and contributed to will enable us to ask more probing questions.

Notes

1. Peter H. Wilson, *German Armies: War and German Politics, 1648–1826* (London: UCL Press, 1998), passim, describes the issues in these wars to which Saxony periodically contributed troops, thereby developing goodwill among the other participating powers and securing favors for Saxon ambitions.
2. T. C. W. Blanning, *The Culture of Power and the Power of Culture: Old Regime Europe, 1660–1789* (Oxford: Oxford University Press, 2002), 60; from Karlheinz Blaschke and H. Kretzscmar, "Obersachsen und die Lausitzen," in *Geschichte der deutschen Länder: Territorien Ploetz* (Würzburg: A. G. Ploetz-Verlag, 1964–71), 2 vols, ed. Wilhelm Sante, 1:490.
3. George Stauffer, "Leipzig," in *The New Groves Dictionary* (NY: Grove's Dictionaries, 2000).
4. Gloria Flaherty, "Bach's Leipzig as a Training Ground for Actors, Musicians, and Singers," in *Music and German Literature: Their Relationship since the Middle Ages*, ed. James M. McGlathery (SC: Camden House, 1992) addresses this topic.
5. Jonathan I. Israel, *Radical Enlightenment: Philosophy and the Making of Modernity, 1650–1750* (Oxford: Oxford University Press, 2001), 107; from Johann Goldfriedrich, *Geschichte des deutschen Buchhandels vom Westfälischen Frieden bis zum Beginn der klassischen Literaturperiode (1648–1740)* (Leipzig: Börsenvereins der Deutschen Buchhandler, 1908), 83.
6. Jonathan Israel, *Radical Enlightenment*, 144–45.
7. Richard L. Gawthrop, *Pietism and the Making of Eighteenth-Century Prussia* (Cambridge: Cambridge University Press, 1993), 191–92. The Canstein Bible Institute, established

in 1711, produced bibles cheaply; the Elers Press produced the other works. (From Oskar Söhngen, "Festrede," in *Die bleibende Bedeutung des Pietismus* (Witten and Berlin: Cansteinsche Bibelanstalt, 1960) 14; Joachim Böhme, "Heinrich Juylius Elers, ein Freund und Mitarbeiter A. H. Franckes." PhD diss., F. U. Berlin, 1956), 157.

8. Israel, *Radical Enlightenment*, 106–7; Albert Ward, *Book Production, Fiction, and the German Reading Public, 1740–1800* (Oxford: Clarendon Press, 1974), 175, n. 2; quote is from J. Schmidt, *Geschichte des geistigen Lebens in Deutschland von Leibniz auf Lessings Tod* (Leipzig, 1862–64), ii, 186.

9. George Stauffer, "Leipzig: A Cosmopolitan Trade Centre," in *The Late Baroque Era: From the 1680s to 1740*, ed. George J. Buelow (London: Granada Group/Macmillan Press, 1993), 269. For other descriptions of Leipzig, see Karl Czok, "Sächsischer Landsstaat zur Bachzeit," *Beiträge zur Bachforschung* 1 (1982): 25–31; and Stauffer, "Leipzig," in *The New Groves Dictionary*.

10. Christoph Wolff, *Johann Sebastian Bach: The Learned Musician* (New York: W. W. Norton, 2000).

11. George B. Stauffer, *New York Times*, Sunday, April 2, 2000.

12. Robert Marshall, "Towards A New Bach Biography," *Musical Quarterly* 84/3 (Fall 2000): 497–525, 499.

13. See Peter H. Wilson, *Absolutism in Central Europe*, Historical Connections Series (London/New York: Routledge, 2000) for in-depth historiographical treatment. Also H. M. Scott, "The Consolidation of Noble Power in Europe," in *The European Nobilities in the Seventeenth and Eighteenth Centuries* (NY/London: Longman, 1995), 2 vols; and Rudolph Vierhaus, *Germany in the Age of Absolutism*, tr. Jonathan B. Knudsen (Cambridge: Cambridge University Press, 1988), 91–97 (originally *Deutschland im Zeitalter des Absolutismus (1648–1763)* (Göttingen: Vandenhoeck and Ruprecht, 1988). Ulrich Siegele, "Bach and the Domestic Politics of Electoral Saxony," in *Bach* (Cambridge: Cambridge University Press, 1997) locates Bach's professional difficulties in Leipzig in the context of a power struggle between Saxon absolutism and the feudal Estates' rights for the city under traditional constitutional arrangements.

14. They remained autonomous territories until the legal dissolution of the Holy Roman Empire and their alliance—without Prussia and Austria—under Napoleon as the Confederation of the Rhine. German unification, with Prussia, would wait until the end of the nineteenth century. Regarding the political anomaly called the "Holy Roman Empire of the German Peoples," see Peter H. Wilson, *The Holy Roman Empire, 1495–1805* (London: Palgrave Macmillan, 1999).

15. Scott, "The Consolidation," 37.

16. Mack Walker, *German Home Towns: Community, State, and General Estate, 1640–1871* (Ithaca: Cornell University Press, 1971), 111. Scott, *The European Nobilities*, examines the differences in Prussia, Austria, and the European nations in the relationship between the aristocracy and the sovereign courts and those concerning the ongoing political power and viability of this estate.

17. W. H. Bruford, *Germany in the Eighteenth Century: The Social Background of the Literary Revival* (Cambridge: Cambridge University Press, 1935, rpt. 1952), 61, from J. M. von Loën, *Der Adel* (1752), 128, 129. Also James Sheehan, *German History, 1770–1855: The Oxford History of Modern Europe* (Clarendon Press, 1989; paper rpt., 1994), 133.

18. Walker, *German Home Towns*, 110–11.

19. Walker, *German Home Towns*, 197, quoting from unpublished writings, in Franz Rosenzweig, *Hegel und der Staat*, 2 vols (Munich: R. Oldenbourg, 1920), 1:188–92

(rpt. Aalen: Scientia Verlag, 1962). "Consequently," Walker says "everybody devised his own system of estates: because nobody ever found a really satisfactory one" (111). This claim is corroborated in Johann Michael von Loën, "Free Thoughts concerning the Betterment of the State," appended to his novel *Der redliche Mann am Hofe* (Frankfurt am Main: Johann David Jung, 1st ed., 1740). Nonetheless the political system remained; especially in Prussia, these distinctions would determine political and social realities well into the nineteenth century.

20. Wilson, *Absolutism*, 13. These two distinctions represent only a small portion of the interpretations Wilson discusses.

21. To cite one glaring example, in the seventeen territories and nations covered in Scott, *European Nobilities*, only Austria and Prussia represent the German-speaking territories.

22. Wilson, *German Armies*, is unusual in its comprehensive treatment of the Saxon experience, here in war and international politics; see especially 129–37, 183–85, and 252–53.

23. Dominic Phelps, <http://www.history.ac.uk/reviews/paper/phelpsD.htm>, suggests this reason in a recent book review but points out that since the archives have been accessible, "the migration of academics into the fertile lands of the Dresden archives has been slow, particularly in comparison to the quantity of work produced on Bavaria, Hessen-Kassel, Württemberg and Brandenburg-Prussia." He refers to a "research vacuum."

24. Scott, *European Nobilities*, 1:37 re: *Acta Borussica* (Berlin: P. Paney, 1892–1970).

25. Stefan Berger, "Prussia in History and Historiography from the Eighteenth to the Nineteenth Century," in *The Rise of Prussia*, ed. Philip G. Dwyer (Essex: Pearson Education Limited, 2000), 30.

26. Sheehan's *German History*, whose focus begins in the last third of the 18th century, relies on the Prussian orientation but introduces aspects of Saxon distinctiveness when the information is available. A breakthrough in Saxony particularities is noted in James Retallack, ed., *Saxony in German History: Culture, Society, and Politics, 1830–1933* (Ann Arbor: University of Michigan Press, 2000), which, however, concentrates on the century leading to 1933.

27. Blanning, *The Culture of Power*, describes the fall of Saxony and the rise of Prussia during the 1740s (70–72)—the last decade, incidentally, of Bach's life. Also see Philip G. Dwyer, "Introduction," in *The Rise of Prussia*. The military experiences of Saxony and Prussia are detailed in Wilson, *German Armies*, passim.

28. Otto Hintze, "The Hohenzollern and the Nobility," in *The Historical Essays of Otto Hintze*, ed. Felix Gilbert (New York: Oxford University Press, 1975), 44.

29. Otto Hintze, "Calvinism and Raison d'Etat in Early Seventeenth-Century Brandenburg," in *The Historical Essays*, 139–40.

30. Bodo Nishan, *Prince, People, and Confession: The Second Reformation in Brandenburg* (Philadelphia: University of Pennsylvania Press, 1994), 1. The political and religious reasons for the court's choice of the Calvinist reform—the religious values inherent in the reform and the political implications as embraced by the Netherlands—are discussed by both Hintze, "Calvinism" (98–100), and Nishan (see especially 248) but are beyond the scope of our discussion.

31. Edgar Melton, "The Prussian Junkers, 1600–1786," in Scott, *European Nobilities*, 79–80. Walker, *German Home Towns*, refers to laws documented in the 1680s that gave responsibility for tax-collecting, previously handled by guildsmen, to "tax-collection officers" (155–56).

32. For more detail see Sheehan, *German History*, 59–60. Vierhaus, *Germany in the Age of Absolutism*, 101–2, maintains Brandenburg-Prussia was a militarized state by the second half of the seventeenth century, for prestige in Europe and for political power at home rather than for defense purposes. Also see Wilson, *Absolutism in Central Europe*, 76, 94–95; and Dwyer, "Introduction," in *The Rise of Prussia*, 13–15.

33. Hagen Schulze, "The Prussian Military State, 1763–1806," in *The Rise of Prussia, 1700–1830*, ed. Philip G. Dwyer (Harlow: Pearson Education Ltd., 2000), 208; Wilson, *Absolutism*, 30–31. Hintze, "The Hohenzollern," describing the resolution of tensions between the Great Elector and nobility, who wanted the army dissolved after the 30 Years' War, says "the role of the nobility underwent a complete change." In "the new military and centralized state," the nobility's representative assemblies "became unimportant and powerless provincial representations" when "above them appeared the new officialdom of the unified state, overwhelmingly superior in force and power" (46–47). Melton, in "The Prussian Junkers 1600–1786," disagrees with Hintze's evaluation of the tensions (93).

34. The Treaty of Westphalia, among other legal treaties of the Post-Lutheran Reformation period, is discussed in chapter 2.

35. Dwyer, "Introduction," 5–6.

36. Karin Friedrich, "The Development of the Prussian Town, 1720–1815," in Dwyer, *The Rise of Prussia, 1700–1830* (Harlow: Pearson Education Limited, 2000), 135.

37. This section, unless otherwise indicated, is excerpted from Hans-Gert Roloff, "Christian Weises Lebensweg," in *Christian Weise: Gedenken anlässlich seines 350 Geburtstages* (Christian-Weise-Bibliothek Zittau, 1993, 11–19; and Roloff, "Christian Weise—damals und heute," in *Christian Weise Festschrift* (Bern: Europäischer Verlag der Wissenschaften, Peter Lang AG, 1994). I want to thank Barbara Becker-Cantarino for making a copy of Christian Weise: *Gedenken* available. Her primary research on Weise, "Frauengestalten im Werk Weises und in seiner Zeit," appears in the *Festschrift*.

38. Klaus Günzel, "Christian Weise—Pädagog und Literat," in *Christian Weise: Gedenken*, 20–24, passim; from a lecture entitled "Christian Weise, 1642–1708—Versuch einer Würdigung."

39. Evelyn Preuss, "Political Role Play and Political Ethics in Christian Weise's Drama *Masaniello*," Master's thesis, University of Iowa, 1997, discusses the ethical ambiguities inherent in the socio-political perspectives Weise portrayed in the school play *Masaniello*; see especially 115–17.

40. Romain Rolland's article, "A Humorous Novel by an Eighteenth-Century Musician," in *A Musical Tour through the Land of the Past* (New York: Henry Holt, 1922), tr. Bernard Miall, is a critique of Kuhnau's novel.

41. Roloff, "Christian Weises Lebensweg," 17: "weitem grösseren Erfolg."

42. Friedrich Herbert Wagman, *Magic and Natural Science in German Baroque Literature* (New York: AMS Press, 1966), 135. Other novels by Weise are *Die drey Haupt-Verderber in Teutschland* (1691) and *Der politische Näscher* (1678).

43. Joachim Menzhausen, "Five Centuries of Art Collecting in Dresden," in *The Splendor of Dresden* (New Haven: Eastern Press, 1978), 21.

44. Wilson, *German Armies*, 185. Helen Watanabe-O'Kelly, *Court Culture in Dresden: From Renaissance to Baroque* (Houndsmills/New York: Palgrave, 2002), 193, locates Johann Georg III on the field of battle in 1683, 1688, 1689, and 1691, when he died in battle.

45. Roloff, "Christian Weises Lebensweg," 17–19.

46. Günzel, "Christian Weise—Pädagog und Literat," 21: "bürgerlich-emanzipatorischen Denken."

47. Gianfranco Poggi, *The Development of the Modern State: A Sociological Introduction* (Stanford: Stanford University Press, 1978), 58.

48. Vierhaus, *Germany in the Age of Absolutism*, 39 for Leibniz quote, with no further reference. On ennoblement, see 39–43. Vierhaus, unfortunately, generalizes about the changes from the Prussian context.

49. Otto Hintze, "Military Organization and State Organization," in *The Historical Essays*, 201. In "The Commissary and His Significance," *The Historical Essays*, 271, Hintze describes how "military administration became inseparably entangled with civilian and police administration; the whole internal police system that gradually developed from this bore a militaristic cast." Also for the army's functions and growth in the Prussian state, see Rodney Gothelf, "Frederick William I and the Beginnings of Prussian Absolutism, 1713–1740," in Dwyer, *The Rise of Prussia, 1700–1830*, 59–67, where he states that the cost of the army approached 75% of the annual peacetime budget (60); Dennis Showalter, "Prussia's Army: Continuity and Change, 1713–1830," 220–22; Hagen Schulze, "The Prussian Military State, 1763–1805," 206–10; and Scott, *European Nobilities*, 1:40—all in agreement with Hintze's earlier assessment.

50. Gotthold Ephraim Lessing, *Nathan the Wise, Minna von Barnhelm, and Other Plays and Writings*, in *The German Library*, vol. 12, ed. Peter Demetz (NY: Continuum Publishing, 1991).

51. Gothelf, "Frederick William I," passim, and especially Gawthrop, *Pietism*, 237–69, provide comprehensive studies in English of Prussian policy under Frederick William I.

52. Hintze, "The Hohenzollern," in *Historical Essays*, 47–48; and Melton, "The Prussian Junkers 1600–1786," 84–85. Hintze addresses the distinctive role of Calvinism in the developing Prussian ideology in "Prolegomena," *Historical Essays*, 91–154, passim.

53. See Gothelf, "Frederick William I," 60–61 and Friedrich, who in "The Development of the Prussian Town" concluded that Prussian mercantilist policies extending into the 19th century had been a failure and that "absolutism" was a myth (150). Mack Walker, in *German Home Towns*, agrees with Friedrich's negative evaluation of the Prussian economy (155).

54. Friedrich, "The Development of the Prussian Town," 135–36 and 136 n. 19. See Gawthrop, *Pietism*, 258–59, for examples of specific economic policies followed by this regime.

55. Gawthrop, *Pietism*, 260–61, from Carl Franz Reinhardt, "Denkschrift über Staat," quoted in Carl Hinrichs, *Die Wollindustrie in Preußen unter Friedrich Wilhelm I* (Berlin: P. Parey, 1933), 407–9 and 278.

56. Johann Michael von Loën, "Free Thoughts Concerning the Betterment of the State," short essays appended to *The Honest Man at Court* (Columbia, SC: Camden House, 1997), tr. John R. Russell, 208 and 209 respectively. Originally *Der redliche Mann am Hofe* (Frankfurt am Main, 1740).

57. Menzhausen, *The Splendour*, 21.

58. Helen Watanabe-O'Kelly, *Court Culture in Dresden* (Houndmills: Palgrave, 2002), 223–25.

59. Sheehan, *German History*, 132, from Jerome Blum, *The End of the Old Order in Rural Europe* (Princeton: Princeton University Press, 1978). The loss of lands was of utmost significance to the nobility; it was the basis of their wealth and standing: the connection of noble to land, the identification through "von" of the *Herr* to *Herrschaft* (Sheehan, *German History*, 129).

60. BWV 212, *Mer hahn en neue Oberkeet* (We have a new master). Its text uses Saxon peasant dialect. The bureaucrat was Carl Heinrich von Dieskau.

61. Siegele, "Bach and Domestic Politics," 20–21.

62. Wilson, *German Armies*, 253.

63. Blanning, *The Culture of Power*, 72.

64. Peter Gay, *The Enlightenment: The Science of Freedom* (New York: W. W. Norton, 1969), 485. The philosophers' "reserve, their refusal of pressing invitations, and their outright hostility" were more significant than either their accepting his patronage—as Voltaire and Christian Wolff had—or their words of praise (485). Voltaire was admittedly self-serving (462–63).

65. "Forkel's Biography of Bach," in *The New Bach Reader: A Life of Johann Sebastian Bach in Letters and Documents*, ed. Hans David, Arthur Mendel, and Christoph Wolff (New York: W. W. Norton, revised 2000), 426.

66. Gay, *Science of Freedom*, 485.

67. Michael Marissen, "The Theological Character of J. S. Bach's *Musical Offering*," in *Bach Studies* 2, ed. D. R. Melamud (Cambridge: Cambridge University Press, 1995), 91.

68. Ibid., 87.

69. Maria Teresa Giannelli, "Joel Sheveloff, Quaerendo Invenietes (Vendemiatio Secunda) (Presentazione)," *Musica Poëtica: Johann Sebastian Bach e la tradizione europa*, ed. Maria Teresa Giannelli (Genova: ECIG, 1986), 469–88. Sheveloff is working on the final version of his work.

70. The term "public sphere," as it is used here, does not carry the political implications of "the bourgeois public sphere" used by Jürgens Habermas in *The Structural Transformation of the Public Sphere: An Inquiry into a Category of Bourgeois Society*, tr. Thomas Burger (Cambridge, MA: Polity Press, 1989). Not referring necessarily to Saxony, Peter Wilson explains the flawed application of Habermas's theory to Germany's early modern period, in *Absolutism*, 80–83.

71. Johann Adolph Scheibe, *Der critische Musikus* (1737–40). Reprinted in English with an introduction, in David, Mendel, and Wolff, eds, *New Bach Reader*, 337–53. Wolff, in his *Johann Sebastian Bach*, discusses the dispute, especially 1–2 and 431–32.

72. Werner Neumann, *Bach-Dokumente 1* (Leipzig and Kassel: Bärenreiter), no. 92; David, Mendel, and Wolff, eds, *New Bach Reader*, 105.

73. Martin Geck questioned unanimity between community sensibilities and official orthodox theology in 1967 in "The Ultimate Goal of Bach's Art," *Bach* 35/1: 35, tr. Alfred Mann; originally, "Bachs künstlerischer Endzweck," in *Festschrift für Walter Wiora*, ed. Ludwig Finscher and Christoph Hellmut Mahling (Kassel: Bärenreiter, 1967). However his perception of discrepancies was limited to the infiltration of Pietism.

74. Israel, *Radical Enlightenment*, 62.

75. See note 9 above.

Chapter Two

Tumultuous Philosophers, Pious Rebels, Revolutionary Teachers, Pedantic Clerics, Vengeful Bureaucrats, Threatened Tyrants, Worldly Mystics

The Religious World Bach Inherited

Carol K. Baron

The religious world Bach inherited was as complex and diverse as our own. During the early period of the Enlightenment, which overlapped with Bach's lifetime, more complex frames of reference subjected religious ideas—beyond those that separated Lutheran orthodoxy, Calvinism, and Catholicism, the three officially recognized religions in the German territories after the Peace of Westphalia (1648)—to question and examination.[1] Among the educated populations, scientific inquiry, mathematical logic, metaphysics, a variety of splinter religions, philosophy, orthodox dogma, and less defined goals of spiritual renewal competed for attention. Some of the empirical claimants to ontological truth were themselves infused with mystical currents that emanated from scientific as well as religious circles, as was even Lutheran orthodoxy (which was devoted to the ongoing process of defining, interpreting, and disseminating Luther's teaching), despite the fact that orthodox dogma resisted the slightest deviations for fear of heresy.[2] In the wake of the devastation caused by the religious fanaticism of the Thirty Years' War (1618–48), Germans eagerly sought new ways to envision a future in positive religious terms. The religious focus of the *Aufklärung* absorbed the best minds: theologians of every persuasion, scientists, mathematicians, mystics, philosophers, political scientists, propagandists, and the educated lay public. Often overlapping, their inquiries probed the rational, the spiritual, the revealed, the mystical, even the skeptical, as well as the realm of magic and the occult.

The distinctive urgency of the religious aspect of the Enlightenment in the German states has been attributed to the revolutionary birth of Protestantism in Germany, where religious developments continued to be expressions of "inner renewal."[3] Perhaps, also, Germans needed this ongoing religious focus as they attempted to understand the destruction and brutality they had suffered during the Thirty Years' War in the name of religious "truth"—experiences of horror and cruelty still vivid in collective memory. The Saxon philosopher-mathematician Gottfried Wilhelm Leibniz (1646–1716) addressed the problem of belief in an omniscient and loving God when faced with the unfair situations life presents— the dilemma of Job—and developed a complex theodicy.

Ironically, the most contentious issue in modern Bach scholarship concerns Bach's religious beliefs, since the prominent place devoted to Bach's religious or non-religious sensibilities in the scholarship of the last forty years, including this essay, bears out George Stauffer's observation that the lack of sufficient biographical material, discussed in chapter 1, has led to "the tendency of every age to recreate Bach in its own image."[4] Thus, Friedrich Blume portrays Bach as a secular musician because the new Bach chronology revealed that Bach composed three almost complete annual cycles of church cantatas during the first three years of his tenure in Leipzig—their composition was not the lifelong occupation hitherto assumed.[5] Gerhard Herz describes the ensuing inflammatory dispute provoked by Blume. Based on the rediscovery of Bach's annotations in his copy of the "Calov Bible," Herz weighs in heavily on the side of the image of the Lutheran orthodox Bach (but it is notable that the Bible was acquired in 1733 after most of Bach's religious works had been composed); yet Herz concedes that Bach would have been willing to compose religious music for the Catholic Church of the Saxon court.[6] Robin Leaver cites Günther Stiller's evidence from extant ecclesiastical documents of the practice of strict orthodox ritual in Lepizig's principal churches[7] as well as the persuasiveness of the preponderantly orthodox items listed in the 1750 inventory of Bach's personal library to conclude also that Bach adhered to Lutheran orthodoxy. Leaver goes still further in his article "Johann Sebastian Bach: Theological Musician and Musical Theologian," where he asserts that "to suggest that he [Bach] was only a musician and 'not a theologian' is . . . seriously misleading."[8]

Some of the most valuable contributions to Bach scholarship have relied on interpretations of the music that are rooted in Lutheran orthodox hermeneutics. They contribute informed commentary to our knowledge of orthodox theology and aesthetic and religious insights into the rhetoric, symbols, and imagery Bach articulated musically. Among these works I point particularly to the work of Michael Marissen and Eric Chafe.[9] Yet Christoph Wolff, in his recent monumental biography *Johann Sebastian Bach: The Learned Musician*, believes that

Bach "saw himself, if only privately, as a biblical interpreter in the succession of these eminent theological scholars" represented in his library (335); that Bach functioned as a theologian by directing the congregation's attention to "the presence of God's grace through music" (339). However, Wolff derives Bach's compositional processes from "the philosophical-scientific methodology of his day" and the rationalist's *empirical* pursuit of God. Contributing to a major upset, Wolff points to the limited nature of Bach's library, based on information from the posthumous inventory, which only represents "largely old-fashioned theological items left" after "the more appealing library materials were removed and distributed" (334–35).[10] The heart of the contentiousness in the foregoing cross-section lies in the fact that these portrayals are all rooted in religious reflections and practices of Bach's contemporaries. Bach and his work are brilliant but still somewhat inscrutable facets in the complex, kaleidoscopic prism that reflects the German religious world addressed in this chapter.

I want to suggest that thinking about Bach's religious world reflexively and dialogically may help break through the seemingly impenetrable interpretive barriers contributing to this standoff. I believe this approach is appropriate because there has never been a time in religious history so like the late seventeenth and early eighteenth centuries in Germany as exists now in the United States, parts of Europe, and the Middle East. Now, as then, new directions seem to be emerging simultaneously in all systems of religious belief. Since the 1960s, religious movements outside the mainstream have been trying anew to make sense of the human dilemma. There are an unprecedented number of religious movements unaffiliated with conventional religions.[11] A widespread interest in gaining spiritual and mystical knowledge, in incorporating eastern mysticism and spirituality into traditional western religions, in healing and rebirth—all find expression today, even in the most rationalistic, liberal, universalist orientations. At the same time, orthodox and fundamentalist believers feel threatened. The focus of religion on "truth" has led to conspicuous manifestations of intolerance, and fundamentalist beliefs driving genocidal passions and the desire for martyrdom inform our everyday awareness. The universality of such fervid religious experience may be startling to recognize but necessary to acknowledge.

And now, as then, beliefs based on both revelation and scientific empiricism are simultaneously compelling and competitive paths to truth. And these paths evolved in forms similar in their variety and complexity. Widely reported discussions among physicists and theologians since Einstein's "unified field theory" and, especially, the recent debate between the physicist-theologian John Polkinghorne and physicist Steven Weinberg recall intellectual disputes during Bach's lifetime.[12] The Newton-Leibniz debate in particular comes to mind, at the center of which lie Newton's belief in a providential God who intervenes to correct imbalances and contradictions found in nature, and Leibniz's belief in a world that needs no correction since it is "the best of all possible worlds," created by an omniscient God.[13] Comparing the "mathematical" logic in the theosophical systems of Leibniz and Baruch Spinoza (1632–77), although both represent the non-providential camp, was another source of controversy. Furthermore, recent interest in historiographical, archeological, and philological Bible studies follows in the steps of Bach's colleague at the St. Thomas School, Johann August Ernesti (1707–81). Highlighted in periodicals for the general reader, all these paths to religious experience could gain ground among the educated public of Bach's time and be further disseminated from there.

This suggestion of bringing a reflexive frame of reference to the religious beliefs and sensibilities of Bach's contemporaries, to find similarities in ourselves and our contemporaries, could lead to unwanted subjectivity—and the danger of misreading the past is a legitimate concern. However, its corollary also has its perils: missing familiar signs for fear of inappropriate projections. Recognizing shared religious sensibilities, obsessions, and metaphors helped detect these complex patterns of religious thought that permeated Bach's community. We see tensions in Bach scholarship falling away: "Either/or" becomes "this and that" as comparable and expected levels of multiplicity, complexity, and inconsistence follow. Multilayered perceptions and interactions that are at least as subtle and complex as those found in Bach's social equals may then be sought in the gifted composer.

This chapter concentrates on manifestations of religious thought and practice in the Leipzig community in the context of the absolutist regimes of the Wettin dynasty in Saxony and in dynastically related Thuringia where Bach was born. The chapter also highlights interactions in the religious and political spheres between Leipzig and the neighboring Prussian city of Halle, located less than twenty miles away and since 1694 a competing university center. Major figures—clerics, philosophers, teachers, propagandists, cameralists—who made their livelihood as government bureaucrats moved between these centers to escape censorship or, worse, threats to their lives for breaching local religious policies. In another context, this chapter could have been the "tale" of these neighboring cities moving, at the will of their pragmatic rulers and empowered clerics, between forms of religious intolerance and uniformity, and tolerance and diversity.

1. The Telling Seventeenth Century

Religion and Politics: Imperial Treaties

Leipzig's enigmatic religious picture mainly lies in discrepancies between legal statutes agreed to by the territorial rulers constituting the Holy Roman Empire of the German Nation and the progressively independent social and intellectual public sphere that developed during the last quarter of the seventeenth century. A milestone in German history, the 1555 Peace of Augsburg protected

Lutheranism through imperial agreements that legalized Protestantism for about half the German population and established the principle of *cuius region, eius religio*—the ruler's religion determines the official religion of his territory—thereby establishing the principle of state religions. There were approximately three hundred autonomous territories and rulers in the Holy Roman Empire, which included spiritual and imperial estates as well as the imperial cities and the lesser noble estates. The Peace of Augsburg gained religious significance by delegating religious authority to secular rulers, in keeping with a doctrine Luther adopted when his principles were threatened by both Catholics and extremist Protestant groups, notably in the Peasants' Revolt: a doctrine controversial by the middle of the seventeenth century. The Peace of Augsburg gave the new Lutheran rulers the political power to resist the Catholic emperor's authority in their lands; after the Elector of Brandenburg and Duke of Prussia, Johann Sigismund (r. 1608–19), converted to Calvinism (the Reformed Church) in 1613, it protected the religious authority of the Lutheran nobility in his lands.[14] Indeed, it had introduced a peaceful period that lasted until 1618.

However, the nature and extent of the religious tensions and additional schisms that developed in the territories during this period became dramatically clear in the Thirty Years' War (1618–48), when theological rivalries and enmities grew fanatical. Jonathan Israel describes the "inter-confessional conflict" from the mid-sixteenth to the mid-seventeenth century as "Europe's prime engine of cultural and educational change," wherein "no sphere of activity remained free from the unrelenting demands of confessional and theological rivalry."[15] The Peace of Augsburg was superseded at the end of the Thirty Years' War by the treaties of the Peace of Westphalia (1648), which granted official recognition to Calvinism in addition to Catholicism and Lutheranism.

Westphalia altered the doctrine of "*cuius region, eius religio*" established at the Peace of Augsburg. While reasserting the authority of territorial rulers and city magistrates over religious matters—reaffirming Luther's principle—it gave these rulers the freedom to convert without affecting the religions of their subjects, which officially remained those in existence in 1624. Calvinist policies attracted many members of the aristocracy. There exists the precedent of the Cöthen dynasty, for whom Bach worked prior to moving to Leipzig, which had adopted Calvinism as the official religion as early as 1596 and became a plurireligious population accepting Lutherans. When Brandenburg-Prussia's Hohenzollern dynasty converted to Calvinism in 1613, its subjects and most of the nobility remained Lutheran. Religious accommodations in the German territories after the Thirty Years' War became as numerous as there were territories and rulers.

Inherent in this arrangement was the potential for religious pluralism and tolerance. These treaties, however—agreements between states—did nothing to eliminate intolerance between followers of the three confessions or to extend tolerance to the numerous other religious, spiritual, and mystical movements that had splintered off from the "official" religions: these splinter movements represented the range between belief and skepticism found in Anabaptism, Spiritualism, and Socinianism.[16] However, Westphalia also established the "absolute" powers of the territorial leaders by granting them the right to raise armies and conclude political treaties independently of imperial consent—the age of absolutism was thus ushered in. Although old loyalties to the Empire were reasserted, the Empire was thereby weakened. Political ambition was progressively secularized, but the realignment of dynastic and territorial religious identities became new fronts for asserting absolutist power; especially Prussia and France come to mind—the first using religion to enhance obedience for population control, and the second revoking the Edict of Nantes in 1685.

Religion and Absolutist Goals

The economic policies pursued by the absolutist governments reflected the interests and personalities of the dynastic families; and the "political and psychological consequences" of these policies had consequences for the religious sensibilities of the general populations.[17]

Saxony

The Saxon dynasty's progressively luxury-prone interests after the Peace of Westphalia seem to have been only weakly identified with the Lutheran orthodox concerns of its subjects. The electors interceded in religious matters only if disputatious theological polemics threatened the peace. Thus, in the 1650s Johann Georg I (r. 1611–57) befriended the respected and prolific theologian Abraham Calov (1612–86), prominent in German Protestant territories, but their relationship was disrupted when Calov surrounded himself in the syncretistic controversies (see discussion below).

The association of music and liturgy may expose religious ambivalence at the Saxon court, but the situation that really existed still remains an open question. Helen Watanabe-O'Kelly claims that Saxon court culture was "distinctively Lutheran" until the conversion of August the Strong (r. 1694–1733) to Catholicism in 1697. She says that Johann Georg II (r. 1657–80) composed sacred music himself and—pointing to compositions called "historia," a term applied to dramatic compositions going back to the middle ages and supplanted by the term "oratorio"—that "more works of Lutheran church music were written during his reign than at any other time."[18] The situation, however, may be more complicated for the period being considered, and I cannot resolve the contradiction that exists with the evidence that follows. According to Mary E. Frandsen, the Electors patronized religious ceremonial music under the direction of Italian composers and conductors who gave no thought to Lutheran ritual. When Heinrich Schütz (1585–1672) was replaced because of age, Johann Georg II hired Catholics who had been students of Roman Jesuits and replaced the seasonal themes of the Lutheran service with texts that "express instead an ardent love for Christ in very personal terms, eschewing the concept of corporate worship." They used Latin texts "that reflect the traditions of Jesuit mysticism into a Lutheran context."[19] Frandsen identifies texts used between 1660 and 1680 by the composers Vincenzo Albrici and Marco Giuseppe Peranda and points out discrepancies with Lutheran practice. She focuses on texts "imbued with the language of carnal love": "the suffusion of terms like 'languish,' 'burn,' and 'longing' suggests an unquenchable desire for union with Christ," and "colors the speaker's words with a passion that would seem to have transgressed the bounds of spiritual love."[20]

The unresolved issues point to the need to clarify the significance of the use of Latin as opposed to German texts and the confessional nature of the ecclesiastical calendar, celebrations, and services in Dresden. Also, since German Lutheran poetic texts of this and earlier periods also used erotic imagery, how are they different from their Latin counterparts? Ernst Stoeffler cites Josua Stegmann (1588–1632) and Joachim Emden (1595–1650) as among the earliest Lutheran authors whose works "exhibit an excessive sweetness . . . [and] religious eroticism," which he associates with "medieval mysticism." Among numerous later authors of this tradition in devotional literature, Stoeffler mentions John Rist (1607–67) and John Lassenius (1636–92). The extremely popular texts by Heinrich Müller (1631–75), which were certainly dependent on this kind of mystical imagery, were in Bach's library. If there were converging cultural contacts between the Italian and German mystical traditions, they also have not been sufficiently studied.[21]

Under Johann Georg III (1680–91), Italian opera burst on the scene when the Italian Carlo Pallavicino was hired in 1685 as both *Kapellmeister* and opera composer.[22] With August the Strong's conversion, the Saxon court in Dresden in the eighteenth century became the major center for the Neapolitan style of Catholic church music in Germany aside from Vienna.[23] Among Bach's contemporaries in Dresden composing Catholic masses, oratorios, and other works to sacred texts were Jan Ditmas Zelenka (1679–1745), Antonio Lotti (1667–1740), Giovanni Alberto Ristori (1692–1753), Johann Adolphe Hasse (1699–1783), and Johann David Heinichen (1683–1729).

The Saxon electors exhibited an affinity for the elegance and formality of Catholic ritual, probably associating them with the cosmopolitan French and Viennese courts. Elegant court rituals may also have been a tool of Saxon absolutism to enhance the image of the court's power and mythic status among its subjects. These court ceremonies would also have served as an absolutist stratagem to diminish the importance of lesser nobility and magistrates who protected Lutheran orthodoxy.

Brandenburg-Prussia

The Hohenzollern dynasty's conversion to the Reformed Church in 1613 was vehemently opposed by nobles and commoners alike: the success of the first reformation of Luther three generations before precluded the success of the second. Affirming their legal rights under the Peace of Westphalia, the nobility and the Lutheran Church were initially strengthened by the dynasty's conversion to the Reformed Church. Since attempts to enforce the second reformation failed, Brandenburg became, by default, the first imperial territory in which a limited form of toleration was legalized and, more or less, practiced—but not for long. Beginning with the reign of Frederick William, the Great Elector (r. 1640–88), Calvinists were favored over Lutherans for government positions. Attempts to justify poly-confessionalism resulted in further hardening the lines between the two confessions.[24] The Electorate's solution to the Lutheran resistance they confronted was, ultimately, faced head on during the reign of Elector Frederick III (r. 1688–1713; King Frederick I from 1701) when he invited Lutheran Pietists during the last decade of the seventeenth century to join him in facilitating the state reforms with which Brandenburg-Prussia would be identified. This critical juncture in Prussian history overlapped with the crisis in the theology department at the university in Leipzig—felt at the Dresden court as well as in the Leipzig community—that is described below. The religious, psychological, and intellectual consequences, in large part determined by the personalities of their rulers, were that Saxon and Prussian subjects became two cultures bound by physical proximity, their fluctuating loyalties to the German Empire, and the dynastic competition within it.

Tolerance and Heresy Entwined

Although the object of the Peace of Westphalia was to achieve religious tolerance through the secularization of interterritorial agreements, intolerance was persistent. Indeed, attempts at poly-confessionalism like that in Brandenburg-Prussia, limited to Lutherans and Calvinists, inspired insecurity and inflexibility. In many parts of Saxony, theologians, who saw their role as defining pure doctrine and teaching a system of dogma to be learned by rote, were no more than a step removed from the magistrates and landed nobility who asserted their role as defenders of Lutheranism with accusations of heresy, while the Electors shared guilt through their indifference. Indeed, this was the age of witch hunts. In 1666, the Leipzig jurist Benedikt Carpzov (1595–1666) boasted "that he had passed the death sentence on 20,000, mostly witches."[25] The traditional system of criminal law under which Carpzov operated drew its alleged authority from the Bible but was really based on convenient fictions.

> Benedikt Carpzov's *Practica nova rerum criminalum*, which appeared in 1635 and was reprinted nine times until 1723 . . . was the leading authority, as he was the

recognized greatest jurist of his time, to whose court at Leipzig were submitted questions from all quarters. During his long career, up to 1666, he is reputed to have signed 20,000 death sentences. . . . In [his book] he always has a biblical text to justify any conclusion reached, whether the inquisitorial process with torture, the death penalty for adultery, bigamy, heresy, blasphemy, coining, theft, or the most ferocious death-penalties with added hot pincers, cutting-off of arms, the wheel and the stake.[26]

While accusations of heresy could only have been made with extreme caution against the urban merchants, guild members, and professionals, who were vital to the workings of a city as economically significant to the Saxon electorate as Leipzig, often cruel and arbitrary justice was dispensed in the landed estates and smaller cities under the advisement of Leipzig's juridical experts following Benedikt Carpzov's *Practica nova rerum criminalium*. The practice of witch trials in Saxony ended in 1727.[27]

Even prior to the Peace of Westphalia, Abraham Calov, a prolific author of the most important and learned Lutheran dogmatic literature, emerged as a major actor in the so-called "syncretistic controversies." Calov's work intersects with some details in Bach's conflicted biography, because Calov annotated the edition of the Lutheran Bible that Bach acquired in 1733. From 1645 through 1686—overlapping with Carpzov's prosecutorial activities—the syncretistic controversies within the Lutheran Church reached all the Lutheran territories and a schism threatened Lutheranism. Instigated by efforts to encourage tolerance—to unify the principal Protestant confessions or, at least, find shared principles that could foster tolerance—the controversies gave rise to further intolerance. Although many theologians participated in the controversies, the conflicting positions were defined primarily by two Lutherans, George Calixt (1586–1656) and Abraham Calov. Calixt questioned the authority of fixed dogma, favoring instead free inquiry and investigation, with concentration on only a few essential dogmatic principles. Calov accused Calixt and his sympathizers of being heretics and crypto-Calvinists. The disputes reached the public from pulpits and in broadsides. In 1650, Calov went to the Wittenberg parish at the invitation of Saxon Elector Johann George I (r. 1611–57), and by 1660 was dean of faculty at the university in Wittenberg. With increasing insistence, he pressured the Elector to excommunicate the syncretists in Saxony and other territories by force. A threat to the peace, this suggestion was ignored. However his polemical ferocity led to electoral edicts ordering restraint: in 1655, by his mentor Elector Johann Georg I; and, in 1669, by Elector Johann Georg II (r. 1657–80). In 1662, Prussia's Frederick William, the Great Elector (r. 1640–88), forbade his subjects to study philosophy or religion at the university in Wittenberg because of Calov's strenuous opposition to Calvinism. Under orders forbidding religious polemics, Calov published his *Historia syncretistica* anonymously in 1682. Johann Georg III (r. 1680–91) banned the work and destroyed all the copies he could find, but an edition appeared in 1685 with Calov's name. When Calov's inflexibility led to his losing the support of his Wittenberg colleagues, he turned his aggressive entreaties to other faculties. This conflict lasted until his death in 1686.[28]

Calov's religious intolerance was also directed against Socinians. In 1684, he published in Leipzig a collection of essays, composed over an extended period, entitled *Socinismus Profligatus*.[29] Modern Lutheran theologian Robert Preus offers this explanation of why orthodox Lutherans like Calov and his supporters were as hostile to the syncretism of the Lutheran George Calixt as they were to the heterodox views of Socinians:

> When one is convinced that purity of doctrine and doctrinal certainty are attainable, one will take doctrine seriously and will often be quite intolerant toward those who do not share one's convictions. . . . The Lutherans saw in the latitudinarianism of unionism [i.e., liberal standards that would admit to shared principles with other Christians] a threat as dangerous as straight-out heresy. For latitudinarianism and syncretism undermined doctrinal certainty, and here was a challenge to the Gospel itself.[30]

The personal animosity Calov incurred may very well account for the fact that, of all the works in Bach's library, only his work was not claimed—it is the sole extant item from Bach's library. While the level of Calov's exegetical competence was never questioned—in his own time or later—Christoph Wolff's evaluation of Bach's posthumous library inventory as representing old fashioned books seems to validate contemporary opinion.

Preus's explanation of the threats orthodoxy perceived adds to the image of a complex, heterodox religious society. According to Preus, "the Socinian aberration" was one reason for the precisionist demands of the dogmatists. Unlike Poland, Romania, and England, where Socinian congregations had existed since the end of the sixteenth century, in the German territories the extent of Socinian influence at this time can be surmised by the amount of attention Calov's sermons and publications received. They were joined, soon after, by other publications that gained prominence.[31] For example, in March 1694 the Prussian scholar Friedrich Wilhelm Stosch (1648–1704) was arrested and tried by an electoral commission in Berlin for his clandestine 1692 publication and accused of the Socinian heresy. Although copies of his book were seized and condemned from pulpits in Berlin, "the book's extreme rarity and notoriety helped to make it one of the best-known, and most-sought-after, bibliographical curiosities." In its spring 1694 issue, Leipzig's German-language *Monatliche Unterredungen*, one of the journals directed at Leipzig's literate audience, "discussed the scandal of the 'new atheistic book' . . . noting that every *erudit* of any standing had something to say about it."[32] Its dissemination in Saxony was therefore assured.

During this period, when syncretistic conflict and concerns about heresy disturbed religious life in Saxony, Prussia still protected a measure of multi-confessional tolerance. However, a Calvinist ruling a Lutheran state, Frederick William needed to ease the resistance of his legally privileged Lutheran orthodox population to his sovereign authority. Recognizing the economic value of immigration policies that would bring foreign skills and commerce to his region, in 1685, when Louis XIV instituted religious conformity in France by revoking the Edict of Nantes, Frederick William welcomed France's French Huguenots. He also used this population to build his government's bureaucracy and override the rights of his Lutheran population. Distrusting their loyalties, which he feared carried the potential for political disloyalty, the Great Elector was the first Prussian sovereign to challenge the official religious rights of his Lutheran nobles. He built a centralized administration with Calvinist aristocrats recruited from other regions of the Empire—including the French Huguenot refugees—in addition to Prussian aristocrats and talented commoners who converted to Calvinism, many of whom Frederick William ennobled during his reign.[33] Defying imperial law, Frederick William then "asserted the right of even Calvinists (his coreligionists), to hold [state] office, and he rendered ineffective the prescripts of the law of citizenship—on which the nobility had insisted—by according the right of citizenship even to foreigners."[34] Thus he broke the power of the cities and the aristocracy in yet another way. Friedrich William put in place a dynamic and autocratic approach to state-building that his successors continued to pursue. However its further fulfillment during the eighteenth century, reflecting the personalities of his successors, became dependent on a form of population control that pervaded every aspect of life and was tied to strictly disciplined, uniform, and ideological religious practices.

Philosophers for Reconciliation

Although Europe and particularly the German territories could not yet progress in matters concerning reconciliation, toleration, and heresy, the potential for religious war in the future gained the attention of scholars, philosophers, and some rulers. The so called "natural law" of Samuel Pufendorf (1632–94), Germany's most prominent legal scholar, states his objective: "the preservation and promotion of society." His prolix writings are reducible to rules that cultivate "the sociability needed to preserve social peace."[35] His thinking follows directly from the secular moral values propounded in the Peace of Westphalia and develops a civil philosophy dependent on the absolutist power of the sovereign states, in which the power to grant or not grant toleration was vested. Like Calixt, his objective was the reconciliation of the Lutheran and Calvinist churches. It is interesting to note that his 1695 work containing this proposal was published anonymously.[36] Pufendorf rejected the possibility of reconciliation also with Catholics when the proposal for reunification was raised, most notably by Leibniz, because Protestants could not accept the doctrine of papal infallibility. Leibniz outlined his plan for union in 1686 in *Systema theologicum*, which was first published in the nineteenth century, and he also participated in conferences and extensive correspondence devoted to this goal. He was harshly critical of Pufendorf's position.[37] There seems no way to know the degree to which the efforts of Pufendorf and Leibniz were known outside academic and government circles. Apparently reaching only limited audiences and having minimal effectiveness, their ideas were certainly not announced in broadsides and from pulpits.

Secular Life and Spirituality:
Christian Weise and Philipp Jakob Spener

Between 1672 and 1676, works published by Christian Weise (1642–1708) and Philipp Jakob Spener (1635–1705), with intersecting messages, would significantly shape the religious and intellectual character of early eighteenth-century Leipzig. In his widely disseminated work, Weise's rationalized support for socioeconomic change articulated direct opposition to Lutheran doctrine.[38] Weise abandoned his original plan to get his degree in theology at the university in Leipzig. An extremely successful student, he was not invited to join the faculty, undoubtedly because his brilliant debates were peppered by impudent remarks that especially disturbed the theology faculty. Accused of being blasphemous, he retorted that nothing is blasphemous.[39]

Socio-economic change created conflict between Lutheran orthodox doctrine, which was committed to the aristocratic social hierarchy, and the new social hierarchy based on wealth and political clout in the administration of the Saxon state. As ambition and industry replaced inherited privilege, they also mediated the successful commoners' perception of religious authority. Several scholars have noted radical religious implications in Weise's work: In contradistinction to Luther's doctrine of "glorification through abasement" and the passive anticipation of future reward in the afterlife, Weise encouraged social and economic advancement in the here and now, by taking an active role in determining one's earthly destiny. Klaus Günzel writes, "again and again he directs his students towards the values of this world and, at the same time, denies the right of church orthodoxy to question or dispute these values."[40]

Since Weise's ideas directly reached a broad public, his work is especially relevant for studying religious attitudes in the general community. The literary historian Frederick Herbert Wagman credits Weise with having presented "perhaps the best analysis of common superstition" in *Die drey ärgsten Ertznarren in der gantzen Welt*, which Wagman connects directly with the rise of skepticism in seventeenth-century literature. He places Weise among the influential figures of the early German Enlightenment.[41] Weise not only reconceived the organization of society—fostering the social changes described in chapter 1—he also suggested new religious and philosophical paradigms that stand among those of Leibniz and Spinoza, other seventeenth-century skeptics. The differences between the diverse religious and philosophical sensibilities that developed in Saxony, in part following the "popular" socio-economic initiatives fostered by Weise, are strikingly different from the state-controlled authoritarian religious sensibility that evolved in Prussia, where economic change was determined by totalitarian mercantilist policies.

While Weise was an early *Aufklärer* (enlightener) rooted in practical engagement, Philipp Jakob Spener was a Lutheran theologian whose "optimistic eschatology" aspired to an "active faith" and full participation and responsibility for a rewarding life.[42] Both Weise and Spener were close contemporaries of Pufendorf, and their worldview was shaped, like his, by the cruelty practiced during the Thirty Years' War and the depraved behavior it inspired.[43] Spener encouraged social transformation and questioned the passive obedience and focus on fulfillment in the afterlife that was being taught by Lutheran orthodoxy. Stoeffler makes a significant distinction for our purpose (that is, trying to understand Spener's followers in Leipzig) between Lutheran edificatory literature that was "quietistic and *weltflüchtig* (withdrawn)" and resigned to passivity and otherworldly yearnings, and the Arndt-Spener tradition.[44] In 1775, while senior pastor of the ministry in Frankfurt am Main, Spener published his preface to a work by Johann Arndt (1555–1621). Entitled *Pia Desideria: Or Heartfelt Desires for a God-Pleasing Improvement of the True Protestant Church*, Spener's preface was reissued separately the following year, and by the time of the author's death in 1705 it had been reissued four times in German and translated into Latin.[45] Although Spener is known as the "father of Pietism," he actually brought Arndt's ideas to a large public. Spener's suggestions for religious reform seem to have been responses to "the public's desire for more rigorous spiritual teachings . . . and a religious renewal," which was reflected in the large number of German translations of English Puritan authors published by commercial printers during the 1670s and 1680s.[46] Spener seems to have also assimilated ideas from Calvinism. When he went to Strassburg to study with Lutheran teachers there, he was also exposed to ideas of the Reformed tradition. Then in Basel and Geneva, he frequently heard Jean de Labadie preach.

Emphasizing experiential piety and rebirth, Spener criticized the Lutheran clergy for their intellectual orientation, their neglect of pastoral responsibilities, and the abiding corruption at court.[47] He criticized the education of the orthodox ministry, calling for schools that would not be "places of worldliness and indeed of the devils of ambition, tippling, carousing, and brawling."[48] He reopened discussion of the controversial role of mysticism in Luther's teaching but did not embrace mysticism.[49] His revival of Luther's notion of the "priesthood of all believers" held the greatest threat to the orthodox clergy. Originally invoking this notion against Rome, Luther modified his position when it threatened anarchy during the Peasant Revolt. Spener, like Weise and Pufendorf, was not a revolutionary, accepting the existing institutional political structures: he used the notion of a spiritual "priesthood" to encourage individual piety and practice, emphasizing that all believers are among the "anointed," "without distinction," and have "the right to judge their ministers."[50] The discussion groups (*collegium pietatis*) that he initiated for the purpose of reading the Bible and devotional literature drew the harshest criticism against him and his followers. Designed to break down barriers between the minister and congregants as well as "between members of the various social classes among the laity," these meetings were extremely controversial in a class-conscious society.[51] Seeking to reverse the traditionally pessimistic Lutheran view of conditions on earth, Spener cited "biblical prophecies of the conversion of the Jews and the fall of the papacy . . . as proof that 'God promised his church here on earth a better state than this.' "[52] Richard Gawthrop interprets this optimistic eschatology to mean that "either improvement in the Lutheran church would help bring about these events or else the simple occurrence of these events would produce new, zealous converts to Lutheranism, whose impact on the church would be rejuvenating."[53]

Spener's active faith and optimism would undoubtedly have confirmed the life experiences of Leipzig's self-consciously successful community. Nonetheless, although Spener never broke away from the official Lutheran church, and Pietism during his lifetime was not an institutionalized or politically polarizing orthodoxy—as it would become in Prussia by the end of the 1720s—he and his followers were ostracized by Saxony's religious institutions in the Leipzig crisis during the last decade of the century. Heretical issues would only seem to have been transparent in that crisis: the ideas of the protagonists were more complicated than reported in history until recently—I refer particularly to Ian Hunter's work on Christian Thomasius (1655–1728)—and the consequences could not have been foreseen.

2. The Waning Century

Twenty years after Benedikt Carpzov boasted about his juridical successes as the greatest witch hunter, Calov's tirades against heresy ended and the voices of a new generation were heard in Leipzig.[54] All this was happening, incidentally, around the time Bach was born in the Thuringian city of Eisenach. Although Leipzig's citizens, all Saxons, were Lutheran orthodox as determined in 1555 at the Peace of Augsburg, the city's religious life and thought at the end of the seventeenth century were already far more complicated than this would suggest. The religious ideas of post-Reformation Lutheranism, Pietist reformers, and Enlightenment philosophers—both skeptics and rationalist believers—had begun to brush up against each other.

Leipzig's Publishing Industry

Leipzig became an increasingly important center for book production and trades after 1670, when Frankfurt's book fairs became subject to the imperial book censor. In Leipzig, the Saxon Elector controlled censorship and policies were more liberal, permitting works by Catholics, Pietists, and Calvinists as well as Lutheran orthodox works as long as they did not incite disturbances. By the end of the seventeenth century, Leipzig was the publishing center for all of central Europe. The scope of the commercially successful Leipzig publications attests to an eager audience and their intellectual vitality.

In the last quarter of the seventeenth century, journals became the primary international vehicle for disseminating ideas and advertising books. While the earliest journals concentrated on scientific issues, their subject matter broadened with the founding of *Acta Eruditorum*, which was published in Leipzig from 1682 to 1731. Backed by an annual subsidy from the Saxon Elector, this journal was published in Latin to attract an international, albeit thereby restricted, readership. Its contributors and reviewers represented a wide range of interests and positions; they included the political scientist Veit Ludwig von Seckendorff (1626–92), then a prominent political writer in the Saxon court and a friend of Spener; the philosopher-mathematician Leibniz; and the eclectic philosopher-theologian Johann Franz Buddeus (1667–1729), who was a formidable adversary of René Descartes (1596–1650), Spinoza, Leibniz, and Leibniz's disciple-popularizer Christian Wolff.[55] The new conditions for intellectual openness in Leipzig confronted the long tradition of intolerant legal assumptions in which the Leipzig jurists were centrally involved.

Christian Thomasius in Leipzig

The critical journal *Monatgespräche*, founded by Christian Thomasius in Leipzig in 1688 and written in German, was far more important than the *Acta Eruditorum* for Leipzig's literate community. It fulfilled Thomasius's expressed intention of encouraging people to read and debate the issues that were being raised in the world at that time. Jonathan Israel's assessment of its importance sets the stage for our portrait of intellectual and religious Leipzig on its way to becoming the community Bach would encounter: "That a journal devoted to reviewing the latest scholarly books and controversies could not just appear, but flourish, in German, sufficiently illustrates that the intellectual revolution had by this date penetrated well beyond the restricted circles of professional academics, lawyers, physicians, and clergymen who had monopolized erudite discussion in the past and confined it to Latin."[56] In the first volume of the *Monatgespräche*, Thomasius introduced his German reading public to recent intellectual developments by denouncing "the growing Spinozist presence in German culture." Israel believes

Thomasius began with this subject "in part to deflect conservative disapproval from himself," but Thomasius's positions seem to have consistently been subtle and conservative while confronting and exposing all points of view.[57] However, *Monatgespräche* was published only until 1690, when Thomasius was forbidden to teach or publish after defending August Hermann Francke (1663–1727) and the Pietists during the orthodox-Pietist confrontations—the subject of our next section. It was the model for other journals.

Through his innovations as a teacher, journal editor, and legal counsel during the last two decades of the seventeenth century, Christian Thomasius played a critical role in stimulating the intellectual curiosity and confidence that permitted an authentic middle-class culture to develop and thrive in Leipzig. The son of a Leipzig university professor, Thomasius was born and educated in that city and then received his legal education at Frankfurt an der Oder in Brandenburg. He returned to Leipzig, began lecturing there in 1682 and, under the influence of Pufendorf, was named professor of natural law in 1684. Thomasius introduced lectures at the university in the vernacular instead of in Latin—an innovation that alone gained him notoriety; he took the syncretistic position against Calov regarding the Lutheran-Calvinist split and attacked irrational aspects of prejudice, particularly the concept of heresy. Dedicated to fighting the very concept, Thomasius drew lines between politics and religion in the classes he taught in Leipzig and in his *Monatgespräche*. He supported Samuel Pufendorf's civil philosophy as the means to develop an ethical basis for political relationships and opposed the growing metaphysical philosophy.

However, Ian Hunter addresses the " 'unevenness' in Thomasius's intellectual positions," evident throughout his career, wherein he devoted himself to a secular study of politics and constitutional law but remained committed to a "spiritualistic," "pietistic form of Lutheranism."[58] Hunter gives Thomasius credit for recognizing the transformation needed for the principles of Pufendorf's civil government and natural law to take root: the separation of political authority and civil philosophy, which belonged to the secular sovereign state, from religious authority and metaphysical philosophy belonging in the private realm.[59] However, Thomasius, unlike Pufendorf, believed that human intellect could neither comprehend divinity nor formulate moral judgments; therefore, the prince and the desacralized political state needed to bear responsibility for maintaining peace. Individuals need only develop a "privatized religion of faith and grace."[60] To inculcate this separation and promote obedience to the civil state, Thomasius launched a reform program suitable for future lawyers and government bureaucrats based on his *Affectenlehre* (doctrine of the passions), a method for personality assessment that would lead to personal self-control and restraint.[61] His system is described in the long and revealing—here translated—titles of two publications: *New Discovery of a Solid Science, Most Necessary for the Community, for Discerning the Secrets of the Heart of Other Men from Daily Conversation, Even Against Their Will;* and *Further Elucidations by Different Examples of the Recent Proposal for a*

New Science for Discerning the Nature of Other Men's Minds.[62] Once Thomasius was employed at the Prussian university at Halle, his program would be a useful complement to the religious policies of the Hohenzollern rulers.[63] Recent studies of works by members of Leipzig's theological faculty demonstrate that Thomasius's dismissal was, in part, a defense of merged religious and political authority in confessional society, which thereby resisted subordinating religious moral truth to civil authority. It was also a defense of the "theo-rational position" supported by some of Leipzig's theologians. These convoluted arguments, irrelevant in modern societies, are difficult to understand today. Yet we can appreciate that the problem was not the one conventionally cast: "a conflict between religious orthodoxy and enlightened rationalism."[64]

3. Leipzig's Turn-of-the Century Crises: New Paradigms; New Threats

At the end of the seventeenth century, within less than a decade, four critical events occurred in Saxony's religious history: first, Veit Ludwig von Seckendorff persuaded the Lutheran High Consistory in Dresden and Elector Johann Georg III that radical philosophies were currently corrupting Saxon society and the presence of Spener as head of Saxony's Lutheran orthodox confession would inspire stability and a pious transformation. Spener assumed this position but left within five years under unpleasant circumstances. Second, Spener's disciple August Hermann Francke (1663–1727), a popular teacher in Leipzig, was arrested on charges of heresy. Third, at the same time, Thomasius was deprived of his teaching position and the right to publish. Last, Saxony's Elector August the Strong converted to Catholicism in 1697. These four events would affect the Leipzig community's religious, intellectual, and political attitudes during the following years.

Seckendorff and the Pietist Heading Saxony's Lutheran Church; Francke and the Student "Takeover" in Leipzig; Thomasius Banned

In 1685, a year after Calov published his sermons and essays warning of the Socinian threat—the year, incidentally, of Bach's birth and France's revocation of the Edict of Nantes—Seckendorf published his *Christen Staat*. It was an entreaty that something be done about views that were being disseminated in the general population: radical thinkers, especially Spinoza (1632–77), intended "to make 'life in this world' the basis of politics" and challenged faith and Christian authority. His arguments flowed from concerns that identify his place in history. In Seckendorff's opinion, "what was insufficiently grasped in the Germany of his day and inadequately opposed . . . were the consequences of such ideas . . . for politics, the public sphere, and the individual's place in society." His concern was that in these radical notions "nothing is based on God's Word or commandment so that no institutions are God-ordained and no laws divinely sanctioned."[65] A friend of Spener's, he recommended that the Pietist be appointed Senior Court Chaplain in Dresden. Seckendorff was a theorist of cameralism and defended administrative centralization and uniformity, believing that only sovereign control could sustain the "natural harmony" between society's diverse parts. One of his responsibilities, of course, was to protect Johann Georg's "divine" entitlements.

Seckendorff's urgent entreaty and the Dresden Upper Consistory's decision to act point to the general public's access to early Enlightenment ideas. The letter from the Consistory recommending Spener to the Elector is written from the purview of clerics and theologians impotent in the face of uncontrollably dissolute behavior at court, and their need for a charismatic leader.[66] It reports " 'highly dangerous times in the church at present,' " and the need to appoint someone " 'who is prepared not only to edify through sermons, but also to lift this crisis-ridden church through his authority and experience.' "[67] The honor implied by the court's invitation reflects the distinction Spener and his followers had achieved despite the resistance he had been facing ever since the publication of his *Pia desideria*. Spener's appointment in 1686 lasted for less than five years, a period of growing tensions between him and Johann Georg III.[68] He left with an invitation from the Prussian court to take up employment in Berlin.

August Hermann Francke was invited to teach at the university in Leipzig after receiving his degree there in 1685. He helped his professor Johann B. Carpzov II (1639–99) organize the *collegium philobiblicum*, a special group designed to study the Bible in its original languages. He left Leipzig for further theological study elsewhere with theologians in the Spenerian orbit and with Spener himself. Returning to Leipzig in early 1689 to resume his teaching, he now emphasized exegetical and devotional instead of linguistic studies. He attracted a large following among the students, hundreds of whom attended his sessions and neglected their other studies. Gawthrop characterizes the crisis, which demonstrated "the potentially subversive nature of the Pietist movement," as a student "takeover."[69] Francke and his friends also held conventicles in the community. Led by his former teacher Johann Benedikt Carpzov II, the theological faculty lodged complaints with the Dresden authorities in 1690, Francke was arrested, a formal trial was conducted, in which he was unsuccessfully defended by Thomasius, a lawyer as well as a teacher, and he was forced to leave Leipzig.[70]

Thomasius's *Affectenlehre* had been attacked by orthodox faculty members the year before, 1689, as heretical. Its orientation towards the self-restraint of the passions as a way of achieving inner tranquillity clashed with both theological and philosophical approaches to ethics and morality, both of which depended on the concept of "holiness" and on God "from whom these virtues came."[71] When Thomasius defended Francke, Johann Benedict Carpzov II and Carpzov's brother Samuel, pastor to the Saxon court, were among those instrumental in banning Thomasius's work, forbidding him from further lecturing or writing. Thomasius left Leipzig three years later. Both Francke and Thomasius received appointments from Elector Frederick III of Brandenburg (King Frederick I of Prussia from 1701, r. 1688–1713) to the university he opened in Halle in 1694.

Thomasius's place in history rests primarily on his seminal role in ending the European witch trials, the severest way heresy was adjudicated. We skip ahead to 1703 when Thomasius, firmly ensconced as a professor at the university at Halle, published his first attack on witch hunters and witch trials. Henry Charles Lea, paraphrasing Thomasius, writes: "In reciting the names of the principal defenders of witchcraft he [Thomasius] says of [Benedikt] Carpzov, that he is *today* [my emphasis] the monarch and most eminent of criminalists, but the things he brings forward from judicial acts are such evident and crass fables that a man feels ashamed to have read them."[72] In response to Thomasius, Prussia's Frederick William I (r. 1713–40) ordered that all witch trials involving the death penalty be reported to him; he totally outlawed such cases in 1721.[73]

These three episodes in Saxony's religious history and August's conversion to Catholicism had a direct impact on the future of the Leipzig community. Religious diversity and tolerance gained new possibilities, even under the legal restraints imposed by a state religion. At the same time, Prussian military discipline gained new meaning.

State and Religion: New Paradigms for Leipzig and Halle

With the conversion to Catholicism of August the Strong three years after his accession to the throne, Leipzig became progressively more diverse and tolerant for several reasons. Wanting to put his conversion—which removed him even further from his subjects—in as positive a light as possible, August supported tolerant religious policies. Also, some of his subjects were exploring Pietism and remained in contact with the Halle Pietists, and August wanted to avoid a confrontational political situation with the ever more militarized Prussian state. Elector Frederick III opened his new university in Halle, a short distance from Leipzig, as a Pietist center with Spener as consultant and several professors who were recent refugees from the university at Leipzig, the year August acceded to the Saxon throne.[74] Threatened by Prussia's reputation as an aggressive state, August would, time and again, need to temper hostile sermons from Leipzig's orthodox pulpits. Even at the cost of antagonizing orthodox interests, in 1699 August granted the Saxon government's official permission to the Pietist press in Halle to sell its publications in Leipzig,[75] after which the actual hold of Lutheran orthodoxy among the Leipzig faculty waned, although it retained its officially privileged position.[76] At the same time, new and radical ideas entered the public consciousness through the book industry which, because of August's policies, were free from theological censorship.

Figure 2.1. The Dresden Zwinger, photograph, courtesy Deutsche Fotothek.

The meaning of August's conversion was not lost on the community. Any semblance of religious sensibility behind August's conversion may be discounted. His privy counselor Count Fleming maneuvered his conversion to Catholicism to acquire the Polish throne for him as King August II; after this, Fleming, in effect, ruled Poland.[77] August is best known for his reputation as a womanizer, which was already documented in a 1734 publication—supposedly he fathered three hundred children in many countries and courts.[78] During August's reign and that of his son August III (r. 1733–63), Dresden had the reputation of being the most luxurious and ostentatious court in Europe (see figure 2.1).[79] August hired the architect Matthäus Daniel Pöppelman to design "The Zwinger," six connected pavilions, built between 1710 and 1732, to house August's various collections. Bach's contemporaries working in Dresden included Antonio Lotti (1667–1740), the opera composer Johann Adolf Hasse (1699–1783), Johann David Heinichen (1683–1729), and Johann Zelenka (1679–1745). Although August converted to acquire the Polish throne, he apparently encouraged Catholic ritual, following customs, possibly, in place during the reigns of his predecessors. In 1710, he established a Catholic court chapel in Leipzig led by Jesuit priests from Bohemia, which was maintained especially for the visits of the royal family and also served a few Catholic residents in Leipzig as well as Catholic visitors and university students.[80] As a contemporary report tells us, Bach acknowledged the court's favored "Italian style" when he composed the work commemorating the death, in 1727, of August's wife Queen Christiane Eberhardine.[81]

Interchanges between the orthodox and Pietist communities in Leipzig and those in Halle were progressively restricted as religion came under the control of the Prussian state. Diversity and tolerance in Prussia was short-lived. Leipzig, aware of the ascending fanaticism in Prussia's religious and political spheres, needed to be increasingly wary and cautious. Gawthrop and Fulbrook have studied how the "reorientation in Spenerian Pietism, carried out principally by August Hermann Francke . . . contributed decisively to the transformation of the Brandenburg-Prussian state itself."[82] As early as 1692, Elector Frederick III (King Frederick I) affirmed the state's support for Pietism, thereby weakening the status of Lutheran orthodoxy in his territories as designated by the Peace of Augsburg. One of the earliest acts undertaken by his successor, the "Soldier King" Frederick William I, was the dissolution of the estates in 1713, which officially eliminated the legal status and privileges of the clerical estate as well as those of the aristocracy.[83] During this regime the association of state and religion—Prussia and Pietism—became firmly established; religion was linked to Prussia's social and educational structures and to its political aspirations. In the 1720s the orthodox and Pietists in East Prussia still competed for the King's support, but by 1727 Pietist credentials were needed to attain a government position.

This description of Prussia's single-minded goals is intended to prepare the reader for the contrasting multifaceted culture described below in "The Leipzig Files." Under Frederick William I, the Prussian court was itself subject to puritanical measures, a distinctive departure from all other absolutist courts.[84] Trying to control the future, this ruler's 1722 "Instructions for His Successor" condemned the cultural pursuits associated with court life, warning against "opera, comedies, ballet, masquerades, mistresses, drinking and feasting, and other scandalous pursuits of the devil."[85] In the same document, he called for the intensification of mercantilist policies, which were already the most fully developed of any state. The Prussian economy served "state expansion, militarism, and the social disciplining of the population."[86] The point was already made in chapter 1: by the end of his reign, as much as eighty percent of the state's revenues supported the military. His mastery in controlling every level of government even extended to developing a cabinet of commoners who, by their inherent lack of power, assured that the bureaucracy would never exceed his direct control.[87] Historians are in general agreement that Frederick William I's authoritarian efforts emanated from his conviction that he was furthering God's work on earth, that he was accountable to God for his every act, and that by placing himself "in direct dependence on a higher power, his understanding of himself as being God's agent in a quite literal operational sense gave him the boundless self-assurance needed to insist on absolute subordination to his authority."[88] Both this conviction and his methodology were closely aligned with Francke's.

Distinguishing between the messages of Spener and Francke, Gawthrop describes Francke's distinctive spirituality as based on his personal experience of conversion and "fundamentally different" from Spener's religious experiences.[89] He says that Francke and his staff "claimed to be 'merely' media through which God transmitted His wishes for the betterment of humankind," but they were ideologues who set themselves up as "*the* standard for all human conduct" and manipulated "the educational environment in accordance with their 'sacred science.' "[90] Francke's methods included: "breaking the will," "forcing the children to develop the habit of unconditional obedience," "intensive exposure to Pietist spirituality in the classroom," coercion, particularly in the orphanage and school for poor children, "uninterrupted alternation of prayer and work," "continued surveillance," and "supervision well beyond the classroom."[91] Religious indoctrination was even more intense at the university in Halle, with control extended to coercing poor students dependent on scholarships into reporting on the behavior of their fellow students.[92] "The teaching staff in both institutions placed a higher priority on a reform of the will than on scholastic attainment. . . . In the case of the theology program at the university, this meant a " 'born-again' conversion."[93] Fulbrook writes that the economic success of Francke's business enterprises, an aspect of his "active piety," stemmed largely from unpaid labor by the orphanage students and a subsistence level of support for his assistants that was determined by Francke's idea of Pietist values. Like Gawthrop, Fulbrook also addresses the "parallelism between the aims of the ruler and government in Berlin, and those of the Pietists in Halle."[94]

Frederick "The Great" (r. 1740–86) introduced yet another paradigm for the relationship between state and religion. Frederick was an atheist but guarded against sharing his personal religious enlightenment with his subjects—paternalism depended on censorship. The philosophers and cameralist theorists he gathered at his court, including Voltaire and Christian Wolff, were writing and teaching under his patronage; they were obliged to embrace the state's use of religion as a tool for obedience and loyalty as well as, therefore, Frederick's cynicism:[95]

> Popular participation in such a scheme was not so much impious or impudent as simply irrelevant. If the ruler was the physician of his country, supremely knowledgeable and uniquely wise, there was no reason why he should consult his ignorant and superstitious patients. . . . Frederick II, deeply imbued with this rationalism, said flatly that men are governed by two mainsprings of action—"fear of punishment and hope for reward."[96]

A disciple of Voltaire since 1736, Frederick introduced allegedly tolerant religious policies. However, little actually changed, since religious leaders continued to preach submission to the secular power, and "sermons were written with an eye to the authorities. Pastors were employed as civil servants, teachers, promoters of patriotic morale, and . . . as government spies."[97] Philosophical works, published only in Latin or French, were made available only to academics. Gotthold Lessing "observed sarcastically [that Prussia] was a free country: everyone was free to make anticlerical jokes."[98]

4. The Leipzig Files

The orthodox hegemony in Leipzig could not control the diversity of religious ideas that existed by the end of the seventeenth century. They could not stem the explorations of a wealthy, educated, and self-motivated population. Furthermore, the ideas of the orthodox theologians were evolving in directions they themselves could not yet fully assimilate.

Pietism in Leipzig

During the last two decades of the seventeenth century, orthodox theologians tested diversity, temporarily gaining the upper hand when Pietist meetings were disrupted and Francke and Thomasius were forced to leave their positions at the university. However, Spener's Leipzig followers maintained their loyalty after these confrontations and Spener's removal from the Dresden position. Those still interested in exploring Pietism exercised discretion and retreated into covert practices when they were unable to gather openly.[99]

Underlying factors working against Spener and his followers were of two sorts: The first was the orthodox clergy's need to maintain the system of beliefs on which their own positions of authority depended. The second, more significant, was genuine outrage at the interrelated religious and social implications of what and how the Pietists preached, which challenged the teaching that God was author of the social hierarchies on earth, that inequality was necessary to maintain social order, and that equality was reserved for salvation. By returning to Luther's controversial doctrine, the "priesthood of all believers," Spener raised complaints that were essentially theological despite their obvious social and political implications. Johann Benedikt Carpzov's criticism of Spener's 1692 visit to Leipzig speaks from a class-consciousness sensitized by doctrine and its concomitant heresies:

> There came with him . . . a disrespectable entourage which was noticeable immediately upon his arrival. He paid visits to every one, not only to the royal ministers . . . , but to all the preachers and burghers in the city wherever he chanced to go. . . . He started a girls' school [in Dresden] in his house and taught small children the catechism—a chief court preacher of the elector with a children's school that even a village school master could handle! He places himself (in Leipzig) on Sunday in the gallery of the church of St. Thomas where, it is true, honest people stand, but not people of his class.

"Carpzov further criticized the Pietists for allowing servants to sit at the same table with their master."[100]

Francke was banned from Leipzig because, in addition to undermining the traditional university curriculum, he and his friends organized conventicles in the community. These devotional gatherings, held mainly in the evening with-out the benefit of clergy, were investigated, and Dresden's Upper Consistory accused Francke of "having discussions with common people, preaching in the fields" and calling "a linen weaver a 'brother in Christ.'" Mary Fulbrook points to the threat of "such notions of spiritual brotherhood with the lower ranks" to "the maintenance of the social hierarchy."[101] Similar accusations were leveled against Francke after he left Leipzig and went to Erfurt: "Various people . . . from Leipzig and other places had come together, who under the appearance of godliness spread doctrines and arrange all sorts of gatherings by day or night-time."[102] Charges of "orgies of sexual promiscuity" and "secret assemblies" were "regularly made by the orthodox against dissenting societies." The accusations of sexual license reflected the participation of women.[103] When Francke's conventicles again caused similar tensions in Prussia, a commission ordered him to hold his meetings before the evening meal to avoid "suspicions of holding a 'nocturnal conventicle.'"[104]

Espousing false doctrine, heresy, private communion, political insurrection—all are understandable charges. However, the frequent charges of lewd behavior at these prayer meetings and study sessions suggest suspicion and fear that tran-scends a predictably intolerant response to either alternative modes of religious practice or threats such alternative practices might have posed to entrenched bureaucratic powers. Seeking the basis for these charges of lewd behavior opens an opportunity for speculation based on an uncharted hypothesis: it is true that these meetings were not held in a church, nor with an officially designated pas-tor, thereby giving them a provocative and even heretical nuance. In addition, the presence of groups of women congregating in a public setting was prob-lematic at that time and perhaps in itself sufficient provocation for such attacks. However, since these meetings were generally held in outdoor spaces (public meeting places other than a church, a coffeehouse, or a tavern did not exist and, at any rate, are not mentioned in literature), this transparent observation comes to mind: outdoor spaces do not offer a conventional or comfortable setting for sexual promiscuity. Therefore, it is likely that the leap from the presence of women to sexual promiscuity was caused by some irrational provocation.

I suggest that the night, the fear of darkness, was threatening. Note the self-conscious labeling of these meetings as "nocturnal." The hours after dark were not yet associated with respectable, public, social activities. At the end of the seventeenth century the moon offered the best prospect for outdoor light, and artificial illumination was limited to oil and candles (see figure 2.2). Ordinary people had been rising and retiring with the sun until just a few years prior to the first reports of problems with conventicles in Leipzig. It was then that coffee was introduced. The stimulant quickly became popular for private and then commercial use. Coffeehouses proliferated in Leipzig after the first one, "Zum arabischen Coffee-Baum," opened in 1694. The ensuing breakdown of the divi-sions of day and night led to new social patterns in which nighttime activities,

Figure 2.2. Leipzig's new street oil lamps. Engraving, 1701.

both inside and outside the home, eventually became commonplace; but it took time for a conservative society to adjust to such a major change. While these observations are not meant to imply that the introduction of coffee motivated Pietistic sensibilities, they do intend to situate these devotional meetings and the vehement responses they drew within a particular social context, under very specific circumstances.[105]

Although they drove Thomasius and Francke from Leipzig, Leipzig's orthodox theologians did not quell Pietist awareness. Indeed, the reported 1697 arrests evoked an aggressive and constructive communal response. These arrests of alleged "women of the street and . . . rabble" who were found in coffeehouses[106] seem to be undifferentiated from arrests at Pietist gatherings. Shortly after these arrests, there was a rush of activity to reopen church buildings unused since the period of the Reformation. Between 1698 and 1713, no fewer than four church buildings were refurbished and reopened, and joined St. Thomas and St. Nicholas as viable venues for religious study and worship. This activity appears to have been a direct and logical consequence of citizens disturbed by the arrests. Günther Stiller provides evidence that rebuilding the churches was, as he writes, "not the result of endeavors definitely originating with the church authorities or the municipal government but almost exclusively the result of what the church members wished and longed for." The expenses for these renovations were paid for by the merchants and guilds and "actively supported by 'men and women, academicians and merchants' in equal measure."[107] This activity demonstrates a community's solution to its urgent need for additional public spaces where people could presumably express, to some extent, heterodox religious ideas and spirituality. The Leipzig City Council approved a mutually satisfactory compromise, accommodating well-to-do citizens with Pietist and other heterodox leanings while placing them in facilities under the authority of the local consistory.[108]

Transformed Images of Self

Although it would appear, initially, that the private meetings of the middle-classes and "lower-class radical sects with egalitarian conceptions of the priesthood of all believers" held the potential of being real threats to the Elector,[109] circumstances in Saxony played themselves out differently. As described in chapter 1, under Saxony's absolutist government the middle classes developed quite independently of the Electors while cultivating beneficial alliances. Even the craft guilds provided valued services and prospered under Saxon absolutism. Thus, although alleged religious infractions, like the Pietist meetings described above, were not likely to threaten the Catholic Elector, they were threatening to the local consistory and constituted an unwitting confrontation with entrenched religious values. Nonetheless, interest in Pietism among

Leipzig's moneyed and educated elite as well as others in the community was accommodated.

The crucial difference between Spener and the orthodox lay in his belief "in the possibility of the active transformation of this world, the achievement of the Kingdom of God on earth. . . . Pietists believed . . . that it was their duty towards God, for the greater glory of God, to attempt to change conditions in the here and now."[110] Peter Gay discusses the "spirit of industry" that "substituted commercial for heroic, modern for medieval—bourgeois for aristocratic—ideals, which were, precisely, the ideals of the philosophers."[111] They were also the ideals of the German *Aufklärer.* "The recovery of nerve," by which Gay characterizes the underlying motivation for Enlightenment, was manifest in the "celebration of industry" and ultimately the "glorification of merchants."[112] J. S. Bach's oft quoted, seemingly modest statement, "I was obliged to be industrious; whoever is equally industrious will succeed equally well" asserts his community's values.[113] This new secular orientation, echoing the world-oriented ambitions that Christian Weise taught, developed moral and religious correlates compatible with Spener's emphasis on individual responsibility. James Sheehan notes the aggressive application of the religious notion of "vocation" to professional and business pursuits, frankly glorifying personal material success.[114]

Social and economic practices and structures consequently informed the Lutheran notion of "*Stand,*" the hierarchical social strata, during the transition from a feudal to a bourgeois society—redefining class and prestige. Successful commoners challenged the concept of hierarchy based on inherited privilege in both practice and ideology, not only in important commercial cities like Leipzig, Hamburg, and Frankfurt, but in the agrarian estates as well. Sheehan writes:

> In the countryside and at court, in administrative offices and urban drawing rooms, in universities and on the pages of periodical publications, the old elites were confronted by people unwilling to accept without question traditional rank and privilege. These people based their own claims to power and prestige on different grounds: wealth, political competence, educational accomplishment, moral superiority. They came from various places in society: commerce and manufacturing, the civil service and free professions, education and publishing.[115]

Nonetheless, at the end of the seventeenth century interpreting Luther's teachings remained a fluid and vital post-Reformation process among the orthodox, a compelling tribute to his complex and engrossing ideas. And the influence of Spener's teachings, rooted in his reinterpretations of Luther's ideas, represented only one of several new directions religious thinking could take. At the same time, ontological, scientific, and rational inquiries into religious issues produced multiple metaphysical and religious models that could open the imagination to increasingly varied aspects of religion and religious life.

The Spread of Rationalism: Christian Wolff and His Disciples

The mathematician and philosopher Christian Wolff (1679–1754) was a popularizer, publishing in German to reach a wide audience and capable of gathering many professional acolytes as well as a large following. Wolff applied his logical method to many fields, and the titles of most of his works begin with the phrase "Vernünftige Gedanken" ("Rational Thoughts"), which provided an emblem—he "owned" the phrase, so to speak.

Wolff's rational system subjected revelation and theology to reason, using a method derived from Leibniz's concepts of "sufficient reason" and "absolute necessity."[116] Wolff's philosophy posited that reality and nature conform to the laws of logic and unalterable truths like mathematics. He defended the order of the universe, the truth of Christianity, faith, and even revelation through human reason but denied all but "a few—only a few—mysteries reserved to the sphere of the supernatural."[117] In his "Natural Theology," God is the highest form of reason and therefore reason instead of the supernatural can be used to understand religious truth. Ian Hunter defines Wolff's metaphysics as a "civil religion,"[118] carrying a function that would account for its popularity.

Wolff's appointment to the university at Halle initially counterbalanced Thomasius's civil philosophy and Francke's authoritarian religious orientation. After the publication of his metaphysical study *Vernünftige Gedanken von Gott, der Welt und der Seele des Menschen* (*Rational Thoughts on God, the World, and the Human Soul, and All Things in General*) in 1712, the clashes in Halle between the Pietists and Leibnizian-Wolffian metaphysics "created an extremely fraught atmosphere," "in some cases marred by student tumult."[119] Wolff had won over the philosophy department, but when he delivered a lecture upon becoming rector in 1721, entitled "On the Practical Philosophy of the Chinese," the Pietist theologian Joachim Lange (1670–1744) accused him of fomenting atheism akin to that of the mechanistic materialism of Spinoza. Others linked his mathematical method to Descartes and the new sciences. His opponents persuaded Frederick William I that reward and punishment in the after-life were predetermined in the non-Providential aspect of Wolff's system, and that therefore the dissemination of such ideas would destroy military obedience.[120] Tension between the two camps reached crisis proportions, and in 1723 the King expelled Wolff from the university, giving him forty-eight hours to leave Prussia under the threat of death. The King issued two additional decrees in 1725, forbidding the sale of Wolff's books as well as banning their reading and discussion in both universities and private homes.

The scandal and Lange's persistent anti-Wolffian rhetoric increased the demand for Wolff's books elsewhere.[121] Wolff developed followers throughout Germany and internationally. His popularity is demonstrated by the appearance before 1737 of more than two hundred publications discussing the pros and cons of his work, in addition to his own treatises and those by his disciples. Jonathan Israel says that "the conflict which began in 1723 developed into one of the most formative cultural encounters of the eighteenth century and was, arguably, the most important of the age of Enlightenment in Central Europe . . . before the French Revolution."[122] In 1723, Wolff's disciple Johann Gottsched (1700–66) fled Prussia to avoid conscription into the Prussian army, for which as a tall man—Frederick William preferred tall soldiers—he was definitely slated. Settling in Leipzig, Gottsched and his wife promoted Wolff's ideas at the university and in the community and utilized them in their own work. The roles they played in the Leipzig community are described below and in chapter 3.

Heterodoxy Everywhere

Leipzig was a wealthy cosmopolitan commercial center, a university center, a major European center for the book trades, and home to theologians, intellectuals, and German literati. It was the German locale most receptive and most vulnerable to the spirit of controversy that characterized the early Enlightenment. To evade the censors, publications produced for capitalistic, not ideological, reasons used protective tactics when necessary, frequently engaging self-censoring strategies, such as anonymity and negative commentary.

In Leipzig, through one means or another, by the second quarter of the eighteenth century educated commoners were informed about the principle issues in the "religious" quarrels—the nature of God, original sin, Providence, the historical reality of the Trinity—and could identify the main protagonists of the rationalist, deist, Socinian, and atheistic arguments. From the early eighteenth century, censorship was a function of the state and, in Leipzig, a semi-subterranean intellectual and religious culture found a way to survive and grow.

The Example of Johann August Ernesti

On the one hand, Leipzig embraced a religious culture in which new ideas were not fully digested. How could the orthodox religious community have realized the humanistic implications of Johann August Ernesti's philological-historical Biblical criticism? Preus suggests that its scientific and "synergistic" posture, which would apply also to Bach's friend Johann Matthias Gesner, who appointed Ernesti, conflicts with the classical Lutheran orthodox principle expressed in *soli Deo gratia*—a phrase Bach added to many manuscripts. This phrase implies belief in the "monergism" of grace and, therefore, humanity's inherent sinfulness and inability to make moral decisions. Preus acknowledges the hardening of positions in our own time: the "cleavage will still obtain today between a confessional Lutheran orthodoxy . . . and much of modern theology," which he believes cannot be reconciled.[123] Within Bach's church community, was Ernesti's work the sign of a rationalized Lutheranism, a less restricted and experimental Lutheranism, or a misunderstood Lutheranism? Now recall the proponents of "theo-rationalism" among the orthodox theologians in Leipzig who opposed Thomasius.[124]

On the other hand, according to Peter Gay, many people "repelled by orthodoxy bypassed Pietism altogether and studied the Socinians and, after the 1720s the English deists" although, Gay adds, "Wolff's comfortable Christian Rationalism" could provided a "haven": a "gently modernized Protestant orthodoxy . . . , a perfect compromise for literate Christians anxious to justify nonrational beliefs with rational philosophy."[125] Change was indicated by Lessing's father, a Saxon pastor, who "reported that in his youth learned theologians had battled bigotry, but now, in the eighteenth century, it was 'godless deism' and that 'horrible monster atheism' that was the enemy."[126]

Johann Georg Wachter

It would seem that Bach lived in a theological powder keg; yet by the second quarter of the century, the intensity of intolerance, at least in Leipzig, seems to have been much deflated. How else can we explain the fact that in 1722—shortly before Bach arrived—someone with Johann Georg Wachter's reputation was able to get a job at the civic library of Leipzig? Wachter (1673–1757) had lost his library position in Berlin when Frederick William I cut library positions to divert funds to the army.[127] His publication about Spinozism in *Der Spinozismus Jüdenthumb* (1699) was "one of the fullest and most vigorous expositions of Spinoza's philosophy of God, man, and substance available in German," even though Wachter's commentary seemed to be attacking Spinozism, associating it with Judaism and, Judaism with Jewish mysticism. However, he disparaged both the Pentateuch and the New Testament, "implicitly rendering Revelation redundant," and he traced the Christian conception of one God to pre-Mosaic, ancient Greek paganism. In subsequent works for the general reader, he quoted liberally from several works of Spinoza, whom he defended against the attack of atheism and credited with having revealed religious truth, hitherto concealed. In a 1706 publication, *Elucidarius Cabalisticus*, Wachter asserts that " 'natural religion' and philosophical truth reach back in man's consciousness to the remotest times." However, " 'priest and prophets' found they could only bring the common people to awareness of God and morality by exploiting their credulity and gullibility, filling their minds with wild imaginings, 'revelations', and fabricated miracles."[128] Wachter anticipated the studies of the Dead Sea Scrolls linking Jesus and the origins of Christianity with the Essenes. However, for Wachter, this stage was only a link that led back to Greek Platonism and forward through the Kabbalists to Spinoza.[129]

Getting Around the Censor: Rationalism in Leipzig

L. A. V. Gottsched's Die Pietisterey

Because of its popularity, *Die Pietisterey im Fischbeinrock* (*Pietism in Petticoats*), a comedy by Luise Adelgunde Victoria Gottsched (1712–62) published in 1736, is an invaluable document for studying religious proclivities and tastes—the word is used advisedly—in Leipzig's middle-class community.[130] It is based on the French comedy *La femme docteur, ou la théologie janséniste tombée en quenouille* (*The Female Scholar, or Jansenist Theology from the Distaff Side*) by the French Jesuit Guillaume-Hyacinthe Bougeant, in which Jansenist reformers, seeking a spiritual religious experience, are the butt of satire in a Catholic, specifically Jesuit, context. In *Pietisterey*, dramatic parallels are maintained by substituting Leipzig Pietists in a Lutheran orthodox context.

In *Die Pietisterey*, both Pietism and orthodoxy are undermined by rationalist criticism; however the play demonstrates that the citizens of Leipzig were well acquainted with Pietists and their interest in mystical and spiritual ideas, experienced some degree of alienation from Lutheran orthodox practices, felt disdain for the Halle Pietists, and were, at the very least, receptive to rationalism. Its publishing success—there were two printings between 1736 and 1737, eight between 1736 and 1751[131]—attests to the authenticity and "truthfulness" of its depictions, qualities on which comedy depends. Followers of Pietism, orthodoxy, and rationalism are members of one family. The focus on educated women acknowledges the acceptance of women in this reform movement and the number of women who published spiritual and mystical works that were read, especially, by Pietists. This is a Leipzig comedy, written for Leipzig's middle class.

The play also attests to rationalism's hold on Leipzig's literate population. Comparing orthodoxy to "natural religion," the hero-uncle uses rationalist catchwords: "Reason, propriety, and honesty, teach me that" (65). While he does not deny being orthodox—indeed, he defends the orthodox against the irrational intolerance of Pietists—he treats learning the Catechism as irrelevant and refuses confession.[132] However, the uncle blames the Pietists for attracting criticism by their own intolerance of everyone else and by their "lust for sectarianism" (71). Over the course of the play, the Halle Pietists are described as simple-minded and boorish, beggars, frauds, bribers, embezzlers, and prostitutes; the clergy are painted as liars (6, referring to Francke!), hypocrites, child-abusers, and patrons of prostitutes—corrupt in every way. By contrast, the Pietists in the study group are educated women, clearly from Leipzig, and described only as gullible, naïve, argumentative, and emotional.

The circumstances surrounding the publication of *Die Pietisterey* are, in themselves, interesting, demonstrating commercial ruses to avoid the censors. The identities of the author and publisher (Breitkopf), both blatantly disobeying the 1727 electoral ban on anti-Pietist writings, were kept anonymous until after the author's death twenty-six years later, when Johann Gottsched finally revealed his wife's role. The publication was prefaced by an exchange of letters between an anonymous *male* author and *his* anonymous publisher, falsely claiming Rostock in Mecklenburg as its place of publication. In addition to needing protection from the Elector, the author and publisher needed protection from Leipzig's Pietists and orthodox alike. The author claimed that "his friends" had arranged for the publication of the play, which "he" had written for their private amusement and that, apart from giving copies to them, "he" would buy the remainder to keep them from reaching the general public—a plan never carried out, of course. Pietists confiscated copies of the play from bookstores in Königsburg, Prussia, where the play is set. They also smashed the windows of Erdman Neumeister's house in Hamburg, having assumed that Neumeister, an orthodox pastor and outspoken anti-Pietist, had authored *Die Pietisterey*.[133]

Die Pietisterey contains an unusual detail: it acquaints its readers with literature offensive to the orthodox and available at the book markets. In an episode in which plans are being made for a devotional meeting, a "collegia pietatis," the character of the "bookseller" names the best-known writers of Pietist and mystical literature—thirty-one in all!—in effect, a comprehensive directory. Of the eighteen book titles provided, several date from between 1732 and 1736, the years when Gottsched wrote the comedy. The exaggerated length of the list, which does not follow the Bougeant model, would create a highly theatrical effect if the play were performed. The recitation of the titles on the list, saturated with outrageous malapropisms, offers numerous opportunities to mock the mystical language and devotional ideas. Because some titles are very long, merely reading them aloud provides opportunity for satire; juxtaposed, they reinforce the hilarious dialogue. Although such a list would seem to be at cross-purposes with a Rationalist's concern, its inclusion would have been a gleeful affront to the orthodox.[134]

One particular item on the bookseller's list, Pietist Joachim Lange's harsh assessment of the Wertheim Bible (56), thwarted an aggressive international attempt at censorship. Lange had been Wolff's nemesis in Halle in 1723, and Luisa Gottsched would not let the public forget Lange's treachery, now giving him his due through ridicule (56). The Wertheim Bible, which Lange associated with Wolff, was causing an uproar. Its author, Johann Lorenz Schmidt (1702–49), had translated the Hebrew Pentateuch into contemporary German with annotations from naturalist and deist perspectives, treating only creation as miraculous. It was published in 1735, not long before the publication of *Die Pietisterey*. Lutherans, Calvinists, and Catholics alike attacked it, and the encyclopedist Johann Heinrich Zedler (1706–63) reported the battle in his *Großes Universal Lexicon*: Theology faculties condemned it; the Emperor banned its printing and distribution, ordering copies seized in Frankfurt's bookshops by the Imperial Book Commission; and princes of all confessions throughout Germany, including Saxony's, and in Denmark-Norway prohibited it.[135] Schmidt was arrested but managed to escape to Holland. Between 1735 and 1737, approximately fifty publications condemned the work.[136] Although copies of the Wertheim Bible may indeed have been hard to come by, the Leipzig public was well aware of its notorious messages: At the height of its tumultuous reception, it was known through its negative publicity and, not least, through the ridicule of its most eminent critic in *Die Pietisterey*.

Other Subversive Works

Die Pietisterey is one of three unquestionably "subversive" works published in Leipzig between 1730 and 1740 for which the Gottscheds were responsible. Johann Gottsched (1700–66) translated books by Bernard Le Bouvier de Fontenelle (1657–1757), *Histoire des Oracles*, and Pierre Bayle (1647–1706), *Dictionnaire historique et critique*,[137] that expounded skepticism and were most feared by theologians. A professed Christian, Fontenelle nevertheless dismissed the validity of miracles, believing "man's strongest and most unfortunate inclination was the love of mystery. . . . Decades before Voltaire . . . he criticized metaphysics as a vain enterprise, valued common sense above dogma and moderation above rigor."[138] Isaiah Berlin claims that Fontenelle's influence was inferior only to Voltaire's. A Cartesian, Fontenelle identified "progress in the arts (as in everything else) with increase in order, clarity, precision, *netteté* [distinctiveness], whose purest expression is geometry"[139]—these qualities can be used to describe Bach's music. Fontenelle's criticism covers a wide range, from superstitious belief in oracles to the subjectivity of historians, which he regarded as particularly pertinent: " 'What in my view brings home the extent of our ignorance is not so much the facts which really are facts, but which we cannot explain, as the explanations we produce of the facts which are not facts at all,' " a pattern Fontenelle ascribed to " 'human nature.' "[140]

At the center of many religious controversies, Pierre Bayle's ideas are best known from his *Dictionnaire*. Unlike Wolff, he did not reconcile "reason" and "revelation" but left the issue open as Fontenelle did. In 1729, Bayle's *Dictionnaire* was cited in the *Bibliothèque Germanique* as "notorious" for "unsettl[ing] a large number of readers and cast[ing] doubt on some of the most widely accepted principles of morality and religion."[141] It contains heavily annotated entries on religious, philosophical, and historical subjects that clearly convey Bayle's skeptical positions. For example, he argued against the notion that religion was necessary to maintain peace, claiming that atheists could do it, and that the effects of superstition were more pernicious.[142] Adopting the same stratagem Wachter used when writing about Spinoza, Gottsched's translations of Fontenelle and Bayle contain his hostile commentary, the sincerity of which is belied, of course, by the existence of these ambitious translations. They were printed and distributed as commercial enterprises; the annotations were commercial strategies designed to increase sales by making the books more acceptable to the German public and to avoid censors.[143] A propagandist and educator, Gottsched wanted the content of these works known. Continuing in the tradition initiated in Leipzig by Thomasius, Gottsched cultivated the public's interest in the burning issues of his time. These circumstances, nevertheless, indicate that censorship was not assiduously applied in Saxony, at least where commercial interests prevailed.

Two Other Translations

Two other translations appearing during the 1740s that used refutations as pretexts for publication must also be introduced. After translating and annotating the Wertheim Bible, in 1741 Schmidt translated *Christianity As Old As Creation* (1730) by Matthew Tindall (1657–1733). Tindall was the English deist best-known in Germany. Having created a furor in England when it was published there, the book was in 1734 the subject of a Leipzig university inaugural lecture devoted to refuting its errors. Leipzig was therefore prepared for Schmidt's edition, which included, in addition, a prefatory treatise advocating full freedom to publish and freedom of thought. Then in 1744, Schmidt's translation of Spinoza's *Ethics* (c. 1675) was published and included a preface containing his version of Wolff's latest refutation of Spinoza. Although Spinoza's works had been widely discussed, copied, and condemned, this was the first time a work by Spinoza appeared in German or in any vernacular language other than Dutch.[144]

Mysticism in Leipzig: A Heresy; a Spiritual Tool; a Scientific Tool

Mysticism had been a pervasive presence in Leipzig since the last third of the seventeenth century as it was throughout Europe. People of all religions sought answers to life's mysteries—the evasive knowledge of objective reality—in theology, theosophy, mathematics, metaphysics, logic, alchemy, mysticism, and in combinations of these and other modes of thought. Mysticism periodically emerges and recedes in popular imagination and practice in Western religions and not always for discernible reasons. Then as in our own time, mysticism and spirituality, religious enthusiasms and speculation on the fringes of traditional beliefs and practices, made salient incursions through the portals of traditional religious institutions and gave shape to new institutions. Neither the new rational explanations of physical processes underlying creation, mortality, and intelligence nor the moral precepts accompanying and driving newly realized horizons for worldly achievement and success completely satisfied. In pursuing knowledge of life's ultimate mysteries, some individuals sought religious ideas and experiences more satisfying than the conventional ones with which they were raised. Open to spiritual regeneration, some attached themselves to a realm of being that defies uncertainty and transcends ordinary reality. They experienced penetration by God's spirit: God is "*in* us"; looking elsewhere became relatively meaningless. Individuals used their intellect and bodies to achieve fusion in the spiritual realm. In Württemberg, where people continued to suffer from deprivation and insensitive rulers, grassroots movements aspiring to "paranormal" states of mind pursued fervent forms of "practical" mysticism as a way of life.[145] Mysticism, however, was not only this ecstatic experience leading to union and revelation; for some, it was a speculative exercise and devotional aid, focusing on exquisite metaphors to encourage receptivity to the religious message. In Leipzig, where people enjoyed a level of prosperity and optimism never known before, mysticism was experienced speculatively and metaphorically.

The Saxon mystic Gottfried Arnold (1666–1714) was the most prominent of the mystics named by Gottsched in the *Pietisterey*. Arnold had pointedly declared his opposition to institutionalized religions. His *Unparteiische Kirchen- und Ketzerhistorie* (*Impartial History of the Church and Heresy*, 1699), an important view of the history of Christianity, not only questioned the validity of Lutheran orthodoxy but also attempted to vindicate religious "heretics." He asserted that heretics are true Christians and members of all "organized" religions are the heretics, since they turned away from the deepest forms of piety and mystical love, the source of *Sophia* (wisdom). His works best known to contemporaries, *Erste Liebe der Gemeinden Jesu Christi* (*First Love of the Community of Jesus Christ*, 1696), which was published in five editions by 1728, and *Geheimnis der göttlichen Sophia* (*The Mystery of the Divine Sophia*, 1700) emphasized mystical union with Christ. Stoeffler notes that "for Arnold, the normal expression of man's affection for God was so intense that he could only describe it in terminology borrowed from the realm of human sexuality."[146]

The challenge by Arnold and others who professed intensely personal forms of mysticism in the periods preceding and contemporaneous with Bach was as problematic as rationalism to Lutheran orthodoxy. It threw into question the need for the institutional church, the sacraments, confession, the Bible, and so forth. Like the Enlightenment philosophers who examined creation, mortality, and concepts of God and the soul using mathematical and logical tools, the mystical Gottfried Arnold was a heretic, a deviant thinker in respect to the privileged European ways of thinking about God. Stoeffler believes that the mystics' "willful non-conformity seriously hurt the organized religious bodies of their day" and that "what they said and did helped to increase the ever-widening skepticism regarding the church's message."[147] Arnold's separatism removed him from meaningful associations with Pietists of both Saxony and Prussia, despite their mutually shared rejection of orthodoxy. Indeed, more socially meaningful similarities exist between Arnold and Christian Thomasius in their mutual objections to organized religion.

Crossing over territories and religions, Europeans everywhere encountered mystical phenomena in the last third of the seventeenth century. Among French Catholics of the time, François Fénelon (1651–1715) and Madame Jeanne Marie Bouvier de la Mothe Guyon (1648–1717) inculcated the mystical stance of Quietism among their followers.[148] Fénelon and Mothe Guyon were followers of the Spanish-born mystic Miguel de Molinos (1640–97), who preached a form of Quietism in Rome. Molinos's 1675 publication *Guida Spirituale* was translated into German by Gottfried Arnold in 1685; and August Hermann Francke published a Latin translation in Leipzig in 1687. The most improbable heresy of this time was the disastrous Jewish messianism of the followers of Shabbetai Sevi (1626–76) in 1665–66. Sevi, a mystical student of the Kabbala, was believed to be Messiah by "more than 90% of the Jews of the time" as well as by Millenarian Christians.[149] Christians and Jews shared an eschatological belief in the imminence of the Millennium. No less influential a messenger than the charismatic Calvinist theologian Jean de Labadie (1610–74), who had emerged from the Jansenist tradition, announced Sevi's "coming."[150] The new Pietist emphasis on "regeneration" and "sanctification" may have stemmed from Spener's "eschatological hopes."[151] Gershom Sholem notes that "eschatological preaching went hand in hand with the call to repent."[152] Universality and synchronicity—experience shared across both national lines and religious lines—seem to be characteristic of the rise of such enthusiasm and spirituality, then and now.

Again, turning to publications to which the lay community had access, we know that mystical ideas found a place in the imagination of Bach's community through books of popular devotional poetry and prose. The inventory of Bach's library included five books by Heinrich Müller (1631–75), one of the most popular writers of devotional literature. His books were familiar in the same Lutheran homes in which Weise's books, among others, taught rational "political" behavior. In his hymn and prose works, Müller used erotic imagery surrounding "the theme of the devoted soul's intimacies with the Heavenly bridegroom."[153] Mystical ideas also entered popular awareness through the writings of theologians, some of them composers of liturgical texts. Almost half of the religious writers discussed by Luisa Gottsched in *Pietisterey* are German Protestant mystics. Jakob Boehme (1575–1624) is one who, like Arnold, was an enemy of "stone churches."[154] His theosophy—in brief, the world as manifestation of God's "self-actualization"—was denounced as heresy, but his influence was felt throughout Germany, and beyond. Gottsched captured Boehme's idea in *Die Pietisterey* in a reference to seven fountain spirits (*Quellgeister*) from which everything flows. This idea is similar to kabbalistic theosophy's "emanations" of God's attributes.[155] Accusations brought against Boehme of being pagan because he confused nature with God are comparable to those cast against Spinoza and Wolff. Johann Georg Gichtel (1638–1710), another German mystic mentioned by Gottsched, was also an enemy of organized Lutheranism and published the first edition of Boehme's works in 1682. Gottsched's list also includes the English mystic Jane Leade (1624–1704), teacher of universal salvation, and her followers, the German Philadelphians Johann Wilhelm Petersen (1649–1727) and his wife Johanna Eleonora Petersen (1664–1704). The heresy of the Petersens, who were an early influence on Francke,[156] was "call[ing] into question . . . the doctrine of salvation," which "appeared to [their] critics to attribute the incarnation of the divine . . . to all human beings."[157] It is particularly noteworthy because Leibniz wrote a favorable review of Petersen's work and then incorporated the doctrine of universal salvation into his mature theodicy.[158] The theologian Friedrich Christoph Oetinger (1702–82), also on Gottsched's list, attempted like Leibniz, Wolff, and Newton to synthesize science, philosophy, and religion, all of which he believed were mutually validating. Heir to the fervent mystical tradition practiced in Württemberg, in which eschatological speculation played an important role, he was influenced by the Petersens and especially by Boehme.[159] Oetinger used intuition, mysticism, and the Kabbala as points of departure.[160]

Because their beautiful musical settings were regularly heard, Bach's liturgical cantata texts were a principal source for the ongoing awareness of mystical ideas in Leipzig. The image of "mystical union" in Bach's texts represents the soul's longing for union with Jesus through death and salvation. Although the image of death in the cantata texts suggests memories of war and plague, modern scholars have ascertained that death's role in mystical thought had progressively made its way into Lutheran orthodox theology, in keeping with current, albeit controversial, worship practices elsewhere. It did not emerge, however, from within the one-hundred-and-fifty-year orthodox dogmatic tradition but instead represents a heretical tendency at the end of it.[161] In the seventeenth century, the *unio mystica* became a "special step" in the *ordo salutis* (order of salvation) of the Lutheran worship service.[162] This innovation then gained esteem, in part, through the popular work of the late dogmatician David Hollaz (1648–1713), who was influenced by Pietism's "tendency toward synergism" and "preoccupied with psychology in working out an *ordo salutis*."[163] The origin of the liturgical treatment of *unio mystica* is traced to popular devotional songbooks and religious literature composed by lay writers. However, books by writers like Heinrich Müller and Gottfried Arnold, trained theologians albeit mystics and, therefore, outsiders are also a significant source. As subversive as rationalism, mysticism's attraction in the realm of popular religious thought was powerful enough to be absorbed into the practices and rituals of Lutheran orthodoxy. In any case, the erotic imagery of the "Jesus texts" used by the Jesuit-trained composers working for the Saxon Electors in Dresden (which Frandsen suggested were a possible source for the mystical imagery that entered Bach's liturgical texts) is the same as that in the contemporaneous works of Heinrich Müller in Bach's library.[164]

Mysticism also played a role in eighteenth century science, where no lesser practitioners than Newton and Leibniz treated it as an aspect of reality.[165] What we regard as "mysticism and spirituality" in our own scientifically oriented society is not far removed in content from eighteenth-century science and philosophy. A quest for knowledge of God's world, *Sophia*, through mysticism and theosophical speculation drew theologians, scholars, laypeople, mystics, magicians, and scientists. Religious thought and scientific speculation, based on reason and probability, emanated from religious, scientific, and philosophical contexts alike: in Boehme, Petersen, and Oetinger; in Spinoza, Newton, and Leibniz. Their shared goal was to overcome skepticism and validate the existence of God. Empirical science and reason did not answer all questions: mystical thought was a corollary of rationalism. It was the Neo-Platonic course of reason's last resort.

In Leipzig and Dresden, readers enjoyed universally inspiring imagery of near-perfect bliss and existential fulfillment, momentarily assuaging anxiety about life's mysteries. Such imagery even proffered the undiluted joy that Bach's settings depict like no other. We ask ourselves whether some ethos had evolved in Bach's milieu, in Leipzig and where he previously lived, that could explain this special quality in his music.[166]

Interpreting eighteenth-century mysticism in privileged societies—which Leipzig and the other places where Bach was employed certainly were—the English historian Basil Willey suggests one answer. He conflates mystical experience with the optimism of the metaphysicists or "physico-theologists" like Spinoza and Leibniz, as he calls these philosophers: the affirmation that "whatever is, is right" may be and has been made at many different levels, and consequently may mean many different things. It may represent the last insight of the mystic when, in a rapture of contemplation, he has transcended good and evil, and reached an acceptance of all existence as part of a divine pattern.[167] Turning to the general society, Willey suggests that "the affirmation that 'whatever is, is right' may be a cry of satisfaction from a complacent and conservative individual or generation. With a Spinoza or a Leibniz, unquestionably, it represents the conclusion of long and arduous metaphysical reflection. But . . . it generally seems to denote contentment with the existing state of things."[168]

Apropos of Willey's contention, an eighteenth-century equivalent of a chamber of commerce promotion piece from 1725 describes Leipzig as follows:

> Leipzig, the royal and electoral Saxon capital, city of commerce and trade, the eye of the electoral princedom, the mother of the Camenas and muses of our Saxon land, the paragon of all Civilité and the instructor of customs, the pearl of Saxon merchants, the nourishment of all trade, where not only all Europe but also Asia, Africa and America pours together its goods and abundance from afar . . .

and so on in the same vein.[169] This description corroborates Willey's observation that

> in the early and middle years of the eighteenth century the wealthy and the educated of Europe must have known the nearest approach to earthly felicity ever known to man. Centuries of superstition, error, and strife lay behind; most of the mediaeval ghosts had been laid to rest; a revolutionary era had been successfully weathered; and liberty and philosophy and the arts were raising their heads once more.[170]

In his "Treatise on Liturgical Text Settings," Johann Kuhnau, Bach's predecessor, compares Leipzig to the idealized Jerusalem of messianic time: "Let our *Chorum Musicum* sing of your glory to our hearts' content amidst the ever blessed prosperity of the Leipzig Jerusalem, until the end of the world; and let us continue the glorification of your most holy name amidst the perfect choir of angels and the elect in the heavenly Jerusalem, forever and ever. Amen."[171]

Returning to Bach's depiction of joy, the affect associated with many arias and duets—even in settings of texts not containing the sublime spousal imagery of Bride and Bridegroom—we want to dwell on its uniquely vivid actualization. Lutheran orthodoxy and its Leipzig practitioners seem to have left behind Luther's pessimistic "theology of the cross," which promised "joy from the expectation of the blessed afterlife," "the gift of salvation."[172] Like Kuhnau's Leipzig, Bach's music offers the "taste" of joy through arrival and accomplishment, in the here and now, derived from the optimism and "earthly felicity" Willey suggests. The palpable quality of this affect in Bach's music would necessarily have had its source in an emotion known and embraced in the reality of that epoch, and of that composer.[173]

5. Concluding Remarks

The religious complexity of the Leipzig community during the period of the early *Aufklärung* can be bewildering if one is looking for clear definitions of what people believed and how they worshipped. This was an intellectually dynamic period for the wealthy and educated populations in Germany's courts and commercial cities. A burst of scientific and philosophical ideas buffeted religious sensibilities, but it was all theistic in intent. Scientists and philosophers were exploring the same issues but were looking at them from the perspective of nature instead of miracles and creating their own myths about the same mysteries. Religious truths based on evidence found through reason and affirmed by mathematical logic could corroborate as well as challenge revelation. Lutheran orthodoxy and Pietism, spirituality and theosophy, scientific and philosophical reason were pursued with equal vigor, and each, attempting to realize the absolute truth, presented its own view of it. Privileged laypeople, aware of this variety, sometimes cognitively grasped the implications inherent in these approaches and sometimes intuited them, while experiencing the enthusiasm posed by choices and new ways of thinking and acting. The wonder and confusion of cognitive dissonance became the focus of the Saxon public sphere.

The experiences of these roughly sixty-five years mark a period of accelerated change and heightened collective consciousness about life's choices and life's meaning. Changing attitudes were accompanied by unresolved questions about political and religious assumptions, such as the agency needed to maintain a peaceful civil society, the appropriateness of class differences, the appropriateness of passivity and meekness prior to salvation and of conspicuous rewards on earth. Although orthodox structures remained essentially stable, religious practices and ideas acquired nuances rooted in the new optimism and sense of self-worth.

By focusing on the variety of shared religious, philosophical, and spiritual experiences Bach's community shared, this essay attempted to facilitate entry into that vortex of flux and fusions. It encouraged the reader to compare the complexities in Bach's world to the disparate religious parameters in our own. Beyond that, this essay presents the view of a complex world that was worthy, because of its multifaceted aspirations and enthusiasms, of the monumentally great musician who made his way there.

Notes

1. Jonathan Israel, *Radical Enlightenment: Philosophy and the Making of Modernity 1650–1750* (Oxford: Oxford University Press, 2001) sets the period 1680–1750 as "the decisive period of rethinking" (20). Paul Hazard set the period in the title of his *The European Mind: The Critical Years, 1680–1715* (New York, Fordham University Press, 1990); originally *La Crise de la conscience européenne* (Paris: Boivin, 1935).

2. Robert Preus, *The Theology of Post-Reformation Lutheranism: A Study of Theological Prolegomena*, vol. 1 (St. Louis/London: Concordia, 1970), 15, describes the period of Lutheran orthodoxy as several generations of theologians devoted to formulating Lutheran doctrine "solidly grounded on the scriptures" (37). It lasted about 150 years (27), from 1580, shortly after the Formula of Concord, to the 1707 work of David Holaz (1648–1713), "the last important orthodox Lutheran dogmatics" (45 and 65).

3. Peter Gay, *The Enlightenment: The Rise of Modern Paganism* (New York: W. W. Norton, 1966), 328 (henceforth, *"Paganism"*). Political controversy characteristic of the French and British forms of Enlightenment, tied to nationalistic assumptions, was impossible for Germans, who found contentious religious issues "more rewarding."

4. George Stauffer, "Beyond Bach the Monument, Who Was Bach the Man?" the *New York Times*, Arts and Leisure Section, Sunday, April 2, 2000, 1 and 4.

5. Friedrich Blume, "Outlines of a New Picture of Bach," *Music and Letters*, 14 (1963): 214–27.

6. Gerhard Herz, "Towards a New Image of Bach," in *Essays on J. S. Bach* (Ann Arbor: UMI Research Press, 1985), 151–64 passim; quote from 158. Abraham Calov, about whom more below, wrote a gloss on Luther's Bible; Bach's annotations in the Calov Bible are described by Christoph Trautman in *Musik und Kirche*, July/August 1969: 145–60.

7. Robin Leaver, "Introduction," in Günther Stiller, *Johann Sebastian Bach and Liturgical Life in Leipzig*, ed. Robin A. Leaver (St. Louis: Concordia, 1970), 15, tr. Herbert J. A. Boumann, Daniel F. Poellot, and Hilton C. Oswald from the original German, *Johann Sebastian Bach und das Leipziger gottesdienstliche Leben seiner Zeit* (Berlin: Evangelical Publ. Co., 1970).

8. Robin Leaver, "Johann Sebastian Bach: Theological Musician and Musical Theologian," *Bach: Journal of the Riemenschneider Bach Institute* 30/1 (2000): 32–33.

9. Michael Marissen, "The Theological Character of J. S. Bach's *Musical Offering,*" *Bach Studies* 2, ed. D. R. Melamud (Cambridge: Cambridge University Press, 1995), 85–106, and *The Social Designs of J. S. Bach's Brandenburg Concertos* (Princeton: Princeton University Press, 1995). Marissen identifies both works as interpretations of Lutheran orthodox principles. Based on literary and socio-political studies introduced in chapter 1, I would suggest that new *secular* social principles are just as likely interpretations for the meaning of the anomalous instrumentation in the Brandenburg concertos.

Eric Chafe, *Analyzing Bach Cantatas* (New York/Oxford: Oxford University Press, 2000), in which he labels "musico-hermeneutic" elements in Bach's music derived from a specifically "Lutheran 'metaphysical' tradition in music theory" that developed under the influence of the Enlightenment on Lutheran orthodoxy (23).

10. Christoff Wolff, *Johann Sebastian Bach: The Learned Musician* (New York: W. W. Norton, 2000). Joyce Irwin, chapter 4, considers Bach's library "paltry" as inventoried (110, 112). Scholars linking Bach's orthodoxy to the inventory tend to dismiss the significance of inventoried items by Pietists and mystics. The discussion below of Calov suggests why his work would not have been claimed.

11. See especially the seven-year old academic journal *Nova Religio: The Journal of Alternative and Emergent Religions,* and note the study group called "New Religious Movements Group" of the American Academy of Religion.

12. The conclusion of their 1999 debate recalls the language of Christian Thomasius: "The main metaphysical problems remained unsolved. . . . The lack of resolution is inevitable . . . because 'the authority for theology is revelation; the authority for science is experimentation'" (the *New York Times*, Tuesday, April 20, 1999). Paul Hazard, *The European Mind*, reports that Thomasius' "favorite dicta [was]: the light of Nature is one thing; the light of Revelation, another."

13. Israel, *Radical Enlightenment,* 521; also Peter Gay, *The Enlightenment: The Science of Freedom* (New York: W. W. Norton, 1969), 142–43 (henceforth *Science*). Ironically, Leibniz portrayed Newton's conception of gravity as "bogus" and "mere conjecture."

14. See Hagen Schulze, *Germany: A New History* (Cambridge: Harvard University Press, 1998), 52–55 (originally *Kleine deutsche Geschichte* [Munich: C. H. Beck'sche Verlag, 1996]) for interdependent developments in Lutheran doctrine and post-Lutheran Reformation political history in Germany; also F. Ernest Stoeffler, *The Rise of Evangelical Pietism* (Leiden: E. J. Brill, 1965), 185 (henceforth "*The Rise*"). See Bodo Nishan, *Prince, People, and Confession: The Second Reformation in Brandenburg* (Philadelphia: University of Pennsylvania Press, 1994) for the impact of Augsburg on Calvinist-Lutheran relationships in Brandenburg-Prussia (briefly, 4 and 212–16).

15. Israel, *Radical Enlightenment,* 23; also Rudolph Vierhaus, *Germany in the Age of Absolutism* (Cambridge: Cambridge University Press, 1988), tr. Jonathan B. Knudsen, from *Deutschland im Zeitalter des Absolutismus (1648–1763)*, 60.

16. Israel, *Radical Enlightenment,* 23; Vierhaus, *Germany in the Age of Absolutism,* 60.

17. Vierhaus *Age of Absolutism,* 28.

18. Helen Watanabe-O'Kelly, *Court Culture in Dresden from Renaissance to Baroque* (Chippenham: Palgrave, 2002), 5 and 25 respectively.

19. Mary E. Frandsen, "The Sacred Concerto in Dresden, ca. 1660–1680," PhD diss., Eastman School of Music, 1996, 431.

20. Frandsen, "The Sacred Concerto,"433. Erotic language, however, is common to mystical expression and is found, for example, in the Protestant mystic Gottfried Arnold (1666–1714) as well. Frandsen also writes that Vicenzo Albrici "developed the form of the concerto with aria" that "point[s] in the direction of the sacred cantata" (437) which, along with the mystical texts, points to the cantatas later composed by J. S. Bach.

21. Antoine Faivre, *Access to Western Esotericism* (Albany: State University of New York Press, 1994) studies esotericism beginning in the Renaissance. He states that although the influences of Hermeticism, Neoplatonism, and the Kabbalah were impeded in Lutheran territories during the sixteenth century, Paracelsism and its offshoots Boehmenism and Rosicrucianism were influential there (61–66). The

"mystical theology" of Johann Arndt, the precursor of German Pietism, as well as others before him, integrated Lutheran theology with Paracelsian theosophy and alchemy (61). Faivre summarizes high points in the development of the Christian Kabbalah citing works by sixteen scholars (59–60); however, Kabbalistic influence on theology in German territories is not confirmed prior to the 1734 work of Friedrich Christoph Oetinger.

22. Frandsen, "The Sacred Concerto," 437.

23. Karl H. Wörner, *History of Music* (London: Collier Macmillan, 5th ed., 1973), 287.

24. Nishan, *Prince, People, and Confession*, 235–46, *passim*, describes the failed attempts at irenicism.

25. Stauffler, *The Rise*, 182.

26. Arthur C. Howland, ed., *Materials Towards A History of Witchcraft, Collected by Henry Charles Lea* (Philadelphia: University of Pennsylvania Press, 1939) 6:1083. Also see Hazard, *The European Mind*, 172; Stoeffler, *The Rise*, 182; and Trevor-Roper, *The Crisis of the Seventeenth Century: Religion, the Reformation and Social Change* (New York: Harper & Row, 1956), 159.

27. Frederick Herbert Wagman, *Magic and Natural Science in German Baroque Literature: A Study in the Prose Forms of the Later Seventeenth Century* (New York: Columbia University Press, 1942; rpt. New York: AMS Press, 1966), summarizes recorded incidents of executions for witchcraft in different parts of Germany as late as 1775. Peter Gay aptly suggests that the progress of reason was "less the triumph of rationalism than of reasonableness" (*Science*, 31).

28. Paul Tschackert, "Syncretism, Syncretistic Controversies," in *The New Schaff-Herzog Encyclopedia*. Stoeffler, *The Rise*, discusses the issues, 182–84; also see Preus, *The Theology of Post-Reformation Lutheranism*, 1:38–39. Friedrich A. G. Tholuck, *Wittenburger Theologen* (1852) describes the intensity of this conflict and the scandalous and titillating personal attacks on Calov it incited (185–211).

29. Preus, *The Theology of Post-Reformation Lutheranism*, 1:36, n. 10.

30. Ibid., 1:409.

31. Preus, *The Theology of Post-Reformation Lutheranism: God and His Creation*, vol. 2 (St. Louis: Concordia Publishing Co., 1985), 158.

32. Israel, *Radical Enlightenment*, 644. Israel notes that Stosch had really been influenced by Spinoza but "tried and tested legal and ecclesiastical procedures for suppressing Socinianism were readily at hand, and it was easier and more pertinent to indict Stosch in this way," thereby indicating "the strongly theological, anti-Socinian bias" at that time.

33. H. M. Scott, "Introduction: Serfdom and Service Nobility," in *The European Nobilities in the Seventeenth and Eighteenth Centuries*, ed. H. M. Scott (London: Longman, 1995, vol. 2, 4–5. Edgar Melton, "The Prussian Junkers 1600–1786," in ibid., 84–90, discusses the threats the Great Elector perceived during his reign from "elite" members of the Lutheran Brandenburg nobility.

34. Otto Hintze, "The Hohenzollern and the Nobility," in *The Historical Essays of Otto Hintze*, ed. Felix Gilbert (New York: Oxford University Press, 1975), 44. For specific problems confronted in different regions under Frederick William's rule, see 44–47.

35. Respectively, Samuel Pufendorf, *The Whole Duty of Man, According to the Law of Nature*, ed. Ian Hunter and David Saunders (Indianapolis: Liberty Fund, 2003), 56 and "Introduction," ibid., xiii.

36. Samuel Pufendorf, *The Divine Feudal Law: Or, Covenants with Mankind, Represented*, ed. Simone Zurbuchen (Indianapolis: Liberty Fund, 2002), x–xi, and xii.

37. Simon Zurbuchen, "Introduction," in Pufendorf, *The Divine Feudal Law*, xiv–xvii, *passim*. Ian Hunter, *Rival Enlightenments: Civil and Metaphysical Philosophy in Early Modern Germany* (Cambridge: Cambridge University Press, 2001), contrasts the natural law doctrines of Pufendorf and Leibniz (especially 95–98).

38. Materials concerning Weise's influence in facilitating socio-economic change are studied in chapter 1.

39. As in chapter 1, the material on Weise, except where otherwise indicated, is excerpted from Hans-Gert Roloff, "Christian Weises Lebensweg," in *Christian Weise: Gedenken anlässlich seines 350 Geburtstages* (Christian-Weise-Bibliothek Zittau, 1993), 11–19. See note 37 in chapter 1.

40. Klaus Günzel, "Christian Weise—Pädagog und Literat," in *Christian Weise: Gedenken anlässlich seines 350 Geburtstages* (Christian-Weise-Bibliothek Zittau, 1993), 20–24, 21; from a lecture entitled "Christian Weise 1642–1708—Versuch einer Würdigung."

41. Wagman, *Magic and Natural Science*, 9. Wagman characterizes Weise as "perhaps the first important literary figure of the early enlightenment . . . , an opponent of the scholasticism of the German universities, and the outstanding proponent and popularizer of the guiding principle of *Politik* in middle-class life." Furthermore, his " 'political' review-novels exerted a powerful influence on contemporary fiction and called forth numerous imitations."

42. Mary Fulbrook, *Piety and Politics: Religion and the Rise of Absolutism in England, Württemberg and Prussia* (Cambridge: Cambridge University Press, 1983), 25.

43. See Stoeffler's comments in *The Rise*, 181.

44. Stoeffler, *The Rise*, 189; Richard L. Gawthrop, *Pietism and the Making of Eighteenth-Century Prussia* (Cambridge: Cambridge University Press, 1993), 107–8, also discusses sources of Spener's optimism.

45. Peter C. Erb, ed., *Pietists: Selected Writings* (New York/Ramsey/Toronto: Paulist Press, 1983), 5.

46. Gawthrop, *Pietism and the Making of Eighteenth-Century Prussia*, 105 and 113, from Udo Sträter, *Bayley, Sonthom, Dyke und Hall: Studien zur Rezeption der englischen Erbauungsliteratur in Deutschland im 17. Jahrhundert* (Tübingen: Mohr, 1987), 8–18. Also Fulbrook, *Piety and Politics*, 25, and Stoeffler, *The Rise*, who adds that several theologians in the Arndt-Spener tradition directly referred to English Pietists (189). Stoeffler discusses Arndt's mystical ideas (204–9). For Faivre's study of Arndt's mystical ideas, see n. 21 above.

47. The last accusation is controversial, since the clergy would seem to have been powerless against the Electors. Kevorkian, "Piety Confronts Politics: Philipp Jacob Spener in Dresden, 1686–1691," *German History* 16/2 (Spring 1998), 148–49, argues against Spener's thesis that orthodox clergy "furthered the goals of absolutist rulers" and defends their frustrated critical agenda.

48. Erb, *Pietists*, 41, an excerpt from Spener's *Pia desideria*, tr. Theodore G. Tappert (Philadelphia: Fortress Press, 1964).

49. Spener, *Pia desideria*, in Erb, *Pietists*, 44, recommends the 14th century mysticism of John Tauler (1300–1361) and the *Theologia Germanica*. Gawthrop points out, however, that Spener "was considerably less mystical in orientation" than Arndt and "placed little emphasis on knowledge of God, contemplative prayer, or unity with God following rebirth" (*Pietism and the Making of Eighteenth-Century Prussia*, 110).

50. Spener, *Spiritual Priesthood* (1677), in Erb, *Pietists*, 51 and 64 respectively.

51. Gawthrop, *Pietism and the Making of Eighteenth-Century Prussia*, 109; for Spener's goals, see 109–15.

52. Gawthrop, *Pietism and the Making of Eighteenth-Century Prussia*, 107–8, from "The Possibility of Better Conditions in the Church" in Spener, *Pia desideria*. One of Fulbrook's premises is "that the direction of obedience postulated in Lutheran doctrines" depended on political developments and that "the substantive content given to the emotions evoked by religious ideas is formulated in specific political circumstances" (*Piety and Politics*, 188).

53. Gawthrop, *Pietism and the Making of Eighteenth-Century Prussia*, 108, n. 11.

54. Still ongoing, as Hazard tells us, "the country in which sorcerers were hunted down with the grimmest determination was, at that time, Germany" (*The European Mind*, 172). Wagman reports, "by the third quarter of the 17th century the witch-craze had begun to slacken" (*Magic and Natural Science*, 97–98, n. 16), from Howland, ed., *Materials Towards A History of Witchcraft*, 1394. However "the last recorded execution for witchcraft in Germany" took place in 1775, between fifty and one hundred years after the last trials in France, England, or Scotland (from Montague Summers, *The Geography of Witchcraft* [New York: Knopf, 1927], 503).

55. Israel, *Radical Enlightenment*, 143.

56. Israel, *Radical Enlightenment*, 143, from Herbert Jaumann, *Critica: Untersuchungen zur Geschichte der Litereraturkritik zwischen Quintilian und Thomasius* (Leiden: E. J. Brill, 1995).

57. Israel, *Radical Enlightenment*, 640; see 396–97 for other examples of his "cautious" eclecticism, which Ian Hunter, below, characterizes as erratic.

58. Hunter, *Rival Enlightenments*, 198. I raise Hunter's critical view, since Thomasius has hitherto been lionized as a forerunner of radical Enlightenment thought but treated superficially. See also 200.

59. Pufendorf's "natural law" is a moral law that is "natural" because it is "inscribed in man's nature" and is "accessible via natural reason as distinct from divine revelation" (from "Introduction," in Pufendorf, *The Whole Duty*, xii).

60. Ibid., 201. For the distinctive nature of Thomasius's defense of civil philosophy and its divergence from that of Pufendorf and other civil philosophers, see especially 197–98.

61. Ibid., 200.

62. Paul McReynolds and Klaus Ludwig, "Christian Thomasius and the Origin of Psychological Rating Scales," *Isis* 75/3 (September 1984): 546–53, discusses these two publications by Thomasius that contain his ideas on psychological rating scales. Their titles and the fact that the first of these articles initially appeared in a letter to Friedrich III of Prussia (547), dated December 1691, a year after Thomasius was dismissed from his position in Leipzig, seem sufficient evidence for their contributions to the militarized Prussian state described in chapter 1. The authors believe this to be "the earliest instance anywhere of the employment of rating scales in personality evaluation" (546).

63. Hunter, *Rival Enlightenments*, 199.

64. Ibid., 132, from T. Ahnert, "Christian Thomasius' Theory of Natural Law in Its Religious and Natural Philosophical Context" (unpublished PhD diss., University of Cambridge, 1999), 76–82.

65. Israel, *Radical Enlightenment*, 5, from Veit Ludwig von Seckendorff, *Christen-Staat* (Leipzig, 1693), ii, 139–41.

66. Israel, *Radical Enlightenment*, 148–49.

67. Kevorkian, "Piety Confronts," 152.

68. Kevorkian, "Piety Confronts," 162, documents the nature of these tensions and the ensuing negotiations and resolution. Gawthrop points out that "urban patriciates,

court nobles, and princes lived in accordance with the ethic of conspicuous consumption, a way of life Pietist preachers rarely hesitated to criticize" (116–17).

69. Gawthrop, *Pietism and the Making of Eighteenth-Century Prussia*, 117.

70. F. Ernst Stoeffler, *German Pietism During the Eighteenth Century* (Leiden: E. J. Brill, 1973), 6–7. T. Förster, *The Schaff-Herzog Encyclopedia*, 4:367, asserts that "it was inevitable that his success should arouse envy, and it must be confessed that not everything in the movement of Francke and his friends was commendable, as, for instance, the contempt of science and distrust of earnest philosophical study united with self-complacency and conceit among those who were only superficially inspired by the Spirit."

71. Hunter, *Rival Enlightenments*, 205–6. For the conflict and its past history, "between civil and metaphysical law" and its numerous protagonists including jurists and theologians on each side, and their united opposition to Thomasius, see especially pages 205–7.

72. Howland, *Materials Towards A History of Witchcraft*, 1394, from Christian Thomasius, Lehr-Sätz von dem Laster der Zauberey: Aus dem Lateinische Teutsche übersetzt, 1703. See note 54 above.

73. Gawthrop, *Pietism and the Making of Eighteenth-Century Prussia*, 97–98, n. 16.

74. Ernest Stoeffler, *German Pietism*, addresses the open question of whether these Pietist leanings of the Calvinist Frederick were "from religious conviction . . . or an attempt to undercut the power of orthodoxy," the official state religion in Prussia, which was an affront to his absolute rule (42).

75. Gawthrop, *Pietism and the Making of Eighteenth-Century Prussia*, 182; Israel, *Radical Enlightenment*, 106.

76. Another contributing factor, noted by Stoeffler, *German Pietism*, 79, was the death of Johann Benedikt Carpzov II in 1699, after which the theological faculty's more tolerant voices could be heard. Carpzov's brother Samuel Benedikt Carpzov (1647–1707) was a member of the High Consistory and "a true friend of the Pietist [Spener] until his brother at Leipsic [*sic*] became the leader of the opposition and persuaded him to change his attitude." Samuel Carpzov assumed Spener's position when he left Dresden (*Schaff-Herzog*, 2:424).

77. Norman Davis, *God's Playground: A History of Poland* (New York: Columbia University Press, 1982), 492–506 *passim*, details the history of Saxon rule in Poland.

78. Karl Ludwig von Pollnitz, *La Saxe Galante or the Amorous Adventures of Augustus of Saxony . . . together with diverting remarks on the ladies of the several countries thro' which he traveled, translated from the French by a gentleman of Oxford* (London, c. 1750); originally issued anonymously (Amsterdam: Aux dépens de la Companie, 1734).

79. This court is described in W. H. Bruford, *Germany in the Eighteenth Century: The Social Background of the Literary Revival* (Cambridge: Cambridge University Press, 1935, rpt. 1952), 77.

80. Janice B. Stockigt, "Die 'Annuae Literae' der Leipziger Jesuiten 1719–1740: Ein Bach Dokument?" *Bach-Jahrbuch* 78 (1992): 77–80.

81. *The New Bach Reader* (New York: W. W. Norton, 1998), ed. Hans T. David and Arthur Mendel, revised and enlarged by Christoph Wolff, 136, regarding BWV 198, "Ode of Mourning."

82. Gawthrop, *Pietism and the Making of Eighteenth-Century Prussia*, 120–21. Also Fulbrook's chapter in *Piety and Politics*, entitled "From Reform to State Religion: Pietism in Prussia," 153–73, *passim*. Gawthrop's study provides an up-to-date bibliography of related studies and primary source materials; he criticizes earlier

historians who have not adequately distinguished between Spenerian and Franckeian Pietism.

83. See Christoph Wolff's description of Bach's work in Halle in 1713 as organ consultant and then his audition in 1714 for a prestigious position, which he turned down (136 and 149–55). One may wonder if the new political situation influenced Bach.'s decision.

84. Fulbrook, *Piety and Politics*, 50, n. 16, and 166.

85. "Instruction König Friedrich Wilhelms I. für seinen Nachfolger," *Acta Borussica: Die Behördenorganisation und die allgemeine Staatsverwaltung Preussens im 18. Jahrhundert*, vol. 3 (Jan. 1718—Jan. 1723; rpt. Berlin: Verlag von Paul Parey, 1901), 441–70; cited in Fulbrook, *Piety and Politics*, 50.

86. Vierhaus, *Age of Absolutism*, 30.

87. Fulbrook, *Piety and Politics*, 167. Fulbrook quotes an eighteenth-century government minister who called Prussia "not a country with an army, but an army with a country" (52).

88. Gawthrop, *Pietism and the Making of Eighteenth-Century Prussia*, 211–12. Gawthrop presents several sources describing Frederick William I's problems with self-worth, his "continual need for external signs of success," his fear of betrayal and concomitant insistence on obedience—all of which led to his "radical disregard for customary constraints on princely authority" (213–14).

89. Ibid., 139. Regarding Francke's conversion, see also Stoeffler, *German Pietism*, 5. Gawthrop, 137 n. 45, takes historians, including Stoeffler, to task for assuming a close theological link between Spener and Francke, pointing particularly to studies by Johannes Wallman, *Philipp Jakob Spener und die Anfänge des Pietismus* (Tübingen: J. C. B. Mohr, 1970) and "Geistliche Erneurung nach Philipp Jakob Spener," *Pietismus und Neuzeit* 12 (1986). He recommends Francke's own "August Hermann Franckes Lebenslauf" in Erhard Peschke, ed., *Werke in Auswahl* (Berlin: Abhandlungen den sächsischen Academie den Wissenschaften: Philosphische-historische Reihe 53, 1962), "a selection of pedagogical and programmatic writings, and a group of sermons that reveal the essence of his spirituality" (287).

90. Gawthrop, *Pietism and the Making of Eighteenth-Century Prussia*, 153–54.

91. Ibid., 157–59.

92. Ibid., 167–68.

93. Ibid., 164. I have not found studies making the connection between Francke's documented methods and Thomasius's *Affectenlehre*, which would appear to have existed.

94. Fulbrook, *Piety and Politics*, 159. Fulbrook reports an eyewitness account from 1713, early in the relationship between Frederick William and Francke, that describes Francke's shrewd response to the ruler's question about Pietist attitudes towards war: "His Royal Highness must defend the country, but I have been called to preach: blessed are the peacemakers" (165, nn. 22 and 23). He followed this up with a written memorandum defending war, described in Gawthrop, *Pietism and the Making of Eighteenth-Century Prussia*, 209–10.

95. Gay, *Paganism*, 24–27, and *Science*, 484–87, describes their limitations, the impossibility of their rejecting the existing social order, and the evasions they used to protect themselves.

96. Gay, *Science*, 490. Quote from Friedrich der Große: *Die politischen Testamente* (1752), *Klassiker der Politik* 5, tr. Friedrich von Oppeln-Bronikowski (Berlin, 1922), 37.

97. Gay, *Paganism*, 348–49.

98. Gay, *Paganism*, 115; *Science*, 71.

99. Ulrich Siegele's article in this volume provides ample evidence of concealed Pietist sympathies within the Leipzig City Council in the early 1700s, revealed particularly in the confession of one of its members in his last will and testament (see chapter 5, 165).

100. Koppel S. Pinson, *Pietism As a Factor in the Rise of German Nationalism* (New York: Columbia University Press, 1934), 110, from J. B. Carpzov, *Ausführliche Beschreibung des Unfugs welchen die Pietisten zu Halberstadt im Monat Dezember 1692 und die heilige Weynachtszeit gestiftet* ([n.p.], 1693), 14–15 and 55, respectively.

101. Fulbrook, *Piety and Politics*, 94, from Erich Beyreuther, *August Hermann Francke, 1663–1727: Zeuge des lebendigen Gottes* (Marburg an der Lahn: Verlag der Francke-Buchhandlung, 1956), 68–71.

102. Fulbrook, *Piety and Politics*, 94, n. 53, from Gustav Kramer, *August Hermann Francke: Ein Lebensbild* (Halle: Verlag der Buchhandlung des Waisenhauses, part 1, 1880), 75.

103. Trevor-Roper, *The Crisis*, 184. Women wrote several of the books introduced as Pietistic in L. A. V. Gottsched's play *Die Pietisterey*, discussed below.

104. Fulbrook, *Piety and Politics*, 156.

105. I am grateful to Professor Shaul Magid for telling me about Elliott Horowitz, "Coffee, Coffeehouses, and the Nocturnal Rituals of Early Modern Jewry," *Association for Jewish Studies Review* 14/1 (Spring 1989), which traces developments of nighttime synagogue rituals in several European communities in the seventeenth and early eighteenth centuries following the introduction of coffee.

106. Hans-Joachim Schulze, "Ey! Wie Schmeckt der Coffee Süsse" (Leipzig: Verlag für die Fraue, 1985), 16–7; tr. Alfred Mann, "Ey! How Sweet the Coffee Tastes," in *Bach* 32/2 (2001).

107. Stiller, *Johann Sebastian Bach*, 40–41. Quote from P. Kaiser, "Die Geschichte der Matthäikirche," in *Unsere Mattäikirche in 4 Jahrhunderten, 1494–1894* (Leipzig, 1894), 16.

108. Martin Geck wrote that by the time Bach came to Leipzig, a "gentle, affectionate[ly] devout . . ." Pietism had become the "common religiosity," although the dogmatic theology of orthodoxy remained the basis of church services; see "Bachs künstlerischer Endzweck," in *Festschrift für Walter Wiora*, ed. Ludwig Finscher and Christoph Hellmut Mahling (Kassel: Bärenreiter, 1967); translated by Alfred Mann, "The Ultimate Goal of Bach's Art" in *Bach* 35/1 (2004): 29–41, 35.

109. Quotations from Fulbrook, *Piety and Politics*, 94, based on Beyreuther, *August Hermann Francke*, 68–71.

110. Fulbrook, *Piety and Politics*, 25, says that in their world-oriented theology, the Pietists were like the Calvinists.

111. Gay, *Science*, 48; also 49–53. These ideals were those of the new literary style in Germany that substituted the bourgeois revue novel for the heroic or aristocratic novel and glorified the practical ideals of the new elite. See Wagman, *Magic and Natural Science*, for this tendency in the "political" novels of Weise and others, especially 148–49.

112. Gay, *Science*, 24–25; also 49–51 and 401.

113. From "Bach's Character," in "Forkel's Biography," *New Bach Reader*, 459. I think Bach's statement is another example of his efforts to control his own image, adding to those presented in Christoph Wolff's keynote address, Biennial Meeting of the American Bach Society, April 16, 2004. Although Bach's sons were trained to be professional musicians, they received legal degrees, which also points to Bach's

identification with the aspirations of the new social elite. Writers, including Goethe, received arts degrees; therefore a theology degree for a church musician would seem to have been appropriate, at least on the surface.

114. James Sheehan, *German History 1770–1866* (Oxford: Oxford University Press, 1989), 143.

115. Ibid., 132.

116. Ian Hunter, *Rival Enlightenments*, interprets these principles as "sufficient reason" and "contradiction" (266).

117. Gay, *Paganism*, 329; he deprecates Wolff for "vulgariz[ing] Leibniz's complicated thought."

118. Hunter, *Rival Enlightenments*, 276–77.

119. Israel, *Radical Enlightenment*, 541.

120. Hunter, *Rival Enlightenments*, 268–70. Israel, *Radical Enlightenment*, 546, summarizes Buddeus's arguments against Wolff in *Bedenken über die Wolffianische Philosophie* (Halle, 1724): "Wolff's system erodes belief in Providence. . . . [It] . . . precludes . . . reward or punishment in the hereafter 'for it would be senseless were God to punish or reward people who do nothing themselves but merely let happen what the nexus of causes, and the pre-established harmony, brings about. . . . Whether, and how far, this author agrees with Spinoza is not really the point': for there are different varieties of atheism and just as one can be atheistic 'without being a Spinoza, one can cultivate pernicious doctrines encouraging atheism despite diverging on this or that point from Spinoza.'"

121. Israel, *Radical Enlightenment*, 551, from Georg Volckmar Hartman, *Anleitung zur Historie der Leibnizisch-Wolffischen Philosophie* (Frankfurt and Leipzig, 1737; rpt. Hildesheim, 1973).

122. Israel, *Radical Enlightenment*, 544.

123. Preus, *The Theology of Post-Reformation Lutheranism*, 1:407–8.

124. See note 64 above citing Ian Hunter's discussion of the crisis.

125. Gay, *Paganism*, 329.

126. Ibid., 349, from Erich Schmidt, *Lessing: Geschichte seines Lebens und seiner Schriften*, 2 vols (Berlin: Weidman, 2nd ed., 1899), 1:11.

127. Israel, *Radical Enlightenment*, 651–52.

128. Ibid., 649.

129. Ibid., 651.

130. Luise Adelgunde Gottsched, *Pietism in Petticoats and Other Comedies* (Columbia, SC: Camden House, 1993), tr. Thomas Kerth and John P. Russell. Page references to this work will be given in parentheses in the text. Originally *Die Pietisterey im Fischbeinrock, oder die doktormäßige Frau, in einem Lust-Spiele vorgestellet* (Rostock: auf Kosten guter Freunde). However, real publication information would have been "Leipzig: Breitkopf, 1736."

131. William E. Petig, *Literary Anti-Pietism in Germany during the First Half of the Eighteenth Century*, Stanford German Studies 22 (New York:/Frankfurt am M: Peter Lang, 1984), 44, from Wolfgang Martens, "Afterword," in *Die Pietisterey im Fischbeinrocke* (Stuttgart: Reclam, rpt. 1968) There is no evidence it was performed.

132. Similarly, Kevorkian presents evidence that Leipzig congregants avoided confession (177).

133. Neumeister is credited with introducing librettos for the recitative-aria cantatas using poetic meter and rhymes associated with Italian secular cantatas and opera, for which see Christoph Wolff, *Johann Sebastian Bach*, 160–61.

134. There is no evidence it was performed. Petig "views the list of Pietist books as a satirical counterpart to the 'Frauenzimmerbibliotheken,' the recommended lists of books for female readers, which often appeared in the moral weeklies" (70, from Wolfgang Martens, "Obrigkeitliche Sicht: Das Bühnenwesen in den Lehrbüchern der Policey und Cameralistik des 18. Jahrhunderts," *Internationales Archiv für Sozialgeschichte der deutschen Literatur* 6 [1981]: 167).

135. J. H. Zedler, *Großes vollständiges Universal Lexicon,* 54 vols (Leipzig and Halle, 1732–50); Israel, *Radical Enlightenment,* 553.

136. See Israel, *Radical Enlightenment,* 552–54, for the extent of the controversy. Also see Stoeffler, *German Pietism,* 73.

137. Bernard Le Bouvier de Fontenelle, *Histoire des Oracles* (Fontenelle, Paris: 1686; 2nd ed., 1698). Pierre Bayle, *Dictionnaire historique et critique* (Rotterdam: 1697; expanded, 1702 [3 vols]).

138. Gay, *Paganism,* 317–18.

139. Isaiah Berlin, *The Proper Study of Mankind* (New York: Farrar, Straus and Giroux, 1997), 344, n. 1.

140. Italicized in Hazard, *Pietism and the Making of Eighteenth-Century Prussia,* 166.

141. Ibid, 113–14. Quotation from *Bibliothèque germanique* (1729) 18.

142. Gay, *Science,* 524.

143. Jeffrey Freedman, "The Process of Cultural Exchange: Publishing Between France and Germany (1769–1789)" PhD diss., (Princeton University, 1991), although discussing the publications of a specific Swiss publisher later involved in the exchange of German and French works, nevertheless clarifies the relevance of these translated adaptations, which, he writes, "unfolded according to the logic of the market, rather than that of ideology" (4). "When mediated by a commercial publisher, the process of cultural exchange followed the dictates of capitalist profit: it was no respecter of textual integrity, or the *auctoritas* of authorship or the rights of genius."

144. Israel, *Radical Enlightenment,* 657–58. See 655–57 re: Schmidt's complex motives for making this work available.

145. Fulbrook, *Piety and Politics,* 128–29. Today we talk about "meditation," which is experienced on different levels, and about Pentecostal worship, etc.

146. Stoeffler, *German Pietism,* 179. See 176–82, passim, for a summary of Arnold's positions and influence. *Geheimnis der göttlichen Sophia* is excerpted in Erb, *Pietists.*

147. Stoeffler, *German Pietism,* 215–16.

148. Yet Fénelon was a fierce opponent of the Jansenists, a mystically oriented group also devoted to evangelical reform within Catholicism. Regarding the Jansenists, see Hazard, *The European Mind,* 419.

149. Richard Popkin, *The Third Force in Seventeenth-Century Thought* (Leiden/NY/Kobenhavn: E. J. Brill, 1992), 232. For the full story of this apostasy, see Gershom Scholem, *Sabbatai Sevi: The Mystical Messiah 1626–1676* (Princeton: Princeton University Press, 1973).

150. Popkin, *The Third Force,* 362–63.

151. Stoeffler, *The Rise,* 241. Stoeffler assumes that Labadie influenced Spener during his studies in Geneva in the early 1660s (229). Scholem describes the period 1665–1666 as a similar religious "awakening" among Jews worldwide, "with the same emphases on piety, charity, and personal reform" (583).

152. Scholem, *Sabbatai Sevi,* 593.

153. Stoeffler, *The Rise,* 222–23: "To Müller the very essence of personal Christianity was love for God and mystical union with him." Stoeffler says he was "one of the most

influential men of his age." Books in Bach's library included: *Schluß-Kette und Kraftkern* (1663) 2 copies; *Schaden Josephs in allen dreien Ständen* (1681); *Himmlischer Liebes Flamme* (1659); *Die geistlichen Erquickstunden* (1664); and *Rath Gottes* (n.d.)— publication dates are of first editions (found in Robin A. Leaver, *Bach's Theological Library: A Critical Bibliography* [Neuhausen/Stuttgart: Hänssler Verlag, 1983], 13). See also Joyce Irwin, *Neither Voice Nor Heart Alone: German Lutheran Theology of Music in the Age of the Baroque* (New York: Peter Lang, 1993), 72–77 and in this volume.

154. Stoeffler, *German Pietism*, 171.

155. Ibid., 110. Although noting similarities, Gershom Scholem, *Kabbalah* (Jerusalem: Keter, 1974; rpt. New York: Penguin Books, 1978), 200, says there seems to be "no historical connection between them."

156. Gawthrop, *Pietism and the Making of Eighteenth-Century Prussia*, 126 and 130.

157. Jaroslav Pelikan, *Bach Among the Theologians* (Philadelphia: Fortress Press, 1986), 65.

158. Allison P. Coudert, *Leibniz and The Kabbalah* (Dordrecht/Boston: Kluwer Academic Publishers, 1995), xv and 116.

159. Stoeffler, *German Pietism*, calls Oetinger "the most original theologian of the eighteenth century in Württemburg, and perhaps all of Germany" (107).

160. Erb, *Pietists*, 18–19 and Stoeffler, *German Pietism*, 118. According to Antoine Faivre, Oetinger interpreted the Kabbalistic work of Isaac Luria (1534–72) and thereby introduced Hasidism to German Pietists (73).

161. See Wolfgang Herbst, "Johann Sebastian Bach und die Lutherische Mystik" (Inaugural Dissertation der Theologischen Fakultät der Friedrich Alexander Universität, 1958), especially, 159, where he addresses the "influx of mysticism that was conditioned by the times" and concludes that mysticism developed in the Lutheran orthodox community independently of Pietism and from within its own tradition. Also in this regard, Friedrich Kalb, *The Theology of Worship in 17th Century Lutheranism* (St. Louis: Concordia, 1965): "It would . . . be illusory to suppose that ideas of mysticism, which at the time were in the very air, did not creep into the theology and piety of the church"; "thoughts" about mystical union can be traced to Luther but cannot be found in the Gospel or orthodox dogmatics (174–75).

162. Kalb, *Theology of Worship*, 176, acknowledges that his own judgment of its heretical nature was not necessarily shared or even understood by theologians in the seventeenth and eighteenth centuries: "If Orthodoxy is to be blamed at all, it should be faulted not for providing the doctrinal form for the unio mystica thought of the Reformation but for its frequent lack of the critical discernment to recognize that a brand of mysticism foreign to the Gospel was infiltrating in the guise of piety born of the unio mystica" and, furthermore, for its failure to "reckon with the possibility of wrong inferences" (179–80 and 185, respectively). See also Herbst, "Johann Sebastian Bach und die Lutherische Mystik," 31–32.

163. Preus, 65. Hollaz's book, *Examen Theologicum Acroamaticum* was "highly respected . . . , going through eight editions between 1703 and 1763" and "was unrivalled in popularity among the later dogmatics" (ibid.). Compare to Herbst, "Johann Sebastian Bach und die Lutherische Mystik," n. 161 above, regarding Pietist influence.

164. See Herbst, "Johann Sebastian Bach und die Lutherische Mystik," 31, and Kalb, *Theology of Worship*, 176, who point to the likelihood of its source in lay authors before the idea of mystic union was systematized according to the precise intentions characteristic of Lutheran theology.

165. Regarding Newton, see Betty Jo Teeter Dobbs, *The Janus Faces of Genius: The Role of Alchemy in Newton's Thought* (Cambridge: Cambridge University Press, 1991); and Coudert, regarding Leibniz's debt to the Kabbala and his introduction to the Lurianic Kabbala in 1671 by the alchemist Franciscus Mercurius van Helmont (1614–1698) and Knorr von Rosenroth (1636–89). Rosenroth translated and published a compendium of kabbalistic texts in *Kabbala Denudata* between 1677 and 1684.

166. If Bach shared the optimistic Leipzig spirit and articulated it in his music, he would probably also have known it in the locales where he was previously employed. He composed the largest number of his cantatas shortly after he arrived in Leipzig, adapting and integrating works previously composed along with new material (Wolff, *Johann Sebastian Bach*, 269).

167. Basil Willey, *The Eighteenth Century Background* (New York: Columbia University Press, 1949; 11th printing, 1977), 43.

168. Ibid., 44.

169. *Das in gantz Europe beruehmte, gallant and sehenswurdige königliche Leipzig* (1725), Beineke Library, New Haven, Br95/185* (pamphlets and dissertations from the eighteenth century). I am grateful to Joyce Irwin for bringing this item to my attention and providing the translation. See George B. Stauffer, "Leipzig: A Cosmopolitan Trade Center," in *The Late Baroque Era: From the 1680s to 1740* (Granada Group & Macmillan, 1993), 254–95, for an overview of the city's wealth, opportunities for upward mobility, fairs and book trade, architectural innovations, and sacred and secular music-making.

170. Wiley, *The Eighteenth Century Background*, 44–45.

171. In this volume, p. 225.

172. I want to thank Michael Marissen for sharing his in-depth knowledge of Lutheran orthodoxy in correspondence and in his paper, "The Theological Character of J. S. Bach's Musical Offering."

173. Mary Greer, "Embracing Faith: The Duet as Metaphor in Selected Sacred Cantatas by J. S. Bach," *Bach* 34/1 (2003): 1–71, never denies that theology promises union with Jesus in the future, but cites examples of "the joyful dialogue or duet that . . . connotes strong faith" (4) and the "metaphorical embodiment of strong faith and the joy associated with it" (34). In her conclusion she writes, "There appears to be a strong correlation between the joyful mood of many duets and the implication of strong faith. The joyful affect of many of Bach's duet settings seem to be strongly associated with references to the here and now in juxtaposition with the hereafter" (60).

Chapter Three

Family Values and Dysfunctional Families

Home Life in the Moral Weeklies and Comedies of Bach's Leipzig

John Van Cleve

The Leipzig that Johann Sebastian Bach came to know during the second quarter of the eighteenth century fostered the cultural development and economic growth that dominated the German-speaking contribution to European civilization of the day. An adequate understanding of the literature most closely associated with the city and the era, especially the moral weekly and the Leipzig comedy, can only emerge from familiarity with everyday life as well as literary life. Since the late 1960s, German Studies has paid increased attention to the socio-economic determinants that have prevailed during the highly diverse periods of a long literary tradition.[1] This essay participates in that development by considering not only the world of letters, as closely defined, but also those elements of the everyday world that found reflection in literature.

Leipzig: The Trade Center

Since the Middle Ages, the everyday world of Leipzig had revolved around commerce. At Easter and Michaelmas, goods moving between German lands and, to the East, Poland and Russia, to the South, Italy, and, to the North, England and Scandinavia were put on exhibition at trade fairs rivaled in size and importance only by those held in Frankfurt. Wool and silken textiles were heavily represented; spices and wine were frequently offered by French and Italian exhibitors; leather and furs came from the East; and there was an active trade in gold, silver, and precious jewels.[2]

As a natural crossroads for overland trade routes, Leipzig had actually managed to enhance its commercial position during the severe disruptions of the

Thirty Years War (1618–48). The domestic Saxon woolen industry made the city a hub for trade in cloth of all kind, including the Silesian linen that was the German states' single most important export commodity.[3] The wholesale market in Swabian fustian, a blend of cotton and linen, was located in Leipzig, which also served as the north European center for the trade in Italian silk fabric. City merchants organized the markets for tin, copper, brass, and iron produced by mines in Saxony and Silesia. The export trade in metals grew as England and France began to industrialize in earnest.

Two small immigrant communities significantly advanced Leipzig's standing as a commercial center. French Huguenots displaced by Louis XIV's obtuse evictions transferred many of their contacts in the wine, oil, and luxury industries. And resident Italian merchants supported markets in wine and specialty foods. Both communities were active in the rapidly expanding trade in such "colonial" wares as tobacco and coffee.[4]

Much of the commerce that flowed to and from the fair, particularly the Polish fur trade, was handled by Jews.[5] Jews were not permitted residence in Saxony, but they were allowed to stay in Leipzig for the duration of the fair. There they were watched closely and forced to pay heavy taxes and fees. Upon entering Leipzig, Jewish traders were issued entry passes and pieces of yellow cloth that had to be on their persons at all times. At the marketplace, the city collected fees, and at the conclusion of the fair each Jew paid a duty based on at least six hundred talers worth of merchandise bought or sold.[6] It was a strained, temporary tolerance. The contemporary Jewish merchant Glückel of Hameln reports in her journal that the fear of death tortured Jews who traded at the fair, because if a Jewish participant died, all goods were forfeit to the city, which then usually denied the removal of the body for burial in the closest Jewish cemetery in Dessau, thirty miles away.[7]

Finally it should be noted that Leipzig provisioned the royal court in Dresden. Because August the Strong desired an ambience at his residence that would rival Versailles, the traffic in luxury goods from Leipzig to the court, both in perishables and in durable goods, was strong and constant.[8] Several of the merchants who supplied both the Elector's army and his palace were ennobled for their efforts.[9] Such men lived in elegant and expensive Baroque houses that they filled with works of art, thereby reifying their status as leading citizens. Figure 3.1 depicts the house built between 1701 and 1704 for the Leipzig merchant and one-time mayor Franz Conrad Romanus, which was a model for other opulent bourgeois houses built in Leipzig during the early eighteenth century.[10]

A Literary Culture

The central importance of the Leipzig fairs for the book trade rested on the business activity of three local publishers, who led the industry in German-speaking Europe: Johann Ludwig Gleditsch, Thomas Fritsch, and Johann Heinrich Zedler. Their efforts were inadvertently furthered by the Empire when Vienna

Figure 3.1. The Romanus house on Katherinenstraße, corner of Brühl, designed by architect Johann Gregor Fuchs. Engraving by Samuel Blättner, 1704.

tightened book censorship in Leipzig's seventeenth-century commercial rival, Frankfurt am Main. Greater governmental involvement in the industry tended to drive foreign investment from the Hessian city and toward its Saxon rival. Leipzig's importance to German music history was furthered by the efforts of the printer-publisher Bernhard Christoph Breitkopf, and particularly his son Johann Gottlob Immanuel, who standardized and modernized the publication of sheet music.

The catalogues of books offered at the Leipzig fairs constitute an invaluable source of information concerning not only the industry but also its customers through the eighteenth century; the equivalent Frankfurt catalogues become progressively shorter, finally disappearing after 1749. They record dramatic developments in the book-buying habits of the literate population. Albert Ward has determined that in the 1701 catalogue 55 percent of all titles are in Latin. These works were written for theologians and the university-educated audience.[11] Of the remaining titles, 24 percent refer to theological texts in German.[12] These works varied greatly and were of interest to different sectors of society. They included the popular religious materials, written especially for the lay, middle class Protestant reading public, which were the most widely read works between 1700 and 1740. Although few statistics are available for the period before 1700, we know that in addition to religious and devotional works in the vernacular, beginning in the second half of the seventeenth century a vernacular secular literature developed, also edifying in nature, which directed its concerns to the practical and political education of commoners. Not writing about heroes, fantasy, and pastoral romance for the nobility and the scholar, Christian Weise, the most famous of these early secular writers, wrote dramas and novels for the new class of educated professionals—adventure stories with didactic intent. They taught, by example, the "political" behavior needed to work in government and at the courts. Their enormous popularity is known from reported reprints.[13]

By 1740, the progression in the ratio of books from Latin to German is pronounced. The one German book in four of 1701 has become two German books in every three.[14] The surge occurs in two categories: "Imaginative Literature" and "Popular-Moral Works." When Hans-Joachim Kreutzer comments that Leipzig was a center of the scholarly book trade when Bach arrived in the city in 1723, he is correct.[15] However, it is more revealing to note that during the course of Bach's residence in the town, the trade became substantially less "scholar-oriented." Indeed, by 1740 approximately two books in every three were for the non-scholar.

Bach's Leipzig was the site of the most important watershed development in the history of printed German books, the change in target audience from the expert to the layperson. What is known about the changing audience for printed matter in the first half of the eighteenth century? By modern standards, it was very small indeed. As the 1720s began, Leipzig's population stood at just under 28,500 inhabitants.[16] That population put it in the middle of a list of populations of the major cities in German-speaking Europe.[17] In the absence of mandatory public education in Electoral Saxony, only the rudiments of literacy were offered in small private schools, whose student bodies were composed of the children of craftsmen, civil servants, servants, and soldiers. Such schools serviced roughly 1200 pupils, a figure that hardly begins to cover the school-age children in the city. However, simple attendance is not to be equated with literacy. Literary demographer Rolf Engelsing estimates that 25 percent of German children attended school during the eighteenth century, and that of those children fewer than 10 percent actually learned to read and write.[18] In a still overwhelmingly rural, agrarian culture, illiteracy was the norm. Not only were peasants in the countryside and craftsmen in town usually illiterate, but even merchants, the wealthiest members of the developing bourgeoisie, usually could read, write, and cipher only to the extent required in business. Often his correspondence had to be read aloud to the principal of a firm by a younger assistant.[19] The scrivener and scribe of ancient and medieval times come to mind. In the eighteenth century, most of the modest potential audience for the equally mod-est supply of published literature was composed of university-trained profes-sionals, whose numbers included the rapidly expanding stratum of civil servants required to administer the sundry absolutist German states. Furthermore, in the first half of the century, it was still true that even in houses of educated towns-men, girls were forced to lead sheltered lives and leave education and the active life options it could create to their brothers.[20] Books were designed specifically for women. A list of such books from 1705 shows subjects like cooking, garden-ing, geography, politics, and genealogy, in addition to devotional works. The books for and by women in the Leipzig book-fair catalogue of 1740 include many devotional works.[21]

Nevertheless, a "literary culture" developed in the German territories after 1700, stimulated by the increase in available books and "the velocity and extent of their circulation." James Sheehan portrays a society in which non-specialists read extensively—a new occurrence—making an effort to keep up with new publications.[22] Albert Ward says that "any work which appeared at the fair was within a matter of weeks circulated through all Germany, listed in numerous printed catalogues, and announced in many journals, newspapers, learned and political magazines, and the like." Large bookshops opened in many cities.[23] Furthermore, the rise and success of the "moral weekly" and other forms of peri-odical literature was a decisive indication that both a literary culture and a shared public sphere had developed. Sheehan summarizes what is known about these developments:

> Publishers also began to market a variety of newspapers, magazines, and guides to the literary scene. One of the first signs of the newly expanded audience for literature was the extraordinary success of the so-called "moral weeklies", which were based on English models and combined instruction, entertainment, and edification. About ten new moral weeklies appeared every five years between 1700 and 1740, twenty-eight between 1741 and 1745, and twenty-seven from 1746 to 1750. . . . By the 1770s there were over seven hundred periodicals being published in German, as compared to just fifty-eight at the beginning of the century. Some of the most important and influential of these publications were designed to keep readers informed about the world of books and authors.[24]

The developments in the book trades and the growth of a literary culture coin-cided with the converging needs of the absolutist governments and the Enlightenment. In response to the increase in merchants' demands for safe roads and stable economies from the governments of the scores of absolutist petty German states, the princes greatly increased the size of their administrative bureaucracies. The rapidly growing need for civil servants fostered university study, a requirement for appointment, and upward mobility. By the time Bach arrived in Leipzig, a second generation of graduating students was emerging from academic departments committed to the primacy of rationalism, the implementation of empiricism, and the necessity of a reason-based ethics. And the wealth pouring into Europe in the form of colonial trade produced merchants in the wholesale trade who truly lived like princes. In addition, the Enlightenment's critical analysis of all human institutions necessarily undermined traditional assessments of estate membership. The cumulative effect was a weakening of the feudal estate system in favor of a new wealth- and merit-based system of social stratification in which one's stratum came to be referred to as one's "class," in German "Klasse."

Leipzig was in fact one of the first German cities to develop the beginnings of a new social stratification system well-established in England by the end of the seventeenth century. In the European Middle Ages, social status had been determined by one's place in a hierarchy of strata based on political proximity to the ruler. That place was and is referred to with the words "estate" and, in German, "Stand." Virtually all members of the society belonged to estates: nobles and peasants, princes and prostitutes. Membership was based neither on merit nor on wealth but on traditional assessments of the value of each occupation and on the assumption that all such occupations were necessary. The quarter-century of Bach's residence in Leipzig falls within the period of that city's transition from the medieval system to the modern.

As the descendant of a long line of musicians, Bach's position in society, whether in Arnstadt or in Cöthen, is most easily understood as an estate, first because natal status went far in determining estate membership. His father, Johann Ambrosius Bach, was his first teacher; Johann Christoph, a brother, his second. He spent a traditional apprenticeship as a choirboy in Lüneburg, and then it was off to appointments as an organist. All in all, the structure of his early biography varies little from that of a medieval craftsman. The position of music director for the Prince of Anhalt suggests arrival at the status of a young master of his trade; upon assuming that dignity he had effectively risen to one of the higher levels available to the musician estate. And the small towns in which he had lived were still organized under the old social system. Therefore Bach's move to Leipzig entailed not only proximity to the transformation of the literary tradition but also entry into a then emergent *class*, the German bourgeoisie. Each of its members had to mediate between the long-established reflexes of a medieval townsman and the rising economic expectations of a latter-day burgher.

Appropriately enough in that context, literature developed that attempted to engage the bourgeoisie in German letters that relied on new genres and taught lessons in changing expectations for its readers' families. The resident of Leipzig who had access to his city's literary life knew the name Gottsched.[25] Johann Christoph Gottsched viewed literature as a means of continuing the education of his fellow townsmen after their graduation. And they in turn continued to look for guidance to the professoriat that had given them their understanding of the world and that had made their careers possible. The resulting confluence of interests might still have been swept back by the inertia of past literary tradition had it not been for the salubrious atmosphere for intellectual endeavor provided by Leipzig.

Gottsched had taken a master's degree at the University of Königsberg in 1723, and then left Prussia, where his height and physique made him especially subject to military conscription. By 1725 Gottsched was lecturing on literature and philosophy in a tenure-track position at the University of Leipzig. In his lectures, in moral weeklies he edited, and finally in a slender but epochal volume of literary theory he wrote, Gottsched used his first years in Leipzig to begin the work of creating a new tradition on the German stage and in German letters. He attacked, as dangerous to public morality, a contemporary theater scene that featured native farces, wandering *commedia dell'arte* companies, troupes of so-called English Comedians, marionette performances on market squares, and the opera. In each venue he saw a preference for action at the expense of moral instruction. He was repulsed by what he considered a reliance on the exaggerated, the sexual, the obscene in word and gesture. For decades Italian, English, and Scandinavian performers had been entertaining German audiences with wild gesticulation, acrobatic pratfalls, exhibitionism, and non-verbal communication of the most elemental sort. Gottsched was aghast at the contrast between French Classicism with its ancient Greek and Roman models and the improvisational stage of the "Hanswurst," the foul-mouthed, audience-baiting indigenous German clown.

From the year of Gottsched's arrival in Leipzig until the present day, he has occupied an uncomfortable position in German letters. Convinced that German literature and German theater had reached an abysmal state, he set about a rigorous, even aggressive reform. That reform, the reformer's methods, and his personality have occasioned strong reactions from Germanics scholars. On one hand, Marxist scholarship interested in developing an eighteenth-century bourgeois model for its own proletarian culture has seen him not just as a promoter of the national literary tradition but as "objectively necessary" to its development.[26] On the other hand, some scholars have seen fit to continue the attack first mounted against Gottsched and his followers by a well-established Lessing in 1759, a full three decades after the reform had begun. One recent and particularly shrill denunciation finally characterizes the reformer as "anti-music," apparently ignoring the fact that Gottsched collaborated with Bach on occasion.[27] Here, by means of a dispassionate inquiry, I seek to determine what prompted the Leipzig reform and how its champion proceeded.

Gottsched's activity on behalf of German letters took place at the beginning of the literary movement known as the Enlightenment, itself a part of the broader European movement in the natural sciences, philosophy, and related disciplines.[28] Terminological confusion among disciplines is possible since "baroque" is the term commonly applied to Bach's music. In German literary history, the word refers to the dominant movement of the seventeenth century, that is, to the century-long period that immediately precedes Gottsched's Enlightenment, which may be seen as commencing in the 1720s and concluding in the 1780s. As a relatively long-lived movement, the German literary Enlightenment is often understood to pass through phases and to prompt reactive countermovements. The latter seek to develop those spiritual or non-rational creative possibilities deemed underrepresented in self-consciously rationalist Enlightenment thinking. The most widely recognized of such reactive movements are "Sentimentality" of the 1740s and 1750s with its ties to German Pietism, "Storm and Stress" of the 1770s, and finally the movement frequently seen as the complete expression of the "Storm and Stress" or as an extension of the European Gothic, the literary Romanticism of the 1790s. It was Gottsched who opened the door to that reactive diversity by attacking Late Baroque literature as an unmitigated disaster for German letters and stagecraft.

The Leipzig reform was not the first for German literature. Gottsched's effort, however, must be credited with greater success than the previous reform, of exactly one hundred years before, when Martin Opitz had published a poetics aimed at purging the tradition of elements considered low and foreign. Gottsched's success resulted from both his young man's prodigious energy and the openness of his times to both message and message-bearer. Not only did the professor lecture, edit, and write for the cause of reform, but in the 1730s he worked with a well-known acting troupe to develop a "purified" German stage, and he married a talented woman who wrote comedies for that new stage. Because the message came from a university professor, it had particular weight during a time of high prestige for German universities. They were looked to for leadership in the process of bringing the philosophical Enlightenment to the average townsman.

The Moral Weekly

The concept of the moral weekly, and the prototypes for it, came from England.[29] Selections from *The Tatler* (1707–11), *The Spectator* (1711–12, 1714), and *The Guardian* (1713) that had been translated into German made up much of the first continental effort, *Der Vernünfftler* ("The Sensible Man"), which first appeared in Hamburg in 1713. But it was not until the following decade that the genre achieved widespread popularity: first in Zurich (1721), then in Hamburg again (1724), and finally in Halle and Leipzig (1725). In that last year, Gottsched began writing his weekly, *Die vernünfftigen Tadlerinnen* ("The Sensible [female] Scolds").[30]

Pamela Currie, contradicting the wisdom of many scholars who see the readership of the moral weeklies belonging to a cross-section of the German population, limits their circulation to "the higher groups of urban society: the aristocracy, magistrates, university-trained professional men, wealthy merchants, and masters in the more prestigious crafts." Her evidence is based on their costliness and the issues they address.[31] When the moral weeklies began to appear in Hamburg and Leipzig around 1720, literate but less well-heeled people faced a problem, which they solved by joining forces and finances: five or even ten would pay for one subscription.[32]

Serial publication was well suited to an academician accustomed to regular meetings with those he was charged with educating. Gottsched's *Die vernünfftigen Tadlerinnen* rested on the fiction of a group of three women writers who offered their views to those of their sex. Published 1725–26, the weekly appeared first in Halle before moving to Leipzig, which quickly became German-speaking Europe's leading place of publication for serials. With his second Leipzig weekly, *Der Biedermann* ("The Man of Probity"), which first appeared in 1727, Gottsched reset his focus on the family as the locus of practical enlightenment. The underlying assumption that regular inculcation of the subject matter is more appropriate than one-time illumination is apparent in the repetitiveness of both weeklies. Gottsched uses *Der Biedermann* to present a model for family life in lessons designed to entertain as they teach. To that end he employs specificity as well as brevity: he creates a family whose pattern of life and shared ethics reflects his vision of the German bourgeoisie. The home life of the fictional couple, Sophroniscus and Euphrosyne, demonstrates the values to be nurtured at the hearths of civil servants, professionals, merchants, and the lower nobility.

The couple and their family supposedly reside at an estate that borders that of the fictive author of the weekly, Ernst Wahrlieb Biedermann. The latter reports that his surname prompted the idea for the serial and suggested its ethical tone.[33] But the first word in the second issue is "Sophroniscus," who is immediately identified as Biedermann's older and more experienced best friend, and as a man who pursues the common goal of humanity and happiness, on the path of virtue.[34] Figure 3.2 is a facsimile of that page.

Sophroniscus is a landed nobleman who maintains an agrarian lifestyle that emphasizes self-sufficiency, self-improvement, and moderation. As a paterfamilias, he directs all the activities of servants and family members with constant, focused energy. The thought that he might look down on those of lower estate as his inferiors does not occur to Sophroniscus. A well-educated man, he frequently refers to the teachings of the ancient Greeks and Romans as well as to those of modern scholars. Yet his library is not vast, for he believes that it is better to have a few good books rather than many mediocre volumes.[35] Such a man has no time for displays of learning that serve only to enhance social position. At the same time his tastes are cosmopolitan, never subservient to the passing intellectual style or trend. He regularly shares his simple, fervent religious faith with his family and servants. Several times a week, all are gathered before him to hear the lord of the manor discourse on the many examples of God's grace, for which all in attendance should give thanks. His religiosity is neither the

Der
Biedermann.

Anderes Blatt 1727. den 8. May.

HORATIUS.

Vivitur parvo bene, cui paternum
Splendet in mensa tenui salinum,
Nec dulces somnos timor aut Cupido
Sordidus aufert.

Sophroniscus, mein Nachbar, ist mein bester Freund, den ich in der Welt habe, und also eins von den vornehmsten Theilen meiner Glückseeligkeit. Er ist älter als ich; folglich hat er eine Erfahrung und Klugheit, die mich zur Ehrfurcht und Hochachtung gegen ihn beweget: Dem ohngeachtet will er, daß ich mit ihm, als ein Freund mit dem andern umgehen solle. Ich bediene mich dieser vergönnten Freyheit desto williger, je vortheilhaffter und angenehmer mir seine Vertraulichkeit ist. Es gehet keine Woche vorbey, darinnen wir einander nicht zwey oder dreymahl sprechen sollten: Und keine Zeit verläufft uns geschwinder, als diejenigen Stunden, da wir beyeinander sind.

Ich habe des Vortheils erwehnet, den ich aus der Freundschafft meines Sophroniscus ziehe: und hieran könnte sich vielleicht jemand stossen. Ich weiß es auch sehr wohl, daß Freundschafften die aus Gewinnsucht entstehen, auf einem sehr seichten Grunde ruhen. Sie dauren insgemein nicht länger, als der eigennützige Theil was genüsset oder noch zu hoffen hat. Allein man unterscheide nur eine vortheilhaffte Freundschafft von einer gewinnsüchtigen oder eigennützigen: so wird man mich keines Fehlers beschuldigen. Daß ein Mensch nach seinem Vortheile strebet, das ist ihm niemahls zu verdencken. Die Begierde glücklich zu werden ist unserm Wesen so fest eingepräget, daß man ihr nicht wiederstehen kan: Ja man muß ihr nicht wiederstehen; sondern sie auf alle Weise befördern. Sie ist gleichsam die einzige Feder, die das gantze Menschliche Geschlecht in Bewegung setzet, und einen jeden ins besondere treibet, das Gute zu thun und das Böse zu lassen. Sie ist der sicherste Grund der gantzen Sittenlehre: denn was würden doch wohl vor Mittel übrig bleiben, uns zur Tugend zu leiten und von den Lastern abzuhalten; wenn es uns gleichviel wäre, ob wir glücklich oder unglücklich würden? Wenn ich also meinen Freund liebe; so liebe ich ihn bloß deswegen, weil er durch seine Freundschafft mich glücklicher macht, als ich sonst seyn würde, wenn ich dieselbe nicht geniessen könnte: Heißt das aber was anders, als denselben um meines Vortheils halber lieben? Nur das ist der Unterscheid, daß dieser Vortheil nicht eben in Geld und Gut, Essen und Trincken, oder andern dergleichen Dingen bestehet. Ich nehme das Wort Vortheil in einem weitläuftigern Verstande. Ich verstehe dadurch auch die Vermehrung meiner Gemüths-Kräffte, und alle Belustigungen des Verstandes, die aus dem Umgange mit vernünfftigen, gelehrten, tugendhafften und redlichen Leuten ent-

B   sprin-

Figure 3.2. *Der Biedermann*, vol. 2, p. 1 (Leipzig: May 8, 1727).

orthodoxy nor Pietism of Leipzig; indeed, he professes to no particular denomination. Yet, his knowledge of Christian teachings is profound. He prohibits the use of foul language and demands peaceful, harmonious relationships among those with whom he lives. He chose to marry Euphrosyne not because of a dowry, which he refused, but because she shares his views and plays an active teacher's role in the raising of their six children.

Sophroniscus himself instructs his children, but the extent of his devotion to education is most apparent in his selection of Aristides as the children's private tutor.[36] During the seventeenth and early eighteenth centuries, such private tutors were treated more often than not as servants whose sphere of activity was not of great importance.[37] Quite the opposite is the case at this estate. From the onset Sophroniscus impresses upon Aristides that the children are to view him as a friend of their father who also happens to be their teacher and mentor. His salary is to be the then handsome sum of one hundred talers yearly with all living expenses provided. Aristides has worked at the estate fifteen years when the weekly begins to appear and has come to be seen as a brother to the owner. The boys Philalethes and Euphrastus love him and want him to be present at all their activities. His instruction emphasizes the cultivation of reason and understanding that will benefit the German fatherland.[38]

The father's active participation in the raising of his children and the direction both he and the tutor give their upbringing is apparent in the gift of newly published books from the Leipzig fair, an occasion reported at the end of the third issue of *Der Biedermann*. To Aristides himself Sophroniscus gives a history of the German people by a professor at the University of Leipzig. The paterfamilias is impressed not only by the erudition displayed in the analysis of such an important topic but by the style of the writing, which he finds appropriate, beautiful, and "masculine." One son receives a translation of Cicero's volume on duty; the other son a copy of a new German translation of the *Télémaque* of Fénélon (1699). The latter choice is significant because Fénélon was a Catholic archbishop, a political idealist, and a Christian Neo-Platonist mystic. Apparent is the dedication to literature of both the ancients and moderns, to a close awareness of both indigenous German culture and the then ascendant French, to the analysis of the process of education itself, to the importance of the cultivated use of language and, not least, interdenominational broadmindedness. Relatively little space is given over to the religious views and practices of Gottsched's model German family, no particular orthodox confession is cited, and there is no reference to attendance at any Pietist meetings. Still it is apparent that Sophroniscus has an abiding theistic faith. His sentiments lead to a keen awareness of God as the Creator among all who live at the estate.[39]

In *Der Biedermann* Gottsched offers his readers an ideal for family life, an ideal that stresses the importance of education, widely-based education for children and ongoing moral education for adults. In dramatic works written under his influence, such as those considered below, playwrights rely on the tension between this reasoned, virtuous ideal and those behaviors and personalities that are at odds with the reflexes of such a "Biedermann" as Sophroniscus. As the dramatic genre traditionally concerned with the lives of those not in the ruling estates, comedy attracted Gottsched because it took as its traditional genre mission the correction of behavioral and ethical aberrations as they affected the social commerce of townsmen.[40] Smooth and productive social relations were particularly important to members of the emergent middle class in commercial centers like Leipzig, whose merchants, professionals, and civil servants could not be burdened by personality faults that would militate against their personal and professional development.

In practical terms this meant that a typical comedy of the period featured just two kinds of characters: those who would have been received by Sophroniscus as welcome additions to his household and those who evince a defect of character that renders them laughable in the eyes of those who have dedicated themselves to the paths of reason and virtue.[41] Audiences of the day were to recognize the defects, laugh at the characters so afflicted, and resolve to avoid the ethical pitfalls thus illustrated in their daily lives. The resulting body of drama has earned few entries in the canons of eighteenth-century German literature, but it does go far to reveal the cultural reflexes of Bach's Leipzig.

Leipzig Comedy

Gottsched's faithful helpmate in his campaign to create a new German literature, his wife Luise Adelgunde Victoria (Kulmus) Gottsched, wrote one of the very early examples of Leipzig's "enlightened" comedy, *Die Pietisterey im Fischbeinrocke* (1736).[42] There can be no doubt that Pietism's emphasis on a personal, emotionally charged religious experience provoked the Gottscheds. By making the modish and superficial emotionalism of the upper class middle-aged women on stage appear foolish, they meant to generate humor for their eighteenth-century audiences.

"Pietism in Petticoats" dramatizes an episode in the history of the Glaubeleicht family, a surname with meaning like many surnames coined by the playwright. Here it suggests "readily believing" or "gullible." The plot line develops out of the prolonged absence of the common-sensical Mr. Glaubeleicht at precisely the time that his wife has come under the influence of the Pietist theologian Reverend Scheinfromm ("pious in appearance" or "hypocritical"). Mrs. Glaubeleicht has made so many donations to her spiritual leader that she has imperiled the family's financial standing. The depth of her spiritual commitment is suspect from the start. Her passions are aroused not by thoughtful discussions of points of faith but by the mere mention of the names current in the confessional wars of the day: references to leading orthodox Lutheran thinkers cause her to faint, only to be revived by the incantation of the names of Pietist

leaders and their concepts. Reverend Scheinfromm travels from city to city with
a coterie of uncritical female followers, including Mrs. Seufzer ("sigh"), Mrs.
Zankenheim ("home of squabbling"), and the alms gathering Mrs. Bettelsack
("begging sack"). He tries to enhance his financial position not only by draining
Mrs. Glaubeleicht's assets but by trying to arrange a marriage between the sensible Glaubeleicht daughter Luischen and his own dullard son. The man's venal-
ity is apparent in his embezzlement of his followers' contributions, his moral
depravity, and his molestation of a girl during confirmation instruction. In
Luischen, spectators would have immediately recognized a moral touchstone.
Her presence was to prevent them from willingly suspending their disbelief to
such an extent that they forgot the relationship between what they saw on stage
and how they acted after leaving the theater. Luischen responds as Sophroniscus
responds—and as spectators were to respond. The comedy is anything but a theoretical consideration of Pietist tenets; instead, it plays to the criticisms then
held by orthodox Lutherans and promotes the "natural theology" of the
Enlightenment.

However, Luise Gottsched has a broader target in mind than just the born-
again religiosity of her day. Her concerns as a social critic extend to the personality faults adumbrated in the names "Glaubeleicht" and "Scheinfromm." She
points to the problem that exists when only the husbands in families are socially
competent adults, if only because those husbands will occasionally be absent.
Mrs. Glaubeleicht becomes an easy victim of a religious confidence man because
in the absence of educated understanding, she follows belief ("Glaube") uncrit-
ically. Although, as becomes evident at the play's conclusion, the woman is anything but stupid, she is nevertheless undereducated, a flaw that actually
endangers her family. Even as the female playwright holds out some hope in the
form of the younger generation in Luischen, she points to society's complicity
in endangering its members, and especially its children, by leaving wives intellectually defenseless before the machinations of social predators.

By the same token, the reprehensible Reverend Scheinfromm has enjoyed
great success because society is all too easily duped by the appearance of piety.
The rigor of the playwright's critique of Pietism is certainly open to question,
but there can be no doubt concerning the strength of her aversion to those who
would advance themselves by feigning attainments and sustaining appearances
that are wildly at odds with reality. To Biedermann, Johann Christoph
Gottsched's alter-ego, Sophroniscus's religiosity seems admirable—whether it is
Lutheran or Catholic, orthodox or Pietist—because it is genuine. In the absence
of all the customary trappings of religious convention, simple faith itself is powerful enough to underpin the collective morality of a tiny community that is, in a
general sense, profoundly Christian.

Intellectual stylishness and the seductiveness of appearances provided Luise
Gottsched with themes for a one-act comedy that appeared a decade after
"Pietism in Petticoats." In it, the merchant and his family represent a new stock

of heroic literary figures. *Der Witzling* ("The Witling," 1747), is set in the home of the Leipzig merchant Mr. Reinhart ("pure heart").[43] The man is interested in arranging a marriage between his ward, the sensible Lottchen, and the young son of a longtime friend. The play begins with a discussion of the plan, which horrifies the girl. She describes the young Mr. Vielwitz ("much wit") as an arrogant boor. The trusting father figure leaves greatly surprised as his son enters. The latter suggests that Lottchen invite young Vielwitz to coffee so that Mr. Reinhart can gain some first-hand impressions. In fact he suggests that she invite not just Vielwitz but some of his like-minded fellow students from the university. Over coffee the three guests show themselves to be every bit as arrogant as Lottchen represented them and, moreover, opinionated, poorly spoken, and badly educated. Finally, when it is decided that Lottchen will read aloud a letter Vielwitz has written her in hopes of impressing her with his attainments, the girl finds herself reading a letter intended for the young man's father in another city. In the missive each member of the Reinhart family is subjected to ridicule. The true nature of the "witling" has been exposed, and the young man decides to give up his pursuit of Lottchen and leave a city that seems to oppose his every inclination.

The message taken away by the audience is that progeny of the urban merchant class are more than a match for the progeny of the academic elite who seek personal advancement via the appearance of intellectual prowess. The latter may be forces of false and shallow learning, while the merchant's son and his ward evince close knowledge of the leading writers and ideas, both of their own times and of classical antiquity. Their upbringing reflects well on a man meant to be viewed as representative of Leipzig's nascent bourgeoisie. Luise Gottsched explicitly positions that class on the side of her husband's ongoing reform of German letters in the opening scene of "The Witling." Lottchen reports a conversation among young Vielwitz and his friends about Johann Gottsched's *Deutsche Schaubühne* ("German Stage"), a collection of plays by husband and wife, other like-minded playwrights, and French Classicist playwrights in German translations, edited and published in the 1740s in serial fashion.

> Miss Lottchen: [. . .] they were talking about Gottsched's "German Stage." Vielwitz was finding fault with every play in it.
> Mr. Reinhart: [shakes his head]. Well, I never would have thought that! I often read in it in the evening. To be sure, I don't like all the plays myself, but some of them are quite good. And I always think, what I don't like may well please someone else.
> Miss Lottchen: That means you think like a reasonable man, but not like a clever young Vielwitz.[44]

The Leipzig paterfamilias reads for pleasure, as a frequent leisure-time activity. That he does so not to impress other members of his household but for his own edification and delight is evident in his ability to discriminate on the basis of personal literary tastes, which he has taken the necessary time to cultivate. His allowance for the divergent tastes of others indicates support for a literary world that will produce works for a broad array of audience interests. He sees himself as belonging to a cosmopolitan literary public, an evaluation that of course the reader is to apply to Reinhart's hometown. His ward's response indicates not just approval but understanding of, and support for, the development of the discriminating faculty of reason, a development actively championed by the Enlightenment.

The father-as-reader recalls Sophroniscus, who concerns himself not with the number of his volumes but with their quality. The importance that such fathers have is indirectly suggested by the character of the witling Vielwitz, whose upbringing has been in some way deficient. Mr. Reinhart describes the father as a wealthy man who is adept at increasing his own investments and those of others. The message to the readers of Leipzig—the commercial center—is clear: wealth does not guarantee enlightenment; or, as Lottchen observes, "Wealth is no better protection against folly than age."[45]

Lottchen's statement would have been lost on the central character in Hinrich Borkenstein's 1742 play, *Der Bookesbeutel* ("The Book-Sack").[46] This comedy featured enlightened Leipzig burghers in tension with the folly of a Hamburg businessman and his family. The title of the play refers to a particular kind of bag used by the women of Hamburg to carry their hymnals to church during the preceding century but no longer in wide use by the time Hinrich Borkenstein wrote his comedy. The word had acquired a figurative meaning, roughly approximating the English expression "old hat"; through his title, the author alerted the theater audience to be on the watch for outmoded and foolish ways of thinking.

Borkenstein himself was a native of Hamburg, a merchant and the son of a merchant, whose level of erudition contrasted sharply with that of his fictitious Hamburg merchant Grobian ("crude fellow," "lout"). Grobian has refused to finance the academic career of his son Sittenreich ("morally wealthy") at the University of Leipzig, although he is in a financial position to do so, because he and his wife believe that new ideas are suspect. His wife, Agneta, offers the opinion that innovation causes inconvenience; if one simply holds to what one has always done and thought, one spares one's mind all upset.[47] However, Agneta's brother Gutherz ("good heart") has underwritten the student's expenses and, thereby, demonstrated that enlightened impulses are not totally foreign to Hamburg. By contrast, Agneta is such a slave to routine that each meal plan is an entry to the weekly dining schedule, from which deviations are not permitted. Furthermore, food portions are kept small in an effort to save money for the miserly Grobian, and the family retires early each evening, when their neighbors are still up talking, in order to save the cost of lantern fuel.

The complication that sets the plot in motion is a visit in which Sittenreich is accompanied by Ehrenwehrt ("worthy of esteem"), his fellow student from Leipzig, and Carolina, Ehrenwehrt's sister. While Agneta fusses about the necessity of disturbing meal planning to feed three extra mouths, Grobian dreams of making a double marital alliance with wealthy old Mr. Ehrenwehrt senior. Spectators were, accordingly, treated to both the Hamburg family's "old hat" social instincts and their attempt to ingratiate themselves with a Leipzig family, which stands to bring Grobian great financial gain. By the play's conclusion, Grobian is pleased at the betrothal of Sittenreich and Carolina but infuriated by his hapless daughter Susanna's inability to form an attachment with the heir, young Ehrenwehrt. Susanna is the ultimate victim of her father's rejection of education and innovation: she is unable to do more than sew, cook a very few dishes, and sing with her mother. Ehrenwehrt seeks the intellectual equal of his own sister, who is able to hold up her end of conversations with the two university-trained young men.

During the play Grobian repeatedly demonstrates, in exaggerated form, an ignorance of the world that was not unusual for merchants of the day. When the three travelers first arrive at his house, Grobian expresses astonishment at the vast distance they have traversed:

> Grobian: It's supposed to be over a hundred miles by road from Leipzig to here.
> Ehrenwehrt: Oh no, it is only forty or so.
> Grobian: In all my days I've never troubled myself about roads. I'm not of a mind to travel. After all, Hamburg is the biggest and best place in the whole world.[48]

The belief that Hamburg is the largest city on earth would have struck not just university-educated audience members but also those with international trade connections as absurd. When Ehrenwehrt responds with references to London and Paris, Grobian recalls a cousin who visited those cities only to find that few people there spoke German. He thinks that the whole world should speak German: learning to speak in other ways costs such terrible effort and so much money, and leads to the production of strange sounds that resemble the howling of animals. Grobian is later surprised to learn that the howling is, in fact, other languages.

Whereas Luise Gottsched's "The Witling" is directed against those who obtain just enough education to pass themselves off as educated in order to enjoy the prestige and benefits that accrue to the truly educated, Borkenstein's comedy is directed against those who deny that the value of education outweighs its immediate costs. To do so is to put immediate financial advantage before enlightenment—and even before long-range financial advantage. An educated, well-spoken Susanna would have been in a position to attract the attentions of Ehrenwehrt and provide the tie with the Leipzig family Grobian so desires. Grobian, Agneta, and their blank slate of a daughter are a family of fools created to warn the residents of Hamburg, a city then in the midst of an economic boom, that excessive concern for the accumulation of wealth results in the loss of the very human characteristics that make life worthwhile. The contrast with Leipzig, a city well-known for its level of cultural activity, is meant to act as a goad, an incentive to Hamburg audiences to pull their city up to the level of its Saxon rival.

When Gottsched's disciple Johann Elias Schlegel wrote *Der geschäfftige Müßiggänger* ("The Busy Idler") in 1741, he set his comedy in the Leipzig home of a businessman who would have understood many of Grobian's reflexes.[49] Sylvester is a fur merchant who knows about little more than the commodity he trades but is secure in the knowledge that his abilities have produced a flourishing business and a comfortable life. He finds it difficult to understand his stepson Fortunat, to whom Schlegel's title refers. Although the young man attended university and took a degree in law, he now spends his time pursuing hobbies and personal interests that produce no income, develop no marriage prospects, and establish no career options. It is a life style associated, in the minds of audience members, with the popular stereotype of the nobleman who rests on inherited laurels all his life—the life style the nobleman Sophroniscus turned from. Fortunat's great support is a mother who has spoiled her one child to such an extent that he is incapable of summoning the energy necessary to arrive at either a professional or a personal focus for his life. Much of Sylvester's exasperation results from an expectation concerning the upbringing of a merchant's son that theater audiences would have brought to performances of the play.

The three characters in the play bring different types of foolishness to the middle-class audience for their consideration. This audience was, presumably, interested in overcoming all obstacles in the way of attaining the state of perfection represented by the Sophroniscus family. The characters on stage reveal flaws that are familiar to this audience. One flaw was that of eighteenth-century fathers devoting themselves to their sons' vocational training and placement in suitable businesses, while remaining insensitive to productive interpersonal relationships. Although sympathetic and likeable, a straightforward fellow, Sylvester is a bear in the china shop of children, parents, and family ties. The message from Schlegel is that interpersonal relationships, particularly with family members, are more important than career considerations. Another flaw in these characters lies in the parents' lack of cooperation in child-rearing. Here the problem lies in the degree of ignorance evident in Sylvester's wife, which had been the rule in times past. Gottsched, Schlegel, and their fellow Leipzigers anticipated only trouble in a home whose wife and mother was uneducated. Derisive laughter is the response Schlegel wishes to elicit when his matron mouths ineffectual excuses to her husband and toothless warnings to her son. Fortunat's uneducated and over-indulgent mother has sent her charge to the customary educational institutions, but she has not been able to support his developing a sense of direction in life. Finally, Fortunat's idleness contrasted strongly, and in the playwright's mind comically, with the purposeful activity expected of a mature burgher, whose success in all phases of life is due to education and hard work. Ironically, Fortunat's self-indulgence, which trades on the stereotype of the nobleman, contradicts that stereotype by behavior that is intrinsically foolish and leads only to a social posture "appropriate" in a man of higher estate.

In his portrayal of Sylvester's inability to influence his stepson's life, Schlegel indirectly warns the Leipzig's commercial and professional community about the pitfalls of a single-minded devotion to business affairs. In Schlegel's conviction about the importance of interpersonal relationships there resides the beginning of a literary interest in emotional life, which was first explored extensively by Christian Fürchtegott Gellert.

Gellert's comedy *Die Betschwester* (literally, "The Prayer-Sister," in the sense of a "churchy" woman) first appeared in 1745.[50] Gellert was a student colleague of Schlegel at the University of Leipzig, where both young men joined the literary circle presided over by Gottsched. Both were actively involved in the production of the serialized *Die deutsche Schaubühne* ("The German Stage"). The plot of *Die Betschwester* is so slight that it attracted substantial contemporary criticism. Wealthy Simon travels to the home of Mrs. Richardinn to formalize an engagement to the widow's daughter Christianchen. The older woman is, to all appearances, the churchy woman of the title; however, her devotion to the Christian faith is strictly for appearances. The character soon reveals herself to be an avaricious, judgmental, parochial, scheming hypocrite. Her complete disregard for her daughter's education has left Christianchen a complete innocent, whose only contact with the world of ideas is her friend, the sensible Lorchen. The latter demonstrates the true state of affairs under Mrs. Richardinn's roof to both Simon and his travel companion, the older Ferdinand, who is acting as a marriage broker. In the process Lorchen and Simon fall in love, but they renounce their feelings for the sake of the helpless innocent Christianchen, whom Simon will in fact marry and then bring into enlightened adulthood. Lorchen will become the ward of the wealthy and childless Ferdinand.

Gellert's play holds up to ridicule two forms of foolish behavior: false religiosity and the neglect of women's education. The attack on hypocrisy was deemed too subtle by several contemporary critics, who were of the opinion that less sophisticated audience members would understand the writer's attempt to make the churchy woman foolish as an attempt to make "churchiness" foolish, that is, as an attack on religiosity.[51] Despite all the doubts, Gellert's intent is clear and by the mid-1740s was familiar to audiences of the "reformed" stage: the attempt to project a personality trait that is in reality absent is laughable.

The importance of friendship and the emotions that underpin it was especially present in the minds of writers, like Gellert, who participated in the offshoot movement of the later German enlightenment usually referred to as *Empfindsamkeit* ("Sentimentality").[52] Therefore, while the educationally deprived Susanna in Borkenstein's *Bookesbeutel* is an unknowing fool, whose failure to attract a wealthy husband is meant to elicit no pity, in *Die Betschwester* the same character type is outfitted with a shining virtue not present in Susanna: for all her limitations, Christianchen has been able to form a friendship with a sensible young woman. Lorchen, unable to take advantage of Christianchen's weakness in order to break up her friend's arranged marriage, offers to participate in Christianchen's transformation into a wife worthy of the enlightened Simon. She urges him to remove the girl from her mother's pernicious influence and then leave matters to her:

> [. . .] I shall spend time with your fiancée. I will introduce her into society. I will have discussions with her. I will read good books, sensible novels aloud to her. I will teach her as much French as I can. And she will be writing you a letter every other day.[53]

When the subject of remuneration is brought up, Lorchen forswears any interest in making money from the situation. Her only concern is to help her friend Christianchen.

With the emergence of sentimentality as a desired audience response, the days of the Saxon comedy and the central role of Leipzig as a literary center waned. Now, two decades after his arrival in Leipzig, Johann Gottsched's "papal" authority over German letters was eroding. As the center of literary life moved to Berlin, Gotthold Ephraim Lessing, the great leader of the late German Enlightenment, ridiculed Gottsched in print, reviling him for antiquated thinking. It was during the very years when Bach was realizing the possibilities of the Baroque idiom that Gottsched's Saxon comedy provided the German stage and German literature itself with a fresh start. It was a principled new beginning, fully consonant with the intellectual tenor of the times and the social concerns of Bach's Leipzig.

Notes

1. For an English-language example that treats the eighteenth century, see Alan Menhennet, *Order and Freedom: Literature and Society in Germany from 1720 to 1805* (London: Weidenfeld and Nicolson, 1973).

2. Ernst Kroker, *Handelsgeschichte der Stadt Leipzig: Die Entwicklung des Leipziger Handels und der Leipziger Messen von der Gründung der Stadt bis auf die Gegenwart* (Leipzig: Bielefeld, 1925), 143–59.

3. Wolfgang Zorn, "Schwerpunkte der deutschen Ausfuhrindustrie im 18. Jahrhundert," *Jahrbücher für Nationalökonomie und Statistik* 173.5 (1961): 447.

4. See Kroker, *Handelsgeschichte der Stadt Leipzig*, 153–56.

5. Salo W. Baron and Arcadius Kahan, *Economic History of the Jews* (New York: Schocken, 1975), 247.

6. Kroker, *Handelsgeschichte der Stadt Leipzig*, 133–35. See "ratswaage" [*sic*] in Jacob Grimm and Wilhelm Grimm, *Deutsches Wörterbuch* (Leipzig: Hirzel, 1854–1961),

13:364–65 and 370. For the most up-to-date study of Jewish participation and rights in Saxony, see Jonathan I. Israel, *European Jewry in the Age of Mercantilism* (London/Portland: The Littman Library of Jewish Civilization, 3rd edition, 1998), particularly 139–40, 142–43, 204–5.

7. *The Memoirs of Glückel of Hameln,* tr. Marvin Lowenthal (1932; rpt., New York: Schocken, 1977), 126–27.

8. Kroker, *Handelsgeschichte der Stadt Leipzig,* 141–50.

9. Ibid., 161–63.

10. Romanus was the father of Christiane Mariane von Ziegler, who composed several cantata texts for J. S. Bach.

11. Albert Ward, *Book Production, Fiction and the German Reading Public, 1740–1800* (Oxford: Clarendon, 1974), 30–40.

12. Ward, *Book Production,* 164–65.

13. Ibid., 2. Also, Rudolf Vierhaus, *Germany in the Age of Absolutism,* trans. Jonathan B. Knudsen (Cambridge: Cambridge University Press, 1988), 75. For the qualitative change in popular taste by the last two decades of the century, see Ward, *Book Production,* 62.

14. Calculated from raw figures supplied in Ward, *Book Production,* 164–65.

15. Hans-Joachim Kreutzer, *Obertöne: Literatur und Musik: Neun Abhandlungen über das Zusammenspiel der Künste* (Würzburg: Königshausen und Neumann, 1994), 11.

16. Rolf Engelsing, *Analphabetentum und Lektüre: Zur Sozialgeschichte des Lesens in Deutschland zwischen feudaler und industrieller Gesellschaft* (Stuttgart: Metzler, 1973), 48. See also in this volume, 3 and 29n2.

17. Helmuth Kiesel and Paul Münch, *Gesellschaft und Literatur im 18. Jahrhundert: Voraussetzungen und Entstehung des literarischen Markts in Deutschland* (Munich: Beck, 1977), 15.

18. Engelsing, *Analphabetentum und Lektüre,* 48–49.

19. Rolf Engelsing, *Der Bürger als Leser: Lesergeschichte in Deutschland 1500–1800* (Stuttgart: Metzler, 1974), 138–39 and 148.

20. Curt Gebauer, "Studien zur Geschichte der bürgerlichen Sittenreform des 18. Jahrhunderts," *Archiv für Kulturgeschichte* 15 (1923): 101.

21. Ward, *Book Production,* 5 and 73.

22. James J. Sheehen, *German History 1770–1866* (Oxford: Oxford University Press, 1989), 153.

23. Ward, *Book Production,* 39.

24. Sheehan, *German History,* 154–55. From Ward, *Book Production,* 23; Wolfgang Martens, *Die Botschaft der Tugend: Die Aufklärung im Spiegel der deutschen moralischen Wochenschriften* (Stuttgart: Metzler, 1968); and Joachim Kirchner, *Das deutsche Zeitschriftenwesen: Seine Geschichte und seine Probleme,* 2 vols. (Wiesbaden: O. Harrassowitz, 1958–62).

25. For a general overview of the intellectual life of Leipzig, see Georg Witkowski, *Geschichte des geistigen Lebens in Leipzig* (Leipzig and Berlin: Teubner, 1909). The study follows nineteenth-century practice in its emphasis on literary history, the evaluation of which is dated in the analysis of specific texts.

26. Werner Rieck, *Geschichte der deutschen Literatur vom Ausgang des 17. Jahrhunderts bis 1789* (Berlin [East]: Volk und Wissen, 1979), 177.

27. Gloria Flaherty, "Bach's Leipzig As a Training Ground for Actors, Musicians, and Singers," in *Music and German Literature: Their Relationship since the Middle Ages,* ed. James M. McGlathery (Columbia, SC: Camden House, 1992), 107. On the same

page Gottsched is characterized as a "draft dodger," a "smooth operator," and the organizer of "a campaign to abolish from the very face of this planet all traces of opera."

28. For a recent English-language discussion of the "Enlightenment" as a movement in German literature that took place within the larger European context, see John Van Cleve, "Enlightenment," in *A Concise History of German Literature to 1900*, ed. Kim Vivian (Columbia, SC: Camden House, 1992), 123–38.

29. The standard scholarly treatment of the German moral weeklies of the eighteenth century is Wolfgang Martens's *Die Botschaft der Tugend*. For a discussion of the influence of the early English models, see 23, passim.

30. For a study of "Die Vernünfftigen Tadlerinnen," see Susanne Niefanger, *Schreibstrategien in moralischen Wochenschriften: Formalstilistische, pragmatische und rhetorische Untersuchungen am Beispiel von Gottscheds "Vernünfftigen Tadlerinnen"* (Tübingen: Niemeyer, 1997). The English-language title "The Sensible [female] Scolds" is suggested by Thomas Kerth and John R. Russell, "Introduction" to Luise Adelgunde Gottsched, *Pietism in Petticoats and Other Comedies*, trans. Kerth and Russell (Columbia, SC: Camden House, 1994), xii.

31. Pamela Currie, "Moral Weeklies and the Reading Public in Germany, 1711–1750," *Oxford German Studies* 3 (1968): 69.

32. Engelsing, *Analphabetentum*, 49.

33. Johann Christoph Gottsched, *Der Biedermann* (Leipzig: Insel, 1966), 7–8.

34. Ibid., 10–13.

35. Ibid., 11.

36. For a close examination of the role of education in Der Biedermann, see Günther Saße, *Die aufgeklärte Familie: Untersuchungen zur Genese, Funktion und Realitätsbezogenheit des familialen Wertsystems im Drama der Aufklärung* (Tübingen: Niemeyer, 1988), 8–20.

37. See Kiesel and Münch, *Gesellschaft und Literatur im 18. Jahrhundert*, 73–74.

38. Gottsched, *Der Biedermann*, 19.

39. Ibid., 13.

40. The standard work on the comedy in Germany is Karl Holl, *Geschichte des deutschen Lustspiels* (1923; rpt., Darmstadt: Wissenschaftliche Buchgesellschaft, 1964). For a socio-literary survey of the German eighteenth century, see Walter Horace Bruford, *Germany in the Eighteenth Century: The Social Background of the Literary Revival* (Cambridge: Cambridge UP, 1965). For an English-language survey of German eighteenth-century comedy, see Betsy Aiken-Sneath, *Comedy in Germany in the First Half of the Eighteenth Century* (Oxford: Clarendon, 1936). For a study of contemporary response to the comedies, see John Van Cleve, *Harlequin Besieged: The Reception of Comedy in German During the Early Enlightenment*, New York University Ottendorfer Series, vol. 13 (Berne, Frankfurt am Main, Las Vegas: Lang, 1980).

41. For more on the composition of comedy written under Gottsched's aegis, see Kurt Wölfel, "Moralische Anstalt: Zur Dramaturgie von Gottsched bis Lessing," in *Deutsche Dramentheorie: Beiträge zu einer historischen Poetik des Dramas in Deutschland*, ed. Reinhold Grimm (Frankfurt am Main: Athenäum, 1971), 70–72. See also Horst Steinmetz, *Die Komödie der Aufklärung* (Stuttgart: Metzler, 1966).

42. For more on Luise Gottsched, see Veronica C. Richel, *Luise Gottsched: A Reconsideration* (Bern: Lang, 1973).

43. Luise Adelgunde Victorie Gottsched, "The Witling," in Kerth and Russell.

44. Ibid., 285.

45. Ibid., 282.

46. Hinrich Borkenstein, *Der Bookesbeutel* (1896; rpt., Nendeln, Liechtenstein: Kraus, 1968).

47. Borkenstein, *Der Bookesbeutel*, 47.

48. Ibid., 15; my translation.

49. Johann Elias Schlegel, *Der geschäfftige Müßiggänger*, in his *Werke*, ed. Johann Heinrich Schlegel (Copenhagen and Leipzig: Proft und Rothen, 1773). Johann Elias is not to be confused with his nephews, the far better-known August Wilhelm and Friedrich Schlegel, writer-theoreticians of German Romanticism. For more on the Enlightenment playwright, see Elisabeth M. Wilkinson, *Johann Elias Schlegel: A German Pioneer in Aesthetics* (Darmstadt: Wissenschaftliche Buchgesellschaft, 1973).

50. Christian Fürchtegott Gellert, *Die Betschwester*, in *Lustspiele* (1747; rpt., Stuttgart: Metzler, 1966).

51. See John Van Cleve, *Harlequin Besieged*, 90–101.

52. For a general survey of "Empfindsamkeit," see Helmut de Boor and Richard Newald, *Die deutsche Literatur vom Späthumanismus zur Empfindsamkeit*, in *Geschichte der deutschen Literatur von den Anfängen bis zur Gegenwart*, 6th ed., vol. 5 (Munich: Beck, 1967).

53. Gellert, *Lustspiele*, 169–70; my translation.

Chapter Four

Bach in the Midst of Religious Transition

Joyce Irwin

To a historian struggling to grasp the role of music in early eighteenth-century German Lutheranism, the frank admission of a contemporary music theorist that church music styles were confusing and changing is refreshing. Friedrich Erhardt Niedt, writing in the third part of his *Musicalische Handleitung* in 1717, was convinced "that not even a composer can tell me what the correct church style is nowadays."[1] Musical styles, it seems, were changing as quickly and irrationally as dress fashions. Although he recognizes as many as three acceptable genres of church music—motets, concerted music, and arias—his advice to church musicians is deceptively simple: one should inquire as to the listeners' musical preferences before choosing. His solution lies in inclusivity: "In this way he has all the rules of the church style together unmistakably" (38). Such a pragmatic approach defies our efforts to paint a neat picture of church music trends in Bach's time. Were any congregations so unanimous in their taste that the choice was obvious? Certainly German Lutherans as a whole were not unanimous, as the acrimonious debates of the late seventeenth and early eighteenth centuries demonstrate.[2]

Beginning with Theophilus Grossgebauer's 1655 work *Wächterstimme aus dem verwüsteten Zion (Voice of the Watchman from ravaged Zion)*, some Lutherans had divided church music styles into good solid, sober, German music and flighty, tumultuous, Italian music. Grossgebauer charged most of those making music in the churches with being unspiritual people, a charge which was broadened in the hands of subsequent participants in this debate into a demand that church music emanate only from regenerate persons.[3] Gottfried Vockerodt (1665–1717), a Pietist theologian and school rector in Gotha writing in the last decade of the seventeenth century, focused the debate on the question whether there could be any morally indifferent actions. Provoked less by innovations in church music than by student musicians' participation in opera and theater productions, Vockerodt regarded the French-influenced theater of the time as a threat to moral standards and devotion to God.[4] Those who were more in the forefront of culture, such as Johann Beer, novelist and concertmaster at the court in Weissenfels, felt there was plenty of room for harmless recreation in the large middle ground of morally neutral activities. He and his allies painted Vockerodt as another humorless foe of music.[5] In their defense of the moral middle ground, however, they left little room for an artistic middle ground, as if those who preferred older styles of music or called for deeper devotion on the part of musicians were necessarily in an opposing camp.

Niedt was one of the musicians who dared to defy the dualistic preconception that those who criticized the music styles of the time must be Pietists or fools. Not afraid to be labeled a "fool for Christ's sake," Niedt refused to adapt to the values of the gallant world, even if that made him suspect in the eyes of his colleagues (40). Indeed, he reported that he had barely escaped the "Inquisition" that ensued following his warnings that the heart must accord with that which is sung by the mouth. He was protected from the "rage and fury of some clergy" by "a person in high position," who defended him from the expulsion that had driven some of his friends from territory to territory (39).[6]

Other respected musicians who warned against musical abuses include Andreas Werckmeister and Johann Kuhnau. Werckmeister, known in musical circles primarily for his tuning systems, also commented on the proper use of music and chastised church musicians for seeking their own rather than God's glory. In a 1691 work, he charged that there were many music directors, cantors, organists, instrumental musicians, and singers who thought little about honoring God and stimulating devotion in the listeners; in fact, they often slandered others in the search for their own glory.[7] Johann Kuhnau, Bach's predecessor in the St. Thomas cantorate, ended his novel *Der Musicalische Quack-Salber* (1700) with a description of "The true virtuoso and blissful musician" that stresses the importance of a morally upright manner of life and appropriate use of musical skill as a gift of God.[8]

We have no evidence that either Werckmeister or Kuhnau was ostracized for daring to criticize musicians, but Werckmeister recognized that the abuses had led some to take an extreme position: "some otherwise devout and faithful men and theologians have taken offense at music to the extent that they have thrown out the baby with the bath water and do not want to endure good music, the noble gift of God, in worship."[9] Even when positions were more nuanced, the tendency to classify persons of the early eighteenth century into opposing camps— orthodox or Pietist—was characteristic of the time, as we learn from Niedt. Some writers had in fact so escalated the differences of opinion that the ensuing war of words left little space for compromise. Though musicians such as Werckmeister, Kuhnau, and Niedt admitted there was a legitimate cause for concern, others refused to listen to criticism. From the latter perspective, anyone who regarded

musicians' moral state as a prerequisite to good composing or music performance deserved to be classified as Pietist and to be considered an enemy of music.

In time, however, the clear lines of demarcation between Pietist and orthodox
began to blur. When, for example, Pietist leader August Hermann Francke came
to Halle in 1692, he met fierce opposition from the orthodox clergy of the town;
over the next two decades, however, his attention turned away from the more
controversial aspects of Pietism, such as visions and prophecies, to educational
and social reforms. As his accomplishments in Halle gained recognition and
influence both in Germany and throughout the world, opposition from the
orthodox clergy declined. Johannes Wallmann points to Francke's cordial reception in Leipzig in 1719 as evidence that "the Pietism of Halle was no longer perceived as threatening by the orthodox clergy."[10]

Pietism's different manifestations and shifting image complicate the attempt
to describe Bach's relationship to Pietism. Why, if Pietists were opposed to complex
or elaborate church music, would Bach have books by Pietists or pietistically-
inclined writers in his personal library? Why, if Pietists were characterized by an
individualistic, emotional approach to religion as contrasted with a doctrinal,
theocentric approach, would Bach have chosen highly subjective texts, unless he
was a Pietist? The answer may be found partly in the realization that in some
respects people of the eighteenth century, whether Pietist or orthodox, had
more in common with each other than with people of either the sixteenth or the
twentieth century. Another part of the answer is to search for a more satisfactory
understanding of Pietism in relation to music.

The presence in Bach's library of books by Johann Arndt (1555–1621) and
Heinrich Müller (1631–75), mystically-inclined pre-Pietists, or by Philip Spener
(1635–1705), who is credited with starting the Pietist movement, does not in
itself indicate a tendency toward, or an affiliation with, Pietism. If we were able
to compare the theological libraries of his colleagues, those without any such
books would probably be in the minority. Nor is the number of religious works
in his possession in any way extraordinary.[11]

Some insight into the standard content of a well-stocked bourgeois library of
1730 can be gained from *The Well-Designed and Abridged Housekeeping Magazine*
by an author named simply Bornemann or Bannormen.[12] This short book is
directed toward someone who is entrusted with managing a court or some other
aristocratic household, though the author indicates it may also guide those who
aspire to raise their own household to the same level of culture. After some 100
pages listing foods, including appetizers, main courses, and desserts for a princely
meal, then listing necessities for coffee and tea drinking and for pipe smoking,
then, furnishings and equipment for all rooms of the house, including surgical
instruments and emergency supplies, there are finally instructional books
for every contingency, not only material but also spiritual. The three pages of theological and devotional works are listed according to need, such as "for refreshing the spirit," "for repentance, confession and communion," "for thorough

Figure 4.1. "Sing and Play to the Lord in Your Hearts." Engraving from Heinrich Müller's *Geistliche Seelenmusik*, 1659. Courtesy of Herzog August Bibliothek, Wolfenbüttel.

extermination of all evil and fortification of the true faith." Given all the luxuries prescribed for the home, this could hardly be a Pietist household; yet many of the books recommended are those of Spener and the devotional writers before him who are often classified as pre-Pietist or early Pietist: Johann Arndt, Joachim Lütkemann (1608–55), Christian Scriver (1629–93), Heinrich Müller. Many of the authors and some of the works coincide with Bach's list, which leads to the conclusion that these writers were not categorized by the general public according to theological party but according to practical devotional usefulness.[13] Indeed, aside from a few works recommended for "a taste of the controversies," the works are non-technical religious literature in German as distinct from Latin academic theology. As Johannes Wallmann has pointed out, this characterizes Bach's so-called "theological library" as well.[14] A comparison of Bach's library with that of any academic theologian of the time would reveal how paltry his collection was, if the list we have is complete.[15] Bach was on his way toward furnishing his library according to the aristocratic standards of his day, but his theological reading does not appear to have been exceptional for his social status.

An inadequate understanding of the Pietist movement itself has contributed to the problem of evaluating Bach's library. To be sure, scholars have had great difficulty arriving at a consensus in defining Pietism, not agreeing on whether the central characteristic was theological, ecclesiological, or devotional. The most widely acknowledged elements are individualism and subjectivity, but these are also the most nebulous and least specific. As Wallmann notes, these are characteristics of a movement encompassing all of Europe as it turned away from the Aristotelianism of scholastic philosophy, from confessional polemics, and from static external religious traditions. To this extent, it "runs parallel with the European Enlightenment," he points out.[16] From a slightly different perspective, Elke Axmacher interprets Pietism as playing a transitional, mediating role between orthodoxy and Enlightenment in such theological issues as the shift away from an atonement-centered view of the crucifixion to mystical love of Jesus, the focus on conversion, on experience, on renewal of life. In all of this, Pietism stands very close to the Enlightenment, but we must be clear that it is not an Enlightenment that—as an interpretation of the movement influenced perhaps too much by French or English sources would have us think—sought to empty religion of all that is non-rational but one which instead sought to actualize the natural in religion.[17] Pietism above all was an attempt to put belief into practice, to show that it made a difference in the way life was lived; the movement therefore criticized those persons whose lives could not be distinguished from unbelievers and those religious ceremonies that did not contribute to improving moral behavior or increasing religious devotion. Carol Baron suggests that many elements of Pietism were shared with other contemporaneous movements such as Jansenism and Hasidism.[18]

The rejection of theory in favor of practice characterized areas of eighteenth-century life other than religion. Expounding on the principles of musical composition, Johann David Heinichen identified the theoretical approach as outdated, though a source of lingering controversy: "The main . . . cause for dis-agreement is the failure of both sides to agree on the first principle on which everything in music depends: whether music and its rules are regulated by the Ear or by the so-called Reason? The old musicians side more with Reason, but the new with the ear".[19] Heinichen sided decisively with the new: "As we must now admit unanimously that our *Finis musices* is to stir the affections and to delight the ear, the true *Objectum musices*, it follows that we must establish all our musical rules according to the Ear".[20] Heinichen attributed a poor understand-ing of Reason to earlier composers who used mathematical devices to arrange notes so that they looked good on paper. Reason rightly understood, he asserts, serves the ear as music's proper end and employs all its skill toward the goal of pleasing the ear.

In some respects, then, the goal of Pietists and of eighteenth-century musi-cians was similar: to move away from an abstract, theoretical method based on intellect to a practical method focusing on the response of the whole person. When we make such a comparison, however, we must keep in mind that this gen-eral description applies to Pietism in the broader sense, defined by Wallmann as "a religious line of thinking going back to Johann Arndt, reflected primarily in literary texts such as devotional works and spiritual poetry marked by pietistic characteristics."[21] Pietism in the narrower sense, by contrast, is "a socially tan-gible religious renewal movement which separates itself from orthodoxy and the beginning Enlightenment and organizes itself independently through forma-tion of groups and congregations."[22] Only in this narrow sense is it possible to distinguish clearly between Pietist and orthodox; Pietism in its broader sense was more a defining characteristic of the age than a mark distinguishing one person from another. Bach's choice of Pietistic texts for his cantatas, therefore, reflects the type of poetry available to him and the linguistic style of the age, not an affili-ation with a religious movement.

Pietism in the broader sense shared much with the musical approach espoused by Heinichen, which aimed at moving the affections. Although emo-tionalism is not the defining characteristic of Pietism that some would have it be,[23] the emphasis on involvement of more than just the mind did lend itself to strong feelings and religious experiences. August Hermann Francke, next to Spener the most significant Pietist leader, is said to have responded to the ques-tion "What is the love of God?" with a statement placing priority on feelings: "It is of such a nature, that it must be felt, in order to be understood."[24] This shared emphasis on emotional response, whether to music or to God, has led some observers to wonder why there was so much antagonism between Pietists and musicians. The distinction between the broader and narrower senses of Pietism helps to clarify that the commonalities are found in the broader view; the nar-rower group of Pietists recognized that the emotional response might be to the external stimuli and not to the stirrings of the Holy Spirit. In such a case the result is shallow emotionalism, not a change of heart.[25]

It was, indeed, not Pietists but orthodox and Enlightenment thinkers who developed the connection between music's power to move the affections and religion's ability to stir feelings. Whereas music had consistently been credited with the power to move hearers to greater devotion, the development of the "doctrine of the affections" in music lent itself to this purpose. In the German arena this doctrine is attributable primarily to Athanasius Kircher, a Jesuit polymath whose 1650 work *Musurgia universalis sive ars magna consoni et dissoni* influenced German musical thought for much of the next hundred years.[26] It drew on the psychological/scientific understanding of the day, based on ancient medical writings, which taught that the affections had a physiological basis in the balance of humors or bodily fluids (black bile, yellow bile, blood, and phlegm) that determined one's temperament. To hear music is a physiological sensation that has repercussions through the body on the psyche.[27] In the late seventeenth century in Germany, the opera was the context in which music's ability to stimulate these responses was most fully explored. In 1700, however, Erdmann Neumeister, pastor in Hamburg, saw the potential of this style of music for expressing and arousing religious affections as well.[28] He proposed the cantata style as a modified operatic form for church. Given that there had been considerable controversy regarding the permissibility of Christians performing or attending operas, it was predictable that cantatas of this sort would be seen as a secular perversion of church music. The guidelines for church music style and theatrical style had been regarded as quite distinct by most Lutherans up to this point, even if some musicians had flouted the rules.[29]

After Neumeister's innovation, writers knew they needed to be cautious in treading unfamiliar territory. In Johann Kuhnau's "Treatise on Liturgical Texts Settings" of 1709, we observe both a hesitation to blur the distinction between church and theatrical style ("by displaying here nothing of the madrigal style that pertains to arias and recitatives, I can more easily avoid any suspicion of writing theatrical music") and yet an awareness that the old distinctions were no longer generally understood or accepted ("only very few people know the essential difference between the church and theatrical styles").[30] Similarly sensitive to both old and new ways of thinking about musical style, Gottfried Tilgner, writing the preface to the 1717 edition of Neumeister's cantatas,[31] defended the new style against its critics by assuring them that there were still restrictions on church style. Not everything is appropriate or acceptable. If a text concerning the suffering of Christ were to be set to the melody of a folie d'Espagne, or a Resurrection text to a courant or gigue, the person responsible would have to be considered a simpleton if not a godless blasphemer. The use of recitatives, on the other hand, is completely appropriate; after all, the Our Father, the words of institution, the Gospels, and other religious texts are sung by the clergy in this manner. As for the many textual repetitions and da capo musical repetitions in arias, critics should remember that the Psalms also have several examples of repetitions (Psalms 148, 150 and especially 136). A single statement does not stir the listener's affections and move the spirit as effectively as does repetition.

Most of all, however, the objections seemed to center on the desire to dissociate sacred music from secular: some seemed to consider music that was the least bit cheerful to be a deadly sin; many thought that too many instruments playing at the same time disturbed the sacred quiet of the Sabbath; above all the critics objected to adapting melodies that were known to listeners from worldly contexts. This often happens, notes Tilgner, in those locations where the same person is responsible for music in both church and opera house. Tilgner responds that circumstances can often excuse something which in principle is objectionable, but furthermore the process has frequently gone the other direction (most religious melodies have been appropriated for worldly, even drinking songs), and this does not disturb anyone's devotion in the worship service. Both Tilgner's preface and Kuhnau's treatise serve to caution twentieth-century interpreters who too blithely talk about the unity of sacred and secular in the Lutheran tradition on the basis of Luther's doctrine of vocation[32] or of the legend of his using drinking songs as the basis for his chorales. Even if this is a theologically sound position, it was not uniformly accepted among Lutherans. Neumeister's cantatas would not have created such a stir had the unity of sacred and secular been a foregone conclusion.

Whereas the two decades following Neumeister's innovation were a time of caution in advocating theatrical style in church music, Gottfried Ephraim Scheibel, writing in 1721, offered a whole-hearted defense of stylistic unity. He admitted that the general opinion held by the best musicians and composers was that church style had to be different from secular style.[33] He would accept this opinion, however, if only someone could explain to him how joy and sorrow and other affections could be divided between the two. The object might differ, admittedly, but the affection is the same. The musical tone which gives pleasure in the opera can do the same in the church, just with a different object of the pleasure.[34] Crucial to this position is a positive understanding of affections and sensations as natural phenomena. Following the humoral psychology mentioned with respect to Kircher, Scheibel explains the physiological aspect of affections. Every sensation is either internal or external; the former affect the soul, the latter the body. Music acts first on the external senses, but then the soul receives the idea from the senses and begins to move into action. The response varies from person to person, however, depending on one's temperament, whether melancholic, sanguine, choleric, or phlegmatic. Melancholic persons, because of their thick blood and slow circulation, prefer slow, sad, serious music. The frequent musical dissonances correspond to dissonances of the spirit such as fear and sorrow, and thus by natural sympathy melancholic persons are moved by such music. Scheibel's explanations, as we see, are not moral judgments on the state of a person's soul but rather analyses of different personality types as based on physiological types.

Scheibel's perspective is remarkably different from Luther's theology of music in the seventeenth century. One of the passages of Scripture commonly used to demonstrate music's value was the story of David playing the harp for King Saul, reported in 1 Samuel 16:23. The biblical text describes Saul's problem as an evil spirit, and Martin Luther had treated it as such. Because the problem had a supernatural basis, Saul's cure, according to Luther, did not rest primarily in the sound of the music but in the words of the Psalms which David must have sung as he played. Much as Luther believed in the value of music, it was the text, not the tune, that was essential; the Psalter is "a sweet, comforting, delightful song, even if one reads forth or says the bare words without notes."[35] The Word of God, not the sound of music, has the power to drive away demons: "For it does not go well with the evil spirit when God's Word is sung or preached in correct faith."[36] David's contribution to the cure, as Luther saw it, lay not in his musical skills as such but in the faith from which he sang. The same point was brought out in the following century by a popularizing Lutheran theologian, Christoph Frick, who wrote a book on music: "David struck a spiritual song from the bottom of his heart and sang on in fervent devotion to Christ."[37] Another early seventeenth-century theologian, Balthasar Bidembach, credited David most of all with choosing appropriate music, which meant that he avoided styles of music associated with non-religious purposes: "David did not play a dance on the harp . . . no entertaining melody which sounds nice to the ears, for the devil does not let himself be driven away by nice sounds [klingen und lauten]; rather, David would have played spiritual melodies, though neither did the tone itself drive the devil away, but David undoubtedly sang along. And he sang no mercenaries' or knights' songs nor bawdy songs; instead, he sang a Psalm or a song of God's omnipotence, goodness and gracious promises."[38] Medical historian Werner Kümmel, who cites Bidembach in an essay on melancholy and the power of music, shows that with some notable exceptions, the pre-eighteenth-century interpretation of this passage rejected naturalistic explanations. Interestingly, a sixteenth-century effort at a naturalistic explanation came from a marginal character of the Reformation who bordered on Anabaptism: Martin Borrhaus, in his biblical commentaries of 1557, expounded on the four genres of music and their differing effects on the affections, concluding that soft, fast, well-ordered sounds called forth a happy mood.[39] Some elements of a naturalistic explanation were introduced by Catholic theologians and Calvinist physicians, but not until Kircher's work became known in Germany did this approach enter Lutheran thought, and even then the naturalistic humors and the supernatural spirits often mingled in a single theory.[40]

To say that nature and supernature were not clearly distinct in the early modern mind, however, is not the same as to say that sacred and secular were not clearly distinct. I would venture to suggest that it was only with the adoption of a naturalistic approach that the secular could be fully affirmed and a secular style adapted for sacred purposes. Indeed, Scheibel approaches not only the psychological effects of music but also religion itself from an empirical perspective. Rather than regarding worship as biblically grounded or as a response to divine commandment, he sees worship as emerging from a natural impulse: "It is grounded in nature that when a human being recognizes God he will as a consequence honor Him outwardly with words and deeds."[41] In comparing forms of worship, therefore, Scheibel uses not biblical or theological arguments but practical observations of human behavior. Granting that for genuine believers any form of worship is appealing, he nevertheless believes that the vast majority of people do not fit into that category and need to be enticed to come to church (27). A service without external appeal or embellishment will not stimulate them in the right direction. If they hear only the hymns they have heard since childhood, they will sing them mindlessly and be lulled into an inattentive state. When their senses are engaged, however, their minds will also respond (28); if they have been moved by beautiful music, they will be more receptive to the sermon (29).

This is equivalent to the commonplace notion that music is an aid to devotion, but Scheibel's analysis has a more behavioristic slant. Presented in terms of observation about human nature, the position moves away from the standard Lutheran view that music is a gift of God and that the heart and voice must be attuned to God for the music to be acceptable. Scheibel does not place priority on the spiritual state of the performer except as it affects the hearer. The public persona of the church musician is important in order not to offend listeners and preachers with godless living. Furthermore, if the musicians are not noble and Christian, it is not likely that they will be able to increase the listener's devotion (55–56). A respectable, sober lifestyle is also important for the sake of the music; too much pleasure-seeking and carousing leads to carelessness, whereas a musician and composer must be attentive to the smallest details (57). Still, the musician needs to get around in the world and to learn the state of church music in different locations in order to keep up to date. Scheibel's musician is no world-denying ascetic but lives honorably according to the moral standards of a Christian society. Although musical skill is of utmost importance, virtuous living reinforces that skill. There is therefore no direct conflict with those who said that a Christian musician must first of all be Christian, then a musician; yet the emphasis is significantly different, for the reasoning has such a strong practical basis. Not the danger of eternal damnation but the risk of social dishonor and musical ineptitude are the motivating factors for a morally upstanding life.

Scheibel's practical reasoning is evident also in one interesting side issue: the question whether women should be allowed to sing in church. He would rather have them sing in church than in the opera and considers it a waste that they may not use their considerable talents to the glory of God and the edification of others. Good boy sopranos are rare, because they have too little experience and last such a short span of time, and falsetto singers are not always available; therefore women could readily fill the need. Scheibel has no illusions about changing tradition quickly in this area, but, in his common sense approach to Scripture, he dismisses the biblical argument against women speaking in church as not applying to this issue (59–61).

That women were appearing on German stages was in itself a relatively new phenomenon, but that Scheibel wanted to extend this practice to the church was just one aspect of his aim of bringing church music into the main stream of the musical culture. Since the opera is the place where the techniques for moving the affections have been developed, operatic style should serve as the model for achieving the same end in a religious context. Scheibel offers several examples where through some textual changes the same music and poetic form could be used in both opera and church cantata.[42] Because he does not see a distinction between religious joy or sorrow and worldly joy or sorrow, except insofar as they are directed toward different objects, there need be no distinction between religious and worldly music. If music's purpose, as he indicates, is to move the affections rather than, say, to glorify God directly, then it must be evaluated in terms of how effectively it accomplishes that end.

This explanation of the use of the same music for both sacred and secular texts can be applied to Bach's compositions. In many instances, Bach borrowed music from one of his compositions to use in another, often transferring it from a secular to a sacred context. This parody practice has puzzled Bach interpreters, giving rise to explanations both practical (Bach was too busy to compose new music for every occasion)[43] and theological (he regarded all of life as sacred and did not distinguish between sacred and secular music).[44] While these factors may have played a part, the rhetorical explanation provided by Scheibel is the most helpful: the art of arousing emotions is common to both religious and secular music. The parody process—far from being a shortcut—requires skill in the use of musical figures and a careful attention to the relation between text and music.[45]

Scheibel's work was mentioned very favorably by one of the most prolific and influential musical commentators of the century, Johann Mattheson. In his *Critica Musica* (1722), Mattheson praised the work not only because Scheibel had first praised him but, more importantly, because "I have never read anything like it which is so much in accordance with my own sentiments."[46] In this section Mattheson was concerned with the quality of poetic texts being used by composers and with musicians' skills in setting texts effectively. To this end Scheibel's eighth chapter treating musical texts is accorded special note by Mattheson.[47] Another viewpoint the two men held in common was the advocacy of female singers in church. Mattheson reported in 1739 that he had introduced female singers at the cathedral against considerable opposition, but that they had eventually become well accepted, even though no other church choir in Hamburg yet allowed women.[48]

Although we cannot know whether Bach was aware of Scheibel's work, Bach practiced much of what Scheibel advocated: the use of recitatives and arias for giving expression to religious affections, the adaptation of music used in secular contexts to sacred texts, and the concern for relating poetry and music skillfully and effectively. Mattheson called on Bach among others to speak out in support of the theatrical church style against its critics: "Speak! Bach, Graupner, Händel, Heinichen, Hurlebusch, Keiser, Stöltzel, Telemann, and everyone else in today's world who knows how to move hearts through the art of music (Ton-Kunst)."[49]

This last phrase suggests a significant difference between advocates of operatic cantata style and its critics. Emeritus professor of law Joachim Meyer, writing in 1726 about the "recent spread of theatrical church music," charged that this style did not fulfill the two goals of "honor of God and edification of neighbor" ("*die ehre Gottes und des Nechsten Erbauung*") but that it served more to build the reputation of the musicians.[50] This formulation of the two-fold purpose of church music was standard in the Lutheran tradition; the degree of emphasis placed on each one was the deciding factor in differentiating theological positions, with the orthodox emphasizing more the honor of God and the Pietists stressing the edification of the neighbor.

As the eighteenth century dawned, however, subtle changes in the formulation of music's two-fold purpose signaled a new view of music more characteristic of the Age of Enlightenment. With Friedrich Erhard Niedt's identification in 1700 of the goal of music as "the honor of God and the recreation of the spirit" ("*Gottes-Ehre und Recreation des Gemüts*"),[51] we observe a shift away from a more other-directed, devotional emphasis to a self-directed, pleasure-oriented emphasis. Indeed, in the same chapter Niedt also uses another phrase which even more clearly expresses the element of pleasure: "to the honor of God and the permissible pleasure of the spirit" ("*zur Ehre Gottes und zulässiger Ergetzung des Gemüths*"[52]). Nevertheless, Niedt acknowledges the danger of excessive or impermissible pleasure in music-making and warns that those who misuse music for the purpose of arousing lustful desires are "musicians of the devil" whose music is a "disgraceful bawling."

The two phrases, "to the honor of God and the permissible pleasure of the spirit" and "the honor of God and recreation of the spirit" appear in Bach's *Generalbasslehre* of 1738, along with the admonition that where this is lacking there is a "devilish bawling." While the wording is not exactly that of Niedt, the resemblance is so strong that we may assume some connection between Niedt and Bach. As a student of Johann Nicolaus Bach, Johann Sebastian's cousin, Niedt may have been transmitting Bach family methodologies that Johann Sebastian also learned from his forebears.[53] We should probably refrain from relying too much on these phrases for an insight into Bach's theology, since we cannot know whether he chose this formulation over other possible wordings or merely adapted a text close at hand. Nevertheless, it is more reasonable to interpret his position from within the eighteenth-century context than to reach back to earlier Lutheran ideas. Efforts by some Lutheran scholars to equate the term *Recreation* with spiritual rejuvenation in a strictly theological sense are in my view not persuasive.[54] Rather, use of the term "permissible pleasure" dismisses the relevance of the strict Pietist position that was suspicious of the pleasures connected with music. The term appeared in Christopher Rauch's 1682 defense of operas, where operas are grouped with other recreational activities such as walk-ing, hunting, socializing in pubs, and playing board and card games.[55] Rauch did find theological significance in such recreation for its ability to refresh the soul and strengthen the "animal spirits," but his position was developed in opposition to those Pietist critics who believed there was no middle ground between morally beneficial and morally detrimental actions. Johann Beer, writing in 1697 in a continuation of the controversy about operas, charged his Pietist opponent Vockerodt with turning "permissible" activities into sins and making everything a matter of conscience.[56] In reaction to the "precisionists," referring to the Dutch Calvinists who may have influenced Vockerodt, Beer began to defend recreation as a morally neutral area. A decade later, Johann Kuhnau makes a similar dis-tinction between religious devotion as evoked by sacred music and "innocent pleasure" as evoked by theatrical music.[57] Bach undoubtedly knew Kuhnau's *Treatise*, at least after he moved to Leipzig, but we cannot assume that he was aware of the controversial context of the terms "permissible pleasure" or "recre-ation." Nevertheless, his choice in 1738 of the formulation including the term "permissible pleasure" rather than the one calling for "edification of the neigh-bor," which he had used earlier in Cöthen for his *Orgel-Büchlein*, places him among those progressive Lutherans who affirmed the value of aesthetic pleasure.

It was primarily in the expression of affections and the endorsement of pleas-ant affections that the theoreticians and composers of cantatas differed from their critics. Throughout the seventeenth century, reform-minded preachers had warned against mere titillation of the ears. Music without a text that could be understood "may serve for pleasure and delight but not for edification in Christianity," wrote Christian Kortholt in 1672.[58] Johann Conrad Dannhauer, one of Spener's professors in Strasbourg, disapproved of the "new ridiculous Italian jumps and siren songs that aim not at the joy of the spiritual heart but at wanton worldly joy."[59] Suspicion of auditory pleasures in the history of Christian attitudes toward music goes at least as far back as Augustine, who wavered "between the danger that lies in gratifying the senses and the benefits which, as I know from experience, can accrue from singing."[60] Although the mainstream of Lutheran orthodoxy emphasized the "benefits" when citing Augustine, there were frequent reminders from reform-minded theologians of the need for balance and caution in regard to the senses. Therefore, when Scheibel chal-lenged those who wanted to distinguish stylistically between sacred and secular music and demonstrated that religious joy or sorrow differed from non-religious joy or sorrow only in the object of the affection, he was breaking with previous tradition. Similarly, Mattheson, in saying "The sense of hearing is also, so far as we know, an attribute not of the body but of the soul,"[61] affirmed the unity of physical and spiritual nature to a degree unknown in the Lutheranism of previ-ous centuries.

When Bach wrote a memorandum in 1730 to the town council of Leipzig ask-ing for better support for his music program, he appealed to changing tastes in music as a major reason for needing a funding increase. His apparent recognition of the listeners' taste as a criterion for musical selections in the church is reminiscent of Niedt's earlier advice to choose music according to the listeners' preferences.

> Now, however, that the state of music is quite different from what it was, since our artistry has increased very much, and the *gusto* has changed astonishingly, and accordingly the former style of music no longer seems to please our ears, and considerable help is therefore all the more needed, in order to choose and appoint such musicians as will satisfy the present musical taste, master the new kinds of music, and thus be in a position to do justice to the composer and his work—now the few *beneficia*, which should have been rather increased than diminished, have been withdrawn entirely from the *chorus musicus*. It is anyhow somewhat strange that German musicians are expected to be capable of performing at once and *ex tempore* all kinds of music, whether it come from Italy or France, England or Poland, just as may be done, say, by those virtuosos for whom the music is written and who have studied it long beforehand.[62]

Whether Bach was sincere in wanting to adapt to changing musical tastes or was using the argument as a ploy to accomplish his own goals is not our concern here.[63] For understanding the context in which Bach lived, it is important to observe that he was very conscious of living in a culture that differed greatly from that of his forebears. The people he needed to please were not the opponents of foreign culture, such as Grossgebauer and Vockerodt, but the bourgeois citizens of a cosmopolitan society. By 1730 the controversy between Pietism and orthodoxy was largely irrelevant to Bach. The emerging new culture was one in which, as seen in Bornemann's *Housekeeping Magazine*, a reader of devotional literature might take delight in a multi-course gourmet meal followed by coffee and pipe smoking. Whether we apply the label "gallant" or "Enlightenment," the new world view affirmed secular activities as aspects of a whole person in a divinely created world.

Writing in 1752 to defend the use of dance rhythms in church music, Caspar Rüetz, cantor in Lübeck, illustrated this perspective when he asked, "If we should not bring into the church even the least thing that belongs to dancing, we would have to leave feet and hands, indeed the whole body, at home."[64] For him the dance floor was no dishonorable or sinful place but rather "the school of elegance, courtesy and bodily dexterity."[65] And if church music could promote "hopping and jumping in the hearts of upright Christians,"[66] why should rhythms that produce such spiritual pleasure be avoided?

The progression from Scheibel's affirmation of the oneness of sacred and secular affections through Mattheson's identification of the ear as an attribute of the soul to Rüetz's recognition of dance rhythms as producing spiritual pleasure coincided roughly in time with Bach's tenure in Leipzig. The cantatas he produced during those years, incorporating many dance rhythms and sometimes parodying his own secular works, are evidence that these progressive writers were the ones providing a theological basis for Bach's compositional process. No longer was it possible to distinguish church style from theatrical or other secular styles. In the age of the Enlightenment, the natural world, which included the human body and its pleasures, was part of the evidence for God's existence and goodness, not a temptation and distraction from the spiritual realm.

Notes

1. Friedrich Erhardt Niedt, *Musicalische Handleitung*, part 3 (Hamburg: Bey sel. B. Schillers erben, 1717), 37. Further references to this work are cited in the text using the page number alone.

2. See Dorothea Beck, *Krise und Verfall der protestantischen Kirchenmusik im 18. Jahrhundert* (Inaug. diss., Halle-Wittenberg, 1951).

3. See Joyce Irwin, *Neither Voice nor Heart Alone: German Lutheran Theology of Music in the Age of the Baroque* (New York: Peter Lang, 1993), ch. 10, esp. 111–12.

4. Vockerodt drew attention to the issue by organizing a school presentation in 1696 in which Roman emperors Caligula, Claudius, and Nero were depicted as failing in office because they succumbed to the allure of theater and music. The program is described in his invitation, *Der Fürstenschule zu Gotha Hohe Förderer und Gönner . . . werden zu Denen öffentlichen Reden welche von Falscher Artzeney unrichtiger Gemüther gehalten werden sollen . . . eingeladen* (Gotha, 1696). Vockerodt's major presentation of his position is found in *Mißbrauch der freyen Künste insonderheit der Music* (Frankfurt: J. D. Zunner, 1697).

5. Beer's initial and most significant publication in this controversy was *Ursus murmurat (The Bear Growls)* (Weimar: Johann Andreas Müller, 1697). Others who opposed Vockerodt included Johann Christoph Wentzel, rector in Altenburg, and Johann Kristof Lorber, who wrote a long poem praising music, *Lob der edlen Musik* (Weimar: Johann Andreas Müller, 1696).

6. Niedt was born in Jena in 1674, matriculated at the University of Jena in 1694, and left for Copenhagen in 1700. Although there were some Pietist sympathizers in Jena, the university was a stronghold of Lutheran orthodoxy. Pamela L. Poulin, in her introduction to Friedrich Erhardt Niedt, *The Musical Guide, Parts 1 (1700/10), 2 (1721) and 3 (1717)*, trans. Pamela L. Poulin and Irmgard C. Taylor (Oxford: Clarendon Press, 1989), xviii, wonders whether Niedt left Jena for religious reasons or in hopes of finding employment.

7. Andreas Werckmeister, *Der edlen Music-Kunst, Würde, Gebrauch und Mißbrauch* (Frankfurt and Leipzig: Theodor Philipp Calvisius, 1691), 12–13.

8. Johann Kuhnau, *Der Musicalische Quack-Salber* (Dresden: Johann Christoph Mieth and Johann Christoph Zimmermann, 1700), 510–33.

9. Werckmeister, *Musicalische Paradoxal-Discourse* (Quedlinburg: Theodor Philipp Calvisius, 1707), 33.

10. Johannes Wallmann, *Der Pietismus* (Göttingen: Vandenhoeck & Ruprecht, 1990), 68.

11. Robin Leaver writes, "At his death Bach possessed a significant collection of theological books, which looks more like a pastor's working library than the library of a musician" ("Johann Sebastian Bach: Theological Musician and Musical Theologian,"

Bach: The Journal of the Riemenschneider Bach Institute 31/1 [2000], 32). This claim is made without any comparison to other personal libraries. One Lutheran pastor-theologian, Johann Friedrich Mayer, who had owned the copy of Luther's works that Bach bought in 1742, had a collection of about 18,000 books. For evidence of other vast book collections and of the growth of libraries during this period, see Jonathan I. Israel, *Radical Enlightenment: Philosophy and the Making of Modernity* (Oxford: Oxford University Press, 2001), 119–41.

12. Bannormen [Bornemann], *Der wohlangelegt- und kurtz gefasste Hausshaltungs-Magazin* (Frankfurt and Leipzig, 1730), 113–15. The book can be found in the Herzog August Bibliothek, Wolfenbüttel, call number Oe 84.

13. Works included in both lists are Arndt's *Wahres Christenthum*, Luther's *Hauss-Postille* and *Tischreden*, Heinrich Müller's *Erquickstunden* and *Liebes-Flamme*, August Pfeiffer's *Anti-Melancholicus* and possibly also *Lutherthum vor Luthern*, which may be the work listed as Pfeiffer's "Christenthum" in the list of books in Bach's estate. (Concerning this title, see Johannes Wallmann, "Johann Sebastian Bach und die 'Geistlichen Bücher' seiner Bibliothek" *Pietismus und Neuzeit*, 12 [1986]: 172.) Authors represented in both lists but with different works include Geyer, Hunnius, Olearius, and Spener. Hutter's *Compendium* does not appear in Bach's list, but it is generally accepted that he was well-schooled in this text. With fifty-six titles, the Housekeeping list is slightly longer than Bach's fifty-two.

14. Wallmann, "Johann Sebastian Bach und die 'Geistlichen Bücher' seiner Bibliothek," 173.

15. Christoph Wolff suggests that the books listed in Bach's estate may be only those that remained after works of more interest had already been removed. See Wolff, *Johann Sebastian Bach: The Learned Musician* (New York: W. W. Norton & Co., 2000), 334–35. Granted, the estate list cannot be compared with a published catalogue of a personal library available for purchase. To argue, however, on the basis of the estate list, that Bach's theological library was remarkable is unconvincing. A brief sampling of personal library catalogues as found, for instance, in the Herzog August Bibliothek in Wolfenbüttel reveals lists of theological works well over 100 pages long. See, among others, *Librorum ad Humaniora Studia, Litterariam, Civilem atque Ecclesiasticam Historiam* of Jacob Burckhard (Magdeburg, 1748), which contains 220 pages of philosophical and theological works and *Catalogi Bibliothecae Christiae* (Leipzig, 1757), with 138 pages of theological entries. For more titles of catalogues of private collections, see Gerhard Loh, ed., *Verzeichnis der Kataloge von Buchauktionen und Privatbibliotheken aus dem deutschsprachigen Raum*, 1607–1730 (Leipzig: Dr. Gerhard Loh, 1995).

16. Johannes Wallmann, *Der Pietismus*, 7.

17. Elke Axmacher, *"Aus Liebe will mein Heyland sterben." Untersuchungen zum Wandel des Passionsverständnisses im frühen 18. Jahrhundert*, Beiträge zur theologischen Bachforschung 2 (Neuhausen-Stuttgart: Hänssler, 1984).

18. See her article in this volume, 35–85.

19. Johann David Heinichen, *Der General-Bass in der Composition*, as translated by George J. Buelow, in *Thorough-Bass Accompaniment According to Johann David Heinichen* (Ann Arbor, Michigan: UMI Research Press, 1986), 310.

20. Ibid., 311.

21. Wallmann, *Der Pietismus*, 10.

22. Ibid., 10.

23. See Irwin, *Neither Voice nor Heart Alone*, ch. 9–11, and "German Pietists and Church Music in the Baroque Age," *Church History* 54/1 (March, 1985): 29–40.

24. From the Memoirs of August Hermann Francke, quoted in Dale Brown, *Understanding Pietism* (Grand Rapids, Michigan: William B. Eerdmans, 1978), 113.

25. Irwin, *Neither Voice nor Heart Alone*, 138–39.

26. Regarding Kircher's musical ideas, see Ulf Scharlau, *Athanasius Kircher (1601–1680) als Musikschriftsteller* (Marburg: Görich and Weiershäuser, 1969). For a general understanding of Kircher, see Joscelyn Godwin, *Athanasius Kircher: A Renaissance Man and the Quest for Lost Knowledge* (London: Thames and Hudson, 1979).

27. For a history of ideas concerning the relationship between music and the human body, see Werner Friedrich Kümmel, *Musik und Medizin: Ihre Wechselbeziehungen in Theorie und Praxis von 800 bis 1800* (Freiburg and Munich: Verlag Karl Alber, 1977).

28. See Philipp Spitta, *Johann Sebastian Bach*, trans. Clara Bell (London: Novello, Ewer & Co., 1884), 1:473. Neumeister's first four cantata cycles were not originally sold to the public but were sent to court chapels—the first to Weißenfels, the second to Rudelstadt, the third and fourth to Sachsen-Eisenach—and often disseminated informally by hand-made copies. In 1717 Gottfried Tilgner gathered these together and had them printed along with the new fifth cycle for wider distribution.

29. Irwin, *Neither Voice nor Heart Alone*, ch. 3.

30. Johann Kuhnau, "A Treatise on Liturgical Text Settings," in this volume, 219–26.

31. Gottfried Tilgner, "Preface," in Erdmann Neumeister, *Fünffache Kirch-Andachten bestehend in theils eintzeln, theils niemahls gedruckten Arien, Cantaten und Oden* (Leipzig, 1717).

32. A major tenet of Luther's theology was the "priesthood of all believers," by which he claimed that there is no essential difference between priests and laypersons, just a difference of occupation. Christians who do not have the vocation of preaching and administering sacraments nevertheless have spiritual status and contribute through their work, be it farming, carpentry, civil administration, or any other necessary and honorable vocation, to the good of the whole body of Christ. See, in particular, his "An Appeal to the Ruling Class of German Nationality As to the Amelioration of the State of Christendom," in John Dillenberger, ed., *Martin Luther: Selections from His Writings* (New York: Anchor Books, 1961), 407–12.

33. Gottfried Ephraim Scheibel, *Zufällige Gedancken von der Kirchen-Music wie sie heutiges Tages beschaffen ist* (Frankfurt and Leipzig: [Zu finden beym authore], 1721). (This volume 227–49).

34. Ibid., 35.

35. Martin Luther, "Von den letzten Worten Davids," in *D. Martin Luthers Werke* (Weimar, H. Böhlau, 1883–), 54:33.

36. Ibid., 34.

37. Christoph Frick (Friccius), *Music-Büchlein* (Lüneburg: J. und H. Stern 1631; reprint Leipzig: Zentralantiquariat der Dt. Demokrat. Republik, 1976). See further Joyce Irwin, "Shifting Alliances: The Struggle for a Lutheran Theology of Music," in Irwin, ed., *Sacred Sound: Music in Religious Thought and Practice* (Chico, California: Scholars Press, 1983), 59–60.

38. Quoted in Werner Kümmel, "Melancholie und die Macht der Musik: Die Krankheit König Sauls in der historischen Diskussion," *Medizinhistorisches Journal* 4(1969): 201.

39. Ibid., 201.

40. Ibid., 206–7.

41. Scheibel, *Zufällige Gedancken von der Kirchen-Music*, 19. Further references to this work are cited in the text using page numbers alone.

42. See translation in this volume, 238–40.

43. Malcolm Boyd, *Bach*, 3rd ed. (Oxford: Oxford University Press, 2000), 179.

44. Jaroslav Pelikan, *Bach Among the Theologians* (Philadelphia: Fortress Press, 1986), 139.

45. On Bach's mastery of this oratorical art, see Arnold Schmitz, "Die oratorische Kunst J. S. Bachs: Grundfragen und Grundlagen" in Walter Blankenburg, ed., *Johann Sebastian Bach* (Darmstadt: Wissenschaftliche Buchgesellschaft, 1970), 61–84. Michael Marissen, in "On the Musically Theological in J. S. Bach's Church Cantatas," *Lutheran Quarterly* 16/1 (2002): 48–64, argues that Bach sometimes finds meaning in a discrepancy between musical affect and verbal content, an argument that forces us to recognize that Scheibel's treatment is a helpful aid, not a complete guide, to the understanding of Bach's use of musical affect.

46. Johann Mattheson, *Critica Musica, d.i. Grundrichtige Untersuch- und Beurtheilung Vieler . . . Musicalischen Schrifften*, part 2 (Hamburg: [Auf Unkosten des Autor], 1722), 96.

47. Ibid., 101, fn.

48. Johann Mattheson, *Der vollkommene Capellmeister* (Hamburg: C. Herold, 1739), 868.

49. Johann Mattheson, *Der musicalische Patriot* (Hamburg: [Ans Licht gestellet von Mattheson], 1728), 218.

50. Joachim Meyer, *Unvorgreiffliche Gedancken über die neulich eingerissene theatralische Kirchen-Music* ([Lemgo], 1726), 3. Meyer (1661–1732) had at different times been cantor, professor of music, and professor of law and history at the Gymnasium in Göttingen. In 1717 he left teaching to practice law.

51. F. E. Niedt, *Musicalische Handleitung* 1 (Hamburg: Benjamin Schiller, 1700), quoted in *Bach-Dokumente II: Fremdschriftliche und gedruckte Dokumente zur Lebensgeschichte Johann Sebastian Bachs, 1685–1750* (Kassel: Bärenreiter, 1969), 334.

52. Ibid., 334.

53. Poulin, introduction to Niedt, *The Musical Guide*, xiii.

54. Oskar Söhngen (*Theologie der Musik* [Kassel: Johannes Stauda-Verlag, 1967]), 273, and Günther Stiller, *Johann Sebastian Bach and Liturgical Life in Leipzig* (St. Louis: Concordia Publishing House, 1984), 209, interpret the word "Recreation" theologically as new creation or "restoration." As I have argued in *Neither Voice nor Heart Alone*, 143–46, however, ordinary use of the word, then as now, had the connotation of pleasant leisure activities.

55. Christopher Rauch, *Theatrophania, entgegen gesetzet der so genanten Schrifft Theatromania* (Hannover: Wolfgang Schwendimann, 1682), 47.

56. Johann Beer, *Ursus Vulpinatur, List wieder List, oder Musicalische Fuchs-Jagdt* (Weissenfels: [In verlegung des Autors], 1697), 54.

57. See Johann Kuhnau, "A Treatise on Liturgical Text Settings" in this volume, 214–26.

58. Christian Kortholt, *Offentlicher Gottesdienst der alten und heutigen Christen: Absonderlich soviel die Sontags-Feir betrifft* (Frankfurt am Main: Wilhelm Serlin, 1672), 57.

59. Johann Conrad Dannhauer, *Catechismusmilch, oder Der Erklärung des christlichen Catechismi* (Strasbourg: Spoor, 1642), 1:524.

60. Saint Augustine, *Confessions*, trans R. S. Pine-Coffin (Baltimore: Penguin Books, 1961), 239 (Book 10, 33).

61. Johann Mattheson, *Der neue Göttingische aber viel schlechter, als die alten Lacedämonischen, urtheilenden Ephorus* (Hamburg: Verlag des Verfassers, Johann Christoph Kissner, 1727), 6.

62. J. S. Bach, "Short But Most Necessary Draft for a Well-Appointed Church Music," in Hans T. David and Arthur Mendel, eds., *The Bach Reader* (New York: W. W. Norton & Co., 1966), 123.

63. See the discussion of this question in Laurence Dreyfus, *Bach and the Patterns of Invention* (Cambridge, MA.: Harvard University Press, 1996), 33–35.

64. Caspar Rüetz, *Widerlegte Vorurtheile von der Beschaffenheit der heutigen Kirchenmusic und von der Lebens-Art einiger Musicorum* (Lübeck: Peter Böckmann, 1752), 35.

65. Ibid., 34.

66. Ibid., 41.

Chapter Five

Bach's Situation in the Cultural Politics of Contemporary Leipzig

Ulrich Siegele

Edited and abridged by Carol K. Baron with translation
assistance from Susan H. Gillespie with Ruben Weltsch

*This study describes the negotiations over the appointment of a new cantor for the
Thomasschule following Johann Kuhnau's death.[1] The negotiations give a clear picture of
the position that the Leipzig town councilors assigned to Bach within the cultural-political
context of the time. They also shed light on the members of the Leipzig Town Council who
were responsible for filling this position. Their deliberations take place within a specific
political context, in which the town councilors were committed to factions created by the prevailing political forces functioning at that time: one protecting the city's prerogatives of self-
government that were rooted in the traditional system of estates, the other supporting the
absolutist aims of the current electoral government. The author's recent article, "Bach and
the Domestic Politics of Electoral Saxony,"[2] describes the political structures in place in
Saxony during the first half of the eighteenth century, which are represented by these factions, and how the tensions they created conditioned the fulfillment of Bach's vocational
goals—both assisting and restricting them—while they may also have played a role in
shaping Bach's music. As the members of the Leipzig Town Council sought appropriate
candidates and deliberated on their qualifications, they articulated concerns that also
included the complex philosophical and religious ramifications that emanated from this
political situation.*

When the appointment of a new cantor for the Thomasschule became necessary
following Johann Kuhnau's death on June 5, 1722, there were two factions in
the Leipzig Town Council. One faction desired to see the position of cantor
filled along the lines of the traditional teaching post. The occupant of the office
certainly should know music as well as possible, but he should be equally competent in the realm of academic instruction—a teacher and musician in one. I will

Figure 5.1. Marketplace with Leipzig Town Hall on right, with small shops below. Engraving by Johann Stridebeck, ca. 1700.

call this faction the "Cantor faction." The other faction wanted to see the position filled along the lines of a modern municipal music directorship. The occupant should be highly qualified, if possible even a musician with the highest possible qualifications, with skills as a composer, performer, conductor, and organizer. Furthermore, he should be exempted from the instructional responsibilities hitherto attached to the position in order to concentrate solely on music. I will call this faction the "Kapellmeister faction."

The entire Town Council, which had thirty-two members in 1723, was organized into three constituent councils and three mayors, comprising one sitting and two non-sitting councils, each of which was chaired by one of the mayors. They took turns performing their duties, according to an annual rotation, for terms of office that extended from September of one calendar year through August of the next, with the transition occurring on the last Monday in August. The entire council met only when there were issues of the utmost importance to discuss. Decisions that exceeded the competency of one council but did not require the involvement of all three were made by the Executive Council, which was composed of the most senior members of all three councils and known as the Council of Elders or the *Herren Seniores*.[3] The Executive Council was the body invested with decision-making power when it came to the appointment of the new cantor.

The Leipzig Town Council was an oligarchy wherein wealth and power created a ruling elite that governed the city. At this time, those who held seats on the Council were generally university graduates trained in jurisprudence and, most often, the heirs of Leipzig's wealthiest merchants, members of the patrician families who were committed to their own special interests. Prepared to be administrators, legislators, and judges, they held positions in all of these capacities, frequently at the same time. Through its constituent members, the Council influenced or controlled most aspects of local society— taxation, the judicial system, church and school governance, and the University— although each of these institutions exercised, and sometimes fiercely guarded, their autonomy. The councilors simultaneously held Council seats and were on the boards of the churches, the consistory (the Electoral authority in ecclesiastical and educational affairs), the University, the assessors' office, the judicial courts, and so on. Furthermore, previously elected members nominated and elected people to fill Council seats that were vacated.

Access to seats on the Council was also possible through so-called, "Electoral recommendation." These seats were gained by lawyers who had honed their legal skills as court advisers and administrators. In the event of contention between the interests of the city and the Electoral government, one could expect the first loyalty of these councilors to be to the Elector. Although Leipzig was an electoral territory and, in that sense, its town council constitutionally represented the sovereign, intrusion by the Elector violated the feudal concept of the city as an estate (like the estate of the nobility) with its own self-governing privileges and powers that limited the power of the electoral prince. Efforts to expand electoral power under absolutism were experienced as attempts to impinge on previously understood privileges, a source of sensitivity particularly in Leipzig, where self-esteem was born of economic power and concomitant political clout. Even under absolutism, the Leipzig city government could exert considerable negotiating independence and power because its services to the Elector were irreplaceable: supplying goods and money. (The paths of access to the city government, as well as its oligarchic nature, are demonstrated in the two model biographies toward the end of this chapter.)

This rotating system of government can be characterized as an all-party coalition of three parties, in which one party was in charge. A balance of power within this kind of system was guaranteed by the fact that while the head of government could act decisively during his year in office to promote the realization of his own faction's ideas and sideline the ideas of the other two parties, he also had to reckon with the fact that in the two following years the other two parties would be in a better position to realize their ideas, while his ideas could be pushed aside.

The Executive Council consisted of the three mayors plus nine additional members. The following is a list of the twelve men who served on the Executive Council in 1722, in their prescribed order of voting. Their age at that time is given in parentheses, and the faction to which they owed allegiance, when known, is indicated as CF (Cantor faction) and KF (Kapellmeister faction). The three mayors were Abraham Christoph Platz (64, mayor since 1705), CF; Gottfried Lange (50, mayor since 1719), KF; and Adrian Steger (60, mayor since 1721), CF. Other members were Johann Franz Born (53), KF; Johann August Hölzel (55), CF; Gottfried Wagner (70); Zacharias Jöcher (46); Gottfried Konrad Lehmann (61); Johann Ernst Kregel Sr., CF; (70), Johann Job (58), CF; Johann Jakob Kees (45); and Peter Hohmann Sr. (59). One must picture a group with an average age of about sixty. The mayor in office in 1721/22 was Adrian Steger; in 1722/23 it was Gottfried Lange. Mayor Platz was the spokesman of the Cantor faction; his second was Mayor Steger. The spokesman of the Kapellmeister faction was Mayor Lange; Johann Franz Born seconded him. The official minutes of their meetings are a record not so much of their deliberations as of the resulting decisions.[4] Generally eschewing the majority vote to arrive at decisions, the Executive Council debated pros and cons and made its selections, subject only to confirmation by election in the Three Councils. The minutes document the objectives and power relations that characterized the two factions, which determined such immediate decisions as who would be permitted to audition and who would be chosen. They also document the conditions under which the office-holder would be permitted to exercise his responsibilities.

There was one other "party" or constituency, whose interest, or at least choice, consisted primarily in being kept informed about what was being negotiated—the public. Newspapers, which focused on individual candidates and their public appearances, satisfied the interest of the public; the topics covered in the news articles were arrivals in Leipzig, auditions, and the results of the voting.[5] The news reports did not always serve merely to inform the public about the actual status of the negotiations, but were intended, at times, to create public opinion and influence the course of the negotiations. This type of public relations, or information policy, was mastered and utilized by the Kapellmeister faction, which in this respect as well, showed itself to be a child of the times.

The point of substantive controversy between the two factions, throughout the five stages needed to appoint a new cantor, was the question of instruction. What was at stake in the issue of instruction was the very definition of the office of cantor. From the very outset, three positions are presented: first, the traditional principle of the Cantor faction that instruction was an inseparable part of the office and consequently had to be carried out by the officeholder personally; second, the progressive objective of the Kapellmeister faction that instruction should be removed from the office, which should henceforth be devoted solely and completely to musical tasks; and third, the concession of the Cantor faction that, as a one-time exception to the traditional principle, this officeholder would be permitted to arrange a substitute for teaching on a private basis. The third position, the concession, was eventually exacted at the election of Bach. When the Cantor faction made its compromise proposal, they stipulated that there be no public, legal act of redefinition, in other words that the traditional definition of the office be upheld, because the compromise was temporary, to last at most through the life of the particular office-holder.

The First Stage

The first stage of the negotiations consisted of the nomination and election of Telemann, followed by his declining the position. The Executive Council first took up the question of Kuhnau's successor on July 14, 1722. Steger, the mayor in office, introduced the six applicants: Johann Friedrich Fasch, Kapellmeister of Count Morzin in Bohemia, 34 years old; Georg Balthasar Schott, organist of the Neue Kirche in Leipzig, 36 years old; Christian Friedrich Rolle, cantor in Magdeburg, 41 years old; Georg Lenck, cantor in Laucha on the Unstrut, 37 years old; Johann Martin Steindorff, cantor in Zwickau, 59 years old; and Georg Philipp Telemann, music director in Hamburg, 41 years old. In order of preference, the Kapellmeister faction proposed Telemann, Fasch, and Schott; the Cantor faction proposed Rolle, Lenck, and Steindorff. Telemann, "already known" as a musician, was particularly well known in Leipzig, where he had made a name for himself by dint of various musical activities while he was still a student at the university. These included the founding of the city's first Collegium Musicum, which was still flourishing—a vivid image that kept the memory of its founder alive. There was just one obstacle to his candidacy: Telemann wanted to be relieved of teaching duties and concern himself solely with music. The Kapellmeister faction, eager to secure a renowned musician, was prepared to accommodate him in every possible way. Not so the Cantor faction. At the same time, it was clear to the Cantor faction that it was powerless against Telemann who, as even Platz had to admit, was "known for his skill in music" and who also had old obligations he could call on. His nomination *primo et unico loco* was a foregone conclusion. Nominating an opposing candidate would only have compromised that candidate and the faction. The question of academic instruction remained the only outstanding issue.

The mayor in office, Steger, stated that "in regard to the schoolwork, Telemann was prepared to make an arrangement with one of his junior colleagues."[6] This meant that the cantor would contract with a lower-ranking colleague at the school to take over the cantor's five hours of academic instruction at the cantor's own expense (that is, without recourse to public funds). Despite this proposed solution, Mayor Platz made a motion to ask Telemann how he envisioned solving this matter: "One would at least have to hear how he plans to arrange for instruction and how he would settle it." A motion passed stating that "first (that is, before the audition and above all before the election), they would communicate with him in this regard, and the duties at school could be conveyed to him." The Cantor faction was willing, in this particular case, to consent to the privately contracted exemption of the officeholder from teaching—as a one-time exception. The Kapellmeister faction still hoped, thanks to the compelling force of Telemann's personality, to achieve their goal of a purely musical definition of the office. Telemann was duly invited and arrived on August 1, eighteen days later.

On August 5, the fourth day after Telemann's arrival in Leipzig and four days before his audition, a newspaper carried the following four items (numbered by the author): "1.) On Saturday past, that is the first of the month, the famous virtuoso from Hamburg arrived here, 2.) who, it is said, will receive the cantor's position recently vacated due to the death of cantor Kuhnau of far-reaching fame and 3.) will audition next Sunday in the Church of St. Thomas, 4.) after which he will return to Hamburg and there take his leave." This report would not be particularly surprising if it contained only items one and three, concerning Telemann's arrival in Leipzig and the time and place of his audition. What is astonishing for a newspaper article are items two and four. In advance of the audition, it carries the report that Telemann will receive the position. This clearly prejudges, not so much the audition as, the election itself. What is more, even before the audition, Telemann's subsequent actions are reported, namely, his return to Hamburg to take his leave, for which reason a final decision about the filling of the position cannot be expected in the immediate future. As I see it, items two and four were a bit of public relations by the Kapellmeister faction, one objective being to address the Cantor faction. Item two presents Telemann's election as a foregone conclusion and as unproblematic. Given that Telemann was the most famous musician in Germany, there could be no doubt that his audition would be a success; the public regarded it as a *fait accompli*. If the Cantor faction had attempted to prevent or even create difficulties regarding the election by referring to the academic duties of the cantor, it could hardly have counted on the understanding of this public, which was interested primarily in the external activities of the cantor and only secondarily, if at all, in his activities within the closed environment of the school.

On August 9, the tenth Sunday after Trinity, he gave his audition. On August 11, the Executive Council met to bring the matter to a vote. Steger opened the proceedings for a roll-call vote. Mayor Lange commented that the Kapellmeister faction had nominated Telemann as their first choice because he was "the most famous composer." Lange cast his vote for him and added, "The matter of instruction could be deferred for now." Johann Franz Born also cast his vote for Telemann and, at the same time, claimed the right to consult with the consistory, of which he was the director. Then Johann August Hölzel, after casting his vote for Telemann, in turn remarked that "outstanding issues will be resolved by the mayor in office." Johann Job and Peter Hohmann also made reference to the issue: "as regards instruction it would be necessary to make arrangements," and "the schoolwork would be taken care of." On August 13, two days after the Executive Council and the Three Councils met, Steger, the mayor in office, informed Telemann of his election. Astonishingly, no response from Telemann is noted in the minutes. The issue of instruction, if it was discussed at all, was left open. Telemann probably argued that he needed a document discharging him from his Hamburg position before he could accept a position in Leipzig. He probably also proposed the same deadline that he later gave when applying for the position of university music director, namely that he would not be available until Michaelmas, that is, after September 29.[7] On the following day, August 14, Telemann received the equivalent of 20 Reichstaler, to reimburse him for traveling costs, and he left Leipzig.[8] Consequently, the next article, dated August 14, the day after Telemann was informed about the election, merely reported that the audition had taken place and had been a success: "Sunday past, that is, on the 9th of this month, the famous virtuoso Monsieur Telemann gave his audition as cantor here in the Church of St. Thomas, with considerable frequency of high and low pitches and with particular approbation."

Telemann declined the position in a letter sent to Leipzig on or shortly after November 6. On November 20, his declination was publicly made known, as follows: "To date the position of cantor here is not occupied, nor is it known to whom the same should be proffered, because the *musicus* from Hamburg who was elected does not accept it for the present but, as one now hears, remains in his previous position."

The Second and Third Stages

During the second stage of the negotiations, the first list of three candidates was formed. When the Executive Council revisited the issue of Kuhnau's successor on November 23, Lange, whose biography appears below on p. 238, had meanwhile become mayor in office and had the task of reporting that their leading candidate had declined the position (see figure 5.2).

The applicants were introduced once again, because each faction had added one new candidate: the Kapellmeister faction, Georg Friedrich Kauffmann, Kapellmeister in Merseburg, 43 years old;[9] the Cantor faction, Andreas Duve, cantor in Braunschweig, 46 years old.[10] There followed the remaining candidates from the first meeting on July 14: Steindorff, Lenck, Rolle, Schott, and Fasch. Fasch, who had meanwhile become Kapellmeister in Zerbst, was, like Telemann, already known locally, since he had founded the city's second Collegium Musicum. Lange added a phrase to his name, "a skilled individual," that is, a skilled musician.

Telemann's declining the position was more than embarrassing for the Kapellmeister faction: it was a setback, because that faction lost its strongest candidate and, at least for the time being, also the chance to bring about a new definition of the position. The Cantor faction felt stronger and was determined to insist on retaining the traditional definition of the position, without even the concession of a privately arranged exception. Its spokesman, Mayor Platz, was the first

Figure 5.2. Gottfried Lange. Contemporary engraving by Martin Bernigeroth.

to speak, and now he was scornful: "There was no reason to be distressed about the fact that Telemann was not coming." Indeed, the Cantor faction was quite content that Telemann was not coming, for he did not fit the traditional principle that they represented. "One should think mainly about the service of the cantor, such that the person being considered would not only understand music but would also be able to instruct." This principle should now be implemented.

But Platz was not in a position to reject the Kapellmeister faction's new leading candidate. He conceded that "Fasch could be permitted to audition," but according to the principle *musiciren und informieren*—he should make music and also instruct. (Telemann, obviously, had not been auditioned in instruction.) When it came to teaching, this much was certain: Fasch and every other candidate of the Kapellmeister faction would fail. But even if Platz had been unable to do anything about the fact that Fasch was first on the list, this time the candidate of the Kapellmeister faction would not be the sole candidate. Platz nominated Rolle and Duve to audition, adding, "one of the two." And Steger, to be certain about paralyzing Fasch, expressly insisted on the application of the principle *musiciren und informiren*. The discussion continued with Johann Franz Born bringing forward two other candidates for discussion, which his faction would have nominated for second and third place, namely Kauffmann and Schott. He added that he "had had Schott," the cantor of the Neue Kirche, "in mind," because placing all the churches under a unified directorship would ameliorate the problematic relationship that persisted between the musical director of the two principal churches and the music director of the Neue Kirche. The other two mayors acknowledged current problems, but expanding Schott's responsibilities always occupied the lowest rung on the scale of the Kapellmeister faction's priorities.

As a result of this meeting three candidates were slated to audition: Fasch, Duve, and Rolle; Kauffmann and Schott remained only as possible candidates. (Lenck and Steindorff were never mentioned after their names were introduced.) On this list, two candidates of the Cantor faction followed the Kapellmeister faction's one candidate. The most important development at this stage was the Cantor faction's successful imposition of its principle of an audition not only in music but also in instruction, thus managing to give its candidates a significantly greater chance than the candidate of the opposition. Helped by Telemann's declining the position, the Cantor faction was able to deflect the attempt to redefine the position and maintain its traditional definition without qualification—even without the concession of a one-time exception.

The auditions, however, had run into some problems of timing, for the first Sunday of Advent was not far off. It would fall on November 29, six days after the meeting; after this, there would be no music for three Sundays. In order to avoid further delay, a rather unusual solution was proposed. All three auditions would be held on the same day, namely the first Sunday of Advent. The first audition would be held in the main service prior to the sermon, the second following the sermon, and the third at the vesper service.

Indeed, before these auditions took place, both factions suffered the loss of their top candidate. Fasch withdrew his candidacy because, as he wrote, "It was not possible for me to leave my employer"; another reason was his refusal to participate in instruction. Rolle asked to be excused for this date. Only Duve would audition. Needing to prevent a candidate of the opposition from auditioning without competition from their own candidates, the Kapellmeister faction substituted Kauffmann and Schott without, however, being authorized by a resolution. The auditions of Kauffmann and Duve were held, as the newspaper reported, "in the Nicolaskirche," and the audition of Schott "in another church."

The Executive Council reopened its discussion of the matter on December 21, the day after the fourth Sunday of Advent, which was the last Sunday of the *tempus clausum*. Lange, the mayor in office, made three announcements. First, there had been two subsequent nominations: "Several others applied," namely Christoph Graupner, Kapellmeister in Darmstadt, 39 years old; and Johann Sebastian Bach, Kapellmeister in Cöthen, 37 years old. Both were potential candidates for the Kapellmeister faction. Second, Fasch had withdrawn his candidacy. Third, "the candidate from Merseburg," that is, Kauffmann, "requested that he be allowed to audition once again."

The third stage of the negotiations now began with the formation of a second list of three candidates. Immediately following Lange's three announcements, the decision is recorded that "Rolle, Kauffmann, and Schott, too, should be permitted to audition, in particular in instruction." The Cantor faction believed it had achieved its goal when Lange announced, "Fasch, however, declared that he could not instruct." But since the audition of their candidate, Duve, was not a success—the newspaper had already covered him with an anonymity from which he would not reemerge—he was no longer under discussion. In consequence, the Cantor faction now had only a single candidate left, namely Rolle.

The negotiations followed a rigidly determined path, whereby a decision had to be made about any candidate under consideration. Graupner and Bach, who were supplemental candidates, were merely mentioned without further discussion. The primary objective of the Kapellmeister faction, once again, was to prevent Rolle from auditioning as the sole remaining candidate, an event that—unless the audition was a catastrophe—would have been tantamount to his election. Kauffmann's request for permission to repeat his audition prevented that. (Kauffmann, himself, aware that the mere fact of his reauditioning had been resisted but, also, that his prospects were good at this time, had not found it difficult to make this request. Evidently, he was confident in his ability to withstand the comparison with Rolle.) By contrast, the introduction of new candidates was a lesser concern. Although, at this time, the Kapellmeister faction was in a better position when it came to potential candidates—now having four against only one on the Cantor faction's list—the permission to go forward with the auditions was conditioned by the Cantor faction's principle of auditioning in both music and instruction, which was now confirmed. The third meeting thus ended with a second list of three candidates, comprising Rolle, Kauffmann, and Schott, in which, conversely now, two candidates of the Kapellmeister faction followed one candidate of the Cantor faction.

The Fourth Stage

The fourth stage had Graupner being elected and declining the position. The Kapellmeister faction had once again found a candidate of the type they needed—a personality comparable to Telemann. At Christmas they presented Graupner. Perhaps he had assumed the role of a candidate even earlier—such as the time of the third meeting on December 21. If that was the case, the Kapellmeister faction would have had two objectives at that meeting: first, to prevent the Cantor faction from achieving its aim of auditioning Rolle as the sole candidate; and second, to gain time so that Graupner could have an opportunity to present himself musically in Leipzig. This could not occur until the end of the *tempus clausum*, during the celebration of Christmas. After the musical presentation by their candidate had been a compelling success, the Kapellmeister faction went into action propagandistically. The following detailed article is datelined the following day, December 26:

> *After the director from Hamburg, Herr Telemann, accepted the call as cantor but later declined the same, the cantor position remains vacant, to the great detriment of the pupils of the St. Thomasschule, and the surviving widow of the late cantor Kuhnau is still enjoying all of the income as of this date. But the following, the forthcoming New Year's Mass, should provide the test from which it should now be possible to learn, very soon, to whom this important post will be offered: namely, Kapellmeister Graupner from Darmstadt, Court Organist Petzoldt from Dresden, or Kapellmeister Kauffmann from Merseburg.*

This version of Telemann's conduct, which is documented here for the first time, has widely influenced history. In the first report of Telemann's declination, dated November 20, it had been stated that Telemann "does not accept it for the present, but . . . remains in his previous position." Now it is stated that he "accepted the call" and then "rejected" it. At the later meeting before the three councils, Lange would repeat this version, saying that Telemann "had promised to do everything, but had, however, not kept his promise"; he "did not keep his word."[11] In actual fact, Telemann had not definitively accepted the position, for he did not sign the bond, the legally binding obligation. To this extent the report of November 20th is accurate. At the same time, the Kapellmeister faction was not altogether wrong, at least from its point of view, to reprove Telemann for behaving badly and even breaking his word. For it was this faction who had arranged that Telemann not be compelled to sign the bond. They did this in order to avoid making a binding commitment with regard to instruction and to committing themselves irrevocably to the compromise proposal of the Cantor faction. Their aim was to protect their freedom to achieve their goal, not to protect Telemann's freedom to accept or decline the position. They believed that Telemann had felt just as committed to them as they had been to him. But Telemann had subscribed to the same pragmatism as the faction that had nominated him: he used the freedom that had been given to him as he saw fit and declined when it seemed useful for him. This was legally unassailable; however it was not in accord with the intentions of the faction that had invented it. The Kapellmeister faction saw itself scorned and abandoned.

But it was not their hurt vanity that caused them to express their opinion to Telemann by means of the press and to make emphatically clear to him what an "important post" he had let slip from his grasp. Historiography would certainly have had an easier time distancing itself from the version of the Kapellmeister faction if it had been able to recognize the fact that the Kapellmeister faction was not trying to promulgate an absolute judgment on Telemann's behavior but instead was pursuing a specific objective in a specific situation. The Kapellmeister faction was concerned not about morals but about tactics. Still, when it came to achieving a tactical objective, morals would serve perfectly well. At the moment when the Kapellmeister faction was preparing to emblazon a new candidate on its banner and fight for him, it had to be concerned about protecting its rear. It had to cast off any guilt that could be associated with the delay in the proceedings and the resulting "great detriment of the pupils of the St. Thomas School." Telemann, who was not coming after all, could still be useful as a scapegoat and be saddled with the sole guilt. The promulgation of this judgment on Telemann had the function of publicly rejecting criticisms that were likely to be, and may even have been, expressed. It thus enabled the Kapellmeister faction to keep its hands free to fight for their newly chosen leading candidate, Graupner. The list of candidates cited in this newspaper report includes Petzoldt, drops both Schott's and Rolle's names, and does not mention Bach.

The Executive Council took up the question of Kuhnau's replacement again on January 15, 1723, twenty-five days after the previous meeting. Graupner was so compelling that the Kapellmeister faction was able to secure the selection of its new leading candidate even before his audition. Faced with the force of a star, the opponents could accomplish little by pointing to the traditional definition of the position. As a result, the Cantor faction was already in a relatively powerless position and was further limited in its ability to act by its continuing shortage of suitable candidates. Hence it did not offer much resistance. Lange, the mayor in office and spokesman of the Kapellmeister faction, avoided taking the previous meeting as his starting point, making his opening presentation in full cognizance of the situation: "The Kapellmeister from Darmstadt, Herr Graupner, has applied and will hold an audition on next Sunday; it would be simply be a matter of conferring the nomination for position of cantor if the audition went well." Graupner was not known in Leipzig in the same way as Telemann and Fasch, both of whom had been founders of a Collegium Musicum; however, he "is well praised in all quarters, as diverse letters prove." Therefore Graupner's person and qualifications were not a problem. The only problem was whether his resignation would be accepted: "Precaution would have to be taken that he would be able to be discharged from his court." The Kapellmeister faction believed that it had taken a dual precaution against being confronted once again with this by now, all-too-familiar ground for rejection by its leading candidate. For one thing, it procured a statement addressing the concern from Graupner "who, however, declares that he is not firmly bound and indicates what motivates him to make a change." In addition, the proposal was made "to write to the landgrave beforehand," that is, to request his discharge officially.

Next in line to speak were two members of the Cantor faction, Mayors Platz and Steger. Mayor Platz was mellow. He had no objection to the person and musical qualifications of the candidate, stating that he "had no special knowledge of Herr Graupner, to be sure, but the latter was a person of stature and seemed to be a fine man, and, he also believed, a good musician." Platz, by the way, had seen fit to express his opinion about a candidate's musical qualifications only twice: this time, in the case of Graupner, and previously, in a similar situation, in the case of Telemann. Next, Platz expressed the usual objection of his faction, without, in this case, pressing for any consequences: "Except one should see to it that he also participates in giving instruction at the school." He agreed about the letter to Graupner's employer. Mayor Steger, by contrast, barely concealed the Cantor faction's annoyance over their defeat and abstained from casting his own vote. "He [Steger] was no musician," and no adherent of the Kapellmeister faction and its principles; he could not evaluate the candidate's musical qualifications by the standards of the Kapellmeister faction. The individuals who were in favor of Graupner's election must therefore take responsibility for it, those for whom the candidate's musical qualifications were paramount, and who understood something about music pursued as an end in itself, which was of no interest to him. He "deferred to the judgment of the mayor in office and what the Kapellmeister from Dresden [Heinichen] had written about him."

Steger makes two procedural motions. The first is that "one could . . . also still hear the others in audition." In part, he was pursuing the specific objective of the Cantor faction by modifiying Graupner's nomination *primo et unico loco* and keeping a chance alive for their currently sole candidate, Rolle. In part, Steger may have been thinking of preparing for the eventuality of Graupner's declining, which could not be excluded. Steger's second procedural motion asked the councilors "in the interim, and until he [Graupner] receives permission to resign, not to bring the matter to the Three Councils." In order to avoid the city's suffering the same embarrassment it had endured in the case of Telemann,

Steger did not want Graupner's election approved by the Three Councils until after his resignation had been confirmed in writing, and he requested postponement. Above all, he wanted the Cantor faction to retain some freedom of action. Mayor Platz expressed his explicit agreement with these provisos. By agreeing only to *hear* the candidates in audition, that is, an audition in music alone, the Cantor faction had effectively ended its insistence on upholding the unaltered, traditional definition of the position. Under these circumstances, the existence of an exception would have to be conceded, minimally, in the form of a privately arranged replacement in instruction. The next speaker, Johann Franz Born of the Kapellmeister faction, voted for Graupner, because he was "so well praised," that is, had such good recommendations, and he added, "Indeed Kauffmann, too, considers him to be better than himself." By conveying Kauffmann's high-minded praise of Graupner, Born indicated that Kauffmann did not want to be measured against Graupner and therefore renounced the opportunity he was given when his request to repeat the audition was approved. (Petzoldt was not included in the formal proceedings at all.) Johann Jakob Kees was absent but, with the exception of Johann Job's abstention, the remaining town councilors voted for Graupner.

Yet this support for Graupner concealed considerable nuances. Johann August Hölzel, a member of the Cantor faction, was impatient with the weakness displayed by Platz and Steger. He opened with a provocation: "Rolle is said to surpass Telemann"—by how much more, then, should Rolle surpass Graupner. With his comment that "one could hear him as well," he added force to Mayor Steger's suggestion that "one could, also, still hear the others in audition." He placed the sole, and hence top-ranked, candidate of the Cantor faction on a par with the leading candidate of the Kapellmeister faction. Soon thereafter, Gottfried Wagner nominated the third candidate and suggested that they "consider whether both Rolle and Bach should also be invited to audition." (Schott was not discussed.) Thus the new list was Graupner, Rolle, and Bach. Gottfried Konrad Lehmann, the supervisor of the Thomasschule (and as such its representative on the Council) was an adherent of the Cantor faction; their candidate Rolle, he said, "is praised as a skilled and learned man"—a man skilled in music and learned in academic matters. Hence he was the only candidate who satisfied the traditional definition of the position. Taking the offensive, Johann Ernst Kregel was "dubious about whether they should hold any more auditions"—possibly out of thrift, or mere annoyance. Hence his objective was to defend Graupner's nomination *primo et unico loco*. Johann Job, an adherent of the Cantor faction, avoided speaking directly in favor of the opposition's leading candidate, stating that he "did not know Graupner personally, but much good was spoken of him." The main problem he saw was the matter of the resignation; he "was only doubtful about whether the latter would be released so easily, for which reason it would probably be good to write to the Landgrave." He was also doubtful with regard to Rolle, since "he was in Magdeburg" and was thus bound to that city. In fact, Rolle had been installed in office in Magdeburg less than a year earlier, on February 13, 1722. Thus, the uncertainty about the candidates' release from their present employment affected not only the leading candidate of the Kapellmeister faction but also the sole surviving candidate of the Cantor faction. Johann Job seems to have been especially interested in the issue of the release. It was well known that Landgrave Ernst Ludwig von Hessen-Darmstadt was in the habit of creating difficulties on this score,[12] and Job may already have put out feelers in Magdeburg or communicated with Rolle directly. In closing, Job, like Platz before him, stressed the principle of his faction but again without drawing any conclusions from it: "As for the instruction, they would have to see to that as well." Johann Franz Born, thinking of the forthcoming auditions, asked "whether the Thomas students should not be placed under obligation, so that if they were needed, wherever they might be, they should be ready to be used." There may have been difficulties in this regard at the time of the auditions on the first Sunday in Advent.

For the moment, at any rate, only the audition of Graupner was publicly announced for January 17, the second Sunday after Epiphany: "This Sunday, here in the church, the princely Kapellmeister from Darmstadt, Herr Graupner, will audition for the vacant cantor's position, by order of the honorable and most wise council; following which the said position will then probably be refilled very soon."[13] The clause, referring to Graupner's holding his audition "by order of the honorable and most wise council," served to protect the candidate against his present employer. However, on January 29, the following is reported: "After the recently held audition, nothing certain has been heard, to date, as to who is to receive said position from the most wise council of this city." This report retracted the earlier announcement of a decision coming "very soon." On February 5, the following announcement was then made: "On the Feast of the Purification [February 2], Msr. Schott, director of the Collegium Musicum, gave his audition in the Church of Saint Nicholas with regard to the still vacant position of cantor." According to the list that had been adopted by the Executive Council on January 15, the next candidate after Graupner should have been Rolle; but Rolle had withdrawn his candidacy. Thus Schott, who had appeared on the list of three names that was approved by the Executive Council on December 21—and, hence, had the right to an audition—could audition in Rolle's place, although it would have been correct for Bach to move up to second place and Schott to third place. In all probability, word of Rolle's withdrawal was received with such short notice that Bach's appointment to audition, which had already been confirmed for February 7, Quinquagesima Sunday, the last Sunday before the beginning of the *tempus clausum*, could no longer be changed, while something could be arranged very quickly with Schott. On February 9, an article appeared stating, "On Sunday past, in the morning, the Princely Kapellmeister in Cöthen, M. Bach, gave his audition here in the Church of St. Thomas in regard to the still vacant position of cantor, and the music performed by the said candidate was much praised by all those who value such things." Riemer records the audition as follows: "On the 7th Sunday, Quinquagesima, Herr Sebastian Bach, currently Kapellmeister in Cöthen, performed his audition for the cantor's position vacated by the late Herr Kuhnau."[14]

After Graupner had successfully completed his audition, he received 40 taler from the municipal treasury on January 20 for his travel expenses,[15] which was double the approved amount, perhaps in recognition of special services at Christmas. He was also given a letter of the same date in which the Leipzig Town Council requests Landgrave Ernst Ludwig of Hessen-Darmstadt to give his gracious assent to the resignation of his Kapellmeister.[16] On or about January 31, on the tenth or eleventh day following his departure from Leipzig, Graupner delivered the letter from the Leipzig Town Council, together with his own letter of resignation. On February 7, the Mayor in office, Lange, received a letter from him.[17] And now, once again, nothing happened for the moment. In a letter dated March 12, Lange inquired of Graupner how things stood and enclosed a letter to Privy Councilor von Kametzky in Darmstadt, to which the court responded in the negative. As a last-ditch effort, Graupner submitted a summary memorandum on March 20, but to no avail. He was called before the Landgrave, who increased Graupner's salary to 900 gulden (equal to 600 Reichstaler Courant), among other improvements. On March 22, the tenth day after the date of Lange's inquiry, Graupner wrote that he was declining. On the following day, March 23, Privy Councilor von Kametzky composed his response and sent it to Leipzig, enclosing Graupner's letter.[18]

The Fifth Stage

The fifth and last stage of negotiations involved Bach's election. The Executive Council addressed the issue of Kuhnau's successor for the last time on April 9. In his opening remarks, Lange, the mayor in office, once again had to announce a declination: "The individual they had thought of in respect to the cantor's position, namely Graupner, could not obtain his release; the Landgrave of Hessen-Darmstadt simply would not grant it." This was the third candidate of the Kapellmeister faction who had declined. The Cantor faction also had a declination to announce, since their only candidate, Rolle, withdrew his candidacy, although it was not mentioned in the minutes.

Three candidates still remain: "Other than these, the Kapellmeister in Cöthen, Bach; Kauffmann in Merseburg; and Schott had come here for consideration." Kauffmann's name was back on the list. With Graupner's declination, the reason for his withdrawal had become irrelevant. The Cantor faction had decided to allow his audition on the first Sunday in Advent to pass as valid, and with this, Kauffmann could once again assume the position that he voluntarily relinquished. Bach moved into first place as a result of his audition. Although

Bach's faction had not previously nominated him as its leading candidate—as they had Telemann, Fasch, Kauffmann, and Graupner—Bach won this designation by himself, by means of his audition. After Telemann declined, Fasch withdrew his candidacy, Graupner failed to gain his release, and Petzoldt was excluded from the formal proceedings, Bach gained first position on the list of candidates.

Since all three remaining candidates belong to the Kapellmeister faction, Lange continued, "but all three would be unable to instruct all the same." No one had yet given an audition in instruction—certainly none of the candidates of the Kapellmeister faction and probably not Duve either, the only candidate of the opposition who had even auditioned. Profiting from the situation that the Kapellmeister faction had been able to create due to the personality of its candidate Graupner, Schott and Bach also avoided this eventuality in early February. Now Lange attempted to perpetuate this situation: "In the case of Telemann, they had already considered a separation." He went for broke, making a motion to "divide" academic instruction and musical tasks, to dedicate the office solely and completely to musical tasks—a new definition of the position. Mayor Platz, whose biography appears below on page 165, the spokesman for the Cantor faction, immediately registered his objection (see figure 5.3). "The last point he finds to be doubtful on considerable grounds," and there then follows the famous infamous statement: "Since they were now not able to get the best, they would have to settle for those of the middle—much good had once been said of a certain fellow in Pirna."

To understand Platz's statement it is first necessary to clarify the presumption on which it is based. These councilors had good heads on their shoulders even in matters of cultural politics, such as filling the cantor's position at the Thomasschule—certainly of lesser importance in the larger scheme of Leipzig's municipal politics. Not a single digression ever occurred during the meetings; nor was there ever a casual comment—or if there was, the individual taking minutes did not make note of it. Every sentence, every word that was handed down was on target. Mayor Platz's statement was pursuing a concrete objective: to give the negotiations a specific turn favorable to the Cantor faction. What was Platz's purpose and objective? At this point, the Kapellmeister faction possessed three candidates, while the Cantor faction had no candidates. According to the rules of play, the game in which the two factions were engaged was at an end. The winner was the Kapellmeister faction, the loser, the Cantor faction. But Mayor Platz was not willing to give up so easily. He sought to use the situation to the advantage of the Cantor faction. This time, both factions were unable to get "the best." Both factions therefore had to accept "middle" candidates, namely those who were farther down on the list. But the Cantor faction did not have a candidate in second place on the list. Therefore they had the right to nominate a candidate to oppose the second candidate of the Kapellmeister faction because, under these circumstances, the election of Bach would have been a selection

D. Abraham Christoph Platz, Appellationsrat und ältester Bürgermeister, konstatierte in der Ratssitzung vom 9. April 1723: „Da man nun die besten nicht bekommen könne, müsse man mittlere nehmen."

Figure 5.3. Abraham Christoph Platz. Contemporary engraving by Martin Bernigeroth.

from among the candidates of the Kapellmeister faction only, that is, without competition from the other side. Nonetheless, Platz's argument was purely formal, referring only to process. On the one hand, he did not intend to make a substantive judgment concerning the qualification of the candidates—he would have considered this presumptuous. Above all, such a judgment could not have influenced the course of the proceedings, since there was no agreement concerning the principles by which the candidates' qualifications should be measured. On the other hand, the formal argument could not be dispensed with lightly, since the Cantor faction had the right to have its own candidate, which could be denied only with difficulty. Hence he nominated a candidate of his faction to face the opposing candidate, Bach. His candidate was Christian Heckel, born in 1676.[19]

It was a clever move, because Heckel, who had been the cantor in his native city of Bischofswerda from 1699, and had served in Pirna in an adjunct status since 1717 and as cantor since 1718, had attended the Thomasschule in Leipzig for seven years prior to accepting his first job. Later he had attended the university for three years. All told, he had spent ten years living in Leipzig, forming relationships and later dedicating his book *Historical Description of the City of Bischofswerda* (Dresden, 1713) to the city of Leipzig. He was not only a proven academic but, thanks to this publication, a proven scholar. As a musician, this student of Schelle and Kuhnau could have submitted a letter of recommendation from the Dresden Court Kapellmeister Heinichen as easily as Graupner did, since Heinichen had become Heckel's daughter's godfather in 1721, and he had no need to worry about the factionalism in Leipzig. At this point, the minutes are broken off, because the secretary had to go next door to the tax collection room and was thus prevented from continuing to take notes.[20] At one time extant, the "replacement copy on loose-leaf sheets has not been preserved."[21] Therefore, the remainder of the meeting must be reconstructed.

It is doubtful that Platz ever believed that he would be successful in an attempt to reopen the process by obtaining permission for Heckel to audition, or that this was even his intention. However, by constructing a legal argument, the Cantor faction was able to propose a motion in favor of its own candidate to oppose the Kapellmeister faction's motion in favor of a new definition of the position. A compromise was arrived at. Each faction withdrew its motion. As a result, the Cantor faction was persuaded to make a concession; namely, it agreed to support the privately arranged exemption of the cantor from instruction, as a one-time exception. It was the same compromise the Cantor faction had already offered at the time of Telemann's nomination. Formally, the compromise was equal, for each faction had withdrawn its motion. The Cantor faction even made a concession; yet despite this concession, it gained substantially as a result of this compromise. It was now evident that the Kapellmeister faction had done itself a disservice by placing its emphasis on personality, while the Cantor faction had gained an advantage by emphasizing the substance of the issue. The victory of the Kapellmeister faction was momentary; the victory of the Cantor faction was lasting. The Kapellmeister faction had gotten its candidate elected—this was overtly evident for the moment; the Cantor faction had secured its definition of the position. Hence, the candidate's position was going to depend on the Cantor faction's consent to the privately arranged exemption from teaching. Furthermore, sooner or later the tenure of this cantor would be at an end; then the traditional definition would be restored to its previous status, unconstrained by any concession—that would become overtly evident in the long run. The term of office that was about to begin was an exception. For the candidate, the compromise was rotten.

Since there was unity regarding the compromise formula and the process to be pursued, Bach was elected by unanimous vote. Before his election was to be confirmed by the Three Councils, in order to avoid any surprises, first Bach needed to make a formal commitment to the compromise, and second, his release needed to be guaranteed, which prior experience had shown was in the interests of both factions. The guarantee was pursued by means similar to those suggested by the Cantor faction in the case of Graupner. Thus these proposals were to be implemented by means of a system of preliminary communication and commitment. The mayor in office, Lange, immediately sent Bach notice that he had been chosen by the Executive Council but that a preliminary declaration of commitment was required on Bach's part before the election was confirmed by the Three Councils. It is probable that Lange enclosed the text of the provisional bond with this communication. Bach had to make five binding commitments, the first of which would become effective immediately upon his final election, and the others later, at the time of his installation:[22] First, he would obtain his discharge from his position in Cöthen and present a document to this effect, for which a period of between three and a maximum of four weeks was given to do so. Bach, wanting to play it safe, requested his discharge immediately. Since the document is dated April 13,[23] he must have already gained assurances about it and had no difficulty agreeing to this point. Second, he would "act in accordance with the school regulations, those already existent or that may yet be imposed." This acknowledgement of the school regulations was inevitable, but not without its complications in view of the new school regulations of November 13, 1723, which had been imposed regarding the distribution of incidental income, especially from burials.[24] Third, he was to "instruct the pupils not only in the regular hours set aside for this, but also *privatissime* in singing, without remuneration." This private instruction was, thus, expressly to be recognized as belonging to the responsibilities of the position, but in the context of the musical aspect of his role. Fourth, he was to "carry out whatever else he is obliged to do, in all respects." Although the performance of all the other duties of the position might appear to be self-evident, this point silently incorporated the principle of the Cantor faction: that the role of instructor was a non-voluntary part of the position.[25] Fifth, he promised, "to the extent that someone may be required to exempt me from instruction in the Latin language, with the fore-knowledge and consent of the most wise and honorable council, to be content to pay that person out of my own means without recourse to the most wise council for any supplemental request." This is the exception to the norm that the Cantor faction had conceded in this single, individual case.[26] Bach believed that he could accept this point without concern, for the exemption from instruction was certainly in accord with his own wishes, and it had probably already been discussed with Mayor Lange. On April 19, ten days after the meeting of the Executive Council, Bach returned to Leipzig and signed the provisional bond. By committing himself to points four and five, Bach ratified the compromise of the two factions. Not until later would he sense the trap he had stepped into.

The Three Councils met to confirm Bach's election three days later on April 22. Two sets of minutes, published as Documents II/129 and II/130 (indicated below as A and B, respectively), have been preserved. The second set of minutes, written by First Municipal Secretary Carl Friedrich Menser, is proficient and covers the most essential matters; the first, from a less competent hand, is less precise but includes a number of welcome elaborations. The two documents confirm and complement each other in various respects. Instruction and release from previous duties were the two points on which everything depended. Beyond them, not much was said or, at least, not much is recorded in the minutes.

These minutes, which read like a play in which the actors have reversed their roles, affirm not a sudden change of heart by the two sides but a ritual, according to which the compromise was implemented. The spokesman of the Kapellmeister faction, Mayor-in-office Lange, recognizes the principle of the Cantor faction that he had previously sought to undermine, now maintaining that Bach satisfies the principle of the Cantor faction (even though he had declared in the meeting of the Executive Council on April 9 that all three candidates, including Bach, "would be unable simultaneously to instruct"). He now states that Bach has, "along with music, instruction; and the cantor would have to instruct in the *Colloquiis Corderi* and in grammar, which he was also willing to do" (A). In the Executive Council, where the conflicts were fought out, his recognition of this principle would have caused disoriented astonishment. Claiming that one of the candidates of his faction satisfied the principle of the other faction would have engendered denial and contradiction. Now, by contrast, when the contradiction has been blunted by compromise, the Cantor faction acknowledged the candidate of the Kapellmeister faction. The spokesman of the Cantor faction, Mayor Platz, stated "he would have to accommodate himself to the instruction of the young people. Bach had the skills required for this, and wanted to do it" (A); and Bach "declares that he will not only instruct the boys in music but also in other school subjects, in proper fashion" (B). Platz, for whom even this compromise went too far, refers to it only indirectly when he says, "we will see how he may go about the latter (the instruction)" (B). Steger follows the previous speaker right down to his choice of words, then speaks openly of the exception that has been agreed to. He states that Bach "has declared that he will show his loyalty . . . not only as cantor, but also as a member of the faculty of the Thomasschule." As *collega quartus*,[27] "he would come to terms with the other instructors who have to act as his substitutes."(A). And "since he declares that he will instruct both in music and in the school, if he was not able to proceed in all respects with respect to the latter, there would be no objection if he were to have it done by another individual" (B). As yet, the key to the role reversal is not visible.

Mayor Platz expressed his displeasure over the long, drawn-out back and forth, and excuses his faction's support of a candidate of the opposition with the admonition not to lose any more time, "since the vacancy was so long, there was cause to move to a vote. It would be desirable for the third try to be successful" (A). Concerning the person of Bach, he commented positively saying, "Bach was said to be of good repute and he was satisfied with his person" (B). Mayor Steger tries to be reassuring. He "thanked them for their carefulness, [stating] the reasons for the delay had been cited, as well as why Herr Bach should be accepted" (A). Steger, who had abstained from the vote on Graupner in the meeting of the Executive Council on January 15, now regretted the loss of Graupner: "He would have wished that Graupner could have accepted it, but now was thinking in the direction of Bach" (B). Then, finally, he gives a positive assessment: "Bach's person was as good as Graupner's" (A).

For all that, in concluding, Steger falls out of the adopted role that was hitherto assumed by the compromise and, trying to salvage what he can for the Cantor faction, imposes the musical ideal of the Cantor faction on Bach: He "would have to make compositions that were non-theatrical"(A). With this, in opposition to the Kapellmeister faction, he insists on compliance with a provision that had been included in the bond signed in 1701 when Kuhnau had been installed in the office of cantor of the Thomaskirche: "for the maintenance of good order in the churches, to organize the music in such fashion that it may not last too long, and is composed in such a way that it does not turn out opera-like but rather engages the listeners in devotion."[28] In Leipzig's principal churches, in other words, the *stylus luxurians theatralis* was to be forbidden, and, at most, the *stylus luxurians communis* permitted. However, Bach's musical qualifications, by means of which he had advanced to first place, were known from his audition. Therefore, hardly a word is said here on this subject.[29]

Gottfried Wagner remarks that "Bach had been praised to him" (A); Johann Ernst Kregel Jr. calls him "a very skilled man" (B). Mayor Lange expresses the most substantial (and also accurate) judgment: "He excels at the keyboard" (A)—admittedly not exactly the description that was expected for the position that they needed to fill. Then, at the close of the meeting, after the Three Councils had unanimously confirmed Bach, Mayor Lange remarked, "It was necessary to think of a famous man," thereby restating, at the very conclusion of the selection process, the goal of his faction. When compared to any opera composer, every organist—even the most famous among them—was less famous. Bach, despite the fact that he was a candidate of the Kapellmeister faction, was a "middle" candidate for both parties.

The newspaper article from the following day, April 23, again citing an anonymous source, stated: "It is said to be certain that the Princely Kapellmeister from Cöthen, Herr Bach, has received and accepted the call as cantor." On May 5, thirteen days after the confirmation of his election, Bach appeared at the city hall, presented his discharge papers, and signed the final declaration of acceptance. Then he was admitted to the council chamber where Mayor Lange told the sitting council that "diverse individuals had applied for service as cantor at the school at St. Thomas, but because he had been judged the most capable among them, they had elected him unanimously." Bach "thanked them most obediently for their consideration, and promised all loyalty and diligence."[30] Eleven months to the day after Johann Kuhnau's death, the position of cantor at the Thomasschule had been filled once more.

The Structure of Sacred Music in Leipzig: Patronage and Factionalism

Fundamental changes in the structure of Leipzig's church music at the end of the seventeenth century, due to the introduction of new worship services, were decisive in regard to Bach's activities in Leipzig. In 1699, the Franciscan or Barfüßerkirche, which had lain unused since the Reformation, was reactivated for religious purposes. In 1710, a new Sunday service was introduced at the university's Paulinerkirche. The introduction of new services brought with it the necessity of providing the music for them. Until then there had been only one musical authority in the city—the cantor of the Thomasschule. Should the arrangements for music at the new services, as well as at the two principal churches, be brought together under his control, with church music production thereby remaining centralized? Or should the traditional position be responsible only for the traditional services of the two principal churches, and new positions be created for the new services, with the possibility of new centers of church music arising? This question had somewhat different implications for the Neue Kirche and for the Paulinerkirche. The Neue Kirche belonged to the city; hence the arrangement between the cantor of the Thomasschule and the Neue Kirche fell within the purview of the municipal authorities. The Paulinerkirche belonged to the university; hence any arrangement between the cantor of the Thomasschule and the Paulinerkirche affected the relationship between the city and the university.

The solution to the city's problem—as regards both the personnel questions and policy implications—was tied to the *de facto* existence of an alternative. When Johann Kuhnau was elected cantor of the Thomasschule in 1701, there was evidently no individual in sight around whom another position could have crystallized. This changed overnight when Telemann appeared on the scene. His musical personality immediately found influential supporters and sponsors. Telemann or Kuhnau—this concrete alternative allowed the factionalism within the Leipzig Town Council to become manifest. The issue was not musical qualification, but what kind of music: not skill, but style. One faction held fast to tradition; the other favored the contemporary alternative. Telemann was given the task of composing (and probably conducting) a cantata for the Thomaskirche every other week.[31] He was presumably there whenever Kuhnau was scheduled to conduct the main music programs at Nicolaikirche, that is, the cantatas, which alternated regularly between the two principal churches. Thus there emerged, alongside the alternation of traditional elements at the two principal churches, an alternation of traditional and contemporary cantata elements at the Thomaskirche. To be sure, Kuhnau and Telemann both composed and performed cantatas; but Kuhnau insisted on its traditional style, whereas Telemann tended to an up-to-date style influenced by the opera. As long as no option existed, it was understood that the city's highest-ranking musician would also have authority over the musical activities of the Neue Kirche.[32] As soon as a practical alternative appeared, the representative of tradition was associated with the traditional genres of chorale and motet, while the representative of the contemporary was entrusted with the genre in which contemporary music could unfold—the cantata.

Creating the position of organist and music director at the Neue Kirche was the institutional prerequisite for establishing a contemporary church music; after this position was awarded to Telemann in 1704, the city of Leipzig had not just one center for church music but two—one traditional and the other contemporary. Each of the two centers had the support of a political faction within the Leipzig Town Council, and the competition between these centers was rooted in the competition between these political factions. As long as the two offices—cantor of the Thomasschule, and organist and music director of the Neue Kirche—were competitively filled, and each of the two factions considered one of the church music centers and its respective director to be the exponent of its musical ideas, an accommodation between these centers and their directors was out of the question. Furthermore, the creation of a second center meant that people who wanted to make music—above all students—had a choice. The reservoir of aspiring musicians no longer came exclusively to the cantor at the Thomasschule, who had previously been the sole official representative of the city. They now divided up, by preference, between the two principal churches and the Neue Kirche. Kuhnau's heartfelt laments about this new competitive state are well known.[33]

The competitive relationship between the Neue Kirche and the principal churches had been problematic throughout Kuhnau's term in office. At the time of Kuhnau's election as cantor in 1701, there had been talk of transferring control over the musical program of the Neue Kirche to the cantor of the

Thomasschule; however, soon after, Telemann's appearance and the concrete possibility of having a choice led to the separation of the two offices. This competitive situation changed only when the faction favoring the musical activities of the Neue Kirche succeeded in determining the selection of Kuhnau's successor, thereby making the contemporary style of sacred music—previously restricted to the Neue Kirche—binding for the city as a whole. If the organist and music director of the Neue Kirche and the cantor of the Thomasschule had belonged to the same faction, competitiveness would inevitably have turned into neighborly consensus.

It is not known what plans existed, or what kind of relationship would have developed, if Telemann had accepted the position at the Thomasschule. Indeed, when Telemann declined the position as Kuhnau's replacement, Johann Franz Born suggested unifying the directorship of all the churches by electing Georg Balthazar Schott, the music director of the Neue Kirche, to be cantor of the Thomasschule as well.[34] The consensual arrangement made for Bach will be discussed below in detail. The very fact that such an arrangement could have been found for Bach, who had never before lived and worked in Leipzig, is a clear indication that such an arrangement must have been considered for Telemann and was a goal of the Kapellmeister faction.

Different criteria had always determined the arrangement between the cantor of the Thomasschule and the Paulinerkirche. Even before the new Sunday service was introduced at the Paulinerkirche on August 31, 1710, Kuhnau had performed certain traditional functions there. The introduction of the new service meant the addition of new functions and, with them, the necessity of deciding to whom they should be entrusted. Evidently, the University was inclined to hire its own organist and to give Kuhnau responsibility for figural music. Also, the city's need for a clear line of demarcation *vis-à-vis* the university prevented Kuhnau from taking on any new functions, limiting even his ability to perform the traditional ones. Fasch and his Collegium Musicum took advantage of the vacuum that was created in this way, aiming to create a third center of church music. Apparently, however, an agreement was reached between the University and the city, probably assisted by Fasch's departure, but primarily facilitated by a compromise between the University and the city. The reason for the compromise can be found in Kuhnau himself: he was a member of the academy and, as a former attorney, ranked higher than Fasch, who was only a student. As a member of the University, he was acceptable to this institution and enjoyed its protection, which the city was obliged to respect. Kuhnau may not have been able to arrive at an arrangement with the Neue Kirche because of the factionalism within the Leipzig Town Council, but thanks to his own status as a member of the academy, he was able to arrive at an arrangement with the Paulinerkirche.[35]

Soon after Telemann was elected cantor of the Thomasschule, he submitted a formal request to the University.[36] The record shows that "Georg Philipp Telemann submitted both an oral and a written request that the *Directorium Chori*

Musici of the *Templum Paulinum* might also be entrusted to him." The University's decision reads: "The *Directorium Musices* shall be conferred on Telemann as per his request, since he is beyond reproach, an excellent *musicus*. At the same time, so it should not appear that the *Academia* would always be obliged to accept the municipal cantor, he should be given his orders but nothing will be prescribed therein concerning how and through whom he should organize the academic music; rather such matters are left to his sole discretion." Telemann's receiving *carte blanche* regarding the details of his service was related to the city, not to him. The University did not want to be constrained by the city's choice of Telemann or any one else for cantor. It wanted to preserve its freedom to fill the position it controlled. In other words, the University was articulating its need to draw a line of demarcation *vis-à-vis* the city. Telemann, for his part, had not yet signed the bond committing himself to the city and, thus, was not yet bound by Provision 14, which specified that he "should and would not accept any *officium* at the University without the consent of the most honorable and wise council."[37]

On this point, however, problems—if any—were likely to come only from the Cantor faction. For the Kapellmeister faction was certainly prepared, from the outset, to agree to Telemann's acceptance of the musical directorship at the University. Its aim was to combine the arrangement at the Neue Kirche, which it had the power to bring about, with an arrangement at the University, which was achievable because of Telemann's persona—thereby, to unite, in one hand, the authority to direct all the music in Leipzig. Organizationally, its aim was to centralize Leipzig's musical life around an outstanding personage, a principal municipal music director who would, if possible, also be the academic music director. Substantively, its aim was to transform Leipzig's organizationally centralized musical life into a center of musical contemporaneity—and not only in the realm of church music. There is little doubt that sooner or later Telemann was expected to assume, once more, the position of the director of the Collegium Musicum. Perhaps the Kapellmeister faction even had a plan, or at least a hope, that he would reactivate the Leipzig opera.

After Telemann (in November, 1722) and then Graupner (in March, 1723) declined the position of cantor at the Thomasschule, the University elected Johann Gottlieb Görner, in response to his application, as its music director on April 3, 1723. The University selected him at a time when it was predictable that the city would elect Bach as cantor of the Thomasschule. The University wanted to act before the election by the city, which was to take place in the meetings of the Executive Council on April 9 and the Three Councils on April 22. Neither in Telemann's nor in Graupner's case had the University carried out such a preemptive action. The Three Councils never confirmed Graupner's election; for this reason, Graupner was never in a position to apply for the music directorship of the University. Before the meeting of January 15, Graupner's election by the Executive Council was predictable; but this did not cause the University to carry out such a preemptive election. Now, however, faced with Bach (and possibly Kauffmann), the University confronted them with a *fait accompli*.

The University wanted its music director to be one of its own. It could accept a candidate from the group of opera composers, because opera composers had been academically trained. Not so the organists; that is why the University rejected the possibility of a candidate from among the organists. In fact, neither Bach nor Kauffmann was academically trained. The non-academics were good enough if all you needed was a clever organ technician. To test the organ in the Paulinerkirche in 1717, they had also considered Kauffmann before inviting Bach.[38] But to elect a non-academic as music director was impossible. In order not to run the risk of having to respond to the request of a non-academic, the University made its decision before the city could act. In this way, when they rejected Bach, they were able to base their decision not only on the general principle that the University was not always obliged to accept the cantor elected by the city, but also on the specific argument "because he applied too late."[39] This particular excuse, however, was sheer mockery. For Bach could not apply before he was legally elected by the city. The University, which did not want a non-academic, had created a circumstance in which, from the outset, Bach could only apply after it was too late.

It is not necessary here to detail the long and complex struggle between Bach and the University. In the end, the occupant of the position of cantor at the Thomasschule and his students were responsible, in matters of polyphony, only for the oldest traditional elements of "common music" at both the Neue Kirche and the Paulinerkirche—namely, motets. To conduct these in person was beneath the dignity of the Kapellmeister and was therefore delegated to the prefects. The contemporary *Musica formalis*, the *Concert Musique*, was, in both places, entrusted to others.[40] Bach rejected the University's compromise offer, in which Rector Ludovici, who had only recently served as vice-rector of the Thomasschule, offered him one half of the salary.[41] Instead, Bach appealed to the sovereign, seeking legal redress by administrative means. Naturally, the University had better options for legal representation. Thus Bach, by trying to get everything, ended up with nothing.

The Kapellmeister faction did not succeed in creating a union between the municipal and academic musical directorships and integrating the University into the musical life of the city. Nevertheless, after Bach's election had been confirmed, Gottfried Lange expressed confidence in the future, stating that it "would be necessary to give thought to a famous man, so that the *studiosi* should be animated."[42] True, the Kapellmeister faction had not been able to secure a famous man, an opera composer and, above all, not the most famous of the famous, Telemann. But the musical qualifications and professional competence that Bach brought to the position were so superior—especially compared with the University's choice, Görner—that they would attract precisely the most musically talented students to collaborate under his direction. This, then, was what actually happened.

Figure 5.4. Night music with Leipzig students. Engraving, 1729.

Bach and the Neue Kirche reached a preliminary agreement either when he assumed his new position or shortly thereafter. The job of directing the cantatas of the first choir in Bach's absence fell to Georg Balthasar Schott (and later to his successor Carl Gotthelf Gerlach). The organist and music director of the Neue Kirche had also been given the function of a second substitute music director of the principal churches.[43] The definitive arrangement fell into place after a change occurred in the position of organist and music director of the Neue Kirche. At the end of March 1729, Schott left his position at the Neue Kirche to become municipal cantor in Gotha. The fact that Gottfried Lange was the mayor in office in 1728–29 and, after September 1728, was the most senior among the mayors, had a favorable impact on the outcome. First, Lange dismissed Schott, who had most likely been elected to and assumed the position at the Neue Kirche in August 1720 during Lange's first year in office, with a gratuity of 24 Speziestaler.[44] This was the equivalent of 32 Reichstaler Courant and was a significant amount considering Schott's annual salary of 50 Reichstaler Courant. Bach took over the direction of the Collegium Musicum, which was not a municipal institution. For the cantor of the Thomasschule to take over the leadership of the Collegium Musicum, which had been linked to the Neue Kirche for almost twenty-five years—since Telemann's time[45]—was a deep intrusion into the structure of Leipzig's musical life. This reorganization of the lines of responsibility is in line with the goals of the Kapellmeister faction, which wanted the cantor of the Thomasschule to become the municipal director, the central figure not only for church music but also for all concert music in Leipzig. Perhaps it was agreed at the time of Bach's installation as cantor that this arrangement would come into play as soon as a change in the position of the organist and music director of the Neue Kirche and, hence, in the leadership of the Collegium Musicum, made it possible. In Bach's opening words when he announced his assumption of the direction of the Collegium Musicum, it is possible to hear his relief that the time of waiting is over: "The latest news is that God has now, too [that is, finally], provided for the honorable Herr Schott and has given him the cantor's position in Gotha."[46] Schott's successor Gerlach was now limited to the roles of organist and music director of the Neue Kirche.[47]

With these changes, the status of the music program of the Neue Kirche changed. As early as 1725, it is true, the five musicians at the Neue Kirche had received an extra gratuity. A year later, it was made into a regular benefit that was awarded annually, upon application; but the designated support began in 1730. In May, 36 Reichstaler were approved for two violins, a viola, and a cello. The Thomaskirche had received the same amount for the same purpose a year earlier. On June 10, Gerlach's salary was doubled, from 50 to 100 Reichstaler, beginning immediately with the third quarter. Further salary increases follow in 1735, 1746, and 1747 until, in this year, his regular income reached 235 Reichstaler.

It is not possible, as a rule, to know in whose mayoral term these commitments occurred, but an unambiguous situation existed in 1730: the four stringed instruments and the doubling of Gerlach's salary were both approved during the term of Jakob Born, who had become the speaker for the Cantor faction after Platz died in 1728. This raises a question. On the one hand, it is indisputable that Gerlach was elected on Bach's recommendation and represented him as music director. Their relationship was collegial, and they belonged, if not to the same, at least to a similar musical trend. On the other hand, it is indisputable that Jakob Born, under whose regime the targeted support of the music program of the Neue Kirche began, was a member of the Cantor faction. I am unable to resolve this contradiction. However, it should be noted in this context that "the inanimate body" of Abraham Christoph Platz was interred "in the burial place that had been set aside by him under the chapel in the Neue Kirche."[48] It would be quite plausible to assume that the new worship services in Leipzig were originally introduced in order to bring the need for a new piety, which had erupted and been suppressed during the Pietist disturbances of 1689 to 1691, into regular ecclesiastical channels.

When Bach became director of the Collegium Musicum, he also assumed the role of directing the city's concert life. At the same time, he had gained access to a core group of qualified instrumentalists whom he could also involve in church music. Bach did not wait long before demonstrating the wealth of instrumental power that he finally had at his disposal. On June 6, 1729, Whitmonday, he introduced the main music, Cantata 174, with a version of the first movement of his third Brandenburg Concerto that he had expanded harmonically.[49] One may wonder why this demonstration took place on Whitmonday rather than on Whitsunday. Perhaps there were external reasons, for example, the availability of a particular instrumentalist. But perhaps Bach did not want its initial presentation to be in the main service at the Nikolaikirche, which was under the supervision of either Johann August Hölzel or Jakob Born—both members of the Cantor faction—but rather in the main service of the Thomaskirche, whose supervisor was Gottfried Lange.

In organizing Leipzig's musical life, Lange had some latitude to accomplish his ideas. At the Thomasschule, as at the University, he came up against barriers that were set by these institutions.[50] In any case, in the eyes of the Cantor faction the restructuring that had been carried out was serious enough. For it gave Bach a leading role in the concert life of the city, as it simultaneously opened up new possibilities for more elaborate forms of church music. Neither was what the Cantor faction had in mind. Moreover, the restructuring brought about by the Kapellmeister faction removed Bach even further from the school and set him on his own feet. It gave Bach, for the first time, a firm organizational basis for his activities as Kapellmeister. To the Cantor faction, it seemed that the delicate balance, which it had tolerated only reluctantly in any case, had been upset and, during Jakob Born's tenure as mayor in the following year, it prepared to strike back.

New Contests in the Executive Council:
The Cantor Faction Seeks Change

The Kapellmeister faction could have gotten along very nicely with the exception allowing Bach to hire a substitute to teach for him, as described above (p. 146). The Cantor faction, however, was unable to accept it; the longer it lasted, the less this faction was able to accept it. After seven years, it launched an attempt to put an end, if not to Bach's tenure then at least to the exception. At the meeting of the Executive Council on August 2, 1730, Jakob Born, of the Cantor faction, who had been a member of the Three Councils during the negotiations for Kuhnau's successor, was now the Mayor in office. He had assumed this position when Platz died in 1728. At the end of this meeting, ostensibly convened to discuss the inadequacy of the school building and the need for reconstruction, Born began to talk about the cantor, which was not on the agenda—obviously to catch the Kapellmeister faction off guard by mounting a surprise attack. He presented a three-step plan: first, a new arrangement under the terms of the exception; second, an end to the exception during Bach's tenure; and third, an end to the exception by means of an end to Bach's tenure.[51]

The first step was a new arrangement under the terms of the exception. Since the agreement concerning the substitute was dependent on the support of the Council, the Council could make its continuing support contingent on a personnel change if it found the substitute no longer adequate. "Monsieur Pezold [sic] had done a poor job of doing what was required [as Bach's substitute]; the third and fourth forms were the seed bed of the entire school, and it is necessary to provide them with a competent individual." Born makes a motion arguing that "one would first have to consider whether it would not be preferable to provide another individual for these classes. Kriegel was said to be a good man; they would have to consider such a resolution."

The second step is an end to the exception during Bach's tenure. The idea that the approval of the exception was itself revocable was not a sudden insight. The bond obligated Bach to the city and did not obligate the city to him. The consistory had agreed to Bach's proposed substitute, Pezold, only conditionally: "at this time," that is, until further notice, "his teaching responsibilities may be left to his colleague from the third form."[52] Finally, the mayor comes to the third stage of his plan, an end to the exception by putting an end to Bach's tenure: "He did not behave in the proper way. In particular, he had sent a choirboy to the countryside without informing the Mayor in office and gone out of town without leave, which he should be forbidden to do and for which he should be reprimanded." The punishment for lack of compliance with the bond was loss of the position. The Mayor speaks only of forbidding and reprimanding, but the goal of this third step of the plan is nevertheless clear—removal from office.

All twelve members of the Executive Council at this time had been councilors in 1722–23; seven had participated directly in the negotiations as members of the Executive Council. The Kapellmeister faction now included Gottfried Lange (supervisor of the St. Thomas Church) and Johann Franz Born; the Cantor faction included Adrian Steger, Johann August Hölzel (supervisor of the St. Nicholas Church), and Johann Job. Lange addressed the third step of the plan and did not cite any facts in Bach's defense; rather, he agreed with the accusations saying, "Everything was true that had been said against the cantor." In this way, he prevented any discussion of the accusations. Furthermore, he agreed with mild disciplinary measures prohibiting and reprimanding Bach. He then immediately turned his attention to the first step and agreed with the motion "to occupy this position with Monsieur Kriegel." By expressing no disagreement, Lange prevented the implementation of steps two and three of Born's plan.

After Lange, Mayor Steger of the Cantor faction responded irritably: "The cantor himself not only did nothing, he refused to give any explanation for it. He gave no vocal lessons, and there were other complaints besides." He stated the goal of his faction without hesitation: "A change would be necessary, there would have to be a break." The argument centers on the need to revoke the exemption from instruction. The only thing to do is make a change in the appointment of the cantor. But at this point Steger could only maneuver within the framework that Lange had lain out; therefore he "concedes that another arrangement should be made," and that there should be a change in the substitute from Pezold to Kriegel. After Steger, Johann Franz Born, another adherent of the Kapellmeister faction, "agrees with the above-mentioned opinions." For Johann August Hölzel, the minutes show only a "Yes." An unidentified member of the Cantor faction must have requested and gotten a resolution demanding a significant punishment: "It was resolved to reduce the cantor's salary." The sole remaining councilor, Jacob Job, felt the need to justify his "Yes": "because the cantor was incorrigible." Bach was indeed incorrigible, not as an individual but as a type—a Kapellmeister could not be corrected or improved into a Cantor.

On August 25, twenty-three days after the previous meeting, Jakob Born reported to the Executive Council that he "had spoken with the cantor, who, however, showed little desire to work."[53] Without authorization by any decision of the Council, he had attempted to implement step two of his plan directly with Bach, asking him to take over instruction of one of the lower classes; Bach refused. Now the earlier motion was confirmed, and the final decision was made to replace as Bach's substitute the third-form instructor, Carl Friedrich Pezold, with the fourth-form instructor, Abraham Kriegel. Bach's payment would now go to the new substitute instead of the old one.

Bach's efforts in search of a new position ("compelled . . . to seek my fortune elsewhere"), as documented in the letter of October 28, 1730 to George Erdmann,[54] can be traced to the pressure exerted by Mayor Jakob Born at the end of his first year in office. Bach could not but regard him as "an odd authority, and not much devoted to music." (Bach establishes his priorities with regard to issues and individuals: he places music above community and his professional competence as the highest-ranking musician above the directive of the mayor who governs the community.) Under the existing circumstances, Bach found that he had to live "in almost constant vexation, envy, and harassment" by the Cantor faction.

It is noteworthy that in his report of his conversation with Bach at the August 25 meeting of the Executive Council, the mayor did not mention *Bach's Draft of a Well-Appointed Church Music*, as far as we can tell from the minutes, which are dated just two days earlier, on August 23.[55] No transmittal letter, address, or record of receipt is extant for this document. Only the location where it was first found, the municipal archive of Leipzig, confirms its relationship to the Town Council. This fact, if it does not indicate that it was simply misplaced, may indicate that it was not Bach's decision to write it but that it was done at the request of the Kapellmeister faction. Lange may have asked for such a memorandum to reorganize Leipzig's church music as part of an offensive response to the policy being carried out by the Cantor faction. If Bach presented the memorandum to Lange personally, and Lange gave it to the registrar's office when he no longer needed it, it would have arrived at the archive without a paper trail. The assumption that Lange requested the memorandum provides a straightforward explanation for its style, in general, and for its numerous details.

The roles that the Leipzig town councilors and their wives played as godparents of Bach's children give us clues concerning their position *vis-à-vis* the Kapellmeister faction and their support of Bach's candidacy. For godfather of his first child born in Leipzig, Gottfried Heinrich, Bach chose Gottfried Lange, who also lent the child his name.[56] The godparents of Elisabeth Juliana Friederica, baptized on April 5, 1726, were Gottfried Wilhelm Küster's wife, Christiana Elisabeth, and Carl Friedrich Romanus's wife, Juliana.[57] The godparents of Ernestus Andreas, baptized on October 30, 1727, were Johann Ernst Kregel junior and Gottfried Leonhard Baudiss's wife, Magdalena Sibylla.[58] The relationship with the Küsters was long-lasting; as late as 1752, after her husband's death, Anna Magdalena Bach stands in for Christiana Elisabeth Küstner, whose husband had succeeded Gottfried Lange as mayor in 1748, as godmother at a baptism.[59]

The End of Bach's Tenure

The failed attempt by the Cantor faction to put an end to the exception in the summer of 1730 forced them to be patient—for a long time, as it turned out. Two decades would pass before it ended, through no effort of theirs, with Bach's death on July 28, 1750. However, even before that happened, there was a decisive change in the leadership body of Leipzig.

When Lange died in November 1748, he had been the longest-serving mayor—for twenty years. Jakob Born moved into his position, so that it was once again in the hands of the Cantor faction; after him came Stieglitz, also from the Cantor faction. The third mayor, Lange's successor from the Kapellmeister faction, was Küstner, a newcomer. This change in leadership had no impact on Bach's tenure in office; however it did affect the choice of his successor and the way he was chosen. The prime minister of Saxony, Count Brühl, discussed the issue of Bach's successor with the senior mayor, Jakob Born, during a visit to Leipzig. Brühl recommended the director of his private orchestra, Harrer, as Bach's successor. He subsequently provided Harrer with a letter of recommendation to Born, which Harrer delivered personally.[60] Brühl's letter proposed a two-step process. The Council would offer Harrer an opportunity to audition, and if the audition were successful (which was not in doubt), the prospect of assuming the position would be officially confirmed. The audition was arranged promptly; it took place on the following Sunday, June 8, 1749, the first Sunday after Trinity, "in the large music concert hall at Three Swans on the Brühl," where it was performed "to the greatest applause."[61] What effect all this had on Bach was probably something to which Born did not devote a single thought. Born decided in favor of a preemptive election, because his faction was sympathetic to the plan. If Bach were to die during the following year, 1749–50, the mayor in office would have been Küstner, a representative of the Kapellmeister faction. In order to prevent all discussion in advance, Born created a *fait accompli*.

At the meeting of the Executive Council on August 7, 1750, after Bach's death, with Küstner as the mayor in office, Born appealed to *force majeure* saying, "He could not very well go against the recommendation."[62] The end of the concession of the one-time exception and the reestablishment of the norm were proclaimed by Christian Ludwig Stieglitz, who had been a member of the Council since 1715 and had participated in the meeting of the Three Councils that had confirmed Bach's election on April 22, 1722. The next day, at the meeting of the Three Councils, Stieglitz again proclaimed, "Herr Bach may well have been a great *musicus*, but no school teacher. Hence in replacing his service as cantor of the Thomasschule, they must seek an individual who would be skilled in both; and he believed that in Herr Harrer (who had been proposed by Count Brühl, the Saxon prime minister) both would be found." The position would once again be filled in accordance with its definition.

Still, the Cantor faction continued to feel threatened by the Kapellmeister faction. As late as October 1, 1755, after Bach's successor had died and the election of his replacement was due to be confirmed by the three councils, Mayor Jakob Born felt compelled to reiterate the principle of the Cantor faction and cite the tenure of Kapellmeister Bach as a negative example and that of his predecessor Kuhnau as a positive example: "The cantor's office should be put on the previous footing, as in the case of Herr Kuhnau, and the new cantor should be concerned with both music and instruction, whereas under Herr Bach many *désordres* had occurred."[63]

The Intellectual Background

The specific controversy between the Cantor faction and the Kapellmeister faction was only a symptom of the differences in their broader intellectual positions. The controversy over the definition and selection of the cantor at the Thomasschule was rooted in differences in their theological convictions. It is likely that the sharpness and durability of this particular controversy derived from this general background. In his autobiography, Mayor Platz, the Cantor faction spokesman during the negotiations over Kuhnau's successor, mentions the name of Philipp Jakob Spener. He sympathized with the non-separatist trend of Pietism within the church. Mayor Steger, his second, is opposed to theatrical, or opera-like, music in church, a position notably linked to Pietism. Stieglitz, who became mayor when Steger died in 1741, had served as supervisor of the Thomasschule since 1729 and, hence, was its expert on the Council, inheriting this position from Gottfried Konrad Lehmann in 1728, who had also belonged to the Cantor faction. Under Stieglitz, Johann Matthias Gesner was appointed rector of the Thomasschule in 1730; and Johann August Ernesti (who had been a tutor in Stieglitz's house since 1730) was appointed first vice-rector in 1731 and then rector in 1734, following Gesner's departure for the University of Göttingen. In the history of academic instruction, Gesner and J. A. Ernesti are closely associated.[64] In working for their respective elections, Stieglitz could not have known where they were going and for what they were preparing the way—the new humanism. He could only know from where they came: the reform pedagogy of August Hermann Francke. All available data thus point to the conclusion that the members of the Cantor faction were inclined toward Pietism.

Not so the members of the Kapellmeister faction, who were oriented in a different direction. This is already evident from the fact that their first three candidates, Telemann, Fasch, and Graupner, came from the opera and thus were involved with the very theatrical music that the Cantor faction rejected. Three of the Kapellmeister faction's candidates—Telemann, Fasch, and Schott—were connected to Collegia Musica; and two of them—Telemann and Schott—were also connected to the musical programs of the Neue Kirche, which represented a new, modern style of composition, musical cooperation, and performance. They also represented closeness to the university and to the opera. Here a new, modern esthetic was being created—the esthetic of the Enlightenment. The musical activities of the Neue Kirche were linked with the name of its initiator, Telemann, the first candidate of the Kapellmeister faction. Its orientation was the Enlightenment.

To avoid misunderstandings: I am not claiming that the members of the Cantor faction were Pietists, and the members of the Kapellmeister faction, followers of the Enlightenment. Adherence to Lutheran orthodoxy was the consensus on which Leipzig society was erected.[65] No one with rank and name, position and honors, could or would have departed from this foundation. But on this foundation, tendencies could develop that, while never fundamentally challenging the common foundation, nevertheless gave it a particular coloration. The members of both factions were committed to Lutheran orthodoxy; but on the basis of this consensus, the members of the Cantor faction leaned toward Pietism, while the members of the Kapellmeister faction leaned toward the Enlightenment. At any rate, these divergent tendencies determined the inclinations of the adherents of these two factions to such an extent that they resulted in an inexorable and long-lasting controversy over the definition of the position of cantor at the Thomasschule and his selection.

The Kapellmeister faction had nominated two groups of candidates—candidates who came from the opera and candidates who came from the organ. The lone wolf Schott had been nominated not on the basis of membership in either of these groups but on the basis of his position as organist and music director of the Neue Kirche, in his capacity as Telemann's successor. The new, international esthetic obviously favored the opera composers; it seemed to flourish on the basis of opera, or theatrical music. But what spoke for the organists? As far as we can see, the organists were rooted firmly, or at least more firmly than the opera composers, in the traditional worldview of Lutheran orthodoxy. What impelled the Kapellmeister faction to nominate them was not primarily their tendency toward the new esthetic, but their complete professional competence. This, too, demonstrates a tendency toward Enlightenment. For the training of professionals, who use rational methods to explore the limits of their fields, present their results systematically and, in this way, make their contribution to the Encyclopedia, was another goal of the Enlightenment. What separated the opera composers from the organists was not their service to the church, for all three opera composers worked extensively for the church, as they would have been expected to do in Leipzig. In this respect, they did not even differ from the cantors. Rather, what the Kapellmeister faction sought was a different type of musician. In one case, they placed the accent on a new esthetic orientation, in the other, on professional competence. Both emphases—an international style and fame and/or competent professionalism—separated their candidates from the emphasis of the candidates of the opposing faction—the music theory of the middle German cantor. The Kapellmeister faction saw in Bach the comprehensively competent musician—they could not have found anyone more competent. This judgment by Lange and his faction corresponded to Bach's own image of himself, because Bach drew his identity from his unrivalled professional competence.

Given the existing constellation of forces, this most competent professional musician was exposed to criticism from two sides. One side faulted Bach for not being an academic; the other, for not having the new esthetic. His defense was on two fronts in the 1730s: on one side against Johann August Ernesti, the protégé of Stieglitz; on the other side against Johann Adolph Scheibe, the student of Gottsched. In the minds of the Leipzig Town Councilors, he represented a competent professional musician; within the universal framework of Lutheran orthodoxy, he represented an element of the Enlightenment.

Two Biographies

The biographies of the principal protagonists in the Cantor faction-Kapellmeister faction conflict are published in the final section of Siegele's original work. These biographies are models exemplifying the different kinds of opportunities available in Saxony for social mobility and gaining access to the highest levels of political and social power during the first half of the eighteenth century. People were no longer strictly limited by their inherited "Stand." Education and ability, wealth and influence—all were possible vehicles for success under absolutism.

Gottfried Lange

The "Memorial in Honor of Gottfried Lange [1672–1748], the Privy Councilor for War to the King of Poland and Elector of Saxony As Composed in the Year 1749 by A Learned Writer and Read in A Learned Assembly"[66] outlines Lange's life and career. The lecture, which was held in Greiffenberg, honors the experienced and famed legal scholar, wise courtier, and diligent director of a respected republic. It describes his birth as honest but not distinguished. His paternal grandfather was a councilor and potter; his maternal grandfather, a citizen and merchant in Greiffenberg. Gottfried's father and older brother were parsons, and his sisters founded four parsonages. He received his schooling from one of his mother's brothers, who was the rector of a primary school in Niederwiesa near Greiffenberg (and later of the lyceum in Löbau), and attended the Gymnasium in Zittau. As a tutor, he accompanied Count Maximilian von Wied not only to the Ritterakademie in Wolfenbüttel, but also to the most distinguished German courts—a preparation for his future services at court. After receiving his *doctor juris* from the Faculty of Law in Erfurt, he complemented his previous studies of history, rhetoric, and contemporary politics with lectures in law, especially public law. At the court in Dresden, after presenting a manifesto, which had been graciously assigned to him, on the subject of the repossession of the Polish throne, he made a pleasant impression with his thorough knowledge of public law and his skillful pen. Despite his positions in Leipzig, he was called to court on several occasions and frequently had to accompany the King to Poland. Since he had devoted much of his energy to this task, he received permission in 1716 to reside in Dresden permanently. On assuming the office of mayor in Leipzig, he was presented with a bejeweled portrait of the king as a sign of royal favor. He had been an assessor since 1715 and, in 1721, he was given a seat in the Jurors' Court. At the time of his death, he was the most senior mayor of the city of Leipzig, director and senior member of the consistory, supervisor of the Thomasschule, and the senior member of the Great Princes' College in Leipzig. He had been married, since 1702, to Rahel, the daughter of M. Joachim Feller, a professor of poetry in Leipzig. Of their seven children, three daughters died in childhood. One married and two unmarried daughters and a single son survived.

The distinctive features of Lange's resumé are evident from the facts given above. He was not from Leipzig but, with interruptions, had spent almost twenty years there—the period of his academic career—before being called to the court of August the Strong and turning from academic work to politics. Nevertheless, to native born, lifelong Leipzigers, Lange would have appeared as an intruder from the outset; his entry was as the King's and Elector's person. Platz, and later Jakob Born too, had close ties to the court; indeed their political roles consisted, at least in part, in fostering these ties for the benefit of the city; however, going from Leipzig to the court was very different than coming from the court to Leipzig.

The sovereign had forced Lange onto Leipzig's political scene.[67] The records reporting his intervention are extant. In 1710 Lange submitted his application to the Leipzig Town Council, proposing that he would accept a seat without salary, for the time being, "until he could expect to be free of his service at court and be truly active in the Council seat." Although the Executive Council did not show particular pleasure over this application, "recommendations from the great" nevertheless required it be looked upon with consideration. At first, Mayor Winckler wanted "not to take the matter seriously," and Executive Councilor Revinus believed that Lange had picked the place "for his retirement," because he did not intend to remain in Poland forever. Nevertheless, he was awarded a seat. A few years later, Lange unsuccessfully tried climbing the Council's hierarchy to become a Proconsul, which implied the expectancy of promotion to Consul, that is, one of the mayoral offices. Consequently, the Elector assigned Lange to the Supreme Court and the Consistory, two Electoral bodies situated in Leipzig. He also secretly exacted the promise of the next vacant mayoral office for Lange, in an arrangement known to Mayors Platz and Gräve. In 1919, at the time a successor to Mayor Schacher needed to be elected, an order was received from the Elector to immediately call Lange to be the new mayor. However, Councilor Steger, never informed of this agreement, had believed that it was his turn to become mayor and was disappointed. Yet, although he protested against being passed over, on March 10, he joined his colleagues in voting for Lange with the understanding that he could work out an electoral order that would designate him as mayor in the future. Steger had attacked Lange's candidacy, but the object of his protestations was the patron.

The circumstances under which Lange had been chosen directly determined Steger's relationship to him. True, Steger was elected mayor shortly after Lange was, but because Lange had been elected outside the usual order of succession, Steger never became a senior mayor. Later, in 1728, he still felt bitter about Lange's move to this rank. The tone in which Steger expressed his opinions about the candidates for cantor and, later, about the incumbent of the Kapellmeister's faction often projected the personal affront that Lange's election continued to signify.[68]

Yet Lange seems to have mastered the difficult situation; the "Honored Memory" stated that he not only won the hearts of Leipzig's citizens but also maintained and enhanced his position at court. Lange's time at court, approximately ten years, must have had a powerful impact on the ideas of a pastor's son about cultural politics. His political origins at the court and his lasting good relations with it must be considered in connection with the goals that he pursued in the realm of cultural politics, above all, with respect to the candidates he considered when it came to choosing Kuhnau's successor. In particular, the candidacy of Bach (whom Lange could have heard in Dresden in 1717) and the well-known ties that Bach maintained from Leipzig to Dresden and its musical scene, should be seen from this perspective. While he did not forget his origins, Lange embraced the goal of making Leipzig's music program the counterpart of that of the Dresden court—a contemporary center of bourgeois music befitting the city's political and, above all, economic importance.

During the first half of the 1740s, Lange's strength began to decline, starting with his hearing. (In his last regular year in office, 1746–47, Jakob Born carried out his duties as acting mayor.) It is striking that Lange's decline, Bach's withdrawal from the direction of the Collegium Musicum, and the founding of the *Großes Concert* all occurred in the same five-year period. Obviously, the cultural-political balance was beginning to shift.[69]

Abraham Christoph Platz

Throughout the negotiations over Johann Kuhnau's successor and up until 1728, Gottfried Lange had an opponent of considerable character in the person of his colleague Abraham Christoph Platz (died 1728), or Plaz, as he himself wrote his last name. Platz was born on April 18, 1658, in Leipzig. His father, Christoph, a merchant in the same city, was the son of Antonius Platz, a merchant in Augsburg. His mother, Ursula Katharina, was the eldest daughter of D. Abraham Teller, a pastor at the Thomaskirche and assessor of the Leipzig consistory. Abraham's mother died on the day after his birth, his maternal grandfather died half a year later, and his father died when the boy was three-and-a-half years old. He was educated by his maternal grandmother and by Johann Gabriel Drechßler, the later Tertius at the gymnasium in Halle. From his fourteenth year, he was on his own. On December 2, 1672, Platz matriculated at the University of Leipzig, starting out in philosophy. He earned the title of

Baccalaureus in 1675 and Magister in February 1675. Destined from his earliest years to become a theologian, he had learned Hebrew as a schoolboy and perfected this language above all others, along with his Rabbinical studies. But difficulties arose that made him feel no longer confident of success, and he switched to law. In this, his mother's brother, D. Romanus Teller, gave him support. He passed his oral examination under the latter's chairmanship on May 23, 1679. The next day he began his travels, which took him to Hamburg, and from there, via Westphalia, Friesland, Holland, the Spanish Netherlands, and England, to France. He spent the winter in Paris, then traveled via Sedan, Dinant, and other towns on the Maas River to Cologne; then, following the Rhine upstream, he visited the principal cities of the Holy Roman Empire and several cities in Switzerland before returning to Leipzig on August 21, 1680. Here an epidemic had broken out, and he retired to the Teller estate, "Kitzscher." In June 1681, he went to Frankfurt-an-der-Oder and on August 9 of the same year he was promoted to the Doctorate. In August 1683, he became a member of the Leipzig Town Council, and on the same day took office as an attorney for the Judicial Supreme Court, which he had been promised as early as 1681. In 1687 he became a municipal judge; in 1699, a vice consul; in 1705, supervisor of the Nicolaikirche (and the Nicolaischule); and shortly thereafter mayor. The latter position was coupled with a position on the Assessor's Court. In the same year, he also received an assessor's position with the Supreme Court; in 1709, a supernumerary; and in 1710, a regular position as councilor of the Appellate Court in Dresden. He was married three times: to Maria Sophia Martini (d. 1702), Anna Magdalena Schwendendörfer (d. 1712), and Margaretha Regina Packbusch. Platz became ill at the beginning of July 1728 with jaundice, but nevertheless fulfilled his official functions. At the end of the month, he even traveled to Dresden for a session of the Appellate Court. On September 3, he returned to Leipzig, drained of all strength, and passed away in the evening of the fifteenth of the month, at about eight o'clock.

Platz himself informed posterity about his life.[70] The full title of his publication, which comprises two unnumbered and 122 numbered folio pages, reads as follows: "Life-chronicle and Final Farewell of Herr D. Abraham Christoph Plaz [sic], Residing at Mockau, Althen, and Plösen; Juris Consultus, Royal Polish and Electoral Appellate Councilor, Assessor, and Elder of the Most Worthy Supreme Court and of the Jurors' Court in this City, respectively; Senior Mayor and Supervisor of the Church and School of St. Nikolai; Accompanied by a Reflection on Genesis XV, v. 1, and Romans VIII, v. 31 and 32. Composed by the Deceased Himself, and Printed at his Behest. Leipzig, printed by Bernhard Christoph Breitkopf. 1729." The parts mentioned in title are presented in this order: "Biography" (1–46), "Reflections on Genesis 15:1 and Romans 8:31–32" (47–72), and "The Last Parting" (72–122). This survey hardly conveys an impression of the many-sidedness and richness contained in this piece. This extraordinary work is at once a calling to account and a testament, the confession and hope of a religious, personal, and public life that was led with self-conscious awareness and piety, with independence toward the world and connection to God, with self-examination and faith, constantly striving for righteousness and modesty.

The first part, "Biography," begins with a justification for this unusual enterprise (1–2). Platz had decided on a simple funeral: "But lest it appear that I hereby want to suppress and annihilate memory and the facts posterity may need—lest I seem to be going without leave-taking—I have decided, not from a desire for vain honors, to leave the following." The biography, in a narrow sense, follows (2–11). As he gathers the data, he includes a reflection about juridical activities as a practicing lawyer (4–7); and of his "*humeur* and the life he led," that is, of his temperament and the conduct of his life (11–17). In a section on "his spiritual and mental condition" (17–23), he includes information about the final state of his health and illnesses (23–24). As far as the "state of [Platz's] mind and soul" is concerned, he himself confesses "that I had not arrived at such a thorough knowledge of my state until the time when the dear man of God, D. Spener, came into these parts" (19). Platz calls Spener a "scholarly, God-fearing, and exemplary theologian" and defends his activities, above all, against his critics, but also against those who falsely claim to follow him (20–21). This biographical section also summarized a prayer (25–38). A treatise on funeral customs (38–46) concludes the first part.

The "reflection" forming the second part is based on the two biblical citations he chose as mottos when he first became mayor in 1705. If he had not decided against a memorial sermon, he would have requested one that explicated these two citations and the hymn, "In the Lord I have put my trust" (45–46). The third part, "The Last Parting," begins with a section that could be entitled "Of the World's Absurdity" (72–76). There follows his leave-taking from particular people, those "on whom I have been dependent in this temporal life or to whom I have been indebted": first, from the capital city Dresden, the sovereign, the ministers and councilors, the Appellate Court (77–79); then, from Leipzig, the Supreme Court, the Council, the Jurors' Court, the clergy, the citizenry (80–90). Finally, Platz turns to personal matters and takes leave from his family, friends, enemies, his subjects in Mockau, Althen and Plösen, and from the entire world (90–98). The leave-taking, like the biography, flows into a prayer (98–100). There follows, as an addendum, a speech about the councilor's oath of office, which he gave in the session of August 29, 1707 (101–20). The document ends with a supplement in another hand about Platz's last illness and his end (120–22).

I want to draw comparisons between certain aspects of the lives of Platz and Lange. Platz and his father were Leipzig citizens. The son of a merchant (89), Platz was able to make a journey, which took a year-and-a quarter, through northern Europe although, he writes, he had to make do with a rather modest sum compared with others (12). He mentions several times that he attained his office "by proper vocation without the slightest undue influence pedaling or politicking" (27–28), that "I did not in my lifetime make a particular effort to gain office . . . Nay, the two most important offices were freely offered to me without my asking" (16), especially the mayor's office, which was obtained "without my expecting it or squandering a single word or facial expression" (46). Platz had "this and that opportunity to be employed at the Court and in other councils, organizations which I did not find it advisable to join for various reasons" (9), later writing, "because I simply did not find myself suitable" (16). His sarcastic description of life at Court follows: "One can rise above all of this by remaining away from things of that kind and by leaving it to those who, as it were, are born and raised for this and to whom it may do greater service" (17).

Regarding this issue, compare the lives of Lange and Platz. Gottfried Lange's father was a village parson in Upper Lusatia. He was able to travel as far as Wolfenbüttel and to the best German courts only as the tutor of a count. At the end of his academic career, he went to the court of August the Strong, obtaining a seat as councilor and then mayor on the strength of the ruler's intervention. The parson's son took a different route than the son of a Leipzig merchant (although this merchant's son had been raised by a pastor's widow). Although the assumption that what Platz expressed was directly aimed at Lange would probably be going too far, the comparison of the two careers intimates what distinct social and individual characters could be united in the Leipzig Council and, in fact, were united when Bach was selected.

Conclusion

Any attempt to reconstruct the social universe in which Bach participated while living in Leipzig is limited by the available sources. Since there is little hope of finding new sources that would unambiguously disclose where Bach situated himself within this universe and where others situated him, we are forced to base such a reconstruction on what is available. More must be considered than has been up until now: the institutions, their particular function and traditions, their structures, their cooperativeness and their conflicts. Yet one must not lose sight of the fact that these institutions were maintained by individuals who were formed by their origins, education, and careers, and who were related to each other through marriage or involvements in other relationships that often joined together various institutions through personal connections. The way to such a reconstruction is lengthy; therefore, it must be left to further investigations to see whether the relationship between Leipzig's government and Bach's conduct in office can be clarified to a greater extent and in greater detail. In doing so, one would need to consider not only the administrative but also the musical side of these relationships.[71]

A review of Bach's tenure in office leads to the conclusion that the Kapellmeister faction assumed the role of patron and fulfilled it to the extent possible. Admittedly, for both sides, disappointment seems to have surfaced rather soon and proved to be lasting. Because it was not able to secure an opera composer but only an organist, the Kapellmeister faction had to compromise its ideal in two respects: First, it could not transform the position of cantor at the Thomasschule into a municipal musical directorship but was only able to achieve a one-time agreement to fill the position with a Kapellmeister. Second, it could not formally achieve the union of the municipal and the academic music directorships but had to be satisfied, informally, by the superiority of its Kapellmeister over the music director of the University.

These were the same two points that made difficulties for Bach during his tenure in office. Bach had decided in favor of Leipzig on the condition that he could look forward to the unrestricted realization of the Kapellmeister faction's goal, as in the cases of the opera composer Graupner and, before him, for the opera composer Telemann. Then, after he was elected and had arrived, he was installed in the position not of municipal music director but of cantor of the Thomasschule—a cantor who could free himself from the specific duties of a cantor by means of a private arrangement.[72] As a result, Bach had to reckon with potential difficulties on the part of the Cantor faction at all times and, in fact, until the end of the 1730s had to struggle against them quite often. Furthermore, when he arrived to take up his post, the position of music director of the University had already been filled, and the all-embracing musical position that he had promised himself in Leipzig was limited in this direction. These were the two shadows that fell on Bach's tenure in office that were based on structural conditions facing the patron and the client, the Kapellmeister faction and Bach himself.

On the whole, Bach encountered noteworthy conflicts during his tenure in office on the basis of only these two structural conditions, even if one must concede that the course and extent of the conflicts, especially the struggle with the University and the battle over the appointment of the prefects,[73] were also rooted in Bach's uncompromising stance and absolute claims, preconditions of his musical greatness. His conflicts were with the University, which did not want a non-academic, and with the Cantor faction, which did not want a non-schoolmaster. With those who wanted him—with the Kapellmeister faction and, also, with the consistory, that is, the Electoral authority in ecclesiastical and educational affairs—he had no conflicts. The approval and rejection that Bach encountered in Leipzig were clearly defined: he was the musical exponent of one cultural-political group.

Notes

1. This article is a translation and abridgment, somewhat reordered, of "Bachs Stellung in der Leipziger Kulturpolitik seiner Zeit," *Bach-Jahrbuch* 69 (1983): 7–50; 70 (1984): 7–43; 72 (1986): 33–67; henceforth *BJb*. All paragraphs in italics are editorial. The author would like to thank the editor for her insightful work.

2. John Butt, ed., *The Cambridge Companion to Bach* (Cambridge University Press, 1997).

3. W. Neumann and H.-J. Schulze, eds, Dokument II/129, also Dokument II/615 from *Bach-Dokumente,* 3 vols (Leipzig and Kassel, 1963, 1969, 1972); henceforth *Dok.*

4. The excerpts from the minutes of the Executive Council, which are the most important source, are published in C. H. Bitter, *Johann Sebastian Bach* (Berlin: W. Baensch, 1881, 2nd ed.; rpt. Leipzig: Zentralantequariat der D. D. R., 1978), with epilogue, person, and subject indexes by H.-J. Schulze (4:102–9)). Note that Bitter's source reference is misleading, since he does not, in fact, draw on "school documents" (Tit. VII B 117) but on the "Executive minutes" (Tit. VIII 60a).

5. All the newspaper reports are taken from H. Becker, "Die frühe Hamburgische Tagespresse als musikgeschichtliche Quelle," in: H. Husmann, ed., *Beiträge zur Hamburgischen Musikgeschichte* (Hamburg: Musikwissenschaftlichen Instituts der Universität, 1956): 22–45; here, 38–41. Of the 14 reports covering the events from the death of Johann Kuhnau to Bach's assumption of the office of cantor, 12 appeared in the *Hollsteinischer Correspondent,* 2 in the Hamburg *Relations-Courier.* The period between the date of the news report and the date of its appearance is usually six or seven days; once it was eight days. I always give the date of the news report, for it can be assumed that a report that could be made by the Leipzig correspondent of a Hamburg newspaper was also known in Leipzig on the same day. See *Dok* II/124, 131, 138, and 140. (All citations according to Becker.)

6. *Editor's note: These quotations are from the minutes of the Leipzig Town Council meetings, which use the indirect speech Siegele retained in this chapter. See note 4 above.*

7. B. F. Richter, *BJb* 1905: 58, together with 51; *BJb* 1925: 2.

8. The equivalent of one Reichstaler is roughly 60 euros or dollars today.

9. F. W. Riedel, "Kauffmann, George Friederich," in *Die Musik in Geschichte und Gegenwart,* ed. F. Blume (Kassel: Bärenreiter, 1949–86), vol. 7, cols. 749–53, henceforth *MGG;* and especially J. Rifkin in *The Grove Dictionary of Music and Musicians* (London: Macmillian, 1980), vol. 9, 830–31, henceforth *Grove.*

10. Church records and Municipal Archive of the city of Braunschweig.

11. *Dok* II/129 and 130.

12. See E. Noack, *Musikgeschichte Darmstadts vom Mittelalter bis zur Goethezeit* (Mainz: B. Schott, 1967), 181–82, 183, also 213.

13. The report is erroneously dated January 18. Since it announces Graupner's audition, which took place on January 17, for "next Sunday," it must be dated sometime before this day, probably on January 16, the day after the meeting of the Executive Council. Moreover, if it were dated January 18, the period of time between the date of the announcement and the date of its appearance, at four days, would be unusually short. With a date of January 16, however, it would, at six days, lie within the normal range. By the way, none of the 13 announcements whose date is beyond question is a Sunday or Monday. This also speaks against January 18, which was a Monday. Graupner's audition, based on the alternation of the two principal churches, was held at St. Thomas.

14. *Dok* II/123.

15. E. Kroker, *Aufsätze zur Stadtgeschichte und Reformationsgeschichte* (Leipzig: H. Haessel, 1929), 140.

16. Text in Richter, *Bach-Jahrbuch* 1905: 54–55, and, not quite complete, in W. Nagel, "Das Leben Christoph Graupners," *Sammelbände der Internationalen Musikgesellschaft* (*SIMG*) 10, 1908–9: 568–612; 591–92.

17. Text in Nagel, "Das Leben Christoph Graupners," *SIMG* 10:592; summary in Kroker, *Aufsätze*, 140. Here Graupner writes that he has presented the letter from the Leipzig Town Council and his own request for release "eight days ago." (January 31, like February 7, was a Sunday. Perhaps Graupner presented his letter and the request a day earlier or later.) Graupner's letter to Lange also documents the fact that "next Easter" (in other words, the end of the *tempus clausum*) was projected as the date on which he would assume the Leipzig position.

18. Graupner's letter of March 22 can be found in Nagel, "Das Leben Christoph Graupners," 593–94, and Kroker, *Aufsätze*, 141. This letter from Graupner to Lange documents Lange's inquiry to Graupner of March 12 and the enclosure to Kametzky, as well as Graupner's memorandum of "last Sunday," March 20. Summaries of the letter from Kametzky to Lange are found in Nagel, "Das Leben Christoph Graupners," 594, and Kroker, *Aufsätze*, 141. Kametzky's note to the files (the marginal note following the Landgrave's conversation with Graupner and before Kametzky's letter to the Leipzig Town Council), which is reprinted in Nagel, "Das Leben Christoph Graupners," 593, belongs to the final phase of the negotiations: between the letter from Lange (dated March 12) and the memorandum from Graupner (dated March 20). On this subject, see also *Dok* II/132.

19. Also see H.-J. Schulze's interpretation of the "fellow in Pirna" remark in *Bericht über die wissenschaftliche Konferenz zum III. internationalen Bach-Fest der DDR* (Leipzig, September 1975) (Leipzig: Deutscher Verlag für Musik, 1977); henceforth *Ber. Lpz 1975*. In 1722, the year to which all other age references are pegged, Heckel was 46 years old. See H. Volkmann, "Christian Heckel, ein sächsischer Kantor des beginnenden 18. Jahrhunderts," *Zeitschrift für Musikwissenschaft* 13, 1930/31:369–84; henceforth *ZfMw*.

20. C. H. Bitter, *Johann Sebastian Bach*, 1:159 and 4:109.

21. Schulze in *Ber. Lpz. 1975*, 75.

22. *Dok* I/91.

23. *Dok* II/128.

24. *Festschrift Georg von Dadelsen* (Neuhausen: Hänssler, 1978), 349–50, n. 59. In fact, there were hardly any funeral ceremonies during Bach's time in Leipzig.

25. Conclusively in *Dok* I/92, item no. 10.

26. Conclusively in *Dok* I/92, item no. 11.

27. The cantor was not actually *collega quartus*, but was supposed to teach in the third and fourth forms (*Tertia* and *Quarta*).

28. *Dok* I/92, item 7; see also Schulze in *Ber. Lpz 1975*, 72.

29. *Editor's note: See Kuhnau's 1710 response to these impositions in chapter 8 in this volume, p. 219.*

30. *Dok* II/133; see also II/146.

31. J. Mattheson, *Grundlage einer Ehren-Pforte* (Hamburg: In verlegung des verfassers, 1740), 359.

32. H.-J. Schulze in: *Ber. Lpz. 1975*.

33. Philipp Spitta, *Johann Sebastian Bach* (Vol. I Leipzig, 1873; Vol. II Leipzig, 1880; 4th ed., Leipzig: Breitkopf und Härtel, 1930), 2:854–55, 858–59, 866–68. See chapter 8, Johann Kuhnau's "Texts for Leipzig Church Music."

34. C. H. Bitter, *Johann Sebastian Bach*, 4:106.

35. See Johann Kuhnau's memorandum in *Zf Mw* 4 (1921–22): 612–14, in which Kuhnau reports that in a specific situation "the most distinguished individuals from the music team at the Neue Kirche . . . voluntarily came and helped me" with the

music in the Paulinerkirche. (I did not choose the word "band," because singers may have been included.) On the one hand, in practice, even in Kuhnau's time, the gap between the Thomasschule cantor—at least when he was directing the musical program of the Paulinerkirche—and the musicians of the Neue Kirche was not unbridgeable. On the other hand, in 1722, when Kuhnau was expected "to loan the boys [of the Thomasschule] to the Neue Kirche for the Passion music," he caused difficulties.

36. B. F. Richter, *BJb* 1925: 2.

37. *Dok* I/92.

38. *Dok* II/88. Along with Kauffmann, Kuhnau had also been discussed, probably first as organist. Elias Lindner, the organist at the cathedral in Freiburg, was mentioned. For evidence, see *Dok* I/50 and *Dok* II/95.

39. *Dok* II/159.

40. On the terminology, see *Dok* I/12, lines 113–14, and *Dok* I/34, line 23.

41. *Dok* II/189, *Dok* I/19, lines 17–18, and *Dok* I/12, lines 163–205.

42. *Dok* II /129.

43. *Dok* II/383, 382, lines 10–22. (It is characteristic that Ernesti would have preferred Bach to be represented by the first prefect, i.e., by someone from within the school rather than a second music director, i.e., someone from outside the school.)

44. D. Härtwig in *MGG* 12, 1965, col. 54; and W. Emery in *The New Grove Dictionary of Music and Musicians* (London, 1980) 16:736; also *Dok* I/20, commentary.

45. W. Neumann, *BJb* 1960: 5–27.

46. Dok I/20.

47. *Dok* II/261. Also see Siegele, "Bach and the Domestic Politics of Electoral Saxony," in Butt, *The Cambridge Companion*, 28.

48. A. C. Plaz, *Lebens-Lauff und letzter Abschied* (Leipzig: B. C. Breitkopf, 1729), 122; discussed below.

49. A. Mendel in Johann Sebastian Bach, *Neue Bach Ausgabe sämtlicher Werke*, edited by Johann-Sebastian-Bach-Institut Göttingen and Bach-Archiv Leipzig (Kassel and Leipzig: Bärenreiter and Deutscher Verlag für Musik, 1954–62), I/14, 65–105.

50. For the problem Bach confronted when he tried to enhance the vocal forces at the Thomasschule, see Siegele, "Bach and the Domestic Politics," 29–30.

51. *Dok* II/280. See *Festschrift Dadelsen*, 346–47.

52. *Dok* II/177.

53. *Dok* II/281.

54. *Dok* I/23.

55. *Dok* II/22. See *Festschrift Dadelsen*, 316–17. For the following see 347–48, especially n. 53.

56. *Dok* II/176. Compare H. Stiehl in *BJb* 1979: 7–18.

57. *Dok* II/204.

58. Ibid., 236.

59. *Dok* III/650a. Compare W. Neumann, *BJb* 1970: 19–31.

60. *Dok* II/583. See Fröde, *BJb* 1984: 53–58.

61. *Dok* II/584.

62. Ibid., 614.

63. *Dok* III/671. See A. Schering, *Musikgeschichte Leipzigs III* (Leipzig: F. Kistner and C. F. W. Siegel, 1941), 343; and Schulze in *Ber. Lpz* 1975: 76.

64. F. Paulsen, *Geschichte des gelehrten Unterrichts*, 3rd edition (vol. 1, Leipzig: Veit, 1919; 2, Berlin and Leipzig: Vereinigung wissenschaftlicher verlager, 1921), here 2:16–33; also 1:567–75.

65. The examination of faith that Bach was forced to undergo was a test of publicly professed faith and only referred to the consensus. I consider it out of the question that the theological tendencies and inclinations of the examiners or the individuals who were being examined could have played a role in the process.

66. In: *Miscellanea Saxonica* VIII (Dresden: Roch, 1774), 38–48, 57–64 (continuation of the life history), 73–77 (conclusion). Christian Gottlieb Jöcher put together a biography in *Allgemeines Gelehrten-Lexicon* (Leipzig: Gleditsch, 1750), vol. 2, col. 2248.

67. In the recent past, the Elector had intervened in imposing his choice for mayor, which led to circumstances that engendered a hostile political situation with the Council, for which please see Siegele, "Bach and the Domestic Politics," 20–21.

68. For the details of his advancement in Leipzig, see Ibid., 21. Furthermore, see O. Günzel, *Die Leipziger Ratswahlen von 1630–1830*, PhD diss., Leipzig, 1923, 115, 121, 128–30.

69. On Lange, see G. F. Otto, *Lexicon der seit dem funfzehenden Jahrhanderte verstorbenen und jeztlebenden oberlausizischen Schriftsteller und Künstler* (Görlitz: C. G. Anton, 1802), 2:376–78. His father Kaspar is found on p. 387, his elder brother Kaspar on p. 388, his brothers Gottlob on p. 378 and Kaspar Gottlob on p. 388. Gottlob's son Kaspar Gottlieb is on pp. 388–90. Lange is documented as an academic teacher of Friedrich Wilhelm Schütz (J. H. Zedler, *Grosses vollständiges Universal-Lexicon alles Wissenschafften und Künste* (Leipzig and Halle: J. H. Zedler, 1743) vol. 35, cols. 1387–91, esp., 1387.

70. H.-J. Schulze seems to have been the first to draw on this publication for Bach's biography (in *Ber. Lpz. 1975*, 74 and 77, n. 22.) A copy is retained in the Bach Archive in Leipzig. The numbers that are given in the following text refer to the pages of the printed publication.

71. See Siegele, "Bach and the Domestic Politics," for a discussion of how political circumstances may have influenced not only musical activity but composition itself.

72. In the so-called provisional bond, Bach first refers to his future place of work as "Thomas-Kirche," but then corrects it by erasure to read "Thomas-Schule" (*Dok* I /91). At a church, he could become a music director and Kapellmeister without difficulty, but not at a school. Perhaps the original version can be traced to the fact that Bach negotiated primarily with Gottfried Lange, and the supervisor of the Thomaskirche had spoken mainly of the development of the music of his church, while touching only in passing on the school (whose supervisor was a member of the Cantor faction).

73. See Siegele, "Bach and the Domestic Politics," 30.

Chapter Six

The Reception of the Cantata during Leipzig Church Services, 1700–1750

Tanya Kevorkian

Scholars have long engaged in the study of Leipzig musicians and their performance of church music during the Baroque era. One question, though, has largely gone unasked: how did the audiences of J. S. Bach and his contemporaries experience the cantata?

Congregants were a lively presence during the act of worship. They made use of nearly every element of the liturgy, of seating arrangements, and of a range of behaviors to articulate their social status, and to support, protest against, or otherwise comment on the form and content of the service. These included selective forms of listening to and participating in the musical parts of the service.[1] In their turn, clerics and musicians tailored the service in response to the congregation's tastes and habits. There is very little direct evidence on the subject of congregations' reactions and behavior during this period, so to reconstruct their experience of the service it is necessary to work with a variety of material, most of it not connected with music. In this article I shall first discuss the general context of the service: the make-up of the congregations, church seating and layout, and the course of the liturgy. I shall then look more closely at the cantata itself, examining its place in the service, as well as clues provided by texts and music.

I shall examine most closely worship on Sunday mornings in Leipzig's two main churches, St. Thomas and St. Nicholas, where the principal services were held. Contemporaries considered them the most important regular public meetings in the town, and the core of an individual's religious life. On these occasions senior ministers preached and instrumental music was regularly performed. St. Thomas cantors, who included J. S. Bach from 1723 to 1750 and

Johann Kuhnau from 1701 to 1722, performed on alternating Sundays in St. Thomas and St. Nicholas. I shall also investigate the morning services in the "New Church" and the University Church.

The Congregations

The service, which started at 7:00 a.m., was preceded by the ringing of bells, which both symbolized the public status of the service and served as a reminder to the population to congregate.[2] As was usual elsewhere in Europe, the wealthy arrived and departed in carriages.[3] Most of the congregation, though, came on foot; in Leipzig, as in most other towns, this entailed a walk of no more than about ten minutes. By 1700 St. Thomas's and St. Nicholas's each seated about 2,500 people in pews allotted to individuals, with additional seats and standing room for about 500 more.[4] The New Church, opened in 1699, had pews for over 1,200 people; St. Peter's, opened in 1712, about 460; and the University Church, opened to the public in 1710, several hundred, with additional standing room in each.[5] While attendance was highest on holidays and other special occasions, and lower during the summer, most seats were occupied during regular Sunday services. References to full churches were frequent, and demand for pews was constant throughout the Baroque era. Thus, by the 1710s around 9,000 people of a total population of almost 30,000 filled the streets heading toward church early on Sunday mornings.[6]

Members of a household separated to sit in their respective pews. Pews were allotted to individuals, not families, and sections of pews were separated by gender.[7] As was customary in Lutheran Germany, women in both St. Nicholas's and St. Thomas's occupied most of the seats on the ground floor. Men, by contrast, held most or all of the balcony seats (St. Nicholas's had three levels of balconies), along with a few pews around the rear and periphery of the ground floor.[8] Women somewhat outnumbered men: in St. Nicholas's 55 percent of pew holders were women; the figure was similar at St. Thomas's.

While people from dozens of occupations were represented in each church, most of the morning congregants at all five churches were property-owning burghers and their families.[9] Seating was mapped socially among these burghers, with status hierarchies reflected in the type of pew held and the location of that pew. The main social division was between local elites (merchants, professionals, and city councillors, and their families) and artisans (bakers, saddlers, smiths, and others, and their families). In the main churches almost half of all pews were occupied by members of the Leipzig elites. In all, 43 percent of pew holders in St. Nicholas's were members of the elites, 43 percent were artisans, and 14 percent belonged to intermediate groups such as shopkeepers and notaries. Figures for St. Thomas's were similar.[10] The elites, who made up less than 10 percent of Leipzig's total population, were thus greatly over-represented among pew holders. Intermediate groups were also over-represented. Artisans were present roughly in proportion to their share of the population. Unpropertied servants, laborers and others, by contrast, who made up around half of the urban population, held almost no pews. They mainly attended afternoon services and services at smaller churches.

There were two types of pews: regular seats, or *Stände*, which were arranged in blocks, and benches, or *Bänklein*, which were attached to the sections of regular pews. Elites held 62 percent of the 1,573 *Stände* in St. Nicholas; members of intermediate groups held 16 percent; and artisans held 23 percent. By contrast, artisans made up 82 percent of the holders of 871 *Bänklein*; only 7 percent of benches were held by elites, and 11 percent by members of intermediate groups. Even among holders of *Stände*, sections of seats were mapped socially. In particular, the best women's pews, closest to the pulpit and with the best view of it—where one could see and be seen—were occupied almost exclusively by elite women. The sections of *Stände* behind the pulpit or farther away from it included more artisans.

Starting in the 1670s, a new arrangement emerged when the very wealthy began enclosing groups of ten to twelve pews around the edges of the churches. Most *Capellen*, as these were known, were constructed around 1700; they came to be built two and three over another, and numbered over thirty in each of the two main churches. They were occupied by the families of leading city councillors and long-distance merchants, and were socially and spatially parallel to opera boxes.

Congregants could be intensely territorial. In 1735 Anna Elisabeth Steinert, wife of a furrier, wrote to request a pew: "I have never been so fortunate as to have my own place [Oertgen] to cultivate my devotions."[11] The following year the shopkeeper Johann Martin went as far as to claim that "such a site and position [a pew] is almost indispensable to the comfortable practice [Uebung] of the worship service."[12] Pews were considered a form of property, and each row of them was equipped with lock and key.

Holding a pew remained an unattainable ideal even for many propertied inhabitants: despite the continuing construction of pews, there was always a shortage. Subletting was a common practice, although considered very inconvenient by the sub-lessees. The poor, visitors to town, and others who had no pew were obliged to stand, milling about in a crowd at the rear of the church.[13]

The Course of the Service

The morning service was divided into three main parts. During the first hour chants, hymns, scriptural readings, and the cantata were performed. This led to the sermon, the central part of the service, which also lasted an hour. Then communion was prepared and administered to the accompaniment of further hymns or a cantata, or both. Finally the pastor read announcements and prayers, and chanted the final blessing. This last part of the service, after the sermon, lasted between one and two hours, depending on the number of communicants, which was highest on major holidays. Throughout the service the organ played an important role in guiding the singing of hymns, setting the mood, and giving instrumentalists a chance to tune (Figure 6.1 depicts the organ in St. Nicholas with its Baroque ornamentation).

People continued to arrive throughout the first hour of the service. In this respect they were like the audiences for contemporary opera all over Europe.[14] The goal for many was to arrive by the beginning of the sermon, the essential feature of the service in the eyes of ordinary inhabitants as well as in Lutheran theology and liturgical theory. Many people also left immediately after the sermon because they did not want to wait for communion to be administered.[15] Leipzig's city councillors acknowledged widespread tardiness and early departure without comment in 1708 and 1713, during discussions about introducing a collection bag; they decided without debate to pass the bag during the sermon, which made sense since that was when the greatest number of people were present and settled in their pews.[16] Musicians also adapted. For example, in *Der vollkommene Capellmeister,* Johann Mattheson recommended to organists accompanying congregational hymns, "As more arrive, the organ must swell as well; and as the congregation gradually disperses, the stops of the organ should diminish, too."[17]

Certainly the duration of the service, and the fact that during winter it began before daylight, helps explain why many people were not there for all of it. Moreover, the churches were unheated, making a long stay difficult to bear during the late autumn, winter, and early spring. Bach himself apparently arrived late to the service sometimes.[18] However, the first hour of the service had a variety of social functions. For example, the Pietist cleric Christian Gerber, in his book on church ceremony published in 1732, ascribed the lateness of the elites to their unwillingness to rise an hour earlier, and to spending too much time dressing, grooming themselves, and drinking coffee. All this suggests that they could make a grander entrance when they did arrive. By contrast, "common people," Gerber wrote, insisted on working before going to church.[19]

Beyond the comings and goings of the congregation, the church was the arena for a variety of other activities during the service. People observed one another and greeted their neighbors as they arrived. From their balcony pews, men, including students (who had their own balcony), could observe the women below. They also courted young unmarried women by visiting them at their pews.[20] Typically insubordinate groups were sometimes responsible for disturbances: students threw objects from their balcony onto women's pews,[21] and "youth and other useless riffraff," in the words of one councillor, retired to spaces behind the *Capellen* to make noise.[22] Communion, a time when music was often performed, was the occasion for another type of unrest, for while

Figure 6.1. Former organ in St. Nicholas's Church in Leipzig, watercolor by Carl Benjamin Schwartz, c. 1785 (Leipzig, Stadtarchiv, RRA 316; by permission).

contemporary illustrations show individuals proceeding in orderly rows to the front of the church, it seems that the actual process was more disorderly. The Pietist Johann Christian Lange wrote in 1695, "During services and especially during communion, a public disgrace and abomination is carried on through excessive opulence in dress, fashionable [*alamodische*] styles and manners, fleshly shoving for precedence, and the envy and jealousy awakened by all these."[23]

Other activities were sanctioned by the city council and clergy themselves. For example, the collection bags passed during the sermon had bells attached and were carried with ceremonial pomp by four artisans dressed in uniform black coats.[24] People were expected to stand for the reading of scriptural texts and the final blessing, and to make other motions such as lifting their hands for prayer, which gave opportunity for subtle forms of non-conformity and social ostentation. Gerber claimed that ministers everywhere had trouble getting all the members of the congregation to stand; in "large and small towns, there are people who think much of their station, cause much vexation during the service by gossiping during singing and preaching, and are not even ashamed of laughing . . . in particular, many imagine that they are too fine to stand with the congregation at the reading of the Epistles and Gospel."[25]

In addition to the variety of sounds and motions that accompanied the liturgy, there were also visual distractions. The churches were richly decorated in a way that invited worshippers' eyes to roam. Attention would focus on the occupants of pews with special status, such as the brides' and grooms' pews, and the truly ostentatious Electoral balcony or pew built in St. Thomas's in 1684, which the Elector and his family used on their occasional visits to Leipzig. Clerics and altar servers wore green, white, red, and violet vestments of precious silks, satins, and velvets, trimmed and embroidered with gold and silver thread. On the balconies were large statues and paintings on biblical subjects, as well as written scriptural passages. The organ shutters, closed during Lent, also had paintings on them. In 1721 the Saxon Elector donated a new, high Baroque altar (see figure 6.2) to St. Thomas's to replace the late Renaissance one. Made of black, red, and white marble, with a large Gloria (sunburst) with gilded rays above it, it was designed and built by the marble sculptor, silversmith, and sculptor of the Dresden court.[26]

The liturgical year included holidays and other occasions marked by an intensification of ceremony and decoration. Celebratory services were rung in more elaborately than ordinary ones, with peals one hour, half an hour, and just before the service, using the full set of bells and special bell changes. The occupational pews for men with a doctorate or licentiate, for city councillors and pastors and their wives, and for court judges, along with the church's altar and epistle lectern were decorated with colorful hangings, of which each church had several sets.[27] Music at celebratory services was also more elaborate than usual, with brass and other instruments being added for festive effect.

Der von Marmor neu erbaute Altar in St. Thomas Kirch in Leipzig.
Joh. Christoph Weigel exc.

Figure 6.2. *The New Marble Altar in the Church of St. Thomas in Leipzig,* print by
J. C. Weigel from J. S. Riemer, *Continuatio annalium Lipsiensium Vogelii,* ms.,
1714–71 (Leipzig, Stadtarchiv; by permission).

In Leipzig all this ceremony reached its height in the decades after 1680. Nurtured by a prolonged period of peace and prosperity, the Baroque style continued to thrive in the city until the 1750s. The culture of church-going was also at its height from about 1680 to 1750. Criticism by Pietist advocates of a simpler religious style, while vocal, did not for the most part influence actual practice in the main churches or the New Church. A major turning point was the Seven Years War (1756–63), which initiated a period of political, social, and cultural turmoil. The various public functions of the service gradually began to be supplanted by other occasions such as the Gewandhaus concerts. Enlightenment rationalists criticized needless ceremony and practices that encouraged "superstition" or distracted from the divine word.[28] In the 1780s and 1790s numerous practices in the main churches were dropped or modified in line with this thinking.[29]

The Question of Attentiveness

Given their widespread tardiness and the variety of activities and distractions facing them, how attentively did congregations listen to the music of Bach, Kuhnau, and others? How much of the often complex music and its religious symbolism did they understand?

Since the place of the cantata in the liturgy was just before and after the sermon, people were coming and going while it was being performed. Given this, and that people conversed with their neighbors, there was a certain level of background noise throughout performances. Further, while it seems that sound projected well from the musicians' balconies, and the acoustic of the churches was well suited for music to be heard,[30] vocal and instrumental forces were quite small. The bulk of most cantatas for regular Sundays featured only one solo voice at a time. The number of instruments playing was also small, although vocal and instrumental forces were increased on holidays and other special occasions.

Measured by present-day standards of punctuality and silence during protestant services, and of regulated applause during concerts of classical music, Bach and his predecessors received less than perfect attention during their performances. However, these standards developed later, and to judge eighteenth-century audiences by modern concert-hall paradigms is to misunderstand them. The expectation that an audience should arrive before the start of a performance, be seated, quiet, and otherwise disciplined was not yet the norm. Historians have begun to discover that, during the eighteenth century in secular concerts and opera houses throughout Europe, it was common practice for audiences to arrive late, wander about, and converse during performances. In secular contexts approval might be expressed by applauding individual arias or concert movements, and even by applause during a performance.[31] And, while it is certain that many worshippers listened carefully to the hour-long sermon, even that was accompanied by the passing of jingling collection bags. The environment would have allowed those who wanted to listen closely to do so, while for others the music would have been peripheral. William Weber has suggested the term "miscellany" to describe audiences' and producers' expectations that a given occasion would fulfill a variety of functions.[32] Also at work was a Baroque performance and reception aesthetic, which involved a layering of visual, aural, and social experiences. This layering was intended to intensify the effect of a given occasion on its audience.

Despite the presence of what we might regard as distractions, there are numerous signs that many congregants did pay close attention to the music, and also that substantial numbers of them were present for much of the service. Starting in the 1710s in Leipzig, librettos for several Sundays' performances of cantatas were sold. They were available in bookstores and in some cases at the church door; they were also sold in other large cities such as Frankfurt and Hamburg, and in smaller towns. Librettos were several pages long, and included only the text of a piece. As the cantor of Delitzsch (a small town near Leipzig) wrote in the 1730s in his introduction to a libretto cycle, "without reading, the musical texts can seldom be fully understood, because of the accompaniment of the instruments, and thus little fruitful and edifying effect is attained."[33] Librettos marked sections such as aria, recitative, and chorale and indicated any scriptural text. In some librettos for Bach's cantatas, only the first line of chorales (based on familiar hymns) was printed. For example, the libretto for *Du Hirte Israel* (BWV 104), first performed on the second Sunday after Easter in 1724 in St. Nicholas's, gives the full text for arias and other sections, but only the first line of the concluding chorale, "Der Herr ist mein getreuer Hirt," followed by the symbol for "etc."[34] This practice indicates that the librettos were intended as a guide to new and unfamiliar lyrics, and not to texts known to the audience. It seems that the librettos sold well. Sales in Hamburg were lucrative enough to ignite a fight over printing rights between Telemann and a Hamburg printer that lasted over thirty years, from 1722 to the 1750s.[35] Passion librettos sold especially well.

The Congregation and the Cantata

While parts of cantata texts were new, the religious messages they expressed were not; also, their specific language and music overlapped in many ways with other parts of the service, and with forms of music often heard outside it. This overlapping made for a high degree of accessibility. The language of cantata texts was the scriptural language of shepherd, sheep, and pasture, of salvation, death, heaven, the soul, trial, and faith. In a largely agrarian society, pastoral references resonated even for city dwellers. Further, cantatas were usually a direct commentary on the New Testament text of the day, which was read from the lectern just before the performance of the cantata. Parts of many cantata texts shifted the third person and past tense of scripture to the first person and present tense, bringing the subject into the listener's immediate frame of reference.[36]

Most of Bach's cantatas, as well as many of those of Georg Philipp Telemann and other New Church composers, featured chorales that were popular hymns,[37] a sign that the composers and their librettists were aiming for accessibility and encouraging ordinary parishioners to become involved with the music. (Kuhnau included fewer chorales.) Hymns resonated with congregants in many ways. Beyond their use in church, they were probably the most pervasively heard music in that society. Beggars often sang them before town gates, on the street, or in front of people's homes in hopes of receiving alms.[38] Hymns were sung during domestic worship and were internalized through repeated singing; they occurred to individuals at moments of stress.[39] Hymnals were important possessions, often given at baptism and confirmation; they saw much use, with their owners underlining passages and writing marginal notes.[40] Many hymn tunes were also used for "secular, even drinking and whoring songs," as one contemporary wrote.[41] Conversely, many hymns made use of melodies from secular songs.

In the context of the service, hymns were the only extended opportunity for the congregation to participate actively. People sang by heart the sixteenth-century hymns of Luther and other reformers;[42] significantly, many of the hymns that Bach used as chorales dated from the Reformation era. A variety of local usages attests to the oral and social rootedness of hymn singing. Sometimes, congregations would substitute one word for another; and in some rural areas only men sang certain hymns.[43] In all areas, since men and women sat in different sections of pews, their experience was that of singing in a block of other men or women. The use of hymnals became common after 1700, in Leipzig as in other towns, especially for singing more recent hymns.[44] By the 1710s most individuals brought their own hymnals to church.[45] From 1732 the numbers for hymns were posted on five boards around St. Thomas's.[46]

The very active association of hymns and lay singing suggests that congregations were especially focused on the cantata when chorales were performed, and that chorales brought the meaning of the whole cantata into focus. It is possible that congregations sang along with the chorales; it would certainly have been difficult for some people to restrain themselves from singing, and there is some evidence that the practice was routine. In a dispute in Hamburg in 1764, Telemann defended his use of a chorale text with words that differed slightly from Luther's original text. He argued that he had already used this text five years previously, when the verses had been "sung with edification by the congregations in all the main churches during the cantata." The cleric Melchior Goeze, by contrast, complained of the "very unfortunate improvement of a new poet" to the original, and asserted that when the altered verses had been used, "The congregation became very confused when the first line and the melody were begun on the choir [balcony], and something completely different was sung from what it was used to. The congregation therefore, and very unwillingly, was forced to fall silent in the midst of singing."[47] Whether or not congregants had approved of the changes (probably some did and some did not), both Telemann and Goeze assumed that they sang with the chorale. Goeze additionally indicates that church singers helped the congregation start by singing the first line of the chorale from the choir balcony, a practice that was followed for regular hymns during at least some services in Leipzig.[48]

This particular dispute concerned performances around 1759 in Hamburg. However, since the practices associated with cantata composition and performance were established by the 1710s and 1720s, it is likely that this practice had also been established for some time. Those practices were roughly similar from town to town. Further, both Telemann and Goeze seem to refer to a custom of long standing.

If hymns were a traditional element of cantatas, the recitatives, arias, and instrumental passages that made up most of a cantata were often newly composed, and reflected the most innovative styles of the time. Influenced especially by the Italian operatic song form, cantatas from the 1690s onward became increasingly innovative, artistically complex, and lively—to some listeners shockingly so. Another secular genre that influenced cantatas was the French court dance, which was very popular in Leipzig. For example, Bach included numerous (untitled) dance movements in his cantatas.[49]

In Leipzig the new theatrical style was initially represented most enthusiastically by Georg Philipp Telemann, who was appointed organist and music director at the New Church in 1704, specifically to perform on holidays and during the trade fairs. Earlier, in 1701, he had been appointed to compose a cantata for performance in St. Thomas's once every two weeks.[50] However, Telemann was primarily involved with secular music at the time, leading a collegium musicum that performed in coffee houses and gardens, as well as in the New Church, and writing over 20 operas for the Leipzig Opera. He imported this secular style into his cantatas. Telemann left Leipzig in 1705, but his successors continued to lead the collegium and to bring the newest styles into the New Church.

Johann Kuhnau made significant strides in adopting a modern cantata style, even if somewhat reluctantly, and he also introduced librettos. Recent recordings reveal an often "modern," full, beautiful sound that belies Kuhnau's somewhat negative reputation.[51] Still, with Bach's arrival in Leipzig in 1723 the new style was more fully integrated into services. Bach embraced the latest Italian and French styles and incorporated them into his music. His secular and sacred works were similar in style, and he often reused, revised, and recombined (parodied) parts of secular vocal and instrumental pieces for sacred use and vice versa.

The innovative aspects of cantata style were familiar to the audience from their visits to the Leipzig opera, which operated from 1693 until 1720, as well as to coffee houses and gardens, dances, and other secular occasions. Perhaps individual members of the congregation recognized specific movements; they more likely recognized the French dances upon which some cantata sections were built. It is possible that some congregants saw the cantata and, more generally, church services as an alternative to the opera as a public venue after 1720.[52] This would have been especially likely during the fairs, when the opera had functioned. During the fairs, held three times a year for two to three weeks each, the town became crowded not only with merchants but also with other visitors who wanted to see new books, hear news from around the world, meet friends and relatives, and absorb the latest in culture. Without the opera, the churches would have become more important as places to mingle and hear music. Cantatas were specifically performed on holidays and at the New Church during the trade fairs. The University Church, opened to the public in 1710, also became known for its festive music during the fairs. A guide book to Leipzig of 1725 declared that the music of the students and their virtuoso leader was "incomparable," and "causes amazement on the part of great men who come from far and wide."[53]

Not all members of the cantata audience approved of the carrying over of secular styles into the church. Pietist critics unflatteringly compared cantatas written in the new style to operatic and dance music.[54] Perhaps the small community of Pietists living in the city followed the advice of the anonymous author of a liturgical and prayer compendium of 1710, who recommended the reading of specific prayers "while there is mere preambling on the organ, or lengthy music being performed (since some people do not particularly value figural and often operatic music)." Such reading of prayers, the author claimed, was a better use of time than "useless chatter."[55]

However, there are many more indications that the new style was welcomed by the public. Gerber wrote, "People are so accustomed to such things that they think the service cannot exist without [organ and instrumental music], or that it would suffer greatly if they were left out."[56] The populace flocked especially on Good Friday to hear performances of highly elaborate Passions, the first of which was composed by Telemann and performed in the New Church in 1717. (Passions were introduced in the main churches in 1721 and 1724; thus Bach's Passions were composed for a newly established event.) The city council encouraged music in the main churches and especially in the New Church as a persuasive strategy intended to attract inhabitants to worship services, as well as to impress visitors.

Numerous factors influenced how Leipzig audiences heard the Baroque cantata. When congregants came to church they did not entirely leave behind the activities of their everyday lives. Social and gender distinctions and concepts of property were carried over into church seating. There was no code dictating prompt arrival or silence, and the service had numerous social functions. Just as the service was in many ways not a departure from everyday social life, the cantata also shared many features with music that congregants heard outside church. The cantata resonated with music and lyrics that were known from a variety of contexts. Such resonance, along with the distribution of librettos, made the music and text of the cantata accessible. This meant that even if many people did not closely follow the cantata, they were aware of its general message, and those who wanted to could listen more closely.

Seemingly in contradiction to these carryovers from secular to sacred, an important goal of the producers of services, one that was also pursued by many congregants, was to step out of everyday routine, to escape the pressures of "the world," and to experience a sense of wonder, awe, and devotion. Musical virtuosity, the emotional resonance of hymns, visual display, and clerical oratory were combined to produce this effect in a way rarely encountered outside the service. Contemporaries were attuned to this artistic layering and its effects on congregants, as their descriptions of services show. The social practices associated with churchgoing, on the other hand, were taken for granted as being a part of any public gathering. This accounts for the paucity of descriptions of those practices, for things that would now be considered distracting were quite normal then.

Notes

1. For more on producers, consumers and appropriation, see M. de Certeau, *The Practices of Everyday Life* (Berkeley: University of California Press, 1984).
2. On the order of service and the place of music in it, see R. A. Leaver, "The Mature Vocal Works and Their Theological and Liturgical Context," in J. Butt, ed., *The Cambridge Companion to Bach* (Cambridge: Cambridge University Press, 1997), 86–122, and G. Stiller, *Johann Sebastian Bach and Liturgical Life in Leipzig* (St. Louis: Concordia, 1984).
3. For Leipzig, see A. Bernd, *Eigene Lebens-Beschreibung* (Leipzig: Heinsius, 1738; rpt., Munich: Winkler, 1973), 209, 279. For references to Hamburg and other mercantile cities, see satires in the moral weekly *Der Patriot*, 1/9:71; 1/16:138 (Hamburg: Kissner, 1724; rpt. Berlin: de Gruyter, 1969). For Rome, see A. Cowan, *Urban Europe, 1500–1700* (New York: Arnold, 1998), 134.
4. In 1708 the city councillors listed the number of pews in St. Nicholas's: 769 men's *Stühle*, 343 men's *Bänklein*, 804 women's *Stühle* and 528 women's *Bänklein*, 2,444 in all, noting additional places where people could sit or stand. Stadtarchiv Leipzig, Stift vII.B.32, *Acta, die Einführung des Klingelbeutels in hiesigen Stadt Kirchen und dessen Wiederabschaffen betr*, 1708, 5. St. Thomas's held about the same number of congregants; councillors noted that "in the two churches of St. Thomas and St. Nicholas there are 6,000 souls during the Sunday morning sermon" (ibid., 16). These numbers correspond to those I arrived at by studying the records on pew turnover.
5. For the New Church, figures are derived from the church's account books (*Rechnungen*), 1698–1700 (Stadtarchiv Leipzig). For St. Peter's, see *Rechnungen*, 1712 (Stadtarchiv Leipzig). For the University Church, see Wilhelm Stieda,

Der Neubau der Paulinerkirche in den Jahren 1710–1712 (Leipzig, c.1930). Stieda's figures specify around 300 pews, but there were probably many more.

6. The dynamic of demand being greater than the supply of pews runs counter to the stereotype of enforced church attendance. On Leipzig in this period, see G. Stauffer, "Leipzig: A Cosmopolitan Trade Centre," in *The Late Baroque Era: From the 1680's to 1740*, ed. G. Buelow (Englewood Cliffs, NJ: Prentice Hall, 1993).

7. In contemporary usage, "pew" (*Stand* or *Stuhl*) could refer either to one seat or to a row of seats. *Stand* or *Stuhl* could refer generically to a *Bänklein* as well as to a larger pew. I use the term "pew" to denote one individual's seat, except where noted.

8. On German churches generally, see R. Wex, *Ordnung and Unfriede: Raumprobleme des protestantischen Kirchenbaus im 17. and 18. Jahrhundert in Deutschland* (Marburg: Jonas, 1984), passim.

9. In early modern German towns, artisans, merchants, shopkeepers, and some other occupational groups generally owned their own homes, which usually included a workshop or retail space. Figures are based on an analysis of the records of 5,706 pew holders in St. Nicholas's between 1686 and 1725, which were made whenever a pew changed hands. Occupations of 65 percent (3,695) of the holders are listed. Adult men were listed by their occupations; women and children were listed as the dependents of their husbands or fathers. See the city council's annual *Rechnungen* for St. Nicholas's (Stadtarchiv Leipzig), and the church's *Einnahmen and Ausgaben* (Archiv der Nikolaikirche, Abt.III.532).

10. The allotment registers for St. Thomas's are not precise enough to allow for quantitative analysis. But other records often mention the pews there as being of the same type and arrangement as St. Nicholas's, and the social make-up of pew holders in both churches was similar. Many individuals held pews in both churches.

11. Archiv der Nikolaikirche, III.160./10, Sep 1735.

12. Ibid., 1 Jan 1736.

13. Writing in 1724 with regard to a *Bänklein* his mother held, Johann Michael Kuffs complained that "because this *Bänklein* is very close to the church door, and on account of the many people standing around, often almost nothing can be heard of the sermon." Kuffs to St. Nicholas's Director, 15 Apr 1724; Archiv der Nikolaikirche, III.160./8.

14. J. Johnson, *Listening in Paris: A Cultural History* (Berkeley: University of California Press, 1995), ch. 1.

15. On late arrival and early departure, see Christian Gerber, *Historie der Kirchen-Ceremonien in Sachsen* (Dresden and Leipzig: Saueressig, 1732), 252–53, 474. In his moral weekly publication set in Leipzig and Halle, *Die vernünfftigen Tadlerinnen*, Johann Christoph Gottsched satirizes a young woman who spends three hours dressing for the service and then rushes off, afraid to arrive after the start of the sermon (1 (1725), no. 7: 48–56; rpt. Hildesheim: Olms, 1993).

16. *Einführung des Klingelbeutels*, 26–29, 35, 38, 39, 85.

17. Johann Mattheson, *Der vollkommene Capellmeister* (1739), cited in *Music and Culture in 18th Century Europe*, ed. E. Fubini (Chicago: University of Chicago Press, 1994), 303.

18. A. Schering, *J. S. Bachs Leipziger Kirchenmusik* (Leipzig: Breitkopf and Härtel, 1936; rpt. Leipzig: Breitkopf and Härtel, 1954), 149–50, n. 3.

19. Gerber, *Kirchen-Ceremonien*, 352–53. Gerber's Pietist critique of mainstream religious practices is echoed by other authors, such as Julius Bernhard von Rohr in his *Einleitung zur Ceremoniel-Wissenschafft der Privat-Personen* (Berlin: Rüdiger, 1728; 20–22, 164–65 and passim; rpt. Leipzig: Edition Leipzig 1990, 35).

20. Gottsched, *Die vernünfftigen Tadlerinnen*, 1, no.3:17–24, no.29:225–32.

21. An Electoral decree of 1722 forbade this practice; see Archiv der Franckeschen Stiftungen, D 57.

22. A. C. Platz to Leipzig city council, July, 1720, Stadtarchiv Leipzig, Stift.x.39.a., *Kirchen-Stühle, Capellen and Begräbnis-Stellen betr.*, Vol. 2, p. 4.

23. Lange to an unnamed "father confessor," 1 Dec 1695, copied into Archiv der Franckeschen Stiftungen, D 57:42–77; 55.

24. *Einführung des Klingelbeutels*, 26–29, 39–40, 46.

25. Gerber, *Kirchen-Ceremonien*, 92–97.

26. H. Stiehl, *Das Innere der Thomaskirche zur Amtszeit Johann Sebastian Bachs, Beiträge zur Bachforschung* 3 (1984), 19–20.

27. Stadtarchiv Leipzig, loose pages in 1699–1700 St. Nicholas *Rechnung: Tit. Herrn D. Thomae Ittigs Superintendentes Investitur betreffend; Einführung des Klingelbeutels*; Archiv der Nikolaikirche, III.160, 1701–17; *Rechnungen*.

28. See K. Gründer and K. H. Rengstorf, eds, *Religionskritik and Religiösität in der deutschen Aufklärung* (Heidelberg: Lambert Schneider, 1989).

29. Even Bernd's account of ceremonies (*Lebens-Beschreibung*, 35) was cast as a lament that the authorities were gradually phasing them out. On later changes, see Stiehl, *Das Innere der Thomaskirche*, 36–8; *Einführung des Klingelbeutels*, 85–96.

30. See A. Schneiderheinze, "Zu den aufführungspraktischen Bedingungen in der Thomaskirche zur Amtszeit Bachs," *Beiträge zur Bachforschung* 6 (1987): 2–91.

31. See W. Weber, "Did people listen in the 18th century?" *Early Music*, 25 (1997): 678–91.

32. Private correspondence, 22 Mar 2000.

33. W. Hoffmann, "Leipzigs Wirkungen auf den Delitzscher Kantor Christoph Gottlieb Fröber," *Beiträge zur Bachforschung*, 1 (1982): 54–73.

34. *Texte zur Leipziger Kirchen-Music, Auf die H. Oster-Feyertage, Und die beyden folgenden Sonntage Quasimodogeniti and Misericordias Domini* (Leipzig: Tietze, 1724).

35. Georg Philipp Telemann, *Briefwechsel*, ed. H. Grosse and H. R. Jung (Leipzig: VEB Deutscher Verlag für Musik, 1972), 28–42.

36. U. Meyer, "Bachs Kantatentexte im gottesdienstlichen Kontext," in R. Steiger, ed., *Die Quellen Johann Sebastian Bachs: Bachs Musik im Gottesdienst* (Heidelberg: Manutius 1998), 371–88.

37. See A. Glockner, *Die Musikpflege an der Leipziger Neukirche zur Zeit Johann Sebastian Bachs, Beiträge zur Bachforschung* 8 (1990).

38. Gerber, *Kirchen-Ceremonien*, 259; Bernd, *Lebens-Beschreibung*, 67.

39. Bernd, *Lebens-Beschreibung*, passim.

40. See P. Veit, "Daheime seine Zeit mit singen, mit Beten and Lesen zugebracht: über den Umgang mit Kirchenliedern im aussergottesdienstlichen Kontext," in Steiger, *Die Quellen Johann Sebastian Bachs*, 329–35.

41. Gottfried Tilgner, preface to Erdmann Neumeister, *Fünff-Fache Kirchen-Andachten* (Leipzig: Grosse, 1716), unpag.

42. Gerber, *Kirchen-Ceremonien*, 246.

43. Gerber, *Kirchen-Ceremonien*, 247–49; Hans Medick, *Weben and Ueberleben in Laichingen 1650–1900: Lokalgeschichte als allgemeine Geschichte* (Göttingen: Vandenhoek and Ruprecht, 1996), 493 and passim.

44. Gerber, *Kirchen-Ceremonien*, 246. See also K. Dienst, " 'Bringe Deine Bibel und Dein Gesangbuch mit zur Kirche . . .' Vom 'Gesangbuch im Kopf' zum 'Gesangbuch in der Hand,' " *Jahrbuch der Hessischen Kirchengeschichtlichen Vereinigung* 47 (1996): 67–74.

45. Adam Bernd quoted a burgher in the 1710s as having said, "nowadays there is hardly anyone who does not have his hymnal with him [in church]" (Bernd, *Lebens-Beschreibung*, 302). Numerous hymnals were sold in Leipzig by the 1710s. See Stadtarchiv Leipzig, Tit. vii.B.34.a. and St. Georg *Rechnungen*, 1721 and 1729.

46. Stiehl, *Das Innere der Thomaskirche*, 35.

47. Telemann to Hamburg council, 16 Jun 1764, and Goeze to Hamburg mayor, 14 Jun 1764, in Telemann, *Briefwechsel*, 46, 60–61.

48. Leipzig chronicler Johann Jacob Vogel recorded that in 1667 the Leipzig town council ordered that in St. Nicholas's, "one of the Choralisten begins the hymns both before and after the sermon during the week, so that the deacons in this church, who have done this previously, be spared." *Leipzigisches Geschicht-Buch oder Annales* (Leipzig: Lanckisch, 1714, 1756), 733.

49. M. Little and N. Jenne, *Dance and the Music of J. S. Bach* (Bloomington: University of Indiana Press, 1991).

50. U. Siegele, "Bach and the Domestic Politics of Electoral Saxony," in Butt, *Cambridge Companion to Bach*, 17–34, 32–33.

51. See the recording *Sacred Music by Johann Kuhnau*, King's Consort, dir. Robert King, with notes by John Butt (Hyperion, CDA67059, rec. 1998).

52. Thanks to Matthew Dirst for this suggestion.

53. Iccander [J. C. Crell], *Das in gantz Europa berühmte, galante, und sehens-würdige Königliche Leipzig* (Leipzig: Martini, 1725), 48.

54. Gerber, *Kirchen-Ceremonien*, 283.

55. *Leipziger Kirchen-Staat* (Leipzig: Groschuff, 1710), unpag.

56. Gerber, *Kirchen-Ceremonien*, 279.

Chapter Seven

From Salon to Kaffeekranz

Gender Wars and the Coffee Cantata in Bach's Leipzig

Katherine R. Goodman

Bach's *Coffee Cantata* was written and first performed in an intellectual atmosphere charged with antagonism about the role of women in cultural life. It amounted to a gender war. Should women read? Should they study? Could they contribute anything significant? Should they be permitted to? Should their names appear in print? Should they face the same criticism as men? Should they be initiated into learned societies? If they were culturally active, would they still be able to perform their domestic duties? Could a husband still command such a wife? Advocates of differing opinions hurled assertions and accusations, fomented intrigue, and engaged in cultural subterfuge. In the 1730s Leipzigers witnessed—and many participated in—this battle. By the time of Bach's death in 1750 an uneasy consensus on acceptable limits for the participation of women in modern intellectual life had been reached.

There is no doubt that Bach and his associates were well familiar with the antagonists in this debate. There is also no doubt that the *Coffee Cantata* figured in it. There is only uncertainty about the particular role Bach and other Leipzig personalities played in its production and in the production of another musical satire on women's intellectual ambitions, "Ihr Schönen, höret an" (You ladies, listen well).[1] Until recently the existence of this gender war has remained largely unacknowledged. Therefore, I begin with a summary of it. Next, since the discourse about coffee briefly intersected with the one about women's cultural role, I outline the development of this beverage as a discursive marker for a certain cultural type. Finally, against this background, Bach's *Coffee Cantata* emerges as something more than a light-hearted musical jest. It was circulated, I propose, as part of the effort at gender containment and pacification.

Gender Wars

When Bach arrived in Leipzig in 1723, women did not write secular texts for publication. The court culture that set the tone in Dresden, Saxony's capital, and even to some extent in Leipzig, Saxony's trade center, modeled itself on Parisian practices: Parisian salons were imitated, for instance, in the home of Leipzig mayor Romanus. Although wives and daughters of professional men imitated certain French fashions and wrote gallant poetry (often with religious overtones) or occasional poetry for family events, unlike their French counterparts they did not publicly challenge male hegemony in the cultural sphere.[2] Leipzig's Scudéry and Bach librettist, Christiane Mariane von Ziegler (1695–1760), was yet to emerge as a cultural force. With the help of Johann Christoph Gottsched (1700–66), however, she soon made her presence felt. Throughout the late 1720s and the 1730s Ziegler aspired to create a woman-centered sociability, derived from aristocratic cultural forms originating in France. Moreover she issued her challenge to the arrogation of literary privileges exclusively to men in a very public manner and quickly inspired contempt and loathing. Gottsched and many of his followers continued to support her, but the times were also changing. Both the social importance of the salon and the gallant forms in which Ziegler wrote represented cultural practices about to pass from the historical scene as it became ever more clear that if women engaged in intellectual work, they would do so from a marginalized position.[3] Gottsched's own wife, Luise, became the model for this new, male-centered cultural practice.

This curious turn of events transpired in a very short period of time. Gottsched arrived in Leipzig in 1724, the year after Bach. He was then still a bachelor of twenty-four. In word and deed he soon promoted the idea that the native intelligence and linguistic ability of women would raise the general level of German culture and ultimately challenge the French claim to superiority. After all, French intellectuals (Madeleine de Scudéry, Pierre-Daniel Huët, Charles Perrault, and others) had argued that the exemplary quality of French culture owed much—if not all—to the linguistic and social skills of women and their roles in the salons. Gottsched presented and modeled his belief in the significance of women's cultural role in his moral weekly *Die vernünfftigen Tadlerinnen* (*The Sensible Lady Scolds*; 1725–26), a periodical in whose production Ziegler collaborated under various pseudonyms.[4] Beyond that, he tutored Ziegler—who had already been writing poetry for several years—in German prose and prosody, promoted her admission to the *Deutsche Gesellschaft* (*The German Society*), and nominated her for coronation as poet laureate to the University of Wittenberg. Gottsched's aspirations to challenge the supremacy of French culture were at stake. At this time in his life, witty salon culture and glorious women poets represented both signs of a superior culture and a means to achieve it. Ziegler was to be one of his soldiers in the cultural wars.

The collaboration of Gottsched and Ziegler was complex. For example, when he first came to Leipzig the young scholar had stubbornly and patriotically refused to recognize French cultural superiority. The beauties of that rival culture, however, had not passed unappreciated in Leipzig, which was also known as "Klein Paris" ("Little Paris"). As the protégé of Johann Burkhard Mencke (1674–1732; Saxon Court Historian and author of gallant poetry), Gottsched was no doubt soon introduced to Ziegler's salon. Within a year of his arrival he experienced a change of heart. In grudging admiration for French literary products, he began efforts to elevate German culture through the elevation of women's culture. He began, in short, his quest for the German Scudéry, for it was this novelist who symbolized in Germany the modern achievements in French literature.[5] And he soon found a Leipzig poet willing to advance the cause of women poets in Germany under the protection of her French predecessor.

Ziegler's wealthy family had long harbored francophile sentiments. Christiane Mariane was the daughter of the notorious mayor of Leipzig, Franz Conrad Romanus (1671–1746). The descendant of a recently ennobled family of lawyers, as mayor Romanus had been responsible for various municipal improvements (the introduction of street lighting [Fig. 2.2] and public sedan chairs, for instance).[6] However, he had irritated his fellow citizens by building a new home modeled more on the scale of a grand *palais* than a typical Leipzig residence. It established a standard for the sort of luxury soon denounced by town leaders. Romanus had also angered local craftsmen by employing artisans who were not members of their guilds. Worst of all, in 1705 he was jailed for passing fraudulent bonds and for embezzlement, undertaken no doubt to help pay for his extravagant home.[7] When local opposition to the poetic affronts of his widowed daughter arose, these offenses would have been recent memories.[8]

The salon that Gottsched visited was held in the second-story corner room of her family's *palais*, a room with a marble floor, inlaid wooden doors, Venetian mirrors, and ceilings stuccoed by Italian masters. Local lawyers and professors brought their wives. Among the professors were Johann Burkhard Mencke and Johann Christoph Gottsched. The governor of Leipzig, Count Flemming (1665–1740), was a family friend and likely attended when he was in town. Ziegler also hosted musical events, either in her home or, before the family sold it in 1727, in the family garden outside the city gates.[9] In one of her secular cantatas she summons relatives of Orpheus to a concert; bids wind, birds, and frogs to cease their singing and listen to well-ordered music; and invites participants to moisten their throats with wine and commence the music.[10]

Scholars have generally assumed that Bach attended the salon of this admirer of Madeleine de Scudéry. The evidence is circumstantial, but convincing: Carl Philipp Emmanuel Bach affirmed that his father had socialized with Ziegler; Bach set her texts to music before they appeared in print; Ziegler played three instruments and sang; she was interested in supporting musicians; her aunt, wife of Ratsherr Carl Friedrich Romanus, stood godmother to the Bachs' daughter Elisabeth Juliane Friederike in 1726.[11] So on some evenings, we assume, Bach escorted his wife the few hundred meters between their house and hers. If Ziegler's chosen social forms were modeled on the style of the woman-centered French salons, so also were her literary forms. She admired the works of seventeenth-century salonières like Scudéry and Deshoulières, and when she decided to challenge male prerogative in the literary sphere, she drew on their works as much as on the gallant forms of her Leipzig colleagues. The French literary Amazons had not only challenged the culture of the male-centered, centralized court of Louis XIV; they had also cultivated new literary forms, especially the novel, which contributed psychological subtlety and linguistic innovation to French literature. Ziegler never wrote a novel, but when she published her first book of verse in 1728 she explicitly drew attention to Scudéry and the gallant tradition of French women who challenged male dominance at court and in literature.

Ziegler could not fail to offend, for "Klein Paris" was orthodox Lutheran. And, unless women there wrote religious poetry, they wrote for domestic consumption. In this milieu Ziegler dared to publish secular poetry, dared to publish under her own name, and dared to accuse men of bigotry. For the most part, her male colleagues in poetry had professional occupations and even they published poetry under pseudonyms. In *Versuch in gebundener Schreib-Art* (*Exercises in the Poetic Mode*, 1728) Ziegler boasted, under her own name, of writing her poetry without the aid of any man. Since many of her male contemporaries were fond of circulating rumors that men had actually written the works attributed to French women, there was a point to this boast. However, there is no reason not to believe Ziegler. In various poems she asserts that men have unfairly kept women from exercising their intellectual capabilities, which she claims equal those of men, and summons other women to join her assault on the German Parnassus. While she virtually eliminated this confrontational tone in her second volume (1729), when she published her prose letters in 1731 she repeated her challenge to other women poets to come forward. There she claims her talents do not rival those of her French models. No one writing in German at that time seriously challenged French hegemony in literature, so her admission may be judged an honest assessment. However, Ziegler also claims she is not even the best among her female compatriots and urges them to come forward and prove her critics wrong about the talents of women. To promote more elevated social discourse, in 1735 she translated Scudéry's *Conversations* concerning polite and gallant behavior. She participated with Gottsched and others in the so-called *Scherzende Gesellschaft* (*Jovial Society*), an informal group that convened for literary purposes and which published the satirical *Neufränkische Zeitungen von gelehrten Sachen* (*New Franconian Journal for Learned Matters*) from 1733 to 1736. This jovial society met occasionally at her home. Laughter accompanied the meetings in which they wrote their barbed and veiled attacks on the bad taste of other Leipzig residents. Such activity was standard practice in that uncouth culture, but it was not standard practice for women—at least not in print. Ziegler's fifth and final book appeared in 1739. In it she continued to advocate the values and virtues of a woman-centered sociability.

For eleven years, then, Christiane Mariane von Ziegler pleaded in print for the public involvement of women in the cultural enterprise, indeed for the central role of women in elevating culture. Her efforts reaped some favorable reception and various honors, but they also earned her vile slander and decidedly ungallant criticism. Sidonia Hedwig Zäunemann (1714–40) and Anna Helene Volckmann (1695– after 1751) added their challenges to her print campaign. With metaphors of Amazons and military affairs they gallantly assaulted male dominance in the literary sphere. Other women, like Christiana Rosina Spitzel (1710–40), watched intensely from afar and with some trepidation.[12] Given the fact of Gottsched's support—along with that of his disciples and other women— for a time it may have appeared that this cultural model would prevail. In 1731 Ziegler was inducted into the learned society for the elevation of German literature, the *Deutsche Gesellschaft*, over which Gottsched had presided since 1727. In 1733 she was crowned poet laureate by the University of Wittenberg. A collection of eulogies written for this occasion was published in 1734.

Beginning with her second book in 1729, however, Ziegler continuously referred to jealous and unfair detractors of both sexes. Some of these assaults were surely brought on by her jovial sniping, but their viciousness exceeded common practice. Largely ephemeral in nature, a few of them found their way into print. In one case, insinuations flew that her salon was used to procure a wealthy wife for a poor academic.[13] In another, an anonymous broadsheet circulated in Leipzig accusing the new poet laureate of having seduced students. In this case the university lodged a complaint with the consistory in Dresden.[14] Anonymous slander was considered a serious offense, but the consistory tried to save face. In 1734 it merely fined the four students accused of circulating the broadsheet. Additionally, however, it reprimanded the University of Wittenberg for making such a controversial move as electing a woman to so exalted a position. The university never repeated the offense.

As a consequence of events such as this, in the mid-1730s Leipzig's roughly 35,000 residents witnessed a particularly intense, and often obscene, debate on the competence and morality of women engaged in writing. If some of the public scandal attending Ziegler's literary endeavors has survived to the present, for the most part we can only imagine what the private debates must have been like. In the case of Gottsched and his betrothed, however, we do not have to use our imaginations, for we possess some epistolary evidence of weakening resolve from Ziegler's staunchest supporter.

On a visit to Prussia in 1729 Gottsched had sought out Luise Kulmus (1713–62) on the strength of poetry she had sent him. They married in 1735. During the intervening six years they conducted an epistolary courtship.

If anything, Luise Kulmus, the daughter of a doctor in Danzig, was better educated, more talented, and at least as ambitious as Christiane Mariane von Ziegler. However, this deeply religious young woman abhorred the literary and cultural direction of Ziegler's efforts.[15] She did not approve of women attempting to usurp male prerogative in the public sphere. Rather she upheld the concept of hierarchy of gender roles, as did both Gottsched and the philosopher, Christian Wolff. Nor was the entire movement of gallant poetry—poetry without a moral purpose—to her liking.[16] Several comments in Kulmus's letters reveal her distaste for women like Laura Bassi, who in 1732 began to lecture in mathematics at the University of Bologna, or Dorothea Erxleben, who in 1740 applied to study medicine at the University of Halle.[17] Kulmus's comments on Bassi suggest that her suitor also found that incident distasteful.

For his part, Gottsched continued to support Ziegler in her more public battles, correcting false statements about her in journals, arranging for reviews of her books, and so on; by 1734, however, he was clearly tiring of this role. In a poetic epistle on the occasion of the death of another woman poet, Hedwig Eleonore Hantelmann, he complained of the energy it took to defend women who dared to challenge conventional standards.[18] The society in which he lived simply would not accept the foreign model he first promoted. For his time, and arguably for the century, Gottsched was the staunchest male supporter of women's participation in the cultural sphere; but as he had once changed his views on literature, so he later changed his views on the nature of that participation. By the mid-1730s, despite his public support of the poet laureate, Gottsched admitted he shared his bride's criticism of Ziegler's literary endeavors. He and his wife would provide an alternative cultural pattern for that participation, one modeled on the role of a guild apprentice. It was a male-centered pattern with a strong tradition in local culture.

After his marriage in May 1735 the distance between Gottsched and Ziegler grew. However, while Gottsched's bride deserves a large portion of the credit for this change in attitude, she was anything but the proverbial "angel in the house"—in any case an image derived from a later time. Luise Gottsched had been trained well by her father, mother, brother, and uncle, and she placed her considerable literary skills at her husband's disposal. As soon as she arrived in Leipzig she began taking lessons in Latin from one of Gottsched's students (Johann Joachim Schwabe) and lessons in composition from Bach's favorite student, Johann Ludwig Krebs (1713–80). She worked tirelessly as her husband's "apprentice" (*Gehülfin*): excerpting texts for him, answering his correspondence, translating texts of his choosing, organizing his library, compiling notes for his history of German drama. All this she undertook with her husband's full support, guidance, and encouragement. Unlike Ziegler, the Gottscheds lived modestly, in the same house as their publisher and his business. She occasionally oversaw the work of students and other academics employed by her husband. At the end of his life, Gottsched claimed that his publications had nearly doubled his salary as professor. Much of the labor for these publications had been undertaken or overseen by his wife. They functioned, in fact, much like a guild enterprise.

After their experience of Ziegler's public difficulties, both Gottscheds were careful to construct a less provocative public identity for Luise Gottsched. In the biography of his wife, which he published one year after her death, Johann Christoph stylized her as his *Gehülfin*—translated variously as helpmate, assistant, or apprentice. This term evokes at least two cultural contexts in Germany: Lutheranism and guilds.[19] While Luther's views on women obliged them to attend to the development of their souls and, hence, promoted at least minimal education for women, his writings also firmly proclaimed woman's destiny to be *Gehülfin* to her husband. However Luther's language may already have been shaped by the tradition of guild structures in which women had long functioned as unofficial and eternal apprentices to their husbands. His construction of this gender role certainly could have derived, at least in part, from common guild practices. Guild masters frequently trained their daughters in their craft so that they could help them and their future husbands. It was understood that daughters would marry men in the same craft.[20] In Germany these structures remained very powerful, often dominating small town politics and social structures. Given their strength, criticism of Ziegler's father for hiring non-local artisans may well have affected the reception of her literary efforts twenty years later.

These guild structures were sometimes adopted by academics. Daughters of academics were educated just enough to be useful in the scholarly enterprises of their fathers and, it was assumed, their future husbands. There are examples of this in eighteenth-century Germany; one of the best known is Dorothea Erxleben-Leporin (1715–62) who became the first woman in Germany to earn a university degree in medicine.[21] While the tradition of musicians in this regard has not been investigated, it is notable that neither Bach nor his contemporaries mention his giving his daughters the musical education that might have preserved them and their mother from destitution. Given his meticulous efforts to train his sons, his lack of care regarding his daughters remains a particular tragedy.[22]

Meanwhile, the Gottscheds' male-centered, guild-like construction of woman's participation in cultural life encountered few of the difficulties Ziegler had faced. Luise Gottsched had both a husband to lend her legitimacy and a different model for the construction of her role in the cultural sphere. No doubt she was still mocked by some critics, yet there is no comparable record of assaults on her talent or character. From the time of her marriage until her death in 1762, Luise Gottsched was known throughout Germany as the nation's most learned woman. The pattern of involvement in cultural production figured by Luise Gottsched was imitated in other families. For instance, Ernestine Christine Reiske (1735–98) began by helping her husband with his editions of Greek orators.[23] After his death, she continued his work and earned the admiration of contemporary scholars, including Gotthold Ephraim Lessing. Over time it was the guild model rather than the salon that would permit women in Germany greater access to cultural work.

While aiding her husband in his literary endeavors, Luise Gottsched also engaged in cultural controversy of her own making. Without a trace of admiration for the accomplishments of the French salonières, she entered public debates either anonymously or as her husband's named apprentice. Among her early efforts are translations or adaptations from the French that either ridiculed pietist or gallant pretensions of women to learning (her comedy *Die Pietisterey im Fischbeinrock* [*Pietism in Petticoats*] and her translations of Deshoulières) or favored philosophy above eloquence in public debate (her translation/correction of Madeleine-Angélique Gomez's *Le Triomphe de l'Éloquence* [1730; German 1735]).[24] To these can be added her satire of the gallant poetry of Gottlieb Siegmund Corvinus (1677–1746) and, more important, her translation of Alexander Pope's *Rape of the Lock* (1712–14; German 1744), itself a satire on gallant forms of female social conduct. Had their aims coincided, Ziegler and Luise Gottsched might have made a formidable alliance; as it was, their views were simply too divergent. Beginning at the latest in 1735, then, Ziegler faced both coldness on the part of Luise Gottsched and flagging support on the part of Johann Christoph Gottsched.

Nor did attacks from clearly hostile members of the public cease. Indeed, in musical Leipzig there were many ways to satirize the intellectual aspirations of women. In 1736 the first edition of Sperontes' (Johann Siegismund Scholze; 1705–?) *Singende Muse an der Pleisse* (*The Singing Muse on the Pleisse*) contained a song connecting women who pursued knowledge to questionable morality, "Ihr Schönen, höret an."[25] In the narrative, a gallant "Doris" is invited to participate in university disputes. Unfortunately "Amor" is bound to preside and the prestige of the university will suffer. However, if she applies to the prorector of the university, she will become a member of the "Orden der Schönsten Musen" ("Order of the most beautiful muses"). In her university courses she will learn lessons of love: "Amors Courtesie." If she learns this gallant curriculum well, in three years she will be able to instruct others. And if she exchanges the cradle for the lectern and becomes a "doctor," the author will kiss her hem and hands.

Sperontes' songbook contained new texts for familiar melodies. Additional texts to the same melodies were published at the back. This assault on women's aspirations to learning was tucked into the first printing in just this manner: the melody to which the text belonged was printed in the front with a different text (*Ich bin nun, wie ich bin*). However, the satire on women's learning was removed from the second. Someone apparently charged the authorities with removing it. Spitta believes it to have been Gottsched.[26]

If Spitta is correct, then eighteenth-century rumors about the origins of the song make it even more interesting, because it was claimed to be a collaborative effort on the parts of Bach and Gottsched. This assertion had been passed to

Georg Philipp Telemann (1681–1767) in far away Hamburg and from Jena gambist Wolfgang Carl Rost (1716–85; who visited Bach frequently toward the end of his life) to Christoph Gottlieb von Murr (1733–1811).[27] This Nuremberg historian transmitted the rumor to Bach's first biographer, Johann Nikolaus Forkel (1749–1818).

There are arguments for and against collaboration by Bach and Gottsched on this song. The attribution is troubling by reason both of the nature of the evidence and of certain apparent inconsistencies. Regarding the evidence: Murr, who had not yet been born when the song allegedly circulated, simply asserted that students were fond of singing this song in Leipzig from 1720 until 1730, and Spitta has merely assumed it was circulated as a broadsheet before Sperontes published it. This places the information in the realm of hearsay.

There are at least two possible points of inconsistency regarding Gottsched's participation in this venture. First, Bach arrived in Leipzig in 1723, and Gottsched, only in 1724. Very soon after Gottsched's arrival in Leipzig he began promoting women's intellectual advancement, at the latest with the publication of *Die vernünfftigen Tadlerinnen* in 1725. If we take this support seriously, and most scholars do, it is difficult to imagine a time when he would have collaborated on a satire of women's intellectual aspirations such as this. Second, most scholars have assumed Ziegler and/or Luise Gottsched were the particular object(s) of the satire. If so, the dating argues against the collaboration. Ziegler's affronts to public standards did not occur until after 1728 and Luise Gottsched—whose behavior could not generally be characterized as gallant— did not arrive in Leipzig until 1735.

However, the arguments surrounding apparent inconsistencies can be countered if we take a more subtle perspective both of Gottsched and of the situation in Leipzig. Gottsched's support of women's intellectual abilities in *Die vernünfftigen Tadlerinnen,* and in the person of Ziegler, must be considered together with the perspective he presented in his second moral weekly *Der Biedermann* (*The Decent Man,* 1727–29). In September 1727 one anonymous correspondent proposed to turn lazy students into diligent ones by banishing men from the podium and hiring only "gallant and learned women as professors."[28] The "decent man" does not immediately respond to this proposal. Rather, three months later he allows several ladies to provide a response. One of these doubts there are women with sufficient systematic training to accomplish the scheme, another worries about the dangers to women's virtue, still another thinks such women would earn only the hatred and envy of other women.[29] Silently, the "decent man" appears to approve the opinion of the woman whom he had introduced as exemplary, eminently respectable, and reasonable: things are best left as they are.

These exchanges are likely fragments of a public dialogue not transmitted to us in much detail. Apparently any proposal to educate women systematically could only be conceived in Leipzig in terms of gallantry.[30] While he did not ridicule the idea in *Der Biedermann*, Gottsched silently and decidedly discouraged it. In this exchange the image of the university as a place where gallant behavior is learned and performed is consistent with the musical satire, and with the traditional image of the university in Leipzig. In consideration of these exchanges our view of Gottsched's support for learned women acquires new contours. The fictional female editors of *Die vernünfftigen Tadlerinnen* resemble more the exemplary ladies later depicted in *Der Biedermann* and should be envisioned as performing their reasonable activities at home. The usual two-dimensional characterization of Gottsched acquires depth and credibility, if we allow him a more complex position. The second apparent inconsistency, relating to the supposition of particular objects of satire, is quickly dispensed with if we cease to assume that either Ziegler or Luise Gottsched was the target of this musical jest. However we are then confronted by a song without meaningful content, unless we assume there were other women seeking education in Leipzig in the 1720s. This is a tantalizing—and, given the exchange in *Der Biedermann*, even probable—but still unsubstantiated hypothesis. Speperontes' inclusion of the text in the songbook in 1736 might still have been aimed at a particular person, and Spitta's assumption that Gottsched occasioned its withdrawal from the second printing could then be based on his recent marriage to a woman who took her education very seriously and not as a matter of gallantry. Viewed from this perspective the possibility of Gottsched's collaboration is not inconsistent with his other actions.

As for Bach's authorship of the melody: if he wrote it, it cannot be determined for which text he may have written it.[31] In the first printing, the lyrics under consideration were only printed as alternate lyrics for the melody. The lyrics printed with the musical notation have nothing to do with women and learning. The intriguing thought that Bach and Gottsched collaborated on a song ridiculing women's learning should probably continue to be viewed with caution. Hans-Joachim Schulze, who revealed the source for these rumors, admits they could have been circulated by foes, in the type of cloak-and-dagger innuendo not uncommon in Leipzig in those days. Readers will have to judge for themselves, but I support the idea of collaboration, because, for me, it adds realistic contours to the usual stereotypical image of Leipzig in the 1730s.

Spitta derived evidence to support Gottsched's intervention in the printing of this text from the fact of its *re*appearance in the second edition of 1741. Whether we are satisfied with this evidence or not, it is certainly true that Gottsched's literary and cultural authority was under severe attack at this time. His influence had diminished. The 1740s mark a significant change in German cultural politics and practices. In fact, this songbook represents a new trend in music. It gave those who were upwardly mobile songs they could sing at home, and it quickly became a classic. It supplied new, lighter, more respectable lyrics for well-known melodies and appeared in many editions throughout the eighteenth century. "Ihr Schönen höret an" became a favorite of the rising middle class. The editor of the songbook, Johann Siegismund Scholze, was probably a member of the *Lustige Gesellschaft* (*Jolly Society*) that subsidized its printing. This society consisted mainly of students and was founded to counter Gottsched and Ziegler's *Scherzende Gesellschaft* (*Jovial Society*).[32] It also had some connection to the *Studenten-Musikverein* that met in Schellhafer's hall (pictured on the title page of the *Singende Muse*, later Hotel de Saxe) under the musical direction of Johann Gottlieb Görner (1697–1778), Bach's sometime rival and opponent.[33] The *Singende Muse* helped usher in the so-called "neuer Gusto." Its easy phrasing reportedly made it possible for ladies to play the pieces.[34] Thus even as it launched a new outlet for women, the new fashion anchored an old belief in their lesser talents. These songs, often lamenting women's fickleness, could now be performed in living rooms. It was a middle-class domestic art form and decidedly distinct from the emerging public culture that was to be the principal domain of men. The emergence of two spheres of cultural activity contrasted sharply with Ziegler's older ideal, for she had situated women squarely in the middle of a single sphere.

Usually Ziegler waited out assaults on her with more or less stoicism. In this case she counterattacked. Like "Sperontes" she supplied a text for a known melody. We possess it in printed form in her last book (1739), but like "Ihr Schönen, höret an," it was probably circulated earlier as a broadside. With great verve the lyrics characterize the arrogance and feebleness of men.[35] She addresses them: "Du weltgepriesenes Geschlechte, /Du in dich selbst verliebte Schaar" ("You world renowned sex, you self-adoring horde") and itemizes male faults, including presumption, bombast, and foolishness. Ziegler was nothing if not spirited, even as she faced defeat.

Coffee

For a time coffee became an icon used to identify gallant women, like Christiane Mariane von Ziegler, who harbored either pretensions to or a desire for learning. The fourth strophe of the lyrics to "Ihr Schönen, höret an" advises women to plan their schedules carefully: at nine they should be gallant and domestic like good children; at ten learn how to capture hearts with a glance; at one to play music; at two to write poetry; at three immerse themselves in letters; "Denn höret von der Eh,/ Hernach so trinckt *Coffee*" ("Then listen to lectures about marriage, and afterwards drink a little coffee").

For citizens of Leipzig, coffee was a relatively new stimulant, and—whether women drank more coffee than did men or whether it only seemed more outrageous—the caffeine habits of women were commented on more frequently than those of men. Coffee was first widely served sometime after 1665, when the Turkish ambassador from the court of Sultan Mehmed IV, Kara Mehmed Pascha, visited Emperor Leopold I in Vienna to establish an embassy.[36] His exotic entourage included 300 people, including colorful Janissaries. He also brought camels and magnificent horses, exhibited rich fabrics, and served coffee in wondrous tents. During the next twenty years the bitter and expensive beverage gradually became the drink of choice in various aristocratic circles, but the drink also caught on outside these circles, and taverns were slowly converted into coffeehouses. The high cost of this foreign luxury, especially in those countries without colonies where the beans could be produced, probably resulted in Saxon coffee being generally rather weak and tasteless. Since the painted flowers at the bottom of Meissen china could be seen through the drink, it was called "flower coffee" (*Blümchenkaffee*). Various substitutes (chicory or other beans) may also have been served. Regardless of its quality, private and public consumption of coffee began to replace that of alcoholic beverages, and this sobering drink accompanied the advance of the Age of Reason, the evolution of middle-class culture, and the dominance of the bourgeois work ethic.

This did not happen without earnest debate regarding the medical and social consequences of drinking coffee. One of many popular treatises on the subject was Daniel Duncan's *Von dem Missbrauch heisser und hitziger Speisen und Getränke* (*On the Misuse of Hot and Fiery Foods and Drinks*) published in Leipzig in 1707. Duncan makes every effort to project a moderate view of this new drug, but he is somewhat alarmed. He claims the misuse of coffee is rapidly expanding among both sexes, but especially among women: "For this sex, which does not have as much to do, [coffee] serves in place of an activity, and women drown their cares in coffee as we drown ours in wine."[37] His concern emanates ultimately from a larger estimation of the physical, mental, and cultural consequences of this trend. In the frontispiece to his treatise four gallant women play cards and drink coffee in an elegantly appointed spacious room (see figure 7.1). The caption reads: "And if we drink ourselves to death at least we do it fashionably." ("Sauffen wir uns gleich zu tode, so geschiehts doch nach der Mode.") The dangers of gallant francophile fashions thus included coffee drinking.

On the medical side, Duncan admits: coffee stimulates both the spirit (*Gemüthe*) and the body.[38] It makes the mind (*Geist*) more subtle and increases its vigor. However, he warns, coffee could lead to impotence in men and to infertility and miscarriage in women.[39] It also generally diminishes the mutual attraction of the sexes.[40] Medically speaking, therefore, excessive coffee drinking seriously endangers procreation. Duncan warns women in particular, since coffee makes one thin and gives one a jaundiced complexion.[41] Furthermore, coffee overstimulates the senses, exhausting them more quickly, and coffee drinkers are therefore more likely to require spectacles or a hearing trumpet.[42] Duncan worries excessively about the physical attractions of women.

Also of interest are his anthropological statements. Duncan argues strongly and sarcastically against the view that coffee, because of its stimulating effect on the brain, will help elevate the level of civilization. Friends of coffee had argued that the moist North has less "Witz und Verstand" ("wit and understanding")

Sauffen wir uns gleich zu tode
So geschiehts doch nach der Mode.

Figure 7.1. Frontispiece from *Von dem Mißbrauch heißer und hitziger Speisen und Getränke* by Daniel Duncan (Leipzig: Gleditsch, 1707). By permission of the Houghton Library, Harvard University.

than the dry South, where civilization was born: coffee allegedly dried the humors.[43] For him this argument is invalid, since the Greeks and Romans drank wine, while it is the Turks who drink coffee. Coffee helps neither the fertility of the brain nor the fertility of the body, he deduces.[44] He scoffs at the idea that all the coffee drunk in France has raised the level of their civilization and belittles recent French cultural products. An excess of coffee actually diminishes mental processes, but the misconception that it stimulates them has led to the misuse of the drug: "This error may nevertheless have been one of the great attractions of coffee. For everyone would like to have *de l'esprit*, wit, and understanding. They think they can never have enough of it."[45] Duncan obviously believes himself to be arguing against a widely held, if not prevailing, view, to wit: coffee would permit Germans to overtake the French in the cultural wars. The campaign to elevate German culture had been launched before Gottsched arrived in Leipzig; and coffee drinkers were among the crusaders.[46]

Many of the views represented by Duncan can be found in other sources as well. In his moral weekly *Der Biedermann*, Gottsched responded to concern for the state of drunkenness in Germany. This problem, he claims in the spirit of international cultural competition, has been overcome: Germans are now as sober as the English, French, and Italians.[47] Perhaps they were! Beer soup, long a staple in the German diet, was not among the culinary entries in Corvinus's gallant dictionary for ladies in 1715. There are numerous entries for items related to coffee, however.

For poets, coffee and tobacco began to replace alcoholic beverages as stimulants. Gallant poets imitating Anacreon had sung the praises of wine and women as inspiration for their creative imaginations. Silesian poet Johann Christian Günther (1695–1723) was sometimes chastised for this; but Leipzig professor Johann Burkhard Mencke also praised the effects of Rhine wine and Burgundy, as did others, including Dresden composer of popular student songs Adam Krieger (1634–66). But Mencke was a professor and published his anacreontic efforts under a pseudonym. Gradually tobacco acquired the same reputation as a stimulant. Before his death Günther praised tobacco for aiding his creative powers in the poem, "Lob des Knastertobaks." In 1728 Daniel Stoppe hoped to become as inspired as Günther by smoking tobacco, but confessed his page remained blank.[48] As coffee became more widely available, it was gradually added to the list of stimulants. Duncan repeats these views, and in an encyclopedia entry from the 1730s Johann Heinrich Zedler (1706–?) asserts coffee "can drive . . . the fog from [your head]."[49] Reason and virtue were sustained by sober individuals. The Age of Reason could not be ushered in by inebriated poets.

Women poets, with an eye toward their social respectability, had sometimes felt constrained in their choice of topics by not being able to sing of wine, women, and war. In December 1725, in the pages of *Die vernünfftigen Tadlerinnen*, Marianne von Breßler (1693–1726) had lodged such a complaint.

However, social conventions permitted women to partake of the sober stimulants. As early as 1724, an anonymous newspaper circulated under the title *Poetische Gedancken ueber das raisonnirende Frauenzimmer-Tobacks-Collegium* (*Poetical Thoughts on the Philosophizing Women's Tobacco Seminar*), thus linking the intellectual enterprises of women with that stimulant.[50]

The use of tobacco was frequently associated with drinking coffee. They were linked in Duncan's treatise and in others. Both stimulants were considered foreign, and their use among women was tied to the influence of French gallant behavior. Thus the correspondent "Tobacophilia" in *Der Biedermann* becomes outraged when she finds a Latin treatise objecting to women's use of tobacco. Her learning is pointedly emphasized when she translates this article for the weekly. The unnamed author of the article asserts the French gallant origins of the use of snuff and smoking tobacco, observes the prevalence of snuff boxes on ladies' dressing tables, and objects to their "unfeminine" habit of taking it, especially while playing cards. "Tobacophilia" opines aggressively that women have as much right as men to use tobacco and worries that if tobacco is forbidden, then coffee soon will be as well.[51] As presented here, the militancy and demeanor of women who asserted their equal rights in Germany belonged to the discourse about gallant French court culture. Along with other immoral behavior, this included claims to the right to study, assertions of learning, the use of snuff, and the drinking of coffee. In Leipzig, as elsewhere, coffee was served in several venues: in coffeehouses, in tents in various private gardens, and in homes. Adam Heinrich Schütz converted a pub into the first Leipzig coffeehouse, *Zum arabischen Coffee-Baum*, in 1685.[52] As was typical in German coffeehouses, he also set up a billiard table and probably at least condoned gambling and games of chance. After his death and the death of his son-in-law, it was owned and managed for decades by his daughter. How this was reconciled with a Leipzig proscription against women working in coffeehouses is unclear. As early as 1697 the municipal authorities had admonished women not to enter these establishments. In 1704 they were forbidden to enter a coffeehouse either to work or to consume coffee. The same ordinance also forbade gambling and games of chance (billiards was permitted) and regulated closing hours, 9 pm in the winter, 10 pm in the summer. This ordinance was passed while Ziegler's father was mayor of Leipzig. However, its efficacy may be doubted. In 1715 an entry in Corvinus's *Frauenzimmer-Lexikon* defines "Caffe-Menscher [*sic*]" (coffee trollops) as "suspicious and immoral women who serve men in coffeehouses and render them all desired services."[53] Moreover, at the command of the Elector, the ordinance had to be repeated in 1716, this time with more detailed restrictions on gambling and penalties of ten *Reichsthaler* for the first offense, twenty for the second. Raids were promised.

By 1725 a travel guide to Leipzig pointed proudly to eight licensed coffeehouses in Leipzig where visitors of high and low birth, men and women, met "because [the establishments] were famous for the large *Assemblée* that gathered there daily, and those attending found amiable diversion either in reading various gazettes and historical books, or in a gaming academy for clever and permissible board games and billiards."[54] By 1732 the number of licensed coffeehouses had increased to eleven. Whether these were quite as respectable as suggested in the travel book of 1725 was naturally a matter of perspective. In 1733 Leipzig resident Zedler informs us that some coffeehouses offer gaming and "other forbidden gatherings."[55] The authorities watch these carefully. Others provide:

> Occasion and opportunity for moral and learned discussions; noble, useful and agreeable acquaintances; reading or hearing the latest news; or otherwise furthering your own or your neighbor's needs and well-being. In Holland and England, no one need shy away from frequenting coffeehouses, whether he belong to a religious or worldly profession.[56]

Zedler's hesitancy in recommending coffeehouses to clerics and other respectable people suggests that he was more familiar with these other coffeehouses from having read about such establishments in Holland and England.

Indeed, English coffeehouses were often gathering places for rising young intellectuals, places where moral weeklies had been produced and consumed. However, in Germany the air of former beer halls seems to have adhered to these establishments for some time. Gottsched and Bach frequented them, and Bach's *collegium musicum* performed weekly in Zimmermann's coffeehouse. Gottsched may even have written some of the articles for his moral weeklies there, but this did not make the coffeehouses respectable.[57] Still, it is just possible that women of standing might have attended the coffeehouse performances of Bach's *collegium musicum*. No one has recorded whether Christiane Mariane von Ziegler, music lover and advocate of gallant behavior that she was, ever frequented a Leipzig coffeehouse.

The summer locations of coffeehouses were more amenable to the presence of ladies, for during the warmer months at least two of them used private gardens just beyond the city gates. There the proprietors erected tents under which they served coffee. In winter Bach's *collegium musicum* assembled on Fridays, from eight to ten in the evening, in Gottfried Zimmermann's coffeehouse in Catharinenstrasse, just a few steps down the street from Ziegler's elegant home; but in summer it met in a garden on Wednesdays, from four to six in the afternoon.[58] The tents nicely evoked the drink's exotic Turkish origins.

Proscribed from entering coffeehouses, women who consumed coffee did so mainly at home. Yet home consumption of coffee was sometimes a semi-public affair and, given its cost, coffee was initially served only by aristocratic or wealthy consumers. Christiane Mariane von Ziegler was known to serve coffee in her salon at five o'clock in the afternoon. In the 1730s, if not earlier, men and women gathered for coffee and cards and some would remain for supper. During the meal clever toasts were exchanged and afterwards literary or word games might be played. Perhaps there were more serious discussions about literary and social topics. Even the form of these gatherings and their activities thus followed models from the aristocratic, woman-centered French salons of the seventeenth century.

Ziegler was not the only Leipzig hostess to serve coffee and entertain guests with cards. One male correspondent to *Der Biedermann* gives a satirical account of a gathering around one of "L—'s" most estimable coffee tables. The author complains that the parents of the hostess had neglected her education: that she could not play the popular card game *L'hombre*, could not smoke a pipe, and could not brew a decent pot of coffee. He compares the assembly to a meeting of state where important issues are decided, like make-up and the best beds for childbirth, issues that might have severe repercussions for the health of the republic. He also mentions that they regularly discuss articles in *Der Biedermann*.[59] It is unlikely that this irony is directed at Ziegler's salon. There are indications that her assemblies of lawyers, professors and their wives discussed other matters—the German language, for instance.[60] Gottsched and Ziegler distinguished their aims and practices from other, less serious, enterprises of a similar nature. This certainly contributed to the local hostility against Ziegler's very public successes as Gottsched's protégée. If Ziegler earned the hostility of those who sat around coffee tables without conducting learned or gallant discussions, still others criticized her from a more "enlightened" perspective. It was a gathering like Ziegler's that Luise Gottsched satirized in her German adaptation of two poems by French poet and salonière, Antoinette du Ligier de la Garde Deshoulières (1637–94). Gottsched adds verses of her own to describe salons as places of coarse manners and "barbarism," frequented by young fops creating peasant-like tumult. And when she translated Pope's satire of gallant behavior, *The Rape of the Lock*, her friend, Dresden artist Anna Maria Werner (1689–1753), supplied illustrations (see figure 7.2). One of these depicts a salon like that of Christiane Mariane von Ziegler. A spacious room with large windows contains several tables, at which are seated both men and women playing cards and drinking coffee.

The frontispiece to Sperontes' *Singende Muse an der Pleisse* suggests images caught in transition (see figure 7.3). An indefinite location for a social gathering is superimposed on the Pleisse River with views of Leipzig, including Schellhafer's hall and Apel's garden in the background. It is neither inside nor outside. Muses make music, a woman makes music while a man listens, other men and women are playing cards, and still other men are shooting billiards. In the middle sits a mixed group over coffee. Does the whole represent a salon? A coffeehouse? A garden? It is some of each. The music in this book, we infer, can be played equally in homes, coffeehouses, and gardens. The frontispiece envisions a universal middle-class taste, even as the music sets out to create it. It is

Figure 7.2. Anna Maria Werner, illustration for Luise Gottsched's translation of
Alexander Pope's *Rape of the Lock: Der Lockenraub* (Leipzig: Breitkopf, 1744). By
permission of the Herzog August Bibliothek Wolfenbüttel.

Figure 7.3. Frontispiece from Sperontes' *Singende Muse an der Pleiße* (Leipzig: 1736).

the "new style," simple enough in its phrasing for women to play. Making music in non-aristocratic homes was a new form of refined domestic entertainment. Serious, professional music soon began to emanate from public concert halls subsidized by the same social group, but a stigma attached to women who performed in these.

The *Coffee Cantata*

Werner Neumann has convincingly dated Bach's composition of the *Coffee Cantata* between late 1734 and early 1735.[61] This places it squarely in the midst of the events I have characterized as gender wars. The text Bach selected had been published in *Ernst-schertzhaffte und satyrische Gedichte* (*Serious-jovial and Satiric Poems*; 1732) by another of his librettists, Christian Friedrich Henrici (1700–64), writing under the pseudonym Picander.[62] The last two strophes of the composition known as BWV 211, however, are not found in this text, an issue to which I shall return. The particular poem Bach chose was apparently very popular, as others also set it to music.[63]

For a time, the image of women as coffee drinkers evoked the image of women engaged in intellectual activities. In particular it evoked the image of women asserting their rights and pretensions to intellectual achievement. As written by Henrici this theme follows a predictable course: a narrator introduces the scene; then Schlendrian, the father, complains of the difficulties children cause and, in dialogue with his daughter Liesgen, tries to convince her to give up coffee.[64] He threatens not to let her go to any weddings, not to buy her more petticoats, not to let her watch passers-by from the window, not to let her wear a silver or gold ribbon on her cap. To her nothing is worth giving up coffee, until he threatens not to let her marry. Thus the father uses his daughter's desire for a man to gain control of her coffee drinking. The daughter's willpower and determination—her unruliness—falter at the thought of not getting a husband. To some extent marriage and coffee drinking are presented as mutually exclusive.

Henrici had already satirized women who drank coffee. In his comedy *Die Weiberprobe oder die Untreue der Ehe-Frauen* (*The Women's Test, or the Infidelity of Wives*; 1725), Frau Nillhornin (Mrs. Hippopotamus) had said she would rather cut off her finger than miss her coffee (II, 1) and Frau Ohnesafftin (Mrs. Juiceless) had said she would be a corpse by evening if she didn't have her daily dose (II, 2). Women who drink coffee are a little out of conventional control, a little too independent. Henrici's texts ally him with popular misogynist views about women in general and, given conventions of the time, about intellectual women in particular.[65] However, the text to Bach's cantata does not end with Henrici's.

If the first eight stanzas of Bach's libretto represent the conservative view, his text as a whole mirrors, on a small scale, the changing public attitude. There are two more stanzas, a ninth and a tenth, and these have the effect of subverting and modifying the preceding eight. In Henrici's eighth stanza the daughter, Liesgen, had agreed to give up coffee so that she might marry and urged her father to find her a husband that very night. In Bach's ninth stanza the narrator returns to inform us that Liesgen has secretly let it be known that she will insist on a clause in her marriage contract that entitles her to drink coffee. The music presents us with a charming, ingratiating, and clever young woman who has out-witted her bumbling and outmoded (the meaning of the word "Schlendrian") father.

Had the cantata ended here, the framing device of a narrator would be nicely balanced and Henrici's satire stood on its head. However, Bach's tenth stanza forms a sort of reconciliation for this domestic comedy, and the opposing positions are represented as non-antagonistic. A harmonious ending is found. In chorus, all three voices (father, daughter, and narrator) agree: "The cat will not leave off chasing mice, maidens will remain coffee sisters."[66] They recall that the grandmother and mother have both been fans of coffee—why should they worry about the daughter? Bach's text mediates the struggle: neither the conservative nor the radical position prevails. A moderate consensus renders the debate moot and harmless.

No one knows who wrote these two stanzas.[67] Music historians have assumed that Bach either had something to do with them or wrote them himself. No one proposes that Henrici wrote them, for he did not include them in later editions of his poetry. While it is certainly fair to assume that Bach had something to do with their writing, existing evidence suggests that he may not have actually written the text of the critical ninth stanza. In the manuscript of the cantata, written by Bach, that stanza begins a new page and uses both a different handwriting and different, unusual writing conventions, for example, the Romanized letter "e," as opposed to that of German script. To me this suggests either a different hand or that Bach copied the text from another source. The handwriting of the tenth stanza conforms to that of the first eight.[68]

The literary style of the ninth stanza suggests its author was well familiar with forms of gallant poetry. Above all, gallant poets sought to end their verses with a witty turn of phrase or meaning, and this the stanza certainly accomplishes. In addition, the joke on Henrici, subverting his text, is typical of literary high jinks in Leipzig at the time. In the absence of evidence and any other suggestions, I would like to speculate that Christiane Mariane von Ziegler wrote it. It is precisely the kind of literary fun in which she, and her circle, liked to engage. In this stanza the woman seemingly gains the upper hand, challenging the father and commandeering her future husband.

In the tenth stanza, however, the happy ending is based on acquired wisdom: Liesgen's mother and grandmother both drank coffee. Readers may reasonably infer that if two generations of respectable married women have drunk coffee, it cannot be that harmful. The significance of coffee as a symbol of female rebellion has lost its potency. So, too, had their assault on male literary prerogatives. Today Bach's reconciliation appears as pacification: coffee and women's intellectual ambitions have been domesticated and contained. It is possible that Ziegler and her cohorts viewed it this way as well.

Speculation about the location of the first performance of the *Coffee Cantata* usually places it in Zimmermann's coffeehouse. It cannot be denied that this is a logical assumption. However, there is no evidence to support it. In the absence of evidence, I propose an alternate scenario. Supposing Ziegler to have been the author of the ninth stanza, I suppose her also to have hosted a performance in her salon. Once on the road of speculation, I may as well venture its entire length and imagine her taking part in the performance. German women at this time did not typically play the transverse flute; however, Ziegler was an exception: she played piano, lute, *and* transverse flute. In the absence of documentation to the contrary we are free to imagine that she played the transverse flute that twice accompanies Liesgen. Perhaps Bach's wife, an accomplished singer in her own right, even sang the role. Or perhaps Ziegler sang the role of Liesgen! When Johann Friedrich Gräfe (1711–87), composer of four volumes of songs (*Sammlung verschiedener und auserlesener Oden*), dedicated the first (1737) to his patron Ziegler, he especially complimented Ziegler's singing.[69] The fantasy of Ziegler's participation in the writing, staging, and performing (either on flute or singing) of Bach's *Coffee Cantata*, therefore, is not without foundation. On the other hand, it may be wishful thinking.

No doubt Ziegler *did* find Henrici's original eight stanzas offensive. Her lyrics to "Du weltgepriesenes Geschlecht" ("You World-renowned Sex") could well include Henrici in the scope of her criticism. The fourth stanza begins: "Ihr klugen Männer schweigt nur stille" ("You clever men just be quiet") and thus echoes both the first line of "Ihr Schönen, höret an" ("You ladies, listen well") and the first line of Henrici, "Schweigt stille, plaudert nicht" ("Be quiet, don't chatter"). However, while we may never know definitively just who wrote the last two stanzas—Ziegler, Bach, or someone else—the *Coffee Cantata* marks the beginning of the end for the gallant effort to include women at the center of cultural production in Germany.

Gräfe dedicated the second volume of his songs (1739) to Ziegler's detractor, Luise Gottsched. Like the tenth stanza of the *Coffee Cantata*, it was a sign of the times. Women who desired to participate in Leipzig's cultural life would do so in the future on the margins, under the aegis of a man and not at the center of their own salons. To be sure, women continued to sit around the coffee table, but the *Kaffeekranz* or *Kaffeeklatsch* of middle-class society typically comprised women only. They gathered regularly in someone's home. At each meeting a wreath (*Kranz*) was placed on the head of the next designated hostess. According to tradition, the *Kaffeekranz* was a site for the circulation of rumors and gossip.

The cultural segregation of the sexes—men in the coffeehouses discussing intellectual and public matters, women at home discussing gossip—appears complete. In 1772 Ziegler's home, the so-called Romanus house, was sold to Georg Wilhelm Richter (1735–1800) who moved his already famous coffeehouse into the spacious second floor in May of that year. It drew intellectual and elite customers from throughout Germany and from abroad. Six or seven rooms were used. Chess and cards were played, music too. Newspapers were available. Two rooms were used for dining in the evenings, and wine was also served. The large billiard room was especially attractive because of its fine wallpaper, beautiful paintings, and good views. It was the very room in which Ziegler had held her salon: an assembly of men and women supposedly engaged in witty, intellectual conversation. However, an etching from 1794, just before Richter's coffeehouse closed, shows only men in attendance (see figure 7.4). Or so it appears, for it is always possible that one or more of these figures was a woman dressed as a man. As early as 1690 there were reports of such cross-dressers in the coffeehouses of England, Holland and Italy.[70] Why not Leipzig?[71]

Figure 7.4. Richter's Coffee House (1794). In Ulla Heise, *Kaffee und Kaffee-Haus. Eine Kulturgeschichte* (Hildesheim, Zürich, New York: Olms, 1987). By permission of the Stadtgeschichtliches Museum Leipzig.

Notes

1. Wolfgang Schmieder, *Thematisch-systematisches Verzeichnis der musikalischen Werke von Johann Sebastian Bach* (BWV) (Weisbaden: Breitkopf and Härtel, 1990), 834.

2. The concept of "gender wars" derives from the belligerent imagery of the German contestants in the events described here, as well as from their French sources. For a discussion of the French precedent, see Joan DeJean, *Tender Geographies: Women and the Origins of the Novel in France* (New York: Columbia UP, 1991). For a fuller discussion of the German events, see Katherine R. Goodman, *Amazons and Apprentices: Women and the German Parnassus in the Early Enlightenment* (Rochester, NY: Camden House, 1999). For another discussion of sociability in Leipzig at this time, see Detlef Döring, *Johann Christoph Gottsched in Leipzig* (Leipzig: Hirzel, 2000), 84–88.

3. The famous Berlin salons around 1800 may be regarded as a reinvigoration of earlier social forms modeled after the French. Berlin hostesses—like Henriette Herz, Rahel Varnhagen, or Bettine von Arnim—succeeded in gathering both men and women in their homes for intellectual discussions. These salons were critical for the

cultivation of German Romanticism. However, in the case of Rahel Varnhagen at least, we know she served tea, not coffee.

4. While it is true that the genre, moral weekly, originated in England, Gottsched's conviction about the role of women in culture clearly derived from the French. The model for Gottsched's weekly had been Joseph Addison and Richard Steele's *The Spectator*. The British publication had not only been produced in a coffeehouse; it was subdivided into sections aimed at the different clientele of various London coffeehouses. Even though Gottsched was allegedly fond of frequenting coffeehouses, his weekly gives no clue to the location of its production. Perhaps this is due to the fictional ruse he (and his co-editors) adopted, namely the weekly was supposedly the production of three women. In a German climate, it would have been unseemly for women to be composing anything in a coffeehouse. Apart from gender politics, moreover, no political issues are raised. It would be 1745 before Gottsched's wife, Luise Gottsched, would translate *The Guardian* (1713) into German.

5. She acquired this position in Germany because of the central role she had played in similar Parisian debates. Huët and Perrault praised advances made in French literature by women: Madeleine de Scudéry, Antoinette du Ligier de la Garde Deshoulières and Henriette de Coligny, Countess de La Suze, in particular, had been placed in the French pantheon of muses. Authors like Nicolas Boileau-Despréaux, favoring classical authors, used Scudéry as an example of modern literary abomination.

6. He had also been the main supporter of Telemann for the post of organist and director of music at the New Church in 1704.

7. Romanus died in Königstein prison in 1746. Among the items his wife continued to send him during his imprisonment was coffee.

8. In 1711, at the age of 16, Christiane Mariane Romanus had married Heinrich Levin von Könitz. Within a few years, he died. She married Captain Georg Friedrich von Ziegler in 1715. He also died within a few years. She bore her two husbands three daughters, all of whom died in childhood. The death dates of her first two husbands and her children are not known; however, after Captain von Ziegler's death, his widow traveled and returned to Leipzig in 1722.

9. On the sale of the garden and transfer of title to Frau Romanus, see Michael Müller and Ulla Heise, *Das Romanushaus in Leipzig* (Leipzig: n.p., 1990), 52.

10. Christiane Mariane von Ziegler, *Versuch in gebundener Schreib-Art/Anderer und letzter Theil* (Leipzig: Braun, 1729), 291–301.

11. Cantatas 68, 74, 87, 103, 108, 128, 175, 176, 183. Not printed in her collections are her texts to Cantatas "Ich bin ein guter Hirte" und "Gott fährt auf mit Jauchzen." In addition, texts of hers were set to music by Kapellmeister Hurlebusch, di Giovannini and Philipp Emanuel Bach. Michael Müller and Ulla Heise, *Das Romanushaus in Leipzig*, 54.

12. See Anna Helene Volckmann, *Die Erstlinge unvollkommener Gedichte durch welche hohen Personen ihre Unterthänigkeit, Freunden und Freundinnen ihre Ergebenheit, vergnügten Seelen ihre Freude, und Betrübten ihr Mitleiden gezeiget, sich selbst aber bey ihren Wirtschafts-Nebenstunden eine Gemüths-Ergötzung gemacht* (Leipzig: Christoph Gottlieb Nicolai, 1736), 9–12 and Sidonia Hedwig Zäunemann, *Poetische Rosen in Knospen* (Erfurt: Johann Heinrich Nonne, 1738), 635. Spitzel's poetry shows the influence of Barthold Heinrich Brockes, who admired God's work in nature; but she lauded Ziegler for her talent and her bravery. Jacob Friedrich Lamprecht. ed., *Sammlung der Schriften und Gedichte auf die poetische Krönung der hochwohlgebohrnen Frauen, Frauen [sic] Christianen Marianen von Ziegler gebohrnen Romanus* (Leipzig: Breitkopf, 1734), 41.

13. Such was the interpretation in Christian Ludwig Liscow's *Sottises champêtres*, published in the summer of 1733.

14. Whether one individual urged the university to appeal to the Consistory is unclear, but it seems to have fallen under the purview of the university because a member of its faculty had nominated Ziegler.

15. Luise Gottsched's comedy *"Die Pietisterey im Fischbeinrock"* (1736; "Pietism in Petticoats") ridiculed Pietists and criticized orthodox Lutherans as well. She and her husband both worked for the acceptance of the rationalist philosophy of Christian Wolff. Nevertheless, the letters she wrote her future husband between 1729 and 1735 bear witness to a profound religious sentiment. See Luise Gottsched, *Briefe*, ed. Dorothea von Runckel (Dresden: Harpeter, 1771–72). Indeed, in his biography of her, Johann Christoph Gottsched informs us that theology was one of Luise Gottsched's favorite pastimes in her youth and one at which she excelled. See Luise Adelgunde Victoria Gottsched, *Sämmtliche kleinere Gedichte, nebst dem, von vielen vornehmen Standespersonen, Gönnern u. Freunden beyderley Geschlechtes, ihr gestifteten Ehrenmaale, und ihrem Leben*, edited by Johann Christoph Gottsched (Leipzig: Breitkopf, 1763).

16. Katherine R. Goodman, "Klein Paris and Women's Writing: Luise Gottsched's Unknown Complaints," *Daphnis* 25, no. 4 (1996): 695–711.

17. Luise Gottsched, *Briefe*, ed. Dorothea von Runckel (Dresden: Harpeter, 1771–72), 1:22 and 24; 2:225.

18. Johann Christoph Gottsched, in *Der Deutschen Gesellschaft in Leipzig Eigene Schriften und Übersetzungen* (Leipzig: Bernhard Christoph Breitkopf, 1734), 223–24.

19. Historians have commonly understood Gottsched's use of this word in the Lutheran sense (a wife as a helpmate of her husband). However, there is a strong argument against this interpretation, as both Gottscheds referred to male scholars who assisted them by the same term, *Gehülfe*. This lends the guild analogy all the more explanatory power.

20. The guild usually became responsible for the family of a deceased master. A widow might manage her dead husband's business for a certain time (often a year) after his death, whereupon any apprentice who married her would usually then be exempted from certain licensing restrictions or fees.

21. For a further discussion of this see Katherine R. Goodman, *Amazons and Apprentices: Women and the German Parnassus in the Early Enlightenment* (Rochester, NY: Camden House, 1999), 215–19, 291–93; Anke Bennholdt-Thomsen and Alfredo Guzzoni, "Gelehrte Arbeit von Frauen: Möglichkeiten und Grenzen im Deutschland des 18. Jahrhunderts," *Querelles: Jahrbuch für Frauenforschung* 1 (1996): 48–76; Katherine R. Goodman, "Learning and Guildwork: Luise Gottsched as *Gehülfin*, in Gabriele Jancke and Michaela Hohkamp, eds, *Nonne, Königin, Kurtisane: Wissen, Bildung und Gelehrsamkeit von Frauen in der frühen Neuzeit* (Königstein: Helmer Verlag, 2004), 83–108.

22. For a detailed study of this see Swantje Koch-Kanz and Luise F. Pusch, "Die Töchter von Johann Sebastian Bach," in *Töchter berühmter Männer*, ed. Luise F. Pusch (Frankfurt am Main: Insel Verlag, 1988), 117–54.

23. Anke Bennholdt-Thomsen and Alfredo Guzzoni, *Gelehrsamkeit und Leidenschaft: Das Leben der Ernestine Christine Reiske, 1735–1798* (Munich: Beck, 1992).

24. Luise Kulmus had translated this defense of eloquence by Gomez (1684–1779) in the early 1730s, and it appeared in 1735. After her marriage, Luise Gottsched listened to her husband's classes on oratory from behind a cracked door in their home.

In 1739 she exercised her newly acquired skills by arguing against the primacy of elo-quence and for the primacy of philosophy (truth) in oratory. This exercise, *Der Sieg der Weltweisheit*, was published, under her married name, together with her original translation of Gomez's text and three other, shorter, exercises in oratory, including the satire of Corvinus.

25. Sperontes, *Singende Muse an der Pleisse*, edited by Edward Buhle (Wiesbaden: Breitkopf and Härtel and Graz: Akademische Druck- und Verlagsanstalt, 1958 [is the same as *Denkmäler Deutscher Tonkunst.* Series I, vol. 35/36]), 100. On women from artisan families attending university colloquia during a short-lived Pietist movement in Leipzig 1689–90, see Hans Leube, *Orthodoxie und Pietismus: Gesammelte Studien* (Bielefeld: Luther-Verlag: 1975), 185–89.

26. Philipp Spitta, "Sperontes 'Singende Muse an der Pleisse.' Zur Geschichte des deutschen Hausgesanges im achtzehnten Jahrhundert," *Vierteljahrsschrift für Musikwissenschaft*, ed. Fr. Chrysander and Philipp Spitta (1885; rpt., Hildesheim: Olms, 1966), 88–92. For more on this song, see Max Seiffert, "Die Sperontes-Lieder: 'Ich bin nun wie ich bin'—'Ihr Schönen höret an' und Seb. Bach," in *Festschrift Fritz Stein zum 60. Geburtstag*, ed. Hans Hoffmann and Franz Rühlmann (Braunschweig: Litolff, 1939), 67–70; and Hans-Joachim Schulze, "Über die 'unvermeidlichen Lücken' in Bachs Lebensbeschreibung," in *Bachforschung und Bachinterpretation heute. Wissenwchaftler und Praktiker im Dialog*, ed. Reinhold Brinkmann (Kassel: Bärenreiter, 1981), 32–42.

27. Hans-Joachim Schulze, "Über die 'unvermeidlichen Lücken' in Bachs Lebensbeschreibung," in *Bachforschung und Bachinterpretation heute*, ed. Reinhold Brinkmann (Kassel: Bärenreiter, 1981), 38–39. Schulze has identified the gambist, who was born in Jena to the son of a *Polizeirat* (police administrator) and was there-fore not in the immediate family of the Rost who ridiculed Gottsched and his learned wife in "Das Vorspiel: Ein episches Gedicht" (1742). Nevertheless this Rost (Johann Christoph, 1717–65) was born to the sexton (*Küster*) at the Thomaskirche in Leipzig. Perhaps there was some family connection, perhaps some confusion about the origin of the assertion (whether Bach or a related member of the family, Rost).

28. "lauter galantes und gelehrtes Frauenzimmer als Professorinnen." See Johann Christoph Gottsched, *Der Biedermann* (1727–29; rpt., Stuttgart: J. B. Metzler, 1975), 81.

29. Ibid., 12.

30. A proposal to provide women with a university education had been receiving some attention in Germany at this time. Probably the source of it was Mary Astell's *A Serious Proposal for the Ladies* (1694).

31. Philipp Spitta disputed Bach's authorship, Edward Buhle and Hermann Kretzschmar claimed it. Seiffert was uncertain; Schulze declared it unknowable and fully disclosed the source of the rumors.

32. The power of the Consistory in Leipzig is demonstrated in an interesting way on Scholze. In 1729 it forced him to wed the widow of a merchant of prepared foods. Most likely the couple had been engaged in extramarital relations. Georg Witkowski, *Geschichte des literarischen Lebens in Leipzig* (1909. Reprint, Munich: K. G. Saur, 1994), 306.

33. Philipp Spitta, "Sperontes 'Singende Muse an der Pleisse,' " 37.

34. In the mid-1730s Bach seems to have noticed public taste deserting his music for this lighter, more "gallant" style. Bach's reaction was not conservative. Rather he began producing students (including Johann Ludwig Krebs) who composed in this

style, and there are suggestions that at least in the context of the *Collegium musicum* he tried to experiment with it. The *"Musikalisches Opfer"* contains elements of this "neuer Gusto." See Christian Ahrens, "J. S. Bach und der 'neue Gusto' um 1740," *Bach Jahrbuch* 72 (1986): 69–79, quotation 72.

35. Christiane Mariane von Ziegler, *Vermischete Schriften in gebundener und ungebundener Rede* (Göttingen: Universitäts-Buchhandlung, 1739), 66–71.

36. He visited Paris in 1669, but the beverage seems to have caught on more readily there.

37. "[Caffe] dienet stat eines Zeitvertreibes, bey diesem Geschlechte, das nicht so viel zu thun hat, und seine Sorgen im Caffe erträncket, gleich wie unser Geschlechte die Seinigen im Weine ertränket" (Daniel Duncan, *Von dem Missbrauch heisser und hitziger Speisen und Getränke* [Leipzig: Gleditsch, 1707], 390).

38. Ibid, 431.

39. Ibid., 96 and 399.

40. Ibid., 383.

41. Ibid., 96 and 63.

42. Ibid., 104.

43. Ibid., 431.

44. Ibid., 435.

45. "Dieser Irrthum mag aber dennoch eine kräfftige Anreizung zum Mißbrauch des Caffes gewesen seyn. Denn alle Leute wolten gern de l'esprit, Witz und Verstand haben. Sie meinen, sie können nimmer zu viel davon haben." Ibid., 456.

46. For more on these cultural wars, especially as they relate to women, see Katherine R. Goodman, *Amazons and Apprentices: Women and the German Parnassus in the Early Enlightenment* (Rochester, NY: Camden House, 1999), 43–48.

47. Johann Christoph Gottsched, *Der Biedermann*, 74–75.

48. Georg Witkowski, *Geschichte des literarischen Lebens in Leipzig* (1909; rpt., Munich: K. G. Saur, 1994), 305.

49. "kan die Dünste aus [dem Kopf] . . . vertreiben." Johann Heinrich Zedler, *Universal-Lexikon* (1732–1750; rpt., Graz: Akademische Druck- und Verlagsanstalt, 1964), 4:540.

50. Georg Witkowski, *Geschichte des literarischen Lebens in Leipzig*, 250. The 1742 sequel of Sperontes' *Singende Muse an der Pleisse* contains a song satirizing women and their use of snuff. No doubt trading on the popularity of Picander's coffee text, the woman's voice says she would rather miss her lover than her tobacco; she can only love a man willing to accept her snuff (ibid., 308–9).

51. Johann Christoph Gottsched, *Der Biedermann*, 138–40.

52. Hans-Joachim Schulze, *Ey! Wie schmeckt der Coffee süße: Johann Sebastian Bachs Kaffee-Kantate in ihrer Zeit* (Leipzig: Verlag für die Frau, 1985), 7. Hans-Joachim Schulze, "Ey! How Sweet the Coffee Tastes: Johann Sebastian Bach's Coffee Cantata in Its Time," tr. Alfred Mann, *Bach: Journal of the Riemenschneider Bach Institute* 32/2 (2001). For other discussions of the culture of coffee in Leipzig and elsewhere, see *Süße muß der Coffee sein! Drei Jahrhunderte europäische Kaffeekultur und die Kaffeesachsen* (Exhibition Catalogue, Leipzig, 1994); Ulla Heise, *Kaffee und Kaffee-Haus. Eine Kulturgeschichte* (Hildesheim, Zürich, New York: Olms, 1987); Wolfgang Schivelbusch, *Tastes of Paradise. A Social History of Spices, Stimulants, Intoxicants* (New York: Pantheon Books, 1992).

53. "verdächtige und liederliche Weibes-Bilder, so in denen Caffe-Häusern das anwesende Mannsvolck bedienen, und ihm alle willige Dienste bezeugen." Gottlieb

Siegmund Corvinus, *Nutzbares, galantes und curiöses Frauenzimmer-Lexikon* (1715; rpt., Frankfurt am Main: Insel Verlag, 1980), 285. Corvinus was a Leipzig lawyer and dandy who wrote gallant poetry to supplement his income. It is likely that he also attended Ziegler's salon.

54. "wegen derer sich täglich darinnen ereignenden grossen Assemblée berühmt, sintemahln alle dahin kommende Personen, theils in Lesung allerhand Gazetten und Historischer Bücher, theils als in einer Academie de Jeux in sinnreichen und zuläßigen Schach-Bret-Damen und Billeard-Spiel [*sic*] sehr angenehmes Divertissement finden" (Johann Christian Crell [Iccander], *Das in gantz Europa berühmte, galante, und sehens-würdige Königliche Leipzig* (Leipzig: Martini, 1725). Quoted in Hans-Joachim Schulze, *Ey! wie schmeckt der Coffee süße* (Leipzig: Verlag für die Frau, 1985), 20.

55. "ander[e] verboten[e] Gesellschaften."

56. "Anlaß und Gelegenheit zu guten erbaulichen und gelehrten Gesprächen, vornehmen, nützlichen und angenehmen Bekanntschafften, auch die neuesten Zeitungen zu lesen, oder zu erfahren, oder sonsten seinen oder des Nechsten Nutzen und Wohlfahrt zu befördern. Wie denn in Holland und England sich niemand scheuen darff, die Caffee-Häuser zu besuchen, er mag seyn Geistlichen, oder Weltlichen Standes." Johann Heinrich Zedler, *Universal-Lexikon* (1732–1750; rpt., Graz: Akademische Druck- und Verlagsanstalt, 1964), 5:112.

57. Newspapers and journals were available in Leipzig coffeehouses at this time. Gottsched is pleased when a reader notes that *Der Biedermann* is read in wine and coffee establishments along with other weeklies. See Johann Christoph Gottsched, *Der Biedermann*, 84.

58. In 1723 in Apel's Garden a coffee bush (planted in 1721) bloomed from May to July. It was one of several early attempts in Germany to grow coffee, all of which failed.

59. Johann Christoph Gottsched, *Der Biedermann*, 150–51.

60. Ibid., 92 and 107–8.

61. Werner Neumann, "Schweigt stille, plaudert nicht: BWV 211," in Johann Sebastian Bach, *Neue Ausgabe sämtlicher Werke* (Kassel: Bärenreiter, 1970): series 1, 40:193.

62. Henrici first published a collection of his very popular poetry under this title in 1727. Parts 2 and 3 followed in 1729 and 1732. There were also various editions of different collections. The first eight strophes of Bach's text appeared in part 3 (1732), 564–67. For more on Henrici and Ziegler as librettists for Bach, see Philipp Spitta, "Mariane von Ziegler und Johann Sebastian Bach," in *Zur Musik. Sechzehn Aufsätze* (1892; rpt., Hildesheim: Olms, 1972), 95–118; and Philipp Spitta, "Über die Beziehungen Sebastian Bachs zu Christian Friedrich Hunold und Mariane von Ziegler," in *Historische und Philologische Aufsätze Ernst Curtius gewidment* (Berlin: A. Ascher & Co., 1884), 405–34.

63. As many as four other compositions have been reported: one by Johann Sigismund Buchberger, another by Bach (reported in two of F. Hauser's Bach catalogues) with a similar text, one anonymous composition copied by C. F. Penzel, and possibly another which Spitta found in a newspaper announcement from 1739. Only the one copied by Penzel is still extant, and its text lacks the two extra strophes of Bach's composition. See Werner Neumann, "Schweigt stille, plaudert nicht, BWV 211," 197–98. See also Hans-Joachim Schulze, "Sächsiche Kaffeemusik im 18. Jahrhundert," in *Süße muß der Coffee sein! Exhibition Catalogue* (Leipzig: n.p., 1994), 69–74.

64. The supposition that Bach wrote this cantata to describe some domestic situation in the Bach household is usually based on the similarity of daughters' names. "Liesgen," however, was a name commonly found in plays and poems of the period and one used many times by Henrici. Moreover, Bach's daughter Elisabeth Juliana Friederica (1726–81) would have been eight or nine years old at the time this composition was written, too young for marital considerations. In addition, Bach himself was allegedly fond of coffee.

65. Ever since Gottsched had arrived in Leipzig he had satirized and ridiculed the type of rather common writing that often passed for wit in Leipzig in the 1720s. Henrici had taken punches in Gottsched's attacks and the two were definitely not on friendly terms. See Georg Witkowski, *Geschichte des literarischen Lebens in Leipzig*, 250–52.

66. "Die Katze läßt das Mausen nicht/ Die Jungfern bleiben Coffeeschwestern."

67. For a discussion of this, see Werner Neuman, "Schweigt stille, plaudert nicht, BWV 211," 196–97.

68. Neumann describes a different *Schreibduktus* for this stanza. Moreover, since it begins on a new page he wonders whether Bach had originally intended lengthening the text at all. Ibid., 198.

69. Clearly intended to capitalize on the success of Sperontes' *Singende Muse*, Gräfe emphasized the advantage of his compositions: the music had been newly composed, each melody expressly enhancing particular lyrics. Given Ziegler's tribulations, in particular the satirical allusions to her career in Sperontes' "Ihr Schönen, höret an" the previous year, this dedication would have been gratefully received.

70. Hans-Joachim Schulze, *Ey! Wie schmeckt der Coffee süße*, 17–18. Additionally, the "Amazon" – a woman dressed as a man – appears as a fictional character in literature around 1800, most notably in Goethe's *Wilhelm Meister* (1796).

71. Carol Baron first suggested this delicious topic. Much of the research on which this article is based would not have been possible without the generous support of the Alexander-von-Humboldt Stiftung. I would like to thank Camille Higonnet for reading an earlier version of this article.

Chapter Eight

A Treatise on Liturgical Text Settings (1710)

Johann Kuhnau

Translated by Ruben Weltsch
Introduced by Carol K. Baron

Introduction

Bach's immediate predecessor at the Thomasschule in Leipzig, Johann Kuhnau (1660–1722), was a person of broadly cultivated tastes, with a decided literary flair that he developed successfully according to prevailing styles. His literary works interest us here since, quite side from being a successful composer, he left us documents that are unique and have been referred to in modern musicological studies as significant statements about current issues in literature, music, and religion—all of which, fortunately for us, drew his attention and are relevant for our study.

In 1700, Kuhnau published a novel entitled *Der Musicalische Quack-Salber* which, translated into English, is *The Musical Charlatan*. It is closely modeled on Christian Weise's earliest and most popular novel, *Die drey ärgsten Ertznarren in der ganzen Welt* (*The Three Worst Arrant Fools in The Entire World*), one of the author's so-called "political" works, through which he taught young men appropriate behavior for working, primarily, in government positions in the electoral states. Weise's works were particularly influential in Thuringia and Saxony. (Chapter 1 cites Weise's works and discusses his contributions to the success of Saxon absolutism and the middle classes.) The protagonist in Kuhnau's adaptation is a clever braggart who pretends to be a musician and is ultimately unmasked, thereby evoking the derision and disdain whose underlying purpose is instructive. The penultimate chapter includes a list of sixty-four items of remonstrances and advice, under the heading "Der wahre Virtuose und glückselige Musicus"

("The True Virtuoso and Blessed Composer"), which summarizes the lessons to be learned.

Kuhnau's "Treatise on Liturgical Text Settings," presented here in English translation, originally prefaced a set of cantatas composed for use at the Thomaskirche during the 1709–10 church year. It is an explanation of the process Kuhnau engaged in his work. Like his novel, it too models itself after a literary form, one that was developed, in this instance, by Christian Thomasius, Weise's most prominent student. Thomasius's significance in Leipzig, his difficulties at the university, and his later influence in the German territories were discussed in chapter 2. Although Thomasius was forced to leave Leipzig, the influence of his publications grew even there and is clearly found in Kuhnau's literary style and intellectual conception.

The following description of Thomasius's literary style by Eric A. Blackall, in *The Emergence of German As a Literary Language, 1700–1775*, creates a context for Kuhnau's work.[1]

> It is studded with foreign words, sometimes as Latin and sometimes French. The technical terms are usually the Latin ones then in existence, the French words are usually taken from general cultured vocabulary at the time. . . . Sometimes Thomasius preserves the case-endings . . . but at other times he does not. . . . He often gives foreign words a termination more current in German than the Latin or French ending, but this "naturalisation" of foreign words is usually confined to those words which we might justly expect to have formed part of the general cultured vocabulary of those days. . . . Sometimes Thomasius alternates between a naturalised [*sic*] and a non-naturalised form. . . . It is also a feature of his style to give both the German and the foreign term for the same concept (22–23).

Although Blackall adds, "the language of Thomasius would not seem to differ very much from that of most other learned men writing in German at that time" (22–23), he chooses to focus on Thomasius's philosophical treatise, *Einleitung zu der Vernunfft-Lehre*, published in Halle in 1691, a year after he fled Leipzig, for these reasons: his personality, the public interest he commanded, "and the audience which he envisaged and consciously wrote for" (19). In his attempts to nurture literary interest among the laity, Thomasius was waging a "war against the tyranny of scholasticism" (21). Furthermore, in the *Einleitung zu der Vernunfft-Lehre*, Thomasius actually dealt with the lack of generally accepted philosophical terminology in German which, he believed, reflected "ill-defined concepts" (24). "His standpoint," writes Blackall, is briefly this: "if a philosophical concept is naturally and normally referred to by a foreign name, then we should continue to use this name. . . . The philosopher should call things by the names they customarily bear, whether these be foreign or native" (24). Having also found relevant precedents in Christian Weise's work, Blackall cites Weise as having stated that: "it would be a good thing if the Germans could denote their virtues without having recourse to foreign expressions. In philosophy, mathematics and politics, however, there were many technical terms which were difficult to render in German" (25–26).

Just as Kuhnau was inspired by Weise's funny but pedagogically purposeful novel, he was inspired by Thomasius's literary concerns when he formulated this treatise on liturgical text settings. Kuhnau's interest in the implications inherent in foreign synonyms and synonymous phrases is as significant as his stated goal, to explain how he sets liturgical prose texts, because it establishes his connection to two major figures of the early *Aufklärung*, Weise and Thomasius. When words in Luther's German version of the Bible did not stimulate his imagination, Kuhnau turned to versions in Hebrew, Latin, Italian, or French to find the inspiration for apt inventions. His objective is always to interpret the meaning and significance of the sacred words as accurately as he can, and to delight and move the spirit of the listener.

Texts for Church Music at Leipzig, for the Ecclesiastical Year Beginning, in God's Name, with the First Sunday in Advent of this Waning Year 1709, and Ending, God Willing, at the Same Time in the Year 1710

Leipzig, printed at Imanuel [sic] Tietz's

Here I present to you to read, Worthy Leipzig, those texts that are to be heard, with God's help, during this liturgical year in the *Choris Musicis* entrusted to me.[2] This time I have tried to show how Biblical expressions [*Sprüche*] can be composed, in keeping with their own beauty and without various extraneous adornments, when they are not associated with arias or other poetic *Paraphrasibus* [paraphrases].[3] I have collected the *Dicta* [words] myself for two texts, namely for the first Sunday in Advent and for the Feast of St. Michael's Day, but in doing so I have blended in various verses of familiar German songs and, since I lacked the time to continue in this manner, I have asked a good friend to undertake this task.

I must, of course, acknowledge that arias, which frame expressive words in appropriate *Metris* [meters] and *Rhythmis* [rhythms], give music a special gracefulness that is not so easily achieved with words sung in prose. Nonetheless I have adhered to my original decision, especially because by displaying here nothing of the madrigal style that pertains to arias and recitatives, I can more easily avoid any suspicion of writing theatrical music. Of course, at this time, only very few people know the essential difference between the church and theatrical styles and that, in both styles, madrigals can be used without *Praejudiz* [damage] to any *Proprii* [proprieties], not to mention the fact that in one as well as the other something expressive must be present to move the spirits. The distinction between them is shown herein: that in the former, one tries to arouse in the listener sacred devotion, love, joy, sadness, wonder, and the like, while in the latter, the effect among pure and innocent music lovers is an innocent pleasure. For most of the others, those sensually minded, the effect is to supply more and more nourishment to their appetites, only rarely dampening the uncontrolled heat of their stirred-up blood, as once Pythagoras is supposed to have done when he played his lovely flute to some young men. When he looked down from his window one night, he noticed these fellows, unable to get into the bedroom of a woman next door, proposing to take her house by storm. He played such *charmante* modulations on his instrument that, upon hearing them, they backed off from their intention and left the chaste woman in peace.

There [in church music], the sacred place and text call for every possible art [artistry? *Kunst*], splendor, *Modestie* and devotion; here [in theatrical music], in secular works, good pieces may appear next to bad, droll, ridiculous, and melodies may creep in that excessively hop about and transgress the rules of art.

Now, since our task is to set only plain words in prose and not arias (although songs may also belong to this *Genere* [genus] and are only distinguished by making up the *cantus firmus*, while arias make up the *figuratum*, and since this [type of setting] deprives them of much of their Grace (Fr.; charm), as already mentioned, there is all the more reason to seize upon every opportunity for invention and variation, without which the music would be hard put to achieve its goals, namely, to delight and move the spirit. This is not the place to speak of the way [*der Art und Weise*] to vary and invent, which I discussed elsewhere, where I showed, for example, that four notes equal in length can be ordered in 24 ways, 5 notes in 120 ways, and so forth, according to the *Praeceptis artis combinatoriae* [precepts of Combinatory Art], by always multiplying the last product by the following *Numero Notarum variandarum multipliciret* [number of notes to be varied] according to the *Progressione Arithmetica* [arithmetic progression]. Mixtures can exist in such a way that each combination would soon produce a different effect on the spirit of the listener. And these variations would be nearly endless if at the same time the length of the notes were modified somewhat, to say nothing of the many other *Modorum* (types) of variation. Here, however, our primary concern is to see how the correct understanding of the words can offer an occasion for invention and how it can be conveyed to the ears with good sense by music. For beyond understanding the *Artificium die Affectus zu moviren* [art of moving the affections][4] and skillfully expressing everything else, I would hold it to be necessary not to be a stranger to *Hermeneutica*, and to always *capirte* [grasp] the correct *Sensum* [meaning] and *Scopum* [objective] of the words. I would say furthermore it is not so absurd when setting German biblical language that in case the words in the mother tongue do not lead directly to an apt invention (as much as we have to thank *GOtt* for Mr. Luther's forceful translation) to take in hand other versions in other languages known to us: Experience teaches us that foreign languages affect us more strongly, as can be observed during Lent when even our uneducated join in singing the *Credo in DEum* [*sic*] *Patrem* with much heartfelt emotion, although they barely understand even a few of its words. Above all, however, the original language can contribute to invention in no small degree. I will point to the beginning of the first psalm to briefly demonstrate the point. Supposing that the first words, Blessed the man [*Wohl dem*], did not arouse my spirit to any invention, I would read the Hebrew words *Ashrei ha-ish*.[6] With an exclamation point this can mean, *O! beatudines huius viri*, Oh! the blessedness of this man. And the French version of the preachers and professors of Geneva reads nearly the same: *O que bien heureux est le personnage*. Indeed, I would *paraphrasire* it further by considering the *Pluralis* [plural form], as follows: What orator, or what tongue is sufficiently capable of *exprimiren* [expressing] with forceful words the blessings [*Glückseeligkeiten*] that such a man possesses in the greatest abundance, indeed, in the greatest perfection! Even though I know well that *ashrei* is not always used with this stress (as I find the words in the Italian bible do not differ from the Latin Vulgate: *Beatus vir* translates literally *Beato l'huomo*), this sort of meditation leads me to express Blessed the man [*Wohl dem*] through an array of many voices or by several choruses or else, should such auxiliary forces be lacking, through many passages, coloraturas and the like, sung in one voice or a few voices. Coming to *ha-ish, huius viri*, or *huic viro*, and thus to the German word *dem* [that is, the man], one could indicate a special effect by repeating *dem* and setting it in unexpected Tonos [keys] that catch the listener's attention, so that this meaning would emerge: Happy the man, the man, I say, who represents, so to speak, a great and prominent *Person* [Fr.] in the theater of the world (taking a cue from the word, *personnage*, used in the French version), one who may most truly be counted among the most blessed, that is to say, one who walketh not, *asher lo halakh, qui non ambulavit, ivit, incessit*. On the one hand, if the Hebrew verb *halakh*, walk, is taken in its *sensu proprio* [literal sense], the opportunity exists to express the word *per gradus* [by steps] and not *per saltus* [by leaps]; on the other hand, if the word is taken correctly, as here, in *sensu figurato* [the figurative sense], the crooked maneuvers of the ungodly are, thereby, understood through many passages wandering beyond the limits of *Modi seu Toni* [mode or key]. Next: that walketh not, *ba'azath r'sha'im, in consilio impionum* [*sic: impiorum*] in the counsel of the ungodly. Here, to be sure, there is no difference between the meaning of these words in the original and in the [Lutheran] version. But, as already mentioned, since one is always more alert reading a foreign, particularly the H. [Heilige] language, one is also led to ponder the *radices vocum* [word roots]: Thus, the word *ya'ats*, which more or less means *consilium iniit, concilium cepit, dedit, consuluit* [took counsel], brings to mind that during *Consultiren* [consultations] there is always debating, pro and con, and fairly frequently a completely unexpected conclusion is reached. With this thought in mind, one should let the *Auditores* [listeners] hear the word council [or counsel? *Rath*] on a strange and unexpected *Tono* [note]. If I proceed to the word *r'shaim, impiorum, motorum, inquietorum, seditiosorum, injustorum,* and so on, of the wicked, it should hit the ear in a harsh dissonance. Since the wicked are like a raging sea, because their emotions [*Affecten*] never know peace or good harmony but are *continuirlich* [continually] in battle with one another, the word for them will not agree with pleasant harmony. *Ub'derekh hata'im lo amad, Et in via peccatorum non stetit* [nor standeth in the way of sinners]: There I noted the word *amad, stetit,* he stands (according to Luther's version, he treads [er tritt]). One might have many *Tonos* [notes] sounding in *Unisono* [unison] and thereby indicate something like this thought: He treads the path of sinners, from which he neither wavers nor deviates, and all his *Affectus* [emotions] are bound up in such evil. Since, however, the *Propositio negativa* ist [statement is negative], thereby implying that the pious do not care to do so, the *particulam negandi* [negative particle] must be sharply heard. For this reason, I find in just about all Italian cantatas the Latin *Non* and their Italian *Nò,* used without any addition [that is, without other words], are repeated many times and with good reason. Regarding the expression of the remaining words, one may be guided by what has just been said about *ambulavit* [walketh] and about *impiis* [impious]. When thinking about the word *hata'im,* which *proprie* [literally] means *errantes, deviantes* [gone astray; turned from the right path], one might well abandon the correct *Modo* [mode] and wander about in foreign *Tonis* [keys] without, however, sounding such dissonances as were heard with the word *r'shaim* [the ungodly]. *Ub'moshav lezim lo yashav, Et in cathedra derisorum non sedit,* Nor sitteth in the seat of the scornful. Besides the possibility of representing the act of sitting unchanging and in unison *in loco stabili et Unisono* [unchanging and in unison], the *lezim, derisores,* or scornful might be perceived by means of instrumental music, while the vocalists could demonstrate that they will not harmonize with them. *Ki im b'torath Yahweh hephzo; Sed in lege Domini desiderium (voluntas, delectatio) ejus;* But his delight is in the law of the Lord [*HErrn*]. In regard to the *conjunctionis adversativae* [adversative conjunction], *ki im,* but, it should come in a completely different *Tono* [key], and the mi would be transformed to fa, or the fa to mi. The pleasure or delight in the law of the Lord [*HErrn*] must, however, *insinuiren* [insinuate] itself into the listener's heart using every conceivable charm. *Ub'torato yeh'ge yomam v'laila, et in lege ejus meditari solet die ac nocte* [and in his law doth he meditate day and night]—there, the act of meditating (called "speaking" in Luther's version) could be represented by a profound and well-advanced counterpoint; or by an ingenious so-called *Grave,* as for day and night, however, which means as much as [*so viel als;* that is, the same as] unceasingly, this could be represented by a particularly noticeable repetition of the words. And so forth. Contemplation of the distinct conjugations in the Hebrew language also can contribute not a little to invention. For example, when the Psalms, now and again, say *bar'khu et Yahveh, benedicite Domino,* Bless the Lord, I find *bar'khu, benedicite,* in *pi'el.* If it were in *kal* it, indeed, would have another connotation and mean, roughly, to bend the knees so that, in this instance, the difference between the conjugations requires no special attention.[7] Nonetheless (since a *Musicus* [composer] in such a situation must, so to speak, jump at every opportunity—as one sees in the diverse magnificats by so many masters, where one always wants to find a new and as yet unheard invention), I might permit myself to treat this verb in *Intensivum* [*pi'el*, intensive form] and *Frequentativum* [repetitive intensive form]. Since both conjugations [*pi'el* and *kal*] are related to each other[8] and, given the emphasis generally conveyed by such aspects in other verbs, I would *mente concipirten Paraphrasi* [mentally conceive the paraphrase] as follows: "Bless the Lord [*HErrn*]; do it often and zealously, on bended knees and with all reverence; continue to do so, let his glory sound forth far and wide and in distinctive ways." And with this in mind, I would not only repeat the *Clausulen* (phrases) and intervals but invert them and vary them in distinctive ways. At this time I will say nothing about *Accentibus* [accents], since it is already only too well known anyhow that they shed much light on the perception of the correct meaning and that, consequently, they can open the way for composers to many inventions with their *Distinctionibus* (distinctions) and *Conjunctionibus* (conjunctions).

In this way one should also *procediren* [proceed] with *Dictis* [texts] whose original language is Greek. I will not present any examples because, against my wishes, this *Praefation* [preface] has already grown too long.

I can already hear some people saying: These are *Speculationes* [speculations] that only the smallest part of the *Auditoribus* [audience] can perceive. I concede this: Yet curious minds do pay attention to such things, and the composer derives, at the very least, the advantage of, thereby, breaking open the path to invention. This being so, he may be somewhat forgiven should he slightly exceed the time set aside for his music when seeking to bring out the correct *Sensum* [meaning] and the *pondus* [import] of the words, as proposed above, just as a preacher of God's Word who thinks about *exhauriren* [exhausting] all aspects of his text would be excused for exceeding the time [that is, allotted to his sermon].

Great *GOTT*, whose praise the angels delight to sing, may this work, dedicated to your most holy name, find grace in your eyes. Ah, if we but had the *nova cantica* [new songs] of the angels! Ah, had we the angel voices, but especially angelpure hearts so that, as you alone are worthy to receive praise, honor and glory, we also would be worthy to offer these rightly to you. Nevertheless, let our *Chorum Musicum* sing of your glory to our hearts' content amidst the ever blessed prosperity of the Leipzig Jerusalem, until the end of the world; and let us continue the glorification of your most holy name amidst the perfect choir of angels and the elect in the heavenly Jerusalem, forever and ever. Amen.

Leipzig, 12 Dec. 1709.

J. Kuhnau

Notes

1. Eric A. Blackall, *The Emergence of German As a Literary Language, 1700–1775* (Ithaca/London: Cornell University Press, 2nd ed., 1978), ch. 2, "The Language of Philosophy."

2. This translation is based on the German edition by Bernhard Friedrich Richter, "Eine Abhandlung Joh. Kuhnaus," *Monatshefte für Musik-Geschichte* 34/9, Jahrg. 1902.

3. A notable aspect of this text is the interspersion of foreign words. Mainly they are Latin, occasionally French. We have kept these in the translation to transmit a sense of their use in the original text where, however, they are not typographically distinguished from the German by italics as they are here. Furthermore, Kuhnau tends to inflect Latin words with German ending, thereby Germanizing them. Since both German and Latin are inflected languages, unlike English, we cannot transmit this tendency, and our decision to keep these Latin (or French) words as primary in the body of the text will occasionally lead to improperly inflected endings. We decided that this treatment was the lesser evil in trying to maintain the integrity of the original text. Note that Kuhnau, also, sometimes capitalizes Latin nouns as if they were German.

4. Note here the particularly delightful mixture of Latin and German and the Germanization of the Latin verb.

5. Nouns referring to God receive two capitals, minimally.

6. The English transliterations of the Hebrew used here conform to modern practice; they replace Richter's German transliterations (see Richter, "Eine Abhandlung Joh. Kuhnaus," 148).

7. *Pi'el* is an ancient Hebrew—ancient, generally semitic—verb form, translated as "intensive" or "emphatic." *Kal* is the basic verb form.

8. The Hebrew word *berekh*, knee, has the same root as *barukh*, blessed, and *bar'khu*, bless.

Chapter Nine

Random Thoughts About Church
Music in Our Day (1721)

Gottfried Ephraim Scheibel

Introduced and translated by Joyce Irwin

In 1722, Johann Mattheson, a prolific writer on all musical matters, as well as a
prominent musician, commented with high praise on a book that had appeared
the previous year.

> In recent days a small German publication of five and a half sheets has come into my view
> which I regard more highly than many volumes with so many words. Not just because the
> author, Mr. Gottfried Ephraim Scheibel, mentions me in several places with perhaps
> undeserved praise—although I am highly indebted to him for the honor he renders me
> in this manner—but because I have never read anything of this sort that conforms so well
> with my sentiments.[1]

In particular, Mattheson quotes Scheibel's counsel that writing poetry to be read
is very different from writing texts to be sung. He agrees with Scheibel that few
of their contemporaries are able to write poetry that communicates the affect to
be expressed in the music. The difference between the two, Mattheson notes, is
that he comments from the perspective of a composer, whereas Scheibel identified himself as a *philosophe*.

A few years later, after Scheibel's 1725 publication of *Poetische Andachten* (*Poetic
Meditations*), Mattheson again praised Scheibel, calling him a "well-disposed theological poet."[2] Later in the same work he labels Scheibel a "theologian and candidate for the ministry."[3]

In spite of his theological concerns, however, Scheibel did not enter the ministry but spent his career as a teacher at the Elizabeth Gymnasium in his home
town of Breslau. His wide interests are revealed in the range of topics treated in

his publications. In addition to the treatise on church music presented here, Scheibel also wrote a short history of church music, *Die Geschichte der Kirchen-Music alter und neuer Zeiten.*[4] His concern for good poetry is evident in his writings on church music, and, similarly, his concern for good church music is expressed in his writings on poetry. His *Die unerkannte Sünden der Poeten* (*The Unrecognized Sins of Poets*), published in Leipzig in 1734, takes aim at both the poetry and the lifestyles of many poets of his day but at the same time lauds those civic societies of poets, such as the Hamburg *Patrioten-Gesellschaft*, that upheld the moral value of poetry. Scheibel credited Mattheson with making him aware of the members of this organization.[5]

One Hamburg poet in particular, Barthold Heinrich Brockes, earned Scheibel's highest esteem, and it was to him that his book on the sins of poets was dedicated. Whereas many poets left Scheibel regretting the time he had wasted in reading their poems, Brockes provided for Scheibel a life-changing experience through his main work, *Das irdische Vergnügen in Gott* (*Earthly Pleasure in God*): "I remember still the completely enrapturing movements that these devout poems, filled with true wisdom, awakened in my soul. They serve to this day as a powerful and blessed motivation to recognize my Creator, the world and myself. I see each creature in nature now with different eyes than before."[6]

These comments help to explain Scheibel's other area of interest and publication, that is, the history and nature of storms and weather. In 1727 Scheibel wrote about a destructive storm that had occurred in 1535 in the city of Oels, not far from his home town of Breslau.[7] Written as a poem, which he offers as a modest imitation of the works of such famous poets as Brockes, Mencke, Neukirch, König, and Richey, the work describes the drama of the storm itself and ends with theological interpretation. The thought of Spinoza receives harsh criticism for mixing the natural and the divine. Only through God's transcendence could the devil's power of destruction be overcome. In a later work entitled *Weather: A Poem about History and Physics*, Scheibel presents a more mature philosophy of nature.[8] Distinguishing between ordinary and extraordinary climatic events, he recognizes that particular meteorological conditions in other parts of the earth may seem quite unusual to him and yet have a natural explanation in the larger context. One should not rush to call unusual phenomena miraculous; nevertheless, whether God makes use of natural or supernatural causes, it is his power and wisdom that is revealed and should be recognized in observing all forms of weather.

This view that God is known through his works in nature is characteristic of a trend in eighteenth-century German poetry, of which Brockes is the best-known representative. As identified by literary historian Uwe-Karten Ketelsen, these writers stood on the foundation of orthodox Lutheranism with its view of the unity of creation but were inspired by the new science coming from England and Holland and sought to utilize the scientific approach for the praise of God and God's creation. "For the advocates of the new perspectives and for the poets of the new nature poetry, the 'outward nature,' the 'natura,' becomes precisely the doxological sign of 'gratia,' not only in the scanty stock of symbols of theophany legitimated through biblical use, such as columns of fire or rainbows, but in principal, that is, in every natural phenomenon."[9] This position has been labeled "physico-theology" and is one of the numerous directions of eighteenth-century thought that are commonly grouped under the term Enlightenment.[10]

Indeed Scheibel, who was born in 1696, was a true son of the eighteenth century and had little in common with the older writers, either Pietist or orthodox, who engaged in the controversy over cantatas in church. Whereas the older generation had yet to be convinced that non-biblical texts were appropriate for church music, Scheibel wanted to move on to the question of what poetic skills were required for good church music.[11] And whereas older writers had yet to be convinced that the operatic style of music could be appropriate in church, Scheibel boldly affirmed this recent innovation with arguments representative of the age of reason rather than evoking the debates of the Lutheran past. In so doing, he provided a theoretical foundation for the generation of composers writing cantatas in the 1720s.

Random Thoughts About Church Music in Our Day by Gottfried Ephraim Scheibel[12]

Chapter One

Concerning Music in General

1. The fact that I have taken it upon myself to write about church music should not lead anyone who begins to read my work to think that he will encounter the marks of an experienced musician or cantor who will prescribe rules and laws for writing a good chorale, for example, or an oratorio of the sort common in church. Let the reader be satisfied that I present myself *comme un philosophe* who offers his thoughts about a matter as his judgment dictates. I cannot deny, however, that various things concerning music in itself are not exactly unfamiliar to me, and I like to think that I am counted among those who esteem and love music.

2. Many a person who has looked around a bit at architecture can make a judgment about a building, and another reasonable person can judge concerning a painting, even if the one has never been an architect or the other a painter. Thus I trust that I will not step on any toes or annoy anyone with my random thoughts about church music if I do not pose as a musician. These thoughts are born from the solitude in which I have lived up to now. That which has driven me to print these few pages is not fame but rather an impulse to serve the public, and thus I hope that I will thereby give pleasure to many a lover of music when he sees that there exist yet others who are of like mind.

3. In case my writing style does not please someone, that person should know that he is taking into his hands my first work. And as everything depends on practice, he will with kind eyes overlook the mistakes that crept in here and there. Whoever has never done anything poorly will never do anything well. Who knows whether or not it will go better in the future? These are only random thoughts; that is, I have with my pen drafted my thoughts about church music just as they occurred to me and as I found reasonable.

4. But now to the matter: I have considered it proper and in good order to report a little about music in general before I proceed to church music as it is practiced today. First of all I have concerned myself with its definition and divisions.

5. If someone asks, "What is music?" I answer thus: *quod sit Ars, quae docet per Mutationem Tonorum Affectus movere*, or, in the vernacular, that it is an art which shows us how one can move the affections through changes of tone. I consider this definition correct. Now, to be sure, I should show what I understand by changes of tone, but I leave that to the musical gentlemen, who have a better grasp of these kinds of things than I. Whoever wants to have a detailed report can find a more thorough treatment in the Jesuit Athanasius Kircher's *Musurgia*, Meibom's *Scriptoribus Musicae antiquae*, and the incomparable contemporary musician Mattheson's *Orchestre* and *Organisten-Probe*.[13] I shall simply stay with the goal or purpose of this art, which is the moving of the affections, factoring the topic in the following manner.

6. As far as its divisions are concerned, music is either vocal or instrumental. The former is in my opinion the oldest and first art, because it is not plausible, indeed it is almost impossible, that people would have begun to play instruments before beginning to sing. For before I can play a melody on an instrument, I must first have the idea for it in my head. The latter may perhaps have arisen, as others with good reason conjecture, from the song of birds, whom people wanted to imitate by means of instruments.

7. Concerning the other division into sacred and profane or church and worldly music, I understand the first to be that which we use in worship; but the second, that which is customary at secular ceremonies, at weddings, parties, and so on, was for a long time unknown, up to the time of King David and the reign of his successors in Judah. In order to institute more orderly and devout worship, he commanded the Levites to practice music partly with singing, partly on all sorts of instruments. From that time on the greatest part of their service was that they had to play psalms and sing certain songs between the forecourt of the priests and the forecourt of Israel while sacrifices were going on. One can read about this in greater detail in Lund's *Levitic Worship*.[14]

8. Let no one think that in my opinion the beginning of church music was not until the time of David; we must go much further back and look at the foundation of worship as God himself ordered it through his servant Moses. For then God commanded horns to be made by which the holidays were heralded and the breaking of the entire camp was announced, when the priests had to go into

the holy of holies and along with the Levites carry away the tabernacle with its equipment packed up.[15]

9. The surrounding pagans learned this kind of music from the Jews. The sacrifice to Baal was carried out with the sound of trumpets and drums. Still today one finds the use of music in the pagodas of the wildest heathens. The practices of the Romans and Greeks are known, and it is thus not necessary to set them forth here. Meanwhile there was also secular music, and as long as there have been people they have also had a natural impulse to this art; and there has hardly been any ceremony where people have not put music to use. They ascribed to music such a virtue that Orpheus also is supposed to have brought back his Eurydice from the Elysian Fields by the help of music.

10. The first Christians introduced their psalms and hymns into music right from the start. Now we must confess that with the migrations of so many barbarian peoples the arts in part went into decline and in part were completely lost; sacred as well as secular music went into darkness. Meanwhile, as studies again began to flourish, music again blossomed as of old and daily was cultivated more and more.

11. At the time of the Reformation, Zwingli wanted church music in particular to be done away with, but I believe that if he had lived in our time, now that musicians have better insight into the doctrine of the affections, he would have judged otherwise. At that time the state of music was still quite bad; it is no wonder that it did not appeal to everyone.

12. Let me add yet this also: that God himself takes pleasure in music. Moses thanked God after the release from the Egyptians' authority and bondage in such a beautiful song that we could scarcely write a better one in similar circumstances. When God wanted to give his law from Mount Sinai, the sound of a strong trumpet was heard. Every day David played the loveliest songs and psalms on his harp for the Lord. In Psalm 150 he wants to make use of all instruments for the praise of God. When he wanted to bring the ark of the covenant into his house, this could not happen without music; he himself sang and played and danced for joy before the ark of the Lord. If David had not understood the charm and effect of music, he would never have come up with these ideas or thought that he was doing God a service thereby.

12. Music is indeed a part of the occupation of angels. When Isaiah saw the glory of the Lord, the angels sang, "Holy, holy, holy is the Lord of Sabaoth; all the earth is full of his glory." Who knows whether the most pleasant instruments were not also heard at the same time? At the birth of our Savior they sang on the fields at Bethlehem, "Glory to God in the highest, peace on earth, and good will among people." Part of the joy of the blessed in heaven will consist of music, for John's Revelation depicts to us how they sing before the Lamb and play on their harps. By contrast the torment of the damned in hell is compared to a howling which is an unpleasant music. Finally, when God wanted to threaten the people of Israel with punishment, he often says that he wanted to take away the sound

of their stringed instruments on their holidays; they should instead sing only songs of mourning and other similar things by which he sought to move them to repentance. From all this is to be seen, as we have already thought, that God was never an enemy of music but rather that it pleases him as well as anything else of which people are accustomed to make use.

Chapter Two

Concerning the Goal of Music or the Movement of the Affections

1. The movement of our affections is commonly ascribed to the human will as either a good that is desired or an evil that is avoided. If now the bad is removed and the good is left, or the good is removed and the bad is left, one's soul experiences all sorts of passions and emotions that are called "affections."

2. These are to be considered not only from a moral but also from a physical standpoint. For since each affect is a sensation of my soul, but every sensation happens either inwardly or outwardly, the former concerns the soul, the latter the body and its organs. One must thus confess that the affections are also moved by physical things, by things which fall into our external senses.

3. From this can easily be determined whether music can move the affections. For once it presents to us an affection, as soon as the soul gets an idea of this affection through the external senses, it begins to act and to move in accordance with this idea. However, it differs from one person to another according to the organs of the body in which it acts, for as the body is constituted it also desires things that are appropriate to it.

4. This is, further, all too certain. For whence came, then, the different inclinations of people if the organs by which the soul acts were not of a different nature and constitution from one person to the next? If this were not the case, then people would have to have the same sort of affections, desire the same sort of things, and shun the same kind of things. One would not know any difference between stingy, ambitious, and sensual people. But since this is not the case and the blood, with which the soul has a special connection, is in one person different—sometimes thicker, sometimes thinner, or a person's nature is sometimes dry, sometimes moist, it is no surprise that the soul also has different operations, and this is precisely what is commonly referred to as temperament.

5. Having laid this groundwork, we now come to the question: How can a sound or tone produce in the soul a movement of the will or an affection? This takes effect quite easily and is perceived in well-appointed music more often than not, yet with different effects because of the different temperaments about which I just spoke, which we will more clearly explain in the following.

6. I take as an example a melancholy person whose thick and cold blood turns away all fluids because of its slow circulation. I let him hear a piece of music and

pay attention to where he takes the most pleasure. As many such persons as I have met, I have perceived that sad, slow, and serious things in music are most pleasing to them. Why? Music with frequently changing dissonances splendidly suits his melancholy nature, which gets along well with the most adverse ideas such as fear, sorrow, and so on, which I can fairly call the dissonances of the spirit, as does an adagio with the slow movement of the blood. Because these are all sympathetic matters, it is no wonder that they are pleasing to him and necessarily move the affection to which he is subject.

7. It looks completely different with a person of sanguine humor in whom the blood is in quick movement; this causes them to have an agile spirit and hence also to take pleasure in agile and quick tone changes. On the other hand, persons of choleric humor, who because of frequent bile are inclined to anger, love agitated melodies, especially where the sounds are overdone, as, for example, when something is set in grandiose manner, as one sees in the case of soldiers who are being encouraged through this to fight anew. Only in persons of phlegmatic humor have I observed that because of their lazy and watery constitution they can be moved only slightly or not at all by music. I would almost like to call them people who are free of affections if it were not the case that they love most of all their drinking songs, which are lacking in art. For they are much too sullen to reflect on a matter, and since in music as in other arts, and indeed even in sciences, they are ignorant, it is no surprise that they find no purpose in music and by necessity can feel no movement of the affections.

8. Thus it follows that those who show themselves most impassioned by music are the persons of melancholic, sanguine, or choleric temperament, and according as these are found mixed in a single person, the affections also will be moved accordingly. Yet when I regard music and its effects without consideration of temperament, it already has such a connection with our passions, as for instance, sorrow, joy, contentment, anger, and so on, that it must necessarily move us. If the mere words of an orator are capable of making our hearts cheerful or depressed, how much more is this true of music, which can depict an affection in an even more lively and penetrating manner.

9. In paragraph 6 above, I have recalled how the dissonances that occur frequently in sad music depict perfectly the dissonances of a melancholy temperament. Happy music can also accomplish this for a cheerful and lively temper; just as the animal spirits are moved in the blood circulation swiftly and speedily, so swift also is the cadence of tones that penetrate through the ear into the seat of the soul and help to increase the affection which flows into it by nature.

10. From this, however, one can easily deduce how it is that music can serve as a medicine for the mind. When a melancholy person hears cheerful music, it can easily happen that while the soul gets a contrary idea it also divests itself of contrary effects. In the same manner a lament can easily squeeze tears out of a person of sanguine humor. And there are many thousands of examples that the most embittered spirits have been softened and calmed by sweet music.

11. The question arises now which kind of music is most moving, vocal or instrumental? My answer to this is that it is when they are combined. A mere voice or a mere instrument serves merely as a pastime and for the private pleasure of the spirit, particularly when it does not last long. When I have heard a virtuoso sing an aria or a lutenist, violinist, and so on, play something, I have frequently been led to admire their skill more than to have my cares driven away. A whole concerto of many instruments may well represent to me the genus of an affection but not by a long way its species, by which I would like to know how to be moved. For example, I hear something cheerful, but I do not know about what I should be cheerful. If the voice is combined with an instrument, however, it makes a far better impression on the spirit and will hold the attention of the listeners better than when both are separated from each other, for it is difficult to keep one's thoughts together. That author who wanted to express various biblical stories with their affections on the harpsichord did indeed let his talent be seen therein, but he will not be able to persuade anyone to the affection that he wanted to get across in them. Insofar as it was not printed above the piece, I had to puzzle for a long time what this or that fantasy was supposed to mean.[16]
So much for music in general.

Chapter Three

Concerning Church Music in Particular

Now that we have thought somewhat about music in general, we want to approach closer to our subject and consider that species or kind of music that is customary in churches. We want, however, merely to concern ourselves with its use, for I consider it unnecessary to introduce much about its history, because it is not my place to provide a historical study here.

2. Accordingly, church music is a piece of external worship by means of which God is honored with singing and instruments and the congregation is edified.

3. This definition shows us first of all that church music is a piece of external worship. It is based in nature that when a person recognizes a god, he, as a consequence, honors the same outwardly with words and works. With words, that he may speak of God and of divine matters with nothing less than respect and humility, for "out of the abundance of the heart the mouth speaks" (Matth.12:34). With works, in order that nothing be omitted that belongs to his honor; and this happens when one praises his good deeds either with the voice or with instruments.

4. When the world was created, outward worship consisted originally of sacrifice; Abel and Cain sacrificed to the Lord from their herds and crops. After the flood, people began to erect temples to honor God, to place priests therein, to choose certain days and times in which a special blessing from God should be

praised, and so forth. God did not disapprove but rather took the greatest pleasure in this, as attested by the establishment of Levitic worship among the Jews.

5. God indeed remains a God of order; and although in the New Testament we no longer have a ceremonial law, still the first Christians soon made a proper order of worship, as they came together on certain days, preached, sang psalms, administered the sacraments, and so on, all of which belongs to the outward worship of God.

6. Whatever some misguided soul may think about this outward reverence to God, it remains true that wherever it is abolished, the inward worship of God cannot possibly exist and religion therefore necessarily falls apart. For it is difficult to conceive of worship that happens merely in the heart and does not allow itself to be observed outwardly by one feature or another. For this reason, when Paul directs us not to abandon the gathering of the saints, he only wants to demonstrate the necessity of outward worship, in order that it not be neglected.

7. Further, church music is a piece of outward worship. We may not ask how music succeeded to this honor, for as people sensed something alluring and even beguiling about it, they decided it was good to make use of it in houses of worship in order to bring minds to attention and encouragement in devotion. It is called only a piece, however, because in this matter neither too much nor too little should be done, considering that other important pieces of outward worship, which are carried out in a certain order, could thereby easily be disregarded. For music is to be regarded as nothing other than a preparation for devotion, just like the exordium in an oration, which is also the reason why the worship service in our churches usually begins with music.

8. Third, church music consists of singing and playing instruments. Singing is divided further into chorales and figured music. Both kinds were introduced into the Latin churches especially at the time of Ambrose and Augustine and at the time of Gregory the Great; and subsequently they were introduced to Germany and France at the time of Charlemagne. Chorales are partly hymns, partly psalms and consist of not such a long extension of tones and repetition of words as is common in figural music. We Lutherans retain the hymns, but the Catholics retain their ancient chants and psalms.

9. As far as figured music is concerned, I think that it is greatly to be preferred over chorales, for in this each word expressing feeling is paid its due, which in chorales is just passed over quickly. In our day the use of figured music consists in singing certain texts that pertain to the time. Spiritual songs or chorales are not for that reason to be rejected, but in them one considers the words more than the melody. We mostly use the organ with them so that the congregation remains on pitch, and an experienced organist can in addition lend some charm to them. Concerning instrumental music we will have an opportunity to reflect elsewhere.

10. Whatever the manner in which music is made in the church, there is no goal other than the honor of God and our own edification. God takes pleasure

in everything that we prescribe in the church for the increase of his glory and to testify to our thankful hearts. . . . And our own edification is thereby considerably increased. If secular music can give us pleasure and often take away our cares, why should we not also have similar pleasure when we hear music being made in church? If we feel this pleasure, we can, as believing Christians will testify, easily think of heaven and remember the blessed condition in which we will find ourselves. . . .

Chapter Four

On the Necessity of Church Music

1. This chapter will not sit well with the enemies of music, and they would prefer that one devote one's efforts instead to making music hateful to people. One finds enough Zwinglians.[17] For that reason I have found it necessary to take away their prejudices and to show how absurd and distorted their conclusions look and what a completely false idea they have about music in general and must necessarily have also about church music.

2. Our worship would come out far too abstract without any outward decoration, to which music contributes the most. I willingly grant that everything could be arranged in church without music; it would be enough if people only sang a few hymns, then listened to the sermon and finally attended communion. But I call this kind of worship nothing else than abstract, because in it one would necessarily have to separate oneself mentally[18] from all secondary concerns, and we would then come into church with the mere intention of reflecting on divine matters and honoring God.

3. Thus it should be, and for true, orthodox Christians any kind of worship is pleasing. But how does it stand with the great mass of the unregenerate? Do they have similar thoughts? By no means. Experience teaches that such an abstract worship service does not sit at all well with them. Their vain disposition does not find in it the slightest thing that appeals to it, and one sees how they scorn the same, usually neglect it, or if they do come to church they do so only because of the people and for the sake of appearance, so that they may not be regarded as atheists. We can say right away that hymns are sung that are familiar to them from their youth, and so they sing them without thinking at all. Here there is no thought of making them more attentive or cheering them up, but rather their mind becomes dull even for listening to the best of preachers. Indeed, since they have the further prejudice that piety makes them melancholy, why is it surprising that they think they are correct when they use as evidence that worship appears melancholy enough?

4. How can one bring them, however, to other thoughts? Such can only happen if we make use in the church of such things (and, to be sure, in appropriate

amounts) as strike them in the face and in the ears. The latter can only happen by means of music; it is capable of bringing them into church even if they had no other intention [than to hear music].

5. I do not deny that my conclusion will displease many, but meanwhile it remains true that it is better to entice people into church than to kindle a revulsion against divine matters in most people through all too abstract worship. For how should the Holy Spirit and the Word of God work in them if they seldom come to church? It is impossible to hope for this with their ridicule; it would have to happen in a direct manner. And this is more likely to happen to the extent that one comes to the aid of their vain disposition through one or another good ceremony in the house of worship.

6. All this has its proper consequences: granted that they come with vain thoughts into the church and merely with the intention of listening to one piece of beautiful music or another, still it is not merely possible but rather fully probable that they can acquire good thoughts. If their affections are moved just once by well-ordered harmony (for it is certain that whoever likes to listen to music is also easily moved by it), then they can easily endure the sermon, because they have at the same time already been prepared for it. If this happens, the Word of God does not fall into stony hearts but into softened hearts where it can bring forth fruit better and sooner than otherwise.

7. God forbid that I would deny the Word of God any power even without music, for then those congregations which cannot introduce music into their churches would be unfortunate. No, rather I am speaking here of such places where one can make good use of it. And I have already recalled above that it is only a part of worship and thus contributes only a portion to edification and the honor of God. I remember that in a certain place on Good Friday there was supposed to be a musical passion before and after the sermon. The people certainly would not have come to church so promptly and in such a great crowd because of the preacher but rather presumably because of the music. Now the musical text was simply the suffering of Christ from the Gospels into which, besides two or three arias, frequent chorales or verses from hymns were introduced. I marveled how diligently people listened and how devoutly they sang along; it was the moving music that contributed the most to this, and even though the service lasted more than four hours, everyone stayed inside until it was over.

8. In my opinion, worship of most Reformed churches, especially in England and Holland, produces so many atheists because it has no great outward appeal, just as with other religions people are made superstitious through frequent ceremonies. As the latter sin by excess, so the former sin by deficit; it is best if one remains in the middle of the road. For ceremonies in religion are like proper clothing for people. And in truth God clothed religion so gloriously at the time of Levitic worship in the Old Testament that it drew the hearts of all people to it. Yet one must proceed cautiously in this and not introduce any other ceremonies like music except those that are useful for devotion and edification.

9. Music takes preeminence over such ceremonies, as experience demonstrates. Thus I do not see why we should not make use of it when it would secure such a glorious benefit. If well-ordered secular music can make us happy or sad in the face of vain and often sinful matters, would it not be good if this happened in the church? It would contribute in great portion to improvement and would increase the zeal in the hearts of listeners for worship. And perhaps people would not run after secular music so much if they could listen to such well-ordered and moving music in the houses of worship.

10. Further we note that when our soul is frequently compelled to an affection, that makes such a sharp impression that it remembers it for a long time. We often see that when people have taken pleasure in a certain occurrence in their youth, as long as they live they remember and frequently still take delight therein because of the sharp impression the affection made at that time. Would it not be good if our souls experienced the same and we frequently obtained good thoughts through one well-composed aria or another? And it would be irresponsible, now that music in our day has nearly reached perfection, as far as both the art and the effect are concerned, if we did not seize the opportunity and use it above all in spiritual matters and in service of the edification of our souls.

Chapter Five

That Church Music, in Comparison with Secular Music, Has Nothing Peculiar to It for Moving the Affections

1. My purpose in this chapter is to show that religious and secular music have no distinctions, as far as the movement of the affections is concerned, and therefore a composer must make use of the same kinds of modes for these. It is a common opinion that the two sorts of music must be different, and the best musicians and composers have affirmed this and have believed that church music must indeed look different from secular music, that one must not make the cadenzas so free, and other such matters. It always seems to me as if they themselves did not know what the movement of the affections is even though they are trying to move them.

2. I would grant them this opinion if they knew how to give me the divisions of joy, sadness, and other affections that they make in their brains perhaps without a basis. It remains one affection, only that the objects vary, that, for example, here a spiritual pain, there a worldly pain is felt, that here a spiritual, there a worldly good is missed, and so forth. Just as I can be saddened concerning worldly things, so I can be saddened about spiritual things; just as I can rejoice about these, so I can rejoice about those. The tone that gives me pleasure in an opera can also do the same in church, except that it has a different object.

3. I do not know what objection one will raise against this. I take a secular composition from a cantata, make a parody[19] on it from religious material, and express precisely the affection which the composition brings with it. Then precisely this affection will be moved just as well as when it was directed toward a secular object, and for that reason it will not lose its power. To show that this is correct, I will take as an example the first aria from scene two of act one in the opera "Jupiter and Semele"; the composer is Mr. Telemann, who will be remembered by those who were in Leipzig five years ago. Semele sings:

Ich empfinde schon die Triebe	I feel already the impulses
Die der kleine Gott der Liebe/	That the little God of love
Meiner Seelen eingeprägt.	Implanted in my soul.
Ach wie kan sein Pfeil erquicken	Oh, how can his arrow refresh
Und die süße Glut entzücken	And delight the sweet glow
Die er in mir hat erregt.	That he has aroused in me.

Whoever hears the composition must allow me this parody uncensured:

Ich empfinde schon die Triebe	I feel already the impulses
Die mein Jesus/ der die Liebe	That my Jesus—who his love
Meiner Seelen eingeprägt.	Implanted in my soul.
Ach! Wie kan sein Wort erquicken/	Oh, how his word can refresh
Und des Glaubens Glut entzücken/	And delight the glow of faith
Den sein Geist in mir erregt.	That his Spirit has aroused in me.

To the same beat is heard the following aria in this very scene:

Meine Flammen sind so schön/	My flames are so lovely
Daß ich mich von aller Pflicht	That I from all duty
Durch ihr sonderbahres Licht/	Through their singular light
Kan hinfort befreyet sehn.	Can henceforth be freed.
Wo ein Gott verliebt will sprechen/	Where a God wants to be called loved
Müssen andre Bande brechen.	Other bonds must break.

I take a religious theme and may change only a few words without harming the composition:

Meine Flammen sind so schön/	My flames are so lovely
Daß ich aller Fleisches-Pflicht	That I from all duties of the flesh
Durch des wahren Glaubens-Licht	Through the true light of faith
Mich kan fort befreyet sehn.	Can see myself henceforth freed.
Wo Gott wil von Liebe sprechen/	Where God wants to speak of love
Müssen irrd'sche Bande brechen.	Earthly bonds must break.

I will present one more aria from the opera "Artaxeris," which was translated from Italian and composed by Monsieur Vogler in Leipzig:[20]

Oeffnet euch/ ihr schönen Augen/	Open up, you lovely eyes,
Lasset euren Wunder Schein	Let your magic appearance
Meiner Seelen Pharus seyn	Be the lighthouse of my soul.
Haltet die beflammten Blicke	Keep the emblazoned looks
Länger nicht von mir zurücke	No longer back from me,
Denn ihr Glantz hemmt meine Pein.	For their shine checks my pain.
Da Capo	

Could not a believing soul on the occasion of the unbelieving Thomas have the following thoughts, which would remain the same affect in the music:

Oeffnet euch ihr Glaubens-Augen/	Open up your eyes of faith,
Lasset Jesu Friedens-Schein	Let Jesus' peace appearance
Eurer Hoffnung Pharus seyn	Be the lighthouse of your hope.
Haltet die beflammten Blicke	Keep the emblazoned looks
Von der Lust der Welt zurücke	Back from desire of the world
Denn ihr Ansehn bringt nur Pein.	For their sight brings only pain.
Da Capo	

4. I have made diligent use of these examples because their compositions are known to me. And I wager that if I were to proceed thus with an entire opera and only change the object of the affections, the same affections would be moved. A certain cantor asked me once to have a composer at a certain university compose a cantata for him on the suffering of Christ. I did it, but asked him at the same time in a letter to set it in theatrical style. Why? I will report right away that he had one of his very good friends write back that he could not do it because there was such a large difference between theatrical and church music; that is to say, in the church one may not move the affections as well as in the theater or in secular pieces.

5. I still think, however, that if our church music today were a little livelier and freer, that is to say, more theatrical, it would be more beneficial than the stilted compositions that are ordinarily used in churches. When, for example, there is supposed to be pleasant music, a serious, slow air is offered, where the 6/8 beat is played yet more slowly, as its nature requires, and thereby the movement of the affections is notably constrained. And this is also the reason why our church music today must suffer along. People are so accustomed to the old humdrum and hammersmith's compositions[21] which contain neither charm nor gracefulness, and most think that whatever sounds nice and old-fashioned and simple fits best in church. Should then a cantata come into their hearing, one set according to the new unconstrained manner, some are astonished by it, others, however, because they have heard similar music in secular settings, think

instantly it is a sin and such free compositions are not fitting in church, as if indeed affections might not be moved in church as well as outside church in an opera or a Collegium Musicum.

6. I do not know why operas alone should have the privilege of squeezing tears from us; why is that not true in the church? No, choral works have to be performed there where one hears counterpoint and whatever else that serves better for an organist playing a prelude than for edifying the listener. It is often said: this or that composer can set a good church piece, but he is not so successful in other matters. I turn it around: if a composer can move the affections in theatrical and secular music, he will be able to do this in spiritual matters, as witness the examples of Messieurs Keiser,[22] Mattheson, and Telemann. Admittedly the lack of apt texts is also to blame, but of that at the end.

7. I gladly grant that minuets, jigs, gavottes, passepieds, and so on, are not appropriate in church because they induce idle thoughts in the listeners. One can be outraged about this, and a composer will have a thousand other fantasies without thinking of the same. But enough of this: I could write much more, but let me stop here; reasonable people will have to give their assent to me on this.

Chapter Six

Concerning the Different Kinds of Church Music

In this chapter Scheibel points out the importance of taking into consideration the liturgical season, the occasion, and the audience when choosing music for church. He notes that instrumental music sometimes exceeds the listeners' attention span and understanding. It is better, he concludes, to combine vocalists and instrumentalists, joining an edifying text to a pleasing sound.

Therefore it is better to stay on the middle path and keep to the best manner of organizing church music, namely when vocalists and instrumentalists make music together through a pleasant mixture. This will not only be pleasing to the ears of the listeners, but it will also keep their attention; and when the composition is well set and the choir or orchestra provided with good musicians, edification will not be lacking.

Chapter Seven

On the Appointment of Musicians in the Church

1. The last words of the preceding chapter give me cause to consider good appointment of musicians in the church. For I take for granted that music loses its power and gives cause for scorn and being spurned, if not outright banned

from church, where there is not a David or (to employ the name of a pagan virtuoso) an Orpheus who can draw the souls of the listeners through his voice or with his instrument. And all that virtue that is attributed to lovers and respecters of music is no virtue if it does not manifest itself in proper form.

2. Experience confirms this in the places where music is well appointed so that people get a true taste of it. In Vienna, Dresden, Hamburg, Leipzig, and so on, where one encounters virtuosos, one sees how music arouses lovers and admirers, and consequently it must have achieved its effect in them.

3. Now it is not altogether bad that this doesn't happen in all cities. Not everywhere are there elegant courts or well-to-do citizens who can afford with little effort to pay the salaries of such persons. And even if this were not the case, church taxes do not yield as much as is necessary to maintain a choir. . . .

4. For it does not depend totally on the quantity; we can instead call it a waste when a choir is filled with greater forces than are necessary and when frequently a church could employ three and more choirs without loss. What purpose does a large mass of singers and instrumentalists serve, and further what is the use of three or four organs in a church? Why does one acquire such costly works, let alone pay castrati from Italy and other such wasteful expenditures when someone else would do just as well if not better than many such capons? If each part or voice is provided with one or at most two persons who excel in what they do, then a choir is well provided. Particularly is this the case nowadays when few arias are sung *tutti*, but most are solos (in which the instruments necessarily must not be heard strongly, because the voice would not be heard above them); and if there are *tutti* works, it is enough if the main voices do their part, even if they consist of single persons.

5. Now we also want to see how it looks when a choir in a church is well appointed. The organization is already known: first come the directors of the choir, or cantors, thereafter vocalists, and finally instrumentalists. These make up a choir, and every member of it must have his virtues.

6. As far as the director of the choir or the cantor is concerned, he must first and above all be a man of Christian and honorable conduct. It is a sad plight when church employees lead a profligate and godless life and have a nasty reputation as drunkards and whoremongers, as avaricious and of a strange disposition. It is a great offense to the people as well as to the preachers. And such people will make little effort at increasing devotion but will just play some music, whatever it may sound like.

7. In particular, a director of music must not be greedy; if he has this as a dominant characteristic, it is bad for the musicians in the church. For he will take aim at the salaries of his subordinates and take into the choir or recommend to the church leaders such people as are satisfied with little, even if they do not understand what they are doing and show themselves to be mere bunglers. Thus he will also not turn much to good musical compositions, because money has to go for that. And since greedy people are commonly headstrong, he will arrange

everything according to his whim and not be much concerned whether it pleases the listeners or not.

8. Much less may he be excessively sensual or dissolute, because otherwise he would be lazy and negligent in his office and would not commit himself to the order that is prescribed, because dissolute people are commonly disorderly. And as a great deal depends on his presence, he would often neglect his office and follow after his amusements and entertainments instead. Not to mention that through his carelessness many errors would creep into his music and thus spoil the best composition, because persons of this disposition usually lack discernment. For to this office belongs an alert and attentive man who cannot tolerate the worst trivialities.

9. On the other hand, he should have gotten around a bit in the world so that he knows where church music is in a good state and makes an effort to institute it in the same manner in the church where he serves. It is necessary for him to be a good judge of instruments and to know how to differentiate between fiddlers and virtuosos; the same is also to be understood about singers. For that reason it is especially necessary for a cantor who wants to instruct others in singing to have a good voice himself, although this does not apply precisely to a director of music, who can hold his office on the basis of pure theory in music.

10. As far as singers are concerned, the same applies that was said in par. 6 above concerning their character and manner of life. Especially must a singer show himself to be a virtuoso in the voice part he sings. To this belongs first that he have a strong and clear voice so that he can be heard everywhere in a large church; second, he must sing clearly and express all words audibly so that the listeners can understand the text. But because such people are seldom found, the director of music can, as long as the singer sings in a good manner even if he has a weak voice, have the instruments play softly in an aria where the singer is to sing a solo. Such things I have observed in operas, where the mass of instruments easily can overpower the best singers. If he speaks indistinctly it would be good, at least where cycles are produced, to let the listeners procure these for themselves, and thus they could easily understand what is sung.[23] Nevertheless, I do not even let anyone pass as a singer if he swallows his syllables and will not open his mouth.

11. Here occurs to me the question, whether it is permitted to make use of female singers for music in the church. Good trebles are rare, partly because they are young and therefore cannot yet have much discernment in the learning of singing, and partly because their voices do not last all too long and because one cannot always have falsetto singers. Thus it happens many times that there is a scarcity and one must often take trebles wherever and however one can. A good female singer could easily replace this scarcity. I know what objections will be raised against me in this matter, and I will also let the objections for the most part pass. But to consider the matter in and of itself, it is my opinion that it could proceed insofar as proper arrangements were made for it;

I consider that would be better and more fitting that a musically trained woman sing religious arias in church than to sing secular and amorous songs in the opera. I concede that at first it would seem peculiar to the people, but as in each case when one gradually becomes accustomed to something and it no longer seems strange, the same would happen here. Miriam and Deborah are renowned in the Bible as good singers. No intelligent and reasonable person should take the words of Paul—that a woman should be silent in the congregation—as a proof for the opposition and extend the natural purpose that Paul had in mind. It would be a shame, since such incomparable subjects and virtuosos are found among women, if they didn't want to use these talents to the glory of God and the edification of their neighbor. I label this only a feeble possibility, however, as music in church is provided without them and will also continue to be arranged without them.

12. Briefly to consider the instrumentalists, it is in and of itself clear that capable people must be used for this, even if they are not exactly Corelli, Vivaldi, Telemann, or Handel on the violin; it is enough if they understand as much as is necessary. As far as the organist, the principal person among them, is concerned, let them be taught by Niedt and Mattheson; the latter published a whole book for instruction called *Organisten-Probe,* wherein they may see how far their capability may be stretched.

13. *For the sake of resonance, Scheibel advocates placing the choir above the congregation rather than on the same level.*

Chapter Eight

On the Subject Matter of Church Music, or How a Musical Text Should Appear

In this chapter, Scheibel discusses the importance of a good text and bemoans the lack of sufficient qualified poets in his time. Much of the chapter deals with faults in specific texts written by Scheibel's contemporaries. Of the poets of his day, he regards Johann Ulrich von König, Saxon court poet, and Benjamin Neukirch, from Scheibel's city of Breslau, most highly. Of most interest in relation to Bach are his comments on cantata cycles.

7. I bear due respect for all poets, and as a lover of poetry I frequently wish I possessed a mere portion of their skill. But it is also true, as is commonly said, that "we cannot all do all things." It is one thing to write a poem to be read and another thing to fashion a musical text. For the latter one must be a poet who understands music and who knows how a composer can best apply his musical imagination. . . .

10. Nothing, however, is more common in churches than to produce annual musical cycles. There are enough texts for this from both the gospels and

epistles, but very few stand the test and are worthy to have a composition made of them, because the composer would certainly have to pull his ideas out by the hair. I will let the thoughts stand, but the words are set in such a manner that not a single bit of imagination can be applied, no matter how much one tries.

11. Of all the cycles, there are none better up to this point than those that the world-famous and excellent theologian in Hamburg, Mr. Erdmann Neumeister—rightly called the German Asaph[24] or David—completed. Whoever reads them must confess that he has in these something special; the poetry is full of fire and devotion, and Monsieur Telemann has shown how they sound even more brilliant. His manner of writing poetry is not constrained but rather completely free and lively; as a result neither his arias nor his recitatives come out too long. He knows just how to bring in the chorales and biblical sayings. In sum, one can only label his affairs the perfect works of a perfect master.

12. A not unsuccessful follower is Mr. Johann Jacob Rambach, who last year had a cycle published. I must confess that he set it to music excellently and mostly also writes unusually brilliantly, but in various pieces I had completely different ideas. . . .

Scheibel relates his different ideas about Rambach's poetry, citing particular metaphors he finds inappropriate.

But these are minor details to which the ordinary person does not pay attention. Otherwise his work is nothing other than praiseworthy, and I wish the author further success in this kind of work. At least I would like to hear a musical setting of it; it should be halfway successful and would have to be edifying. Mr. Franck's[25] cycles on the gospels and epistles are no less praiseworthy and emerge from Mr. Neumeister's method.

13. In our churches, however, various kinds of poems are used for music, namely arias, cantatas, oratorios, or such texts as are put together from these three together and thus make a mixed genus.

14. The first genre, namely the arias, which go into three, four, five, six, or more verses on one air or melody, strike me as mere songs. It is impossible for the same melody that arouses a happy affection in the first verse to fit another where perhaps the poet writes of sorrow and then in the third expresses a completely contrary affection. As is only fitting, these have dropped away completely.

15. Cantatas are the second genre, and these come here from Italy and consist solely of arias and recitatives. At communion and after the sermon at vespers, or other times when there is not a large congregation, they are most fitting, for then a single singer, as is generally used in these, can be heard better than when the church is full. Oratorios, where biblical texts appear intermingled with arias, can be heard better in church when there is a large gathering. For the biblical texts or the sayings from the Bible are usually set tutti, which fills the church, and the arias, which are sung as solos, make a pleasant change.

16. The best and now most common form is when arias as well as cantatas and oratorios are mixed together, where namely arias, recitatives, biblical passages and chorale verses on a single theme are presented. The arias express the strongest affection, the recitatives explain it; the passages from the Bible test it, and the verses from hymns are at the same time "advancing arguments" that expand on the movement. I would add to this a reminder concerning the texts and hymns, that they also must have an element of affect in them, of which Mr. Neumeister is a perfect master.

17. From all of this we conclude: anyone who wants to compose sacred poetic texts must be a good theologian and moralist. For it does not just depend on one's notions; they must also be in accord with Scripture. Otherwise our music in church will consist of empty words that, like empty shells, have no kernel, and it will be mere noise in which God takes no pleasure. A spirit-filled text and a moving composition must be combined.

Conclusion

So much for now concerning church music, in part what its current state is and in part how it might or could be. I had intended to write of the hindrances to church music, but I soon changed my plan when I saw that it has so many enemies that they can hardly be counted and that they make up the majority. I would have to touch on various irregularities in both the ecclesiastical and the political estate, and indeed to name persons who would like to do away with it. What astonishes me most, however, is that I have met music lovers who like to hear music in secular society but are annoyed with it in church. Further I would have had to lament these money-hungry times, in which much is spent for the state but little for the house of God. What I would finally wish is that Almighty God would give constant peace in my beloved home city of Breslau as also in the whole country under the reign of Our Most Gracious Emperor, in order that the voice of weeping might not be heard in our houses of God but rather that of rejoicing.[26] I wish that a Right Noble Worshipful Council of the city of Breslau as well as those who are in positions of authority in the church might proceed in part to improve the good orders and ceremonies and in part to add others to them. Up to this point they have made this place into a blooming Zion that delights and amazes visitors to such an extent that they frequently wish to see their fatherland or city in the same condition. God grant that we may continue to enjoy this blessing; and may God uphold the city fathers with perfect blessing and long life for the common good of the churches and schools. As then Zion itself always on this account calls upon God when it sings: "Grant us peace by your grace, Lord God, in our times, for there is none other that fights for us, but only you alone."[27] Give our Emperor and all authorities peace and good government, that we may under them live a quiet and peaceful life in all godliness and propriety. Amen.

Notes

1. Johann Mattheson, *Critica Musica d.i. Grundrichtige Untersuch- und Beurtheilung/ Vieler Musicalischen Schrifften*, part 2 (Hamburg: [Auf Unkosten des Autor], 1722), 96.
2. Johann Mattheson, *Der musicalische Patriot* (Hamburg: [Ans Licht gestellet von Mattheson], 1728), 7.
3. Ibid., 214.
4. G. E. Scheibel, *Die Geschichte der Kirchen-Music alter und neuer Zeiten* (Breslau: J. J. Korn, 1738).
5. G. E. Scheibel, *Die unerkannte Sünden der Poeten, welche man sowohl in ihren Schrifften als in ihrem Leben wahrnimmt, nach den Regeln des Christenthums und vernünfftiger Sittenlehre geprüfet* (Leipzig: Johann Michael Teubner, 1734), 2.
6. Ibid., preface, iii. At the time of this writing, Scheibel had read four volumes of Brockes's work, which appeared in nine volumes, published in Hamburg from 1730 to 1748.
7. *Das bestürmte Oels, oder das im Jahr Christi 1535, den 1. September am Tage Aegidii entstandene grosse Ungewitter in der Hoch-Fürstlichen Residenz-Stadt Oels, allen seinen merckwürdigen Umständen nach mit poetischer Feder nach Art eines Helden-Gedichts beschrieben* (Breslau: [zu finden beym authore, und Michael Rohrlach Buchhändler], 1727).
8. G. E. Scheibel, *Die Witterungen. Ein historisch- und physikalisches Gedicht* (Breslau: Carl Gottfried Meyer, 1752).
9. Uwe-Karten Ketelsen, *Die Naturpoesis der norddeutschen Frühaufklärung* (Stuttgart: J. B. Metzlersche Verlagsbuchhandlung, 1974), 57.
10. See further Wolfgang Philipp, *Das Werden der Aufklärung in theologiegeschichtlicher Sicht* (Göttingen: Vandenhoeck and Ruprecht, 1957).
11. It is worth noting that an earlier poem by Brockes depicting Jesus's suffering and death had, prior to Scheibel's publication, been set by numerous composers for their Passions and would later be used for part of Bach's St. John Passion, even though, as Paul Henry Lang commented, "Brockes's Passion was more an opera libretto than a Passion text" (*Music in Western Civilization* [New York: W. W. Norton & Company, 1941], 480–81).
12. In this major portion of Scheibel's *Zufällige Gedancken von der Kirchen-Music wie sie heutiges Tages beschaffen ist* (Frankfurt and Leipzig, 1721), passages omitted are indicated by ellipses or by italicized summaries.
13. The learned Jesuit Athanasius Kircher (1601–80) wrote *Musurgia Universalis* (Rome: Corbelletti, 1650), a lengthy volume on music history, theory, and style. Marcus Meibom (1620–1711), Danish polyhistor, published many ancient Greek texts about music along with a Latin translation and commentary in *Antiquae musicae auctores septem* (Amsterdam: L. Elzevier, 1652). The multi-faceted musician Johann Mattheson wrote many works on the music of his time, including *Das neu-eröffnete Orchestre* (Hamburg: der Autor und Benjamin Schillers Witwe, 1713) and *Exemplarische Organisten-Probe* (Hamburg: Schiller u. Kissner, 1719).
14. The works of Johann Lund (1638–86), renowned for his knowledge of ancient Hebrew, were published posthumously by his son Thomas Lund in three parts: (1) *Öffentlicher Gottesdienst der alten Hebräer* (2) *Levitischer Hohepriester und Priester* and (3) *Ausführliche Beschreibung der Hütte des Stifts, wie auch des ersten und andern Tempels zu Jerusalem* (Schleswig: L. Eckstorff, 1695–96). A subsequent edition under the title *Die alten jüdischen Heiligthümer/ Gottesdienste und Gewohnheiten für Augen gestellet/ in einer*

ausführlichen Beschreibung des gantzen Levitischen Priestertums (Hamburg: Gottfried Liebernickel, 1701) was republished several times, an indication of the high regard in which the work was held.

15. See Numbers 1:47–53 and 4:1–49 on the role of the Levites in transporting the tabernacle; on the blowing of trumpets to start the march or to signal festivals, see Numbers 10:1–10.

16. Scheibel may well be referring to Johann Kuhnau's *Biblical Sonatas* (*Musicalische Vorstellung einiger biblischer Historien, in 6 Sonaten auff dem Klaviere zu spielen*) (Leipzig: Immanuel Tietz, 1700), an unusual set of works intended to convey various biblical stories such as the conflict between David and Goliath.

17. Ulrich Zwingli, leader of the early Reformation in Zurich, believed that music appealed to the fleshly elements of human nature more than the spiritual and that it should therefore be eliminated from Reformed worship. The term "Zwinglian" was later applied to critics of art music in church, even when there was no historical linkage with Zwingli.

18. Scheibel here makes use of the Latin word *abstrahere*, to draw away, to elucidate the derivation of the word abstract.

19. Scheibel's use of the German word "Parodie" refers to a borrowing of musical material from one composition for use in another composition. In this context, the word has none of the connotations of humor or ridicule conveyed in the ordinary understanding of "parody."

20. This presumably refers to Johann Gottfried Vogler, successor to Melchior Hofmann at the New Church in Leipzig and director of the Collegium Musicum. Telemann spoke highly of him as composer and violinist, but he was released from office in 1720 after he attempted to escape from paying his financial debts. See Robert Eitner, *Biographisch-bibliographisches Quellen-Lexikon*, 2nd ed. rev'd. (Graz: Akademische Druck- u. Verlagsanstalt, 1959–60).

21. A play on the name of Andreas Hammerschmidt, a favorite church composer of the seventeenth century.

22. Reinhard Keiser (1674–1739) served as music director for the duke of Braunschweig and as opera director and cathedral music director in Hamburg. He was known for his operas, passions, oratorios, and cantatas. Bach used his St. Mark Passion in Weimar and again in Leipzig.

23. Toward the end of the seventeenth century, religious writers began to compile the texts of what were to become cantatas into annual cycles for liturgical purposes. The best known are those of Erdmann Neumeister, published in cycles for the years 1704, 1708, 1711, and 1714. Johann Kuhnau, Bach's predecessor in Leipzig, is known to have had the texts printed and distributed before the service, as Scheibel here recommends. See Ferdinand Zander, *Die Dichter der Kantatentexte Johann Sebastian Bachs: Untersuchung zu ihrer Bestimmung* (Diss., Cologne, 1967), 11.

24. Asaph was a Levite and chief musician of the sanctuary in the time of David (I Chronicles 16:5).

25. Salomo Franck (1659–1725) was connected to the ducal court in Weimar and collaborated with Bach in writing cantata texts during Bach's time in Weimar. During his Leipzig years, Bach continued to use texts by Franck.

26. Breslau, in the territory of Silesia, now belongs to Poland, but from the 14th century had been part of the Holy Roman Empire. Through the spread of German-speaking population into the region, much of Silesia had a German consciousness and turned to Lutheranism at the time of the Reformation. At the end of the Thirty

Years' War (1648), Silesia remained within Hapsburg territorial lands, but concessions were granted to Protestant strongholds like Breslau to continue to practice the Lutheran faith within this officially Catholic land. Nevertheless, Silesia, as an economically desirable territory, remained a source of conflict in the continuing struggles for power between the Hapsburgs and their rivals; in 1740, when Emperor Charles VI died without a male heir, Frederick II of Prussia invaded and took Silesia.

27. A well-known German hymn, "Verleih uns Frieden genädiglich," based on a medieval chant and translated by Martin Luther.

Contributors

CAROL K. BARON is Fellow for Life in the Department of Music at Stony Brook University, where she was Executive Director of the Bach Aria Festival and Institute. Recipient of two major awards for Public Humanities Programming from the National Endowment for the Arts, an Alfred P. Sloan Fellowship, an American Council of Learned Societies grant, and two ASCAP-Deems Taylor Awards, she was Executive Producer for the Public Broadcasting System program *In Search of Bach*, viewed throughout the United States and Canada, and in Europe. She has taught at York College, Hunter College, and Amherst University. Her articles on 20th-century music—primarily, the music and biography of Charles Ives—have been published in American and international musicological collections and journals.

SUSAN H. GILLESPIE is a translator from German to English and founding director of the Institute for International Liberal Education at Bard College. Her translations include works in philosophy and musicology as well as fiction and poetry. Her published translations include essays by Theodor Adorno, Eduard Hanslick, Heinrich Heine, Rudolf Kleine, Hugo Riemann, others; books by Leon Botstein, Theodor Heuss, Helga Koenigsdorf, and Hanns Zischler; letters by Johannes Brahms, Felix Mendelssohn-Bartholdy, and Richard Strauss; and the poetry of Paul Celan.

KATHERINE R. GOODMAN is Professor and Chair in the Department of German Studies at Brown University. She has authored two books on German women's literature, *Dis/Closures, Women's Autobiography in Germany 1790–1914* and *Amazons and Apprentices: Women and the German Parnassus in the Early Enlightenment.* Goodman has also co-edited four books, contributed chapters to numerous other collections as well as published articles and reviews. Her current work focuses on Luise Gottsched. Her contribution to this study was supported by the Alexander-von-Humboldt Stiftung.

JOYCE IRWIN is a church historian, organist and choir director. She received her Ph.D. in Religious Studies from Yale University and taught at the University of Georgia and at Colgate University. She is the author of *Neither Voice Nor Heart Alone: Lutheran Theology of Music in the Age of the Baroque* and the editor of *Sacred Sound: Music in Religious Thought and Practice.* Her other area of publication is women's religious history, with particular focus on Anna Maria van Schurman.

TANYA KEVORKIAN is Associate Professor in the Department of History at Millersville University of Pennsylvania. Her publications focus on the social history of religion and music in Germany during the Baroque Era. Her book, *Baroque Piety: Religious Practices, Society and Music in Leipzig, 1650–1750,* is forthcoming with Ashgate Press.

ULRICH SIEGELE is Professor Emeritus of Musicology at Tübingen University, Germany, where he began his career as a student of classical philosophy and history, as well as musicology. His early work in Bach studies consisted of seminal work concerning Bach's activity as a transcriber and reviser of his own music. In addition to contributing detailed and controversial musical analyses of works by Bach, and penetrating political and social studies of Bach's age and career, his far-ranging studies include analyses of works by Beethoven, Monteverdi, and several twentieth-century composers.

JOHN VAN CLEVE has authored two books, *Harlequin Besieged: The Reception of Comedy in Germany During the Early Enlightenment* and *The Merchant in German Literature of the Enlightenment.* His published articles treat various social issues in the German Enlightenment. He has taught at Augsburg College, and his numerous publications are listed in the bio-bibliography of the *Festschrift* composed in his honor, and presented to him in *1991.*

RUBEN WELTSCH, a gifted linguist and translator, was educated in Berlin, Brno, and Florence and received advanced degrees from Columbia University and the University of Colorado. In 1971 he retired as Director of Libraries at Stony Brook University and was appointed Associate Professor of History. He was a major contributor to *Historical Abstracts* from 1963 to 1997. His publications in European history include work on Archbishop John of Jenstein and the Hussite movement in 14th-century Czechoslovakia, and Karel Havlicek's nationalism in the 18th century.

Index

Eastman Studies in Music

Ralph P. Locke, Senior Editor
Eastman School of Music

The Poetic Debussy: A Collection of
His Song Texts and Selected Letters
(Revised Second Edition)
Edited by Margaret G. Cobb

Concert Music, Rock, and Jazz since
1945: Essays and Analytical Studies
Edited by Elizabeth West Marvin
and Richard Hermann

Music and the Occult: French
Musical Philosophies, 1750–1950
Joscelyn Godwin

"Wanderjahre of a Revolutionist" and
Other Essays on American Music
Arthur Farwell,
edited by Thomas Stoner

French Organ Music from the
Revolution to Franck and Widor
Edited by Lawrence Archbold
and William J. Peterson

Musical Creativity in Twentieth-Century
China: Abing, His Music, and Its
Changing Meanings
(includes CD)
Jonathan P. J. Stock

Elliott Carter: Collected Essays and
Lectures, 1937–1995
Edited by Jonathan W. Bernard

Music Theory in Concept and Practice
Edited by James M. Baker,
David W. Beach, and
Jonathan W. Bernard

Music and Musicians in the Escorial
Liturgy under the Habsburgs, 1563–1700
Michael J. Noone

Analyzing Wagner's Operas: Alfred Lorenz
and German Nationalist Ideology
Stephen McClatchie

The Gardano Music Printing
Firms, 1569–1611
Richard J. Agee

"The Broadway Sound": The
Autobiography and Selected Essays
of Robert Russell Bennett
Edited by George J. Ferencz

Theories of Fugue from the Age of
Josquin to the Age of Bach
Paul Mark Walker

The Chansons of Orlando di Lasso and
Their Protestant Listeners: Music, Piety,
and Print in Sixteenth-Century France
Richard Freedman

Berlioz's Semi-Operas: Roméo et
Juliette and La damnation de Faust
Daniel Albright

Bach's Changing World: Voices in the Community studies the community in which Bach spent the last, longest, and most prestigious part of his life: the Leipzig middle class. These deeply researched and thought-provoking essays by prominent musicologists and scholars of religious history and German culture highlight the dynamic religious, social, and political forces that emerged during the composer's lifetime. Using entertainment venues and all forms of commercially produced and distributed literature—"popular" in that world—as well as "official" documents, they explore Leipzig's distinctive middle-class public culture. Contemporary thought was fragmented, intellectually complex, and unable to assimilate the multiplicity of ideas, beliefs, and values that were simultaneously current. The ambiguities and transitional structures in that early modern world have contributed to the inconsistencies that are part of Bach's legacy.

Bach was an accepted, admired, and trusted member of this community, as evidenced by the commissions for secular celebrations he received from royalty, academics, and merchants alike and from his multiple functions as a church composer. He could only have acquired such prestige by participating in that community as a responsible citizen attuned to its values and concerns. The essays are complemented by important statements (never before translated) about Lutheran church music by two of Bach's close contemporaries, Gottfried Ephraim Scheibel and Johann Kuhnau.

Contributors: Carol K. Baron, Suzanne H. Gillespie, Katherine Goodman, Joyce Irwin, Tanya Kevorkian, Johann Kuhnau, Ulrich Siegele, Gottfried Ephraim Scheibel, John Van Cleve, and Ruben Weltsch.

Carol K. Baron is Fellow for Life in the Department of Music at Stony Brook University, where she was co-founder and administrator of the Bach Aria Festival and Institute.

Praise for Bach's Changing World

"Carol Baron and her colleagues have done Bach studies a marvelous service. This volume should prove to be not only a signal contribution to the too-small bibliography on Bach's cultural contexts but also a ready resource for its desired growth. General readers and music lovers, too, will find this accessible book highly worthwhile."
—Michael Marissen, Professor of Music, Swarthmore College, and author of *The Social and Religious Designs of J. S. Bach's Brandenburg Concertos* and co-author of *An Introduction to Bach Studies.*

"By situating Bach firmly amid the popular debates and issues of a particular place and time, this volume brings us as close to Bach as we are likely to get. This rich scholarly achievement is wholly admirable in scope, detail, and sophistication."
—Leon Botstein, president of Bard College, and music director and principal conductor of the American Symphony and Jerusalem Symphony Orchestras.

"Carol Baron has assembled a marvelous collection of essays, which together illuminate Bach's religio-political world, Bach's Saxony, and above all Bach's Leipzig in rich and sometimes surprising ways. The volume reflects the flair and imagination of its editor and its contributors, as well as making an exemplary and very welcome contribution to the cultural history of music."
—Celia Applegate, Professor of History, University of Rochester, and author of *Bach in Berlin: Nation and Culture in Mendelssohn's Revival of the St. Matthew Passion.*